Born in Calcutta, **Tim Tate** is a multi-award-winning documentary film-maker, investigative journalist and bestselling author. Over a career spanning more than forty years he has written for most national newspapers and made more than eighty documentaries for British and international broadcasters. He is the author of seventeen other non-fiction books, including the acclaimed *Hitler's Forgotten Children* and *Hitler's British Traitors* – hailed 'a brilliant book' by Dan Snow. Tim Tate lives in Wiltshire.

Praise for *The Spy Who Was Left Out in the Cold*

'A highly readable and thoroughly researched account of one
of the Cold War's most intriguing and tragic spy stories.'
OWEN MATTHEWS, author of *An Impeccable Spy*

'Totally gripping . . . a masterpiece. Tate lifts the lid on one of the
most important and complex spies of the Cold War, who passed
secrets to the West and finally unmasked traitor George Blake.'
**HELEN FRY, author of *MI9: A History of the Secret Service
for Escape and Evasion in World War Two***

'The larger than life story of one of the West's most productive
Cold War counter-intelligence agents – a man who to the CIA's
embarrassment turned out also to be a bigamist and a romancer
who claimed publicly to be the last descendent of the Russian Czar
and heir to his fortune. A made for Hollywood page-turner,
it's a fascinating read and highly recommended.'
**SIR DAVID OMAND, author of *How Spies Think:
Ten Lessons in Intelligence***

'A brilliant and gripping exploration of one of the last great
espionage enigmas of the twentieth century. Unputdownable.'
TREVOR BARNES, author of *Dead Doubles*

'A wonderful and at times mind-boggling account of a bizarre
and almost forgotten spy – right up to the time when he's
living undercover in Queens, New York and claiming
to be the last of the Romanoffs.'
SIMON KUPER, author of *The Happy Traitor*

'Gripping . . . fascinating dirty linen from
the early decades of the CIA.'
KIRKUS REVIEWS

The Spy Who Was Left
Out in the Cold

The Secret History of Agent Goleniewski

Tim Tate

PENGUIN BOOKS

TRANSWORLD PUBLISHERS
Penguin Random House, One Embassy Gardens,
8 Viaduct Gardens, London SW11 7BW
www.penguin.co.uk

Transworld is part of the Penguin Random House group of companies
whose addresses can be found at global.penguinrandomhouse.com

Penguin
Random House
UK

First published in Great Britain in 2021 by Bantam Press
an imprint of Transworld Publishers
Penguin paperback edition published 2022

A CIP catalogue record for this book
is available from the British Library.

ISBN
9780552177689

Typeset in Minion Pro by Jouve (UK), Milton Keynes.
Printed and bound in Great Britain by Clays Ltd, Elcograf S.p.A.

The authorized representative in the EEA is Penguin Random House Ireland,
Morrison Chambers, 32 Nassau Street, Dublin D02 YH68.

Penguin Random House is committed to a sustainable
future for our business, our readers and our planet. This book
is made from Forest Stewardship Council® certified paper.

'Intelligence work was, by its nature, a game of liar's poker, played with a marked deck and counterfeit money.'
Nelson DeMille, *Up Country*

Dedicated to Janice Watts, who many years ago gave an awkward and unpromising adolescent a holiday job in her remarkable independent bookshop, and fired a lifelong love affair with the printed page.

She would have had no reason to remember. But he has never forgotten.

Contents

Prelude: 4 January 1961

5 p.m.: Mitte District, East Berlin

In the growing dark, hunched against the bite of the Berlin winter, a Stasi spy kept close watch on the communal entrance to the apartment block at number 54 Wollinerstrasse.

Earlier that afternoon he had logged the arrival of a tall, powerfully built man whose features and distinctive full moustache matched the description of Roman Tarnowski, a Polish intelligence agent now under suspicion by his masters in Warsaw as well as the East German secret police.

Twenty minutes later the door opened and the same man emerged, accompanied by a slight and pretty brunette, evidently some years younger than him; each was carrying only a small bag. The spy noted the time in his log and watched as the couple walked quickly away from the building, heading towards the solitary road sign which marked the border with West Berlin, just 150 metres away.

5.30 p.m.: CIA Berlin Operating Base, American Consulate, Zehlendorf, West Berlin

On the US Mission's telephone switchboard a light flashed for the CIA's Berlin Operating Base emergency number. The caller identified himself with an agreed cover name: Herr Kowalski.

The call signalled the imminent arrival of a mysterious and eagerly awaited defector. Although he had, for almost three years, risked his life to send thousands of pages of top-secret Soviet bloc documents to the West, he had done so anonymously: since the first package arrived in

April 1958, all the CIA had known was the man's self-chosen cover name – *Heckenschuetze*, or 'Sniper' – and that forensic analysis suggested he worked for the Polish Intelligence Service.

6.06 p.m.: Clayallee, West Berlin

A West Berlin taxi pulled up beside the uniformed military police guarding the American Consulate. A heavily set man, sporting a luxuriant moustache, emerged and helped a slim younger woman from it; they looked around, evidently apprehensive, then walked tentatively up the steps and into the safety of US territory.

After some discussion, the man confirmed he was *Heckenschuetze*, and disclosed his true identity: Michał Goleniewski, a Lieutenant Colonel in Poland's intelligence service, Urząd Bezpieczeństwa (UB). Until January 1958 he had held the post of deputy chief of military counterintelligence, and he was currently the head of the scientific branch of Polish foreign intelligence; as well as working for the Polish spy agency he was simultaneously employed by the KGB in Moscow, and had access to many of its most sensitive secrets. His companion, he explained, was his East German mistress; she, too, wished to defect.

The CIA station team was jubilant. 'Agent Sniper', the most senior – and devastating – Soviet bloc intelligence defector the Agency had ever known, was in the bag, and was ready to hand over a wealth of details: names and cover names of Communist spies in the West, as well as the locations of their operations.

Had the Agency been able to look just a few months into the future it might have been less triumphant. But as they prepared to exfiltrate their catch from Berlin, they had no inkling of the problems that Goleniewski's identity would cause – much less the decades of chaos and paralysis which his revelations would inflict on the CIA, the British Security Service (MI5) and the entire network of Western intelligence agencies.

Introduction

E VEN FOR A spy – and whatever else he might have been he was a devastatingly successful spy – the man had a remarkable collection of identities.

To Poland's intelligence service he was Lieutenant Colonel Michał Goleniewski, a decorated former Army officer, married to a Russian woman and the father of three children and who, by the end of the 1950s, headed one of its most important espionage departments, while simultaneously working for the KGB in Moscow. In the same period, members of Poland's anti-Communist movement knew and feared him as Dr Roman Tarnowski, a relentless interrogator of dissidents who worked for the General Prosecutor's Office.

In East Germany, to which he travelled regularly, the files of East Germany's secret police, the Stasi, also recorded his name as Tarnowski – though without the honorific doctorate. Meanwhile, Irmgard Kampf, his East German mistress in the Soviet sector of Berlin, to whom he funnelled thousands of dollars, deutschmarks and pounds sterling – all stolen from Soviet bloc spy funds – believed him to be Jan Roman, a widowed Polish newspaper journalist.

In the United States, the CIA registered him under his self-chosen cover name of *Heckenschuetze*, or 'Sniper', and reported that he was its most valuable undercover agent behind the Iron Curtain: a volunteer spy who smuggled thousands of pages of top-secret intelligence documents and microfilms to America, and who exposed Communist agents throughout Europe and the West.

In Britain, the Security Service, MI5, assigned him its own

cryptonym, LAVINIA, and marvelled at the quality of information he provided about KGB agents who had burrowed into its sister organization, MI6, as well as into some of the country's most sensitive military establishments.

When he defected in January 1961, across divided Berlin and with Soviet bloc intelligence agents hard on his heels, he initially announced himself to US Consular officials as 'Herr Kowalski', before telling them that he was really Lieutenant Colonel Michał Goleniewski. But one week later, as he prepared to board the US Military Transport flight which smuggled him out of Germany, he had become Franz Roman Oldenburg – an invented identity that he subsequently used to rent apartments in Arlington, Virginia, and New York. With the CIA's blessing, he also solemnly gave this entirely fictitious name for his bigamous marriage – the first of two such weddings – to Irmgard Kampf.

Two years later, to a succession of US Congressional Committees meeting in secret, and to successive occupants of the White House, his name was Martin N. Cherico. Yet simultaneously he was the beneficiary of a CIA-sponsored private Bill in the House of Representatives to grant him citizenship, under his real name: Michał M. Goleniewski.

But from early 1964 many of the 'White Russian' diaspora – and with them the most senior official of the Russian Orthodox Church in Exile – accepted his claim to a very different identity and pedigree: they recognized him as Aleksei Nicholaevich Romanoff, the miraculously surviving son of the last Tsar, and self-proclaimed heir to the Imperial Russian throne. It was that highly improbable pretence which would cause him the most trouble.

~

Michał Goleniewski was the most important, yet least understood, spy of the early Cold War. In April 1958, while working simultaneously at the top of Poland's espionage services and the Soviet KGB he experienced a Damascene conversion from the Communist systems which had sustained him since 1945. He volunteered his services as an 'Agent in Place' on behalf of the West and for almost three years risked his life to smuggle thousands of top-secret intelligence and military documents, as well as numerous rolls of microfilm, out from behind the Iron Curtain.

Then, in January 1961, with Soviet bloc spymasters in pursuit, Goleniewski and his mistress, Irmgard Kampf, made a dramatic emergency defection across divided Berlin. He brought with him to the US Consulate yet more top-secret papers and the identities of Communist agents operating undercover in America and Europe. A subsequent CIA assessment of his 'tremendous contribution' to the security of the West recorded that he had provided 'the names and details of 1,693 intelligence personalities, including officers, co-opted workers and agents' – an unparalleled haul which has never been matched.

Amongst the most serious spies Goleniewski exposed were George Blake, the KGB's mole inside MI6; the five members of the 'Portland Spy Ring' which betrayed British military secrets to Moscow; the deputy head of West Germany's foreign intelligence service; a senior Swedish Air Force and NATO officer; and a traitor at the highest reaches of the Israeli government.

The CIA called him 'one of the West's most valuable counterintelligence sources' and 'the best defector the CIA ever had'. It sponsored legislation in Congress to grant him US citizenship, rewarded him with a generously paid contract and installed him in a succession of safe houses. The British Security Service, MI5, praised his information as 'of inestimable value' and was grateful for his 'copious' and 'invaluable' services to UK national security.

On the other side of the Iron Curtain, Goleniewski's information and evidence devastated Soviet bloc spy agencies: in April 1961 a military court in Warsaw tried him – in secret and in absentia – and sentenced him to death. Thereafter Polish intelligence began an extraordinary eight-year operation to track him down, and launched a covert campaign to discredit him in the West.

But, in late 1963, the United States government abandoned Michał

Goleniewski. The CIA reneged on its agreements to pay and protect him, and blocked him from testifying to Senate committees. It harassed him and starved him of money, and secretly briefed Congress and friendly journalists that its former star defector had 'lost his mind'. The ostensible reason for this was Goleniewski's entirely bogus claim to be Aleksei Romanoff, Tsarevich and heir to the Russian throne, who had miraculously survived the 1918 massacre of the Imperial Family, and his demand for an alleged $400 million Romanoff fortune smuggled to the West.

The truth about Michał Goleniewski – the story of his spying for the West, his defection and the CIA's ditching of its former star agent – is much stranger than the fictions devised by him and his spy handlers at the CIA offices in Langley, Virginia. He was at the centre of the most serious espionage scandals of the Cold War, and, as a Zelig-like figure, appears in the background of many others.

But for six decades this has been a secret history, obscured by obsessive official concealment, misinformation and outright dishonesty. As a result, Michał Goleniewski has been largely airbrushed from history, his vital contribution to Western security has remained hidden in the closed files of American and British intelligence agencies, and publicly clouded by deliberate disinformation, as well as by his own erratic and eccentric behaviour.

Goleniewski defected in January 1961. The Cold War espionage secrets he exposed became largely obsolete with the fall of communism in 1989. Yet many of the Western intelligence records detailing his remarkable contribution to the national security of the United States, Britain and its allies remain closed.

As the organization which from 1958 onwards gratefully received Goleniewski's astonishing haul of Soviet bloc intelligence information and microfilms, and after his defection assumed control over him, the CIA unsurprisingly compiled extensive files on its star agent. It has, however, proved remarkably unwilling to disclose them. Freedom of Information Act requests produced – eventually and reluctantly – two brief documents; when challenged about the paucity of this disclosure, the Agency grudgingly handed over a further fourteen pages.

The FBI, which also worked extensively with Goleniewski, has been a little more forthcoming – though the bulk of its intelligence files on him and his information remains resolutely unavailable.

In Britain, the Security Service (MI5) and the Secret Intelligence Service (MI6) are insulated from FOI requests: the Freedom of Information Act 2000 specifically excludes them from public scrutiny. MI5 does now voluntarily send to the National Archives some of its files, created more than fifty years ago, but this disclosure is entirely dependent on its own unfathomable whims.

The Security Service did, after some prompting, disclose that it had created – and still held – a file on Goleniewski, but said that 'after careful consideration we have concluded that we are unable to release it . . . due to the continuing sensitivity of the material contained within it'.

Fortunately, none of these organizations is particularly efficient at hiding all its relevant documents. A painstaking trawl of FOI-released files on related individuals and cases yielded a large number of pages from the otherwise withheld Goleniewski files. They have been heavily redacted to remove references to his name as well as the cryptonyms assigned to counter-espionage operations launched on the strength of his evidence; piecing together these scattered fragments was often akin to completing a jigsaw puzzle without the original image for guidance, but the published memoirs and private papers of four of Goleniewski's CIA handlers helped fill in some of the missing corners.

Yet the most important advance has been the release of the long-secret files of Poland's intelligence service relating to Michał Goleniewski. They are held and available – unredacted – at the Institute of National Remembrance in Warsaw, and offer a very different perspective on the man and his motivations. By consolidating and cross-referencing these extensive records with the declassified American and British documents, a more nuanced, more human, and ultimately more troubling picture emerges of the most important intelligence agent of the early Cold War.

Behind the CIA's public claims that their once-invaluable agent had tragically lost his mind lies a rather more disturbing story – or rather stories – about the reason the Agency cut him adrift, and how that affected Western intelligence. It is a tangled tale which includes the covert recruitment of Nazi war criminals by US government agencies, and a Goleniewski-inspired mole hunt within both the CIA and MI5; both agencies, like Goleniewski himself, became lost, for a decade, in the wilderness of mirrors that is counterintelligence. Their obsessive – and ultimately fruitless – pursuit of an alleged KGB mole, burrowed into their respective senior ranks, tore apart the West's most vital security services just as fatally as their former star defector devastated Soviet bloc intelligence agencies. In the process, the CIA itself became the moving force in driving an already-damaged man to genuine madness.

The true history of Michał Goleniewski, then, is that of a brilliant and courageous spy who was simultaneously a deeply flawed man – as is often the case. Driven, by first-hand experience of the KGB's actions and capability, he risked his life, and that of his family, to volunteer his services and intelligence to the West. His is an extraordinary and largely untold story of Cold War espionage and skulduggery, of treachery and deceit, of passion and betrayal.

But it is also the very human tragedy of a brave man, with a remarkable intellect, who undermined his solitary and fanatical mission with a fatal combination of arrogance, hubris and personal greed – flaws which were exploited and exacerbated by the country he had risked everything to help until its officials drove him so far down the rabbit hole of intelligence and counter-espionage that he ultimately lost his mind.

And it all began, in good spying tradition, with an anonymous and mysterious letter, smuggled across divided Cold War Europe in April 1958.

1

'Sniper'

O N WEDNESDAY, 2 April 1958 a bulky envelope arrived, unexpectedly, at the American Embassy in Bern, Switzerland. Postmarked one day earlier in West Berlin, the package was addressed for the personal attention of Ambassador Henry J. Taylor; it contained a letter to him, typewritten in German, wrapped around a second, sealed envelope addressed to FBI Director J. Edgar Hoover, in Washington DC.[1]

The writer said the envelope contained a lengthy and detailed offer of 'enticing leads to Soviet Bloc spies, which ... would excite American counterintelligence interest'.[2] He asked Taylor to forward it to the FBI – and the FBI alone. He did not identify himself, other than to indicate he was 'a Soviet bloc intelligence officer somewhere behind the Iron Curtain', but he signed his message with a self-chosen code name: *Heckenschuetze*, the German word for 'Sniper'.[3]

On the face of it, Bern was an improbable location for an unsolicited approach by a Communist spy. American intelligence viewed the Swiss capital as an unpromising backwater in the Cold War with Moscow.

It had a meagre track record of attracting defectors or would-be agents, and the little success which had been achieved generally resulted from deliberate American attempts to recruit their opposite numbers. Physical 'walk-ins' were rare: written, anonymous offers of intelligence were completely unknown. So, whereas the KGB used Switzerland as a route into the surrounding NATO countries, the CIA had concentrated the bulk of its efforts in Vienna and Berlin instead.

Taylor, too, seemed an unlikely choice. He was a former newspaper reporter and foreign correspondent during World War II who had developed a personal friendship with Dwight Eisenhower, then the Supreme Allied Commander in Europe; after the war Taylor spent a decade broadcasting talks on NBC radio,[4] before 'Ike' – now elevated to the White House – dispatched him to Switzerland. He was a neophyte in international relations; Bern was his first (indeed, only) appointment as an American envoy, and his appointment as ambassador did little to raise his diplomatic profile.

But if unusual, Sniper's decision was deliberate and strategic. From his insider's role within Soviet bloc espionage agencies, he knew that Moscow had infiltrated spies into all US government departments except the FBI. According to Tennent 'Pete' Bagley, one of a select group of American intelligence officers who worked on the Sniper letters, 'in April 1958 [he] was convinced that CIA was penetrated. He addressed his letter . . . to J. Edgar Hoover particularly to avoid the penetrated CIA learning of him.'[5]

But by sending his offer to the Bureau via Ambassador Taylor, Sniper intended to bypass not just the CIA but also the established hierarchy of the US State Department, which he knew to be equally compromised: in April 1958 the American Embassy in Bern had only a small complement of Agency officers, which limited the risk of leaks to Moscow, and Taylor's unconventional ambassadorial background meant that he owed little if any loyalty to Washington's foreign service mandarins back in Foggy Bottom.[6]

There were, however, two significant flaws in Sniper's plan. The first lay in the running sores of inter-agency rivalry and legal jurisdiction. For more than a decade the FBI and the CIA had been locked in a bitter turf war over intelligence; at the end of World War II, Hoover had, in the words of William C. Sullivan who transferred from the Bureau to the Agency, 'the entire world staked out for the FBI and had opened offices in a great many foreign capitals'. But when the CIA was created in 1947, it was given sole responsibility for espionage; the FBI was ordered to shut down most of its international operations and to turn over all responsibility for running foreign-based agents to the Agency.[7]

The second hurdle was personal: Taylor had recently crossed swords with Hoover over exactly this issue of jurisdiction. Shortly after his arrival in Bern, he formally asked the Director to remove the FBI agent working under diplomatic cover inside the embassy; Hoover grudgingly agreed, accepting a promise that relevant information crossing the ambassadorial desk would not be withheld from the Bureau. It was an undertaking that was never likely to survive its first serious test.

But above all, Taylor's inexperience was the deciding factor that early April morning. When Sniper's letter arrived he had been in post for less than a year. Unsurprisingly, he was not willing to forward, unopened, the mysterious sealed envelope to Hoover.[8] Instead he followed established US government protocol and turned it over to the embassy's CIA station chief – Tennent 'Pete' Bagley.

Bagley, a former US Marine and political science graduate, was also new in his post; an ambitious and rising star within the Agency, he had won acclaim four years earlier for bringing a KGB defector, Petr Deriabin, safely to Washington. He saw Bern as an opportunity to advance his career and 'to be involved in everything that went on'.[9] He was, however, initially unimpressed by Sniper's offer of intelligence: 'that first letter,' he later recalled, 'evoked my suspicions'.[10] Like Taylor, he decided to stay within the tramlines of established US intelligence practice, and forwarded it to the CIA's prime Cold War operating station in Berlin. There, according to Ted Shackley, the officer on whose desk it landed, it met with a similar lack of enthusiasm:

> [It was] written in an impenetrable form of double-talk. Several of us had a go at it, but could make nothing of it. The name Heckenschuss [sic] itself looked as though it ought to be conveying something of deep significance ... It seemed to imply either that the author was fighting a rearguard action or was covering his rear ... Hoping that some day we would hear from Mr. Heckenschuss again, I had the letter filed safely away.[11]

The Sniper saga might have ended there had Bagley not thought to send a copy of the strange message back to CIA headquarters in Washington DC. The Agency then was a far cry from the monolithic organization it would later become; staff were scattered across the capital in a series of ramshackle offices, and communication between the operational espionage branches and the analytical counterintelligence department was often haphazard. It was also, at times, argumentative.

The Sniper letter landed first on the desk of Howard E. Roman, an alumnus of the CIA's wartime predecessor, the Office of Strategic Services (OSS), and a former chief of the Agency's Polish unit. A gifted linguist, fluent in German, in April 1958 Roman was a senior case officer, tasked with running 'Agents in Place' – the most prized spies of all since they risked their lives to operate undercover in their native countries behind the Iron Curtain.

'I was asked to examine the letter to see if we could determine what nationality the author was,' Roman recalled two decades later:

> I could tell by the syntax that this was not a native German. Since the writing was entirely about Poland, we concluded that we were talking to a Pole. We analyzed the typewriter in order to determine whether it was of East European make. We also analyzed the watermarks on the paper. None of this yielded anything that made anybody suspicious.[12]

Roman's initial positive assessment of Sniper's *bona fides* was accepted within the Agency's Soviet and East European sections, but it did not find favour with the increasingly powerful head of the separate – and frequently rivalrous – counterintelligence branch, James Jesus Angleton. Like Roman, Angleton was an OSS veteran, and he had extensive experience of running agents in the field during wartime service in Italy. But the nature of his job – he had been the CIA's counterintelligence chief since December 1954 – required him to take a sceptical view of intelligence offers arriving unexpectedly from behind the Iron Curtain.

Moscow had a lengthy history of 'dangles' and 'provocations' – bogus offers from non-existent spies or disinformation designed to lead Western intelligence down false paths – so when Angleton examined Sniper's odd and elliptical letter he concluded that it was most likely the latter.

But despite his doubts, Angleton decided that allowing the situation to play out a little might prove worthwhile: as he explained to Roman, even if Sniper was a provocation, at some point his Soviet handlers would have to seed genuine intelligence material within his information in order to give it credibility. 'It was the old question,' Roman recalled. 'How much truth is the enemy willing to tell you in order to set you up for the big deception?' [13] The letter was duly passed on to one of the CIA's most highly regarded analysts.

Richards J. Heuer was then thirty-one years old. He had been recruited in 1951 by the Agency's Deputy Director of Operations (and future CIA Director), Richard Helms, while a graduate student at the University of California. A philosopher by inclination and by his first university degree, Heuer 'became fascinated with the fundamental epistemological question, "What is truth and how can we know it?" '[14]

It was this intellectual curiosity which had convinced Helms to hire the young student, and in the seven years since he joined the Agency, Heuer had established a reputation as a cerebral thinker, and was slowly expanding the CIA's understanding of how to spot a bogus defector or a seam of false intelligence.[15] In April 1958 he was coming to the end of a tour of duty on the Polish Desk and, like Angleton, he calculated the odds before deciding that Sniper might be a bet worth placing: '[When] that letter was referred to me for action, some colleagues said it was phony and told me not to bother. I said, "you never know" and "nothing is lost by answering".'[16] Sniper's letter was, however, personally addressed to the FBI Director, not the CIA in whose lap it now lay. Moreover, to protect his existence from leaking back to Moscow, it set out detailed instructions for responding to the approach. The conditions were straightforward, but unequivocal: if the FBI wanted to pursue his offer, Hoover was directed to place a coded advertisement in the classified section of the *Frankfurter Allgemeine Zeitung*, and to provide a safe address to which Sniper could send subsequent packages. But his overriding condition – a requirement which would be deemed as accepted if the advertisement ran – was that the CIA was to be kept completely in the dark.[17]

This posed a tricky problem for Heuer. His instincts told him that the offer was genuine, and the would-be spy potentially extremely valuable, but Sniper's first and most fundamental condition had already been disregarded. 'He was determined to provide important information to the United States,' Heuer later recalled, 'but he needed a secure way to do it.'[18]

Because the Agency had intercepted the letter, and J. Edgar Hoover was blissfully unaware of its existence – and since the CIA was not yet prepared to inform the Bureau of Sniper's approach – Heuer decided on a simple, if deceptive solution. He placed the advertisement himself, posing as the FBI Director, in the classified columns of the *Frankfurter Allgemeine Zeitung*.

He gave Sniper details of a CIA-owned Post Office box in West Berlin, where he could send reports and pick up subsequent requests for additional information; these messages were to be hidden in secret writing concealed within the text of otherwise innocuous correspondence. All of this was carried out in the Bureau's name; from the outset of a relationship which it hoped might prove crucial in the deepening Cold War with Moscow, the Agency deliberately deceived a volunteer Agent in Place over an issue that it knew could cost him his life. It was not an auspicious beginning.

Sniper picked up the coded advertisement within days, and in early May sent his first closely typed report. From that Spring of 1958, and over the next two years – always believing he was dealing with Hoover's FBI – Sniper would mail the Agency a succession of multi-page, single-spaced letters at near-monthly intervals, each providing extensive information about Soviet bloc spies in the West. It was, though he could not have known it, just what the CIA most urgently needed.

2

The Intelligence Gap

MOSCOW WAS AN experienced player in the game of espionage. Throughout the nineteenth century, the Tsar's secret police, the Okhrana, had perfected the technique of infiltrating undercover agents into dissident groups. Immediately after the 1917 revolution, the Bolsheviks' first intelligence organization, the Cheka, adopted its predecessor's methods to penetrate and undermine counter-revolutionary organizations. But, as an exhaustive semi-official history of Soviet intelligence recorded, it also expanded its efforts from purely domestic opponents to target the new state's international enemies: 'Within days of taking power the Chekists began agent penetration into hostile organizations to see what they were secretly doing and to decompose them from inside.'[1] It proved to be remarkably good at this. For the next forty years the Cheka and its successors, the NKVD, MGB and KGB, ran extensive and successful worldwide intelligence operations. The apotheosis of these schemes was a six-year-long internal and global operation known colloquially as 'The Trust'.

Between 1921 and 1926, Cheka agents set up a fake anti-Bolshevik resistance organization which both enabled the Soviet state to identify and nullify its internal opponents and, crucially, to fool Western governments into supporting them. By the time it shut down, 'The Trust' had fed strategic disinformation to the intelligence services of eleven countries and banked substantial donations of hard currency from London and Paris. This sting operation would form the template for subsequent Soviet bloc espionage services throughout the Cold War – including one which badly damaged an American-led attempt to foster resistance in Poland – and was so successful that its techniques were still being analysed in Washington almost half a century after it ended.[2]

In stark contrast, the Central Intelligence Agency was a novice in the Great Game. When Sniper sent his first letter, the Agency had only been in existence for a decade, and was riven by internal rivalries, as well as fighting simmering turf battles with the FBI, the State Department and the Pentagon. It was also at war with sections of Congress.

The CIA was welded together from the chaotic mess of dozens of rival bodies competing for supremacy in America's post-World War II foreign intelligence landscape. The road to its inception began in February 1946 when the US ambassador in Moscow, George Kennan, sent a lengthy telegram to Washington warning that the Kremlin was determined to pursue confrontation with the West:

> We have here a political force committed fanatically to the belief that with US [sic] there can be no permanent *modus vivendi*, that it is desirable and necessary that the internal harmony of our society be disrupted, our traditional way of life be destroyed, the international authority of our state be broken, if Soviet power is to be secure . . .
>
> Everything possible will be done to set major Western Powers against each other . . . Efforts will be made in such countries to disrupt national self-confidence, to hamstring measures of national defense, to increase social and industrial unrest, to stimulate all forms of disunity.[3]

This, Kennan argued, posed an immense and urgent problem: he described it as 'undoubtedly [the] greatest task our diplomacy has ever faced and probably [the] greatest it will ever have to face'. The only way to counter this new menace – at least 'without recourse to military conflict' – was for the United States to place its *unarmed* forces on a war footing: 'It should be approached with [the] same thoroughness and care as [the] solution of [a] major strategic problem in war, and if necessary, with no smaller outlay in planning effort.'[4]

In July 1947, President Harry Truman accepted the need for a single, civilian foreign intelligence organization and signed the National Security Act; the Central Intelligence Agency was born. Its immediate parentage, however, was confused and conflicting: three distinct branches of government jointly controlled the new Agency, and each had different priorities. Truman wanted the CIA to focus on providing him with strategic information on America's enemies; the Department of Defense demanded military information and covert action, while the State Department saw the Agency as a vehicle to bring about worldwide political change favourable to US interests.

It was a recipe for disaster. Although the chain of command was gradually streamlined, throughout the late 1940s and early 1950s the CIA's track record was distinctly poor. It failed to anticipate – or at least provide intelligence which would have predicted – Soviet takeovers in Czechoslovakia and Romania; nor did it foresee China's military support for its fellow Communists in the Korean War. Worse, a succession of covert operations in Ukraine, Albania, Poland and Russia failed drastically. The Agency had supported a succession of local émigré organizations, and financed parachute drops of armed insurgents into several of the Soviet-controlled territories. These volunteer agents were promptly captured – and subsequently killed – by secret police forces lying in wait for them; it was clear that the missions had been betrayed from within, raising the very real spectre of KGB penetration into US intelligence.

In September 1952, CIA Director General Walter Bedell Smith confirmed this sobering assessment, warning that 'Communists' had infiltrated almost every branch of US intelligence. In a sworn deposition, read into the Congressional Record, he admitted:

> I believe there are Communists in my own organization. I am morally certain there are. They are so adept and adroit that they have infiltrated practically every security organization of the government.[5]

In stark contrast to Moscow's success, the CIA had almost no equivalent insight into the Kremlin's global plans, much less what its espionage services were doing to further them. These successive failures were not due to a lack of resources; by 1952 the Agency had a budget in excess of half a billion dollars,[6] operated more than fifty stations worldwide and employed 15,000 people – though remarkably few of them could read or speak Russian. Yet six months later an internal report admitted that their labours had produced distinctly patchy results:

> The adequacy of intelligence on the Soviet bloc varies from firm and accurate in some categories to inadequate and practically non-existent in others. We have no reliable inside intelligence on thinking in the Kremlin. Our estimates of Soviet long-range plans and intentions are speculations drawn from inadequate evidence.[7]

John McMahon, a future deputy director of the CIA, then a young officer stationed in Germany, was more succinct: 'We had no capability there. Our insight into the Soviet Union was zero.'[8]

On 27 December 1952, Moscow very publicly rubbed the Agency's nose in its failures. Headlines in newspapers throughout the Soviet bloc countries celebrated the 'discovery' of a combined American and British intelligence plot to foment an anti-communist revolt in Poland. For four years the CIA and Britain's Secret Intelligence Service, MI6, had fostered the resurgence of a wartime resistance group, the Freedom and Independence Association (Zrzeszenie Wolność i Niezawisłość – most usually referred to as WiN). Both believed that it was a substantial well-trained force, with 500 soldiers inside Poland's Army, 20,000 partisans and 100,000 sympathizers behind them; all they needed were weapons, equipment and money. The Agency and MI6 duly parachuted in guns, ammunition, two-way radios and gold at a cost of $5 million – equivalent to $55 million today.

The anticipated uprising never happened. WiN, as the Kremlin-controlled media reported with relish, had been under the joint control of the KGB and Poland's intelligence service, Urząd Bezpieczeństwa (UB), all along. In a carbon copy of the Cheka's 1920s Trust, the operation – code-named CEZARY – had been designed to identify – and ultimately liquidate – domestic anti-communist dissidents, to deceive Western spy agencies, and to relieve them of hard currency and materiel.

It was another deeply humiliating failure for the CIA, and one which highlighted an urgent need to reassess and recalibrate its covert war on the Soviet bloc of nations. As Theodore 'Ted' Shackley, then a young Agency officer working on Polish affairs, later recorded:

> The sight of my colleagues wrestling with the realization that five years of strategic planning and many millions of dollars had just gone down the drain convinced me that more attention had to be paid to the protection of our own personnel, operations and installations.[9]

That much-needed review was not commissioned for another two years. In July 1954, President Eisenhower ordered Lieutenant General James Doolittle, a decorated World War II Air Force veteran, to conduct an inquiry into 'the security, adequacy and efficacy' of the CIA. His report, sent to the White House two months later, made for largely grim reading.

Doolittle gave the Agency some credit for surviving its early chaotic years, which were marked by a 'lack of continuity in policy direction and management' as well as the 'inheritance of mixed and sometimes mutually antagonistic elements from ... predecessor agencies', but damned the overall American espionage efforts against the Soviet Union as inadequate. He warned that due to continuing rivalry between the Agency and other outposts of US intelligence, 'important covert operations have been "blown" because the CIA and military intelligence units were operating <u>against</u> each other [emphasis in original], without knowledge of each other's interest or activity'.

Not all of this was the Agency's fault, but structurally the organization was not, in Doolittle's estimation, fit for purpose. It had 'ballooned out into a vast and sprawling organization manned by people . . . of dubious competence'. Although many were veterans of wartime intelligence, they were simply not winning the new Cold War against the vastly experienced Soviet bloc espionage services:

> Because the United States is relatively new at the game, and because we are opposed by a police state enemy whose security measures have been built up and maintained at a high level for many years, the usable information we are obtaining is still far short of our needs.[10]

The lack of 'human intelligence' – spies working for the United States behind the Iron Curtain – was a fundamental reason for the often lethal intelligence gap between Washington and Moscow:

> Because of the tight security controls that have been established by the USSR and its satellites, the problem of infiltration of human agents is extremely difficult . . . escape from detection is extremely difficult because of constant checks on personnel activities and personal documentation.
>
> The information we have obtained by this method of acquisition has been negligible and the cost in effort, dollars and human lives prohibitive.[11]

Doolittle concluded by recommending a wholesale reorganization of the CIA and the streamlining of its operations – not least by bringing its various branches, then housed in forty-three different buildings, scattered across Washington DC, under one roof. The costs of constructing what would eventually become its Langley headquarters in Virginia would be vast – but then money was not one of the Agency's many problems.

From its inception, the CIA had been largely insulated from

oversight on Capitol Hill. Notionally, two Congressional Committees – Armed Services and Appropriations (Defense) – had the right to oversee its budget and activities; the reality was, as the Agency itself later acknowledged, that neither truly did so:

> In actual practice, awareness of [the] CIA's and other intelligence agencies' activities was limited largely to the chairmen and ranking minority members of those committees/subcommittees . . .
>
> Oversight, such as it was, was typically worked out by the Director of Central Intelligence and a few senior members of the Congress, with little involvement of the Congress as a whole.[12]

But the CIA was not entirely immune to Congressional scrutiny. The early Cold War saw America convulsed by the high-profile Soviet espionage cases of Alger Hiss, Ethel and Julius Rosenberg, and Rudolf Abel. In the same period, Senator Joe McCarthy's televised 'Red Scare' hearings, and often-sensational testimony before the House Un-American Activities Committee, inflamed public opinion and created a widespread popular belief that Communist agents had infiltrated the United States government and the entertainment industry wholesale. Against this backdrop, the CIA gradually came under attack for failing to protect the country from Moscow's machinations.

In April 1956, Michael A. Feighan, a veteran anti-communist and Democratic Congressman since 1943, took to his feet in the House of Representatives to make a speech outlining the threat posed by Moscow and its satellites:

> The central issue of our times is the case of Russian communism versus human freedom. We Americans have been hoping and praying that communism with all its evils and threats to the peace could be banished from the face of the earth.
>
> Communism carries with it the seeds of its own destruction, but . . . that group of criminals [in the Kremlin] is now embarking upon a new type of warfare against all civilization.[13]

Two years later, he returned to the House floor to make a ringing denunciation of the CIA's record in countering the Soviet menace:

> They do not seem to have qualified men in Intelligence to come up with correct information. You cannot evaluate faulty information and arrive at any useful results. I think it is about time there was a complete investigation by Congress of our intelligence agencies responsible for this faulty information – or intelligence if you use that misnomer – that comes from the CIA.
>
> There is abundant evidence that our top officials are receiving faulty information with respect to critical issues around the world which causes us to make blunders which reduce our prestige in the world.[14]

The speech garnered little attention outside Washington, and had no discernible impact in improving Congressional oversight. But it would not be the last time Congressman Feighan caused trouble for the CIA.

The most glaring gap in US intelligence's armoury of Cold War weapons was the dearth of defectors from inside the Soviet intelligence apparatus. Although the 1949 Central Intelligence Agency Act established 'Program PL-110' – a new power which allowed the Agency to import up to 100 defectors annually outside regular immigration rules[15] – by 1958 the CIA had attracted only three major defectors from within Soviet bloc intelligence circles:[16] a depressingly small return on investment and one which, Doolittle noted in 1954, had attracted the ire of competing US intelligence services:

> The exploitation of Soviet and satellite defectors outside the United States has been a source of annoyance (and even hostility) on the part of some of the military services and other agencies toward CIA . . . steps should be taken immediately to insure full implementation of the defector program.

More damningly, Doolittle had concluded that although 'the Agency is properly focussing a great deal of its effort in this direction, the information thus far obtained was "sporadic and incomplete".[17]

Even so, the limited information these defectors had provided strongly suggested that Moscow's spies had penetrated American and allied intelligence services, but the CIA had not been able to identify these Soviet moles within Western ranks. Worse, either through incompetent tradecraft or from a leak from one of the moles in its midst, one of the Agency's most important informants – Major Pyotr Popov, who operated as an Agent in Place inside the GRU (Soviet military intelligence) – was detected by the KGB and forced to become a double agent, feeding false intelligence back to the US.[18]

The evidence pointing to a Soviet bloc intelligence mole inside the CIA hardened in early 1958. Shortly after arriving in Bern, Tennent Bagley made a tentative – and almost instantly unsuccessful – bid to recruit a young Polish UB officer also stationed there. It was not a high-profile operation, nor even particularly well planned: Bagley surreptitiously delivered a letter to the target, inviting him to consider working for the Agency. Yet, somehow this low-key scheme had been leaked to Warsaw within a fortnight of it receiving the blessing of CIA headquarters in Washington. Inevitably, the approach failed. At the time, this was marked down as little more than a routine and fairly minor flop, but within a year it would be revisited and picked over as evidence of possible penetration by a uniquely powerful unit within the Agency whose job was precisely to protect it – and by extension the United States – from infiltration by Moscow's spies.

Lieutenant General Doolittle's scathing report on the Agency's structures, personnel and capabilities had led to a substantial reorganization of its myriad separate branches. The most significant innovation was the creation of a dedicated and highly secretive Counter-Intelligence Staff.

None of the CIA's own organizational charts of the period,[19] depicting the internal configuration of its departments, show any trace of CI Staff; on paper, the group did not officially exist. On the ground, within the often-overlapping intelligence branches, it quickly became a dominant force, stepping outside its notional boundaries to usurp the responsibilities of other divisions. As a subsequent internal inquiry report noted:

> The CI Staff's name would imply (if the Agency's formal organization were to be taken at face value) that its function was limited to advising a command echelon. In fact such a distinction was never enforced.
>
> 'CIA Staff' was actually a misnomer, because the organization carrying this name did not even concern itself to any appreciable extent with the counterintelligence function of the Agency on a worldwide basis. Rather, it concentrated on the USSR and Soviet Bloc countries.[20]

In doing so CI Staff stepped on the toes of an existing – and rather better qualified – group within the office specifically tasked with countering Moscow's espionage:

> Within the SB [Soviet Bloc] Division, there was lodged the so-called Soviet CI Group, which was in many respects a competitor of the CI Staff . . . and as such was inevitably somewhat redundant . . .
>
> One curious aspect of the organizational problem should be mentioned . . . While the SB Division understandably had a number of competent Russian linguists, the CI staff [sic] did not have a single Russian linguist who could be brought to bear . . .[21]

In theory, the two rival branches were equals inside the Agency's labyrinthine bureaucracy; in reality, and as an internal history noted, while the CI staff had access to all the SB's internal files, 'it had no insight into the activities of CIS'.[22] This imbalance placed enormous power in the hands of the man who headed the CI Staff.

James Jesus Angleton was thirty-seven years old when he took control of the newly formed Counter-Intelligence Staff in December 1954. A tall, cadaverous figure who wore heavy-rimmed eyeglasses and habitually favoured an old-fashioned Homburg hat, he had spent more than a decade in the business of detecting and combatting enemy espionage.

After graduating from Yale and then Harvard Law School, he had been drafted into the US Army in 1943 and posted to the Office of Strategic Services – the CIA's wartime forerunner and America's first foreign intelligence and covert action organization. Since the United States was so new at the spying game – and in the midst of the war faced a steep and urgent learning curve – the OSS relied heavily on British intelligence, which had a long hinterland in the business.

Angleton was assigned to the new counterintelligence branch X-2, 'which had only been established that year under the tutelage of the United Kingdom's Secret Intelligence Service, MI6'.[23] He learned his trade at the feet of an experienced MI6 officer named Harold 'Kim' Philby.

Two of Angleton's experiences during World War II played a vital part in forming his approach to the Great Game. The first was his role in Italy, in which he ran agents inside the Axis countries and, as Germany's defeat became inevitable, negotiated secret surrender deals with SS intelligence officers based in Rome; it was a covert operation which would, in time, impact on the CIA's attitude to Cold War defectors. The second, and rather less hidden, influence was his exposure to the highly successful British 'Double-Cross System' which, under the aegis of John Masterman, a former Oxford University academic turned MI5 officer, turned captured Nazi spies into double agents working on behalf of the United Kingdom.

Angleton absorbed and thereafter took as his guiding principle Masterman's advice: 'The more valuable an agent's service, the more reason to fear a deception. The greater the truth . . . the bigger the lie.'[24]

The practical effect of this adage on Angleton's remarkable intellect was to instil a presumption that every piece of intelligence sourced from behind the Iron Curtain – and every defector offering his services – was a potential double cross or deception: in spy jargon, a 'dangle' or a 'provocation'. As his power increased within the CIA, presumption became paranoia, and he slowly became lost in what he would later call 'the wilderness of mirrors': a constantly shifting landscape in which it was almost impossible to distinguish between reality and reflection. As the Agency's own history records:

> Angleton became convinced early in his career that the Soviet Union's KGB for many years had successfully run major deception operations against the West in general and the United States in particular. He became convinced that the KGB had penetrated [the] CIA at high levels and that it had taken advantage of these penetrations to successfully run agent provocations against the Agency.[25]

It was against this backdrop that the CIA intercepted and took to itself Sniper's sudden and mysterious letter to the FBI. The offer of information on Soviet bloc espionage was on the table and, given the Agency's troublesome run of intelligence failures, it was – in theory – exactly the windfall needed. The question was whether the CIA, and more particularly, James Jesus Angleton, was willing to trust it.

3

'Dear Mr Director'

T HE PROBLEM WAS simple – but fundamental. Who *was* Sniper?
Confirming an informant's identity was the conventional first step in establishing his 'bona fides', but as Tennent Bagley, who handled all the early correspondence recalled, 'We did not know who he was; he even hid his nationality.'[1]

Without Sniper's name, much less which service he worked for, it was impossible for the CIA to determine whether he was real or a KGB 'dangle'; whether his offer of intelligence was genuine or a new Soviet 'provocation'.

And Sniper did not make the task any easier. Early tests on his two letters of April 1958, the one addressed to Ambassador Taylor and the other to J. Edgar Hoover, showed that the writer had adopted good trade-craft: there were no fingerprints, indicating he had worn gloves, and the papers bore no identifying marks which might help analysts work out who had prepared them. All the Agency could do was to sit back and wait for the volunteer agent to get in touch again.

In May 1958, less than a month after his opening gambit, a further Sniper letter landed in the CIA dead drop in West Berlin. Like one of its predecessors, it was typed in German, addressed to the FBI, and began 'Sehr geehrter Herr Direktor' – Dear Mr Director.

However, the writer had evidently anticipated the suspicion that his anonymity would generate, so he now offered proof of his good intentions – copies of highly classified NATO documents which had been obtained by the KGB:

> In order to convict [sic] you that the collection of Top Secret informations [sic] through a source (agent) of the Soviet/Polish intelligence is a factual and true one, I take the liberty, as far as I can, to supply you with certain fragments from the copies of protocols (of NATO). If you will compare these with the originals you will see that my information is true and correct.[2]

The papers he included had come from the NATO Conference, held at the Palais de Chaillot, Paris, on 16 December 1957. It was the first summit attended by the leaders of all member nations, and had been subject to strict secrecy – not least because it discussed the defence strategy of the Western Alliance and unanimously agreed covertly to deploy Intermediate Range Ballistic Missiles in Europe, while simultaneously conducting overt negotiations with Moscow.

Sniper had obtained portions of the most sensitive sections of the debate, including statements by Secretary of State John Foster Dulles 'about the new weapons for NATO defence' and a commitment to add $625 million to a loan fund 'for the economic reserves of the underdeveloped countries of the free world'. Sniper even provided a transcript – including the exact time of its delivery – of President Eisenhower's request that delegates take 'a few moments for silent prayer'.[3]

He also gave precise details of how, and when, Moscow had acquired these documents; they had been sent to Polish intelligence by one of its agents in January 1958 – less than a month after the summit took place. Warsaw had duly shipped them 'via special messenger and through special Mil. Air Plane [sic]' to the KGB and the Soviet Politburo.[4]

The papers strongly suggested that NATO had been penetrated and that one of the delegates or support staff was spying for Soviet bloc espionage services. But the level of detail, and its accuracy, also offered significant proof of Sniper's integrity. And, as further letters arrived in a series of CIA dead drops – because Stasi agents were presumed to be constantly searching them out across divided Berlin, alternatives were set up in the Tiergarten park and a public toilet at Berlin Zoo's train station – the evidence that he was a real and reliable source of much-needed intelligence mounted month by month.

Each new report was always typed, and always in German; each ran to several closely typed pages, and Sniper often enclosed copies of top-secret Soviet bloc documents – although he carefully excised from the material anything that might identify the precise agency from which he had obtained it. The letters were routed, via Bagley's office in Bern, to the Agency's chief European intelligence centre in Berlin; from there they were sent in the diplomatic bag to CIA headquarters.

The Agency's field officers and desk-bound analysts pored over every sentence; soon they became convinced that Sniper was genuine. Although frustrated by the man's continuing anonymity, Richards Heuer summed up the prevailing opinion in Washington: 'In time, we began to take his information seriously, although we still did not know his name or whether he was Polish or Russian. We also wondered how he could have gained access to so much information from both countries.'[5]

In Bern, Tennent Bagley also became a true believer in the mysterious anonymous spy, and soon worked out that Sniper must be a senior Polish intelligence officer, working in conjunction with the KGB. This dual role explained how he came by the wealth of his material: 'It took only one or two more letters from him to persuade me that Sniper was not only genuine but also invaluable . . . He occupied a special position of trust within the KGB and thus learned a lot from his KGB friends, mostly but not all involving operations with connections to Poles and Poland.'[6]

James Angleton, however, remained profoundly wary. As the chief of counterintelligence, suspicion was a default position; gift horses bearing such timely and evidently real Soviet secrets were to be distrusted as a matter of course, and presumed to be strategically placed sources of disinformation.

Angleton's fears were not wholly groundless. 'The Trust' might have seemed like ancient history, but the WiN debacle showed that his adversaries in Moscow and Warsaw had long memories, and an appetite for leading the CIA down a tortuous and costly garden path.

Ironically, Sniper himself added fuel to this smouldering scepticism when, in mid-1959, he forwarded an internal KGB report on the formation of a new unit, dedicated to creating long-form deceptions:

> Following is an extract of a translation of a top-secret paper of a Soviet Bloc state security service on the subject of counterintelligence deception:
>
> 'The basic function of the counter-intelligence organs is to detect and liquidate the espionage activity of foreign agents in our country. However, accomplishment of this task does not fully guarantee neutralization of the operations of capitalist intelligence organs . . . [which] after the brief crisis caused by the liquidation of their agents, reorganize their intelligence centers, alter the forms and methods of operation, and continue with greater intensity their espionage activity against us.'

The solution to this, according to the new KGB strategy, was 'planned and systematically conducted disinformation . . . to undermine the enemy's confidence in their agent network . . . to penetrate deeper into their activities, and to strengthen the position of our counter-intelligence network'.

Specifically, these disinformation operations would 'disguise areas of real intelligence interest; to direct the enemy towards areas and installations and subjects where our counter-intelligence apparatus is well set up to detect enemy agents; [and] to get money from foreign intelligence'.[7]

Sniper's report and enclosure were sent to Heuer for assessment; he immediately recognized their importance in the CIA's counterintelligence war with Moscow:

> Department D, the KGB's disinformation department, had been formed in 1959 . . . [Sniper] was the first CIA source to report in detail on its anticipated functions and significance.

He stated that one of the many objectives of KGB disinformation was the protection of Soviet agents by means of actions designed to mislead Western special services. He listed among specific objectives and types of disinformation operations those designed to discredit accurate information of significance received by the opposition through sources not under Soviet control, such as defectors, thus casting doubt on the veracity of the source of this true information: [he] stated further that, in extreme cases, the KGB would be willing to sacrifice some of its own agent assets to enhance the reputation of an agent penetration of a Western intelligence service.[8]

Although Sniper could not have foreseen it – particularly since he believed he was corresponding with the FBI – his exposure of Department D and Moscow's directive fed James Angleton's paranoia. Trapped in the endlessly shifting kaleidoscope of counterintelligence, Angleton brooded over his suspicion that the man who had revealed the existence of Moscow's disinformation branch was himself a KGB dangle – a new and subtle channel for feeding bogus information to the West.

But other – rival – departments within the CIA were convinced that Sniper was not merely genuine but that most prized of all assets – an Agent in Place. Whilst the Agency was desperate for defectors, experienced field officers knew that the most valuable spy of all was one willing to remain undercover in his home country and service. It was a remarkably dangerous role; the KGB and its satellites across the Soviet bloc were on constant alert for traitors within their midst, and if found, the best a mole could hope for was a swift execution. Sniper, then, had deliberately, and apparently willingly, placed his own neck on the block.

Throughout 1959 he sent ever more detailed letters, mostly at regular monthly intervals. The intelligence they contained was as extensive as it was startling, covering Iron Curtain military secrets, political intelligence and, above all, revelations about espionage activities and agents. To Bagley, the thousands of pages Sniper smuggled out to dead letter drops across Berlin provided 'a rich bounty of leads'[9] – an assessment confirmed by a subsequent internal CIA report:

> These documents included significant positive intelligence, provided numerous clues to penetrations of Western governments, armed forces, NATO, etc., and contained invaluable counterintelligence information . . .
>
> He [Sniper] reported on KGB organization, personnel, and at length on those KGB officers with whom he had been acquainted . . . [and] he produced extremely valuable leads to KGB operations . . .
>
> [He] provided the most complete and detailed charts and organization descriptions of the Polish Security Service and the Polish Military Intelligence Service received on any Communist service. His meticulous attention to detail and his extraordinary memory made it possible to trace all the organizational shifts which occurred in the two services since 1945 [and] the control or influence of the Soviets.[10]

Among the choice morsels Sniper served up were details of Polish intelligence's vigorous recruitment of agents at the Poznan International Fair, the biggest industrial exhibition and trade gathering in Europe, and pointers to the identity of an Italian diplomat who had fallen into the UB's clutches and was being used to acquire Western technological secrets for the benefit of both Warsaw and Moscow.

Sniper also sent detailed information about the numbers of illegal *rezidenturas* – senior Soviet bloc spies living under deep cover and controlling sub-agents – in the West. Sniper reported that there were fifty-three such illegals in the United States and Canada alone, and, quoting conversations with named KGB chiefs, revealed that some were tasked with long-term missions extending far beyond conventional espionage:

> The number of *rezidenturas* would include 'MOB' Networks: 'MOB' comes from the word 'mobilization' and is the name given to sleeper networks which would become active in case of war.

Their missions are primarily sabotage and diversion. They maintain communications periodically but do not engage in clandestine activity.[11]

Much of Sniper's information focused on Soviet penetration. On page after page, he described the scale of operations by Soviet bloc spy agencies to burrow inside Western governments and intelligence services. He provided tantalizing hints about one: an extraordinary scheme, dating back to the last years of the Third Reich, to create an undercover 'false flag' fascist 'stay behind' network, which would operate under Moscow's control in post-war Europe.

Sniper's initial account of the organization suggested the probable existence of a major and deep-cover operation. If true, it pointed to Soviet penetration of America's key Cold War ally – the West German intelligence service. But the information was dense and would require long-term, careful handling: the CIA put it to one side, marked for future investigation.

It had good reason to do so. Among the reams of reports which landed in the dead drops were documents indicating a more pressing problem: a highly developed Polish intelligence programme to entrap and compromise US diplomatic staff during their postings in Warsaw. The CIA recorded the details in Sniper's growing file:

> The UB had a pool of attractive female agents who were used against all Western diplomats. If a Westerner made the acquaintance of a Polish woman outside of the UB pool, an effort would be made to remove the latter from the social scene of the Westerners and substitute one of the female UB co-opted workers or agents. In several cases the association has ended in marriage and the Polish woman ... would be exploited as an access to her husband.[12]

Sniper's letters evidently provided sufficient detail for the Agency to identify and investigate specific cases. The results were disturbing:

> In two cases cited by [Sniper], the Western diplomat has had a
> successful career in his country's service and in both cases the
> KGB has taken the case from the UB ... Both diplomats were
> reported by [the] CIA to the security services of his respective
> country ... There are many other examples of the female UB
> agent marrying Westerners or leaving Poland with the assistance
> of a Western diplomat ...[13]

This 'red swallows' entrapment programme highlighted a growing problem in handling Sniper's intelligence reports. For almost a year the CIA
had kept them to itself, determined that no whisper of their existence
should reach the rival intelligence division of the FBI.

But many of the compromised diplomatic staff regularly travelled to
the United States; worse, some were American foreign service officers
who routinely rotated back to Washington before moving on to other
sensitive postings.

By law the Agency was forbidden from operating inside US borders:
domestic security and counter-espionage was the FBI's exclusive domain.
In December 1958, as Sniper's reports stacked up, the CIA knew it had to
bring the Bureau into the circle. The irascible Director's response was
predictable: 'Hoover was mad as hell when he found out we had been
opening his mail', recalled Howard Roman. 'But [he] agreed to let us handle it as long as we showed the Bureau everything we got from Sniper.'[14]

A few weeks before Christmas, the reports were sent across Washington and delivered to the FBI's Domestic Intelligence Division; here,
at least six senior members of the Espionage Division were tasked with
determining whether Sniper was genuine or a Soviet provocation. One
of them, veteran agent John R. Norpel, later testified in a secret session
of the US Senate Internal Security Subcommittee: 'This information ...
came over from the Central Intelligence Agency which said "We are in
receipt of this information from a source" ... I remember that there was
a great deal of discussion as to his authenticity and credibility, in other
words that he was possibly a plant.'[15]

By February 1959, Norpel subsequently told the Senators, the Bureau had reached the conclusion that Sniper's information 'was valid, and that he was a reliable source'. But because Sniper had identified US diplomatic staff, the FBI was required to inform the State Department; 'after corroborative evidence had been developed to either dispute the claim or establish it', the Bureau sent the reports back across Washington to Foggy Bottom.[16]

Sniper himself remained completely unaware that his letters to Hoover had been diverted into the CIA's clutches, or that the Agency had shared them with the State Department; he continued sending lengthy and detailed reports, and the CIA continued its deception, always signing its responses and requests for additional material in the name of the FBI Director. In doing so, as Tennent Bagley later admitted, it was putting the mysterious informant's life in danger:

> Moscow's satraps viewed him as their special confidant inside the UB and had been turning to him personally with the questions they felt too sensitive to ask through formal liaison. In the process he had come to know a lot about their most secret agents in the West . . .
>
> But in his special knowledge lay [Sniper's] special problem as well. What he had learned about Moscow's moles inside Western intelligence services thwarted his purpose as much as inspiring it . . . the KGB representatives had made it clear to [him] that the CIA – meaning its Soviet bloc staff – was . . . penetrated. If he turned there, he knew, the news would get back to Moscow.[17]

Despite this, the circle of US intelligence agencies, and the number of officers within them, that knew about Sniper continued to expand. It could only be a matter of time before his existence as an Agent in Place would be blown.

The CIA was, in any event, then still riven by disputes over the validity and importance of what landed in their lap. While Bagley and other SB officers were convinced, Angleton as chief of counterintelligence remained deeply hostile, and even those unaligned in the Agency's internal wars were frustrated by the extraordinary volume and detail of the material.

'The letters were very confusing,' Howard Roman recalled. 'Everyone analyzed them differently . . . about four per cent of the information in Sniper's letters turned out to be useful.' The rest, in his view, was 'indecipherable or of marginal interest'; in one letter, sent 'at great personal risk', Sniper wrote 'at great length about a notorious black marketeer who smuggled watches to Soviet military officers in Warsaw & undertook occasional spy missions for both the Russians and the Poles'. He provided the dates on which this relatively petty crook would be staying in a hotel in Vienna, gave a vivid description of the wig he would be wearing as a disguise, and insisted American intelligence agents book an adjoining room; here they were to drill a hole in the wall, pump 'anaesthetizing gas' through it, and then kidnap the alleged criminal. 'That was the kind of stuff that took up a lot of room in his letters,' Roman said. '[But] then suddenly you would get two lines . . .'[18]

In mid-1959 two of those lines rang urgent alarm bells throughout the CIA. Roman was told to get himself on the next flight to London, where a joint team of senior MI5 and MI6 officers would be waiting for him. Sniper had provided new and explicit evidence that the KGB was running two very active spies – code-named LAMBDA 1 and 2 – inside Britain's most sensitive intelligence departments: the Admiralty – and MI6 itself.

4

London

THE MODEST BRASS plate on the facade of the tall, stone-fronted building, a short walk from the Palace of Westminster, announced it as the premises of The Minimax Fire Extinguisher Company.[1] Inside its warren of gloomy and somewhat shabby offices there was, though, no sign of commerce, or of any anti-inflammatory merchandise. Nor had there ever been.

For more than thirty years number 54 Broadway had been the head-quarters of the Secret Intelligence Service, MI6: the agency charged with overseas espionage and counter-espionage, but which did not – officially – exist. The brass plate was a simple yet remarkably effective means of disguising the presence of Britain's premier spies working within the building.[2] That morning in April 1959, however, the small group of middle-aged men gathered in a fourth-floor conference room might have benefited from the products purveyed by the purported occupants of the premises.

The assembled company were all senior officers in three of the West's most powerful and important bulwarks against Soviet bloc espionage: MI6, MI5 and the CIA. They were also, notionally at least, allies in the fight against Moscow's spymasters, but the relationship that each had established with the others during World War II had been beset by tension and acrimony for almost a decade.

That spring morning, the American representative added accelerant to an already combustible situation. 'Sniper says the Russians have got two very important spies in Britain: one in British intelligence, the other somewhere in the Navy,' Howard Roman bluntly informed his counterparts, before alerting them to the existence and presumed background of the CIA's source. 'He's almost certainly in the UB. His German's off, and the Polish stuff is Grade 1 from the inside.'[3]

The revelation was the last news either of the British services needed. The defections in May 1951 of Guy Burgess and Donald Maclean, both Foreign Office officials (and, in Burgess's case, a former agent of MI6), had caused a rift between US and British intelligence – one which forced MI5's then Director General, Sir Percy Sillitoe, to make a transatlantic bid to appease his American counterpart in the FBI. As the official history of the Security Service records, he was not entirely successful:

> Sillitoe flew to Washington to brief, and attempt to mollify, the irascible J. Edgar Hoover in person. As well as undertaking the difficult task of trying to reassure a sceptical Hoover about the current state of British security, he quickly found himself caught in the crossfire between the Bureau and the CIA.[4]

At least part of that 'crossfire' involved a third British spy, Harold 'Kim' Philby. As a senior MI6 officer during World War II he had taken James Angleton under his wing and in post-war Washington tutored him in the art of counterintelligence; in turn, Angleton viewed Philby as a close friend and had trusted him with the details of CIA operations. But investigations by MI5 had convinced the Security Service that Philby was a traitor, a KGB mole within British intelligence, and that he had given Burgess and Maclean the tip-off which enabled them to escape to Moscow. Although he had been allowed to resign from MI6, his treachery was an open secret in London and in Washington. It was a festering sore between Hoover and Angleton, and between American and British intelligence. In October 1955 the fault line became public and unavoidable: at Hoover's instigation, the *New York Sunday News* named Philby as the 'Third Man' in Britain's growing spy scandal, and on 25 October the Labour MP Marcus Lipton put the government on the spot in Parliament:

> Has the Prime Minister made up his mind to cover up at all costs the dubious third man activities of Mr. Harold Philby who was First Secretary at the Washington Embassy a little time ago, and is he determined to stifle all discussion on the very great matters . . . which is an insult to the intelligence of the country?[5]

Prime Minister Harold Macmillan, who loathed espionage and generally sought to avoid discussions with Britain's intelligence agencies, made the fateful decision to provide Philby with a clean bill of health; in doing so, he not only insulted the country, as Lipton had warned, but the intelligence agencies in Washington. It was, then, little wonder that in the words of Peter Wright, one of the senior MI5 men briefed by Howard Roman in April 1959, 'relations between British and American intelligence . . . were at their lowest post-war ebb'.[6]

Roman told the meeting that Sniper had reported on discussions with his colleagues in the KGB, and that they had shown him top-secret documents provided by their moles in British intelligence. The information was fragmentary, and the CIA man made it clear that Angleton remained profoundly sceptical. Nor could Sniper put names to Moscow's pair of spies inside MI6 and the Navy; for that reason he had christened them 'LAMBDA 1' and 'LAMBDA 2'.

On LAMBDA 2 there was very little for MI5 and MI6 to get their teeth into. All Sniper knew was that he had served in Warsaw in 1952, where he had been caught by Polish security trading on the black market; it had then blackmailed him into betraying his country. The information on LAMBDA 1, however, was potentially more helpful: Sniper had been shown three internal MI6 documents which the mole had sent to his masters in Moscow.

One was an excerpt from 'R6', the annual summary of intelligence, listed country by country, which MI6 circulated to its offices worldwide;

Sniper had seen the section covering Poland. The second was a portion of 'RB', a parallel report sent out from London which summarized the latest scientific and technical innovations, as well as their use by the SIS in overseas operations. The third document – 'The Watch List' – was the most sensitive of all: it identified Polish citizens that MI6's Warsaw Station had targeted for recruitment.[7]

The triangulation of these three documents meant, in theory, that MI6 would be able to come up with a list of possible moles; working out which of its officers had access to all of them should have made the job of identifying suspects relatively straightforward. The task was handed to the head of counterintelligence, Terence Lecky, a thirteen-year MI6 veteran; it did not take him long to discover that only ten SIS officers had ever had access to all the reports. But that was the best Lecky could do: as Peter Wright recalled three decades later:

> The records of all ten were investigated, and all were exonerated, including one named George Blake, a rising young MI6 officer . . . Blake, MI5 and MI6 concluded, could not possibly be a spy. The best explanation for the leak, in the absence of any credible human candidate, was a burglary of an MI6 safe in Brussels, which had taken place two years before.[8]

There had, indeed, been a burglary – or rather a series of burglaries; in the early to mid-1950s safes in secure premises in Warsaw and Gdynia (near Gdansk), as well as Brussels, had been raided, but since no one had thought to keep an inventory of what they contained, contemporary internal investigations had quickly dried up. In autumn 1959 the burglary story was passed back to Washington without further qualification; Angleton saw it and added it to his growing list of grudges against Sniper. Before long he, MI6 and MI5 would all have cause to regret their somewhat lacklustre collective response to Sniper's warnings.

In March 1960, Sniper sent a new report to the CIA's West Berlin dead letter drop; it provided far more detailed information on

LAMBDA 2 and included a list of ninety-nine documents the mole had smuggled to Soviet bloc intelligence from January to November 1952. MI5 quickly assigned its own cryptonym to the source: henceforth in British intelligence files Sniper was recorded as LAVINIA, and as an excerpt in its belatedly declassified files shows, his new material was remarkably precise:

> We have recently received from CIA information from LAVINIA which may have a bearing on the leakage from an Attaché's office in Warsaw. LAVINIA reported as follows:
>
> 'In about 1951 an employee of the British Naval Attaché's office in Warsaw was recruited. The employee had access to the secret activities and documents of the Attaché . . .
>
> 'The name of the employee was given provisionally by LAVINIA as HUPPKENER or HAPPKENER or HUPPEN-KORT or some such. The employee was transferred back to England about the beginning of 1953 and assigned to the Admiralty. Because of his importance, he was then taken over by the KGB and continued to work successfully for the KGB in London . . .'[9]

The list of documents LAMBDA 2 had leaked was particularly troubling. Its index specified that they had been 'acquired in the British Embassy by means of Agent Penetration', and included data on the size and strength of British and US naval forces; instructions as to what is needed by British intelligence on Soviet ports and the ports of the People's Democracies'; numerous Allied 'military Intelligence Reports'; and the Admiralty's highly sensitive Manual of Naval Intelligence.[10]

MI5 began an urgent review of old case files and reports emanating from Warsaw. What it discovered made for grim reading, and was certain to increase American suspicions about the security of British intelligence. In May 1960, MI6 forwarded the preliminary results to Washington:

We have now carried out a certain amount of limited investigation on the list of documents provided by LAVINIA and have reached, in conjunction with the Security Service, certain tentative conclusions . . .

Although we have not been able to identify all the documents given in the LAVINIA list, we believe that these documents could have been in existence at the British Embassy, Warsaw, in 1951 and 1952. We also believe that there is no other point in Poland or in the UK where all the documents could have existed at any time.

At one point we considered that the burglaries which took place in Gdynia from 1955 onwards might account for the loss of some of the documents. Although our investigations are still continuing, the possibility that these burglaries can account for the loss of the documents is rapidly diminishing. Evidence to date indicates that most of them probably never went to Gdynia . . .

At the time when we had a Naval Attaché's office in Warsaw (up to Autumn 1955), the papers of this office were kept in a registry strong-room shared with the Military Attaché . . . All of the documents by their nature could have been in the possession at some time of the Naval Attaché or the Military Attaché and thus could have been held in the joint registry strong-room.

The key document – and the one which helped focus the hunt – was the Manual of Naval Intelligence. The version which Polish and Soviet intelligence had been given by their spy was dated 1948; but they had also evidently seen a separate chart setting out a planned, but never implemented, internal reorganization of the Admiralty's Naval Intelligence Branch, dated several years later and which was never held in the same location as the other papers. This led to a doleful conclusion: 'We regretfully conclude therefore that we have to consider two separate leakages of Attaché papers.'[11]

There was, however, worse to follow. MI5 drew up a list of embassy staff who could have had access to documents and compared them with Sniper's rough approximation of the spy's name; there was no 'Huppkener or Happkener or Huppenkort', but there was a 'Houghton'. It was hardly an exact match, but the circumstances of the man's career suggested that he was the most likely candidate.

Outwardly, fifty-five-year-old Harry Frederick Houghton was a nondescript plodder in the lower levels of government service, but his drab appearance masked a history of petty criminality, incipient alcoholism and domestic violence. His flaws and weaknesses made him an easy target for Soviet bloc intelligence, while his mundane position ensured that his country failed to spot the danger he posed.

Born in Lincoln, he had left school at fourteen and joined the Royal Navy, rising during World War II to the rank of Chief Petty Officer and assigned the duties of Master at Arms – a non-commissioned officer responsible for on-board discipline. At the end of the war he joined the civil service, and was assigned to the Department of Naval Intelligence (DNI). In July 1951 he was posted, as an Admiralty Clerical Officer, to the British Embassy in Warsaw, and for a year he was the only member of the Naval Attaché's staff. His wife, Amy, accompanied him and the couple lived together in a cheap apartment block.[12]

As a British government employee Houghton had access to Western goods and produce in a Communist society notably short on luxuries. He quickly exploited his position to trade on the black market – a dangerous, if profitable, enterprise which evidently brought him to the attention of the Polish police. They duly handed him over to the Urząd Bezpieczeństwa (UB), which gave him a stark choice: work undercover for Polish intelligence or face the exposure of his criminal activities to the British Embassy. Houghton elected to betray his country.

It was a decision made easier by his growing resentment at what he considered ill-treatment by his employers and unhappiness with his wife. An internal MI5 letter noted:

> Investigations have shown that during his time there [Warsaw] he
> was disgruntled over living conditions, inefficient at his work and
> drank to excess ... His wife did not take to life in Warsaw and
> seems to have contributed to the low state of her husband's
> morale.
>
> During their time in Warsaw relations seem to have deteri-
> orated steadily and towards the end of their tour Mrs. Houghton
> sustained a broken leg, possibly as a result of violence on the part
> of her husband.[13]

If British authorities in the 1950s took no interest in the home lives of
their employees – even when these included evidence of domestic
abuse – Houghton's other activities should have raised serious concerns.
According to an MI5 summary of his wife's subsequent testimony:

> About two or three months after the Houghtons' arrival in War-
> saw, Houghton started going out between nine and eleven on
> Wednesday nights and would return with bundles of used Eng-
> lish bank notes ... Houghton used to explain these nocturnal
> disappearances by saying that they were connected with his
> black-market activities.[14]

Before long, Amy Houghton had additional cause to worry. Houghton
began making regular late-night phone calls; he 'always turned his wife
out of the room before making these calls and she would hear him talking in soft tones. He also brought Polish nationals to their home, again
kicked her out of [the] room and refused to tell her who the visitors were.'

Unsurprisingly, Mrs Houghton began to suspect that her husband
had been recruited as a spy, and asked him 'if he was working for the
Party'. He replied that he intended to 'string along with the side which
paid him the most money.'[15]

A disgruntled naval clerk with unsupervised access to highly classified documents who was semi-openly trading on the black market and
holding late-night discussions with citizens of a hostile power should

have been noticed by the Admiralty. But even in the security panic which had followed the defections of Burgess and Maclean just two months earlier, the Navy took a lofty view of its duty to protect the privacy of its employees. As it explained in a subsequent attempt at self-justification:

> After Burgess/Maclean case, it was only with greatest reluctance that Govt. [sic] accepted the obligation to keep an eye on private lives and habits of public servants, outside their places and times of duty: even then, they set strict limits to the doing of this (confined to those of known bad habits) and were much criticized ... for going even so far.
>
> To go further and institute a direct system of continuous spying is in excess of the Government's policy announced after Burgess/Maclean, and in excess of what the nation would stand ... We reject McCarthyism in this country at whatever price ...[16]

But if keeping a watchful eye on a clerk who exhibited clear signs of treachery was beyond the pale, clerical incompetence was taken far more seriously. By the end of 1952, the Naval Attaché, one Captain Austen, reached the end of his patience. As he subsequently told MI5's investigators: 'As Naval Attaché's clerk he thought [Houghton] was fairly incompetent and typed with his toes judging by the result. He found his personality unattractive and ... noticed he was drinking heavily.'[17]

This had not, however, persuaded Austen to restrict, or even monitor, Houghton's access to classified material; he could, the attaché admitted, 'quite easily have taken papers from the Embassy for quite a long period without their disappearance being noted'.

Nonetheless, the lamentable typing and heavy drinking were apparently inexcusable: in October 1952, Harry Houghton was sacked from his job at the embassy and sent back to England. Before he left he carried out two final tasks: he sold a large quantity of contraband to his black-market contacts, and he met with his Polish intelligence handlers to arrange his transfer to new masters – the KGB.

But Houghton's personal problems and poor performance in Poland appear not to have given the Admiralty any pause for thought. Within weeks of his return from Warsaw it reassigned him to the Underwater Detection Establishment (UDE), a highly sensitive research unit, based in Her Majesty's Naval Base at Portland, Dorset. Here, for the next seven years, he had access to the research and testing results on some of the Navy's newest weapons.

The posting, however, did not ease his sense of grievance, nor his willingness to take out his unhappiness on his wife. He was drinking more heavily than ever, spending between £10 and £20 a week – equivalent to £225–£240 today – in pubs and off-licences.[18] This incipient alcoholism took an inevitable toll on the couple's home life, and in March 1954 Amy Houghton wrote to her husband's employers, begging them to give him another chance in the Warsaw Embassy:

> He feels a great injustice was done to him when he was with-drawn from Warsaw and he still [has] that on his mind . . . I now know he was accused of many things that were untrue and that he was unable to defend himself of the accusations . . . the pur-pose of this letter is to ask you if you will allow him to go back to Poland.[19]

The Department of Naval Intelligence appears to have ignored the letter and the evidence that Houghton posed a potential security risk. It would not be the last time that the DNI turned a Nelsonian blind eye to a prob-lem in plain sight.

By autumn 1955, Mrs Houghton had had enough. She walked out of their home and, shortly afterwards, made a second attempt to sound the alarm about her husband; this time she reported her fears that he was a spy. A note, dated June 1956, which MI5 discovered in Admiralty files, was clear and unequivocal: 'During the course of recent welfare enquir-ies it is understood that Mrs. Houghton alleged that her husband was divulging secret information to people who ought not to get it.'[20]

Mrs Houghton had solid grounds for suspicion. Her husband regularly disappeared – often for entire weekends. He explained these trips as necessary for meetings with his black-market contacts, but when she searched their home, she found 'a bundle of papers marked Top Secret and relating, in so far as she could understand, to underwater detection equipment and torpedoes'. She also discovered a 'tiny camera' with rolls of film, hidden under the stairs.[21]

The Admiralty, however, dismissed Mrs Houghton's warnings out of hand, blithely pronouncing, 'Hitherto there has been no question of his [Houghton's] integrity. It is considered not impossible that the whole of these allegations may be nothing more than the outpourings of a jealous and disgruntled wife.'[22] It managed to reach this remarkable conclusion despite other corroborative evidence of espionage at Portland. As MI5 noted:

> We also now know that in June 1956 an executive officer at UDE Portland reported to a security officer that certain classified files which were missing from the strong room and subsequently returned surreptitiously after a search had been instituted were thought to have been seen on Houghton's desk. In describing the incident, the executive office mentioned Houghton's apparent affluence and his mysterious trips to London . . .
>
> It must be assumed either that the executive officer's report was made orally or that his written report failed to reach Houghton's personnel file.[23]

Yet the only positive action taken by the Admiralty was to transfer Houghton to a different department within the naval dockyard where, it noted, 'it is believed he no longer has access to classified material'. It was too little, too late. As MI5's investigation showed, Houghton had already recruited a sub-agent. As a filing clerk in the Underwater Detection Establishment, Ethel 'Bunty' Gee routinely handled top-secret documents, including details of Britain's first nuclear submarine, HMS *Dreadnought*. A spinster with little social life, she was nine years younger than Houghton and became his lover; she also supplied him with classified papers for onward transfer to the KGB.

By May 1960, M15 and MI6 had come to the reluctant conclusion that the information provided by Sniper/LAVINIA had exposed a spy – and one who, had the Admiralty been rather less lackadaisical about security, should have been detected several years earlier. Houghton had 'all the elements which any Intelligence Service would look for when considering a target for recruitment. He had difficulties with his wife, he was dissatisfied with his living conditions, he was unsatisfactory at his job . . . did not get on well with his superiors, he was inclined to drink and was cautioned at least once about it. He was, in general, thoroughly disgruntled.'[24]

MI5 duly assigned cryptonyms to Houghton and Gee – REVERBERATE and TRELLIS. From that spring onward, watchers from local police and the Security Service's A4 branch kept the pair under near-constant surveillance; they reported that the couple frequently drove up to London for clandestine rendezvous with a mysterious and, given the drabness of London in mid-1960, somewhat flamboyant businessman. It seemed probable that the man was Houghton and Gee's handler, but cross-referencing his photo with that of all known Soviet bloc intelligence officers – *rezidenturas* who operated semi-openly under diplomatic cover inside Soviet bloc embassies – produced no match; he was completely unknown, raising the unpleasant spectre of a hitherto undetected espionage ring. Tugging on the single strand of LAVINIA's information had begun to reveal something far bigger and more dangerous. It had also firmly established – in British minds at least – his credentials as a reliable source.

The CIA, however, was another matter. As MI5 contemplated the unwelcome prospect of owning up to yet another embarrassing security breach, the CIA began demanding answers: what, it asked, had come from Sniper's lead? Internal correspondence between one of the investigators and MI5 management recorded the dilemma:

I agree that this latest information goes a long way to establishing the reliability of [LAVINIA]. May I now take you up again on the point which we discussed recently in my office, namely whether anything can be said to CIA at this stage on the progress of your investigations?

John Briance [MI6's liaison officer in Washington DC] has already been tackled on this point by CIA Headquarters and with your agreement I told him that CIA could be informed that your investigations were proceeding satisfactorily and that nothing had emerged so far which in any way invalidated the information provided by [LAVINIA] . . . Would you now be agreeable to CIA being told:

(a) that an interview with REVERBERATE's former wife has provided information, strongly suggesting that REVERBERATE has been engaging in espionage for a number of years

(b) that he had a girlfriend with current access to UDE Portland

(c) that on a recent visit to London he and Miss Gee were observed to make a clandestine contact

(d) that your conclusions from the above lead you to think that REVERBERATE still has a current intelligence role

This last item is particularly important, as Angleton has always maintained that one of the weakest features in [LAVINIA's] reporting has been that he has given no leads to any current Polish or R.I.S. [Russian Intelligence Service] agents. To learn that REVERBERATE was still an active spy would go a long way towards silencing the critics of [LAVINIA] in CIA . . .[25]

The senior management of both Britain's intelligence services did not, however, relish the prospect either of being completely honest about their latest spy scandal, or of incurring Angleton's ire at being proved wrong about agent Sniper/LAVINIA. By the end of the 1950s, the balance of power in Western intelligence had shifted away from London and was now firmly in the grip of Washington DC. Britain's diminishing world role and the rise of American power – compounded by the Burgess/Maclean scandals – meant that the CIA was very much the senior partner, with MI5 and MI6 relegated to junior status.

Accordingly, British intelligence chiefs decided to offer up only a 'guarded' conclusion that 'there were firm indications that REVERBERATE had spied and that there were indications that he may be currently active and have recruited a sub-source who has more access to classified information than he has'. No mention was to be made to Angleton of Houghton and Gee's mysterious businessman contact, or the possibility of a wider and much more dangerous espionage ring.

Nor, with the original source still operating undercover behind the Iron Curtain, was it possible to arrest the British suspects; doing so would almost certainly alert Moscow to the existence of a mole within the KGB or its satellite agencies. For the moment, MI5 could only step up its surveillance on Houghton and Gee, and try to reassure the CIA that Sniper/LAVINIA had delivered vital genuine intelligence.

MI5 did not know – because the CIA chose not to inform it – that Angleton's grumblings about Sniper were completely unfounded. Sniper had, as Washington well knew, already identified other Soviet spies in three other Western countries. And their individual histories all showed that American intelligence had been severely compromised.

5

Stockholm

COLONEL STIG ERIK Constans Wennerström was fifty-three; tall, handsome and athletic, his clean-cut features matched exactly the image of a dashing military pilot. On the diplomatic cocktail circuits in Stockholm, Moscow and Washington DC he was known as charming, likeable and urbane, a safe and trusted senior officer in Sweden's Air Force and a veteran representative of his country's foreign ministry.

In the files of the Soviet Union's military intelligence service, however, he had a different name and a less exalted reputation; the GRU knew Wennerström as Agent EAGLE, a clever, if noticeably avaricious, spy who held the honorary rank of major general. By mid-1959, when Sniper sent a warning that a senior Swedish Air Force officer had been recruited by the Russians, Wennerström had been in the pay of Soviet intelligence for at least ten years, and had passed on to his masters some of the West's most sensitive military secrets. But he was also an unusually promiscuous traitor; for more than two decades he had sold his skills to the espionage services of no fewer than four nations – often simultaneously.

Washington knew this: its agencies had been amongst those who recruited him. What's more, they had done so fully aware that he was working for rival spy networks. And they did so twice.

~

From the earliest years of the Cold War, Scandinavian countries repre-sented both a threat to, and an opportunity for, the USSR and its espionage chiefs. In 1949 the North Atlantic Treaty Organization, NATO, united twelve countries – the USA, Britain, France, Canada, Belgium, Luxembourg, the Netherlands, Italy, Portugal, Iceland, Denmark and Norway – in a mutual defence alliance with the specific aim of countering Soviet expansion and influence in Eastern Europe. Combined land and sea exercises and a network of NATO bases, built along the borders with Russia and its client states – some of which would house first-response nuclear weapons – provided tangible evidence of the threat.

But the growing standardization of equipment, gradually ensuring that alliance members' armed forces adopted American military terminology, procedures and arms, provided an opportunity for the USSR. The halls and conference tables of NATO, staffed by officials of twelve predominantly European nations, presented Moscow with the potential for a back door into US military plans and technology. The leak of minutes from the 1957 summit in Paris, which Sniper had sent in his first dispatch of Soviet bloc intelligence, was testament to the KGB's success in prising open that door.

It had also led to the first prosecution resulting from Sniper's letters: in February 1959, Einar Blekinberg, a former Danish diplomat, was tried and convicted for his role in providing the NATO papers to Polish intelligence: he was sentenced to eight years in prison.[1]

Sweden, although not a NATO member, held particular promise for the KGB. In 1952 it had signed a mutual defence treaty with Washington, and began purchasing state of the art US war materiel, much of which was to be installed in a strategic series of new airbases along its borders. This semi-detached role ensured that Stockholm had privileged access to the Pentagon and US intelligence while simultaneously flying slightly below the radar of the CIA's counter-espionage efforts.

By April 1949, when the twelve nations signed up to the incorporation of NATO, Stig Wennerström had already been slotted neatly into Moscow's game plan.

~

He was born in August 1906, the son of a captain in Sweden's defence forces assigned to the Vaxholm Fortress guarding the entrance to Stockholm Harbour. By his own subsequent account it was a traditional military upbringing – 'an ordinary officer's home, where there were no excessive or remarkable habits of any sort'[2] – and at the age of twenty-three he joined the Navy; a year later he transferred to the Air Force and in his off-duty hours began learning Russian, believing this, added to his fluency in German, would assist his career.

He proved to have sufficient talent for languages to be sent on a defence department scholarship to study at a university in Latvia, then an independent nation but formerly a Russian colony, on the Soviet Union's western border.

As a young and handsome officer with considerable free time on his hands, Wennerström was quickly invited to the parties and receptions hosted by the Swedish Embassy in Riga, mingling with diplomats and military officials from Russia, other European nations and the United States. Among them was the man who would spark his taste for espionage:

> There was an American in the city, an American officer, who was studying Russian the same way I was. But he was actually an intelligence agent and . . . his language studies served mostly as camouflage for the illegal activity . . . He was in the British intelligence service, which may perhaps sound a mite peculiar. But . . . at the time there existed, practically speaking, no American intelligence service, whereas the British one was very active.[3]

One of the tasks of this unnamed agent was to don Latvian military uniform and slip over the border into Russia to gather intelligence on Soviet forces. He offered Wennerström the opportunity to join one of these sorties; although the young Swedish officer declined, it gave him a tantalizing glimpse of the spy business: 'I want to emphasize that these matters aroused great interest on my part . . . it was the first time that I got the least idea that things such as this really existed . . . [and] it is here that my subsequently great interest in intelligence service was awakened.'[4]

The outbreak of World War II gave Wennerström his first genuine opportunity to begin a career in espionage. In 1940 he had risen to the rank of captain and was posted, as air attaché, to the Swedish Embassy in Moscow. The Nazi–Soviet non-aggression pact was then still in force and while Western Europe was ablaze, the Soviet capital was at peace; a melting pot of diplomats, military and intelligence officers from all the warring powers as well as those not yet embroiled in the conflict. Sweden was officially neutral, though it subsequently allowed Hitler's armies free passage through its territory, and as a Russian-speaking officer of a notionally unaligned nation, Wennerström was in a unique position to gather highly sensitive information.

The Swedish intelligence service was the first to task him with spying. It ordered him to unearth data on the Soviet air force and airfields along the USSR–Finnish border. He obtained some of this information from scouting missions but much of it came from contacts he cultivated in the Nazis' embassy. He began sharing the fruits of his own research with German intelligence and soon became a spy simultaneously for Stockholm and Berlin.

He was evidently good at espionage, since the files of the German Military Intelligence service, the Abwehr, recorded his name as an agent, together with the fact that it had paid him by providing roubles at a knock-down rate.

When he was recalled to Sweden in 1941 he continued spying for the Abwehr and through diplomatic receptions at the Soviet Embassy made valuable contacts with Russian staff officers; these served him well, and in 1947 he was invited to witness a display of the first USSR jet aircraft in Moscow. Shortly before he departed, however, he was approached by a US intelligence officer at a party in the American Embassy; he made Wennerström an offer which proved impossible to refuse.

Because the United States had begun the Cold War with little or no network of agents in Europe, it had co-opted the former head of the Abwehr on the Eastern Front, General Reinhard Gehlen, funding his nascent and eponymous network as a de facto arm of US intelligence. In the process, it had also acquired Gehlen's wartime files which detailed the identities of foreign spies who had worked for Nazi Germany:

> My name was among those on some of these lists or records, and I had been set down as a 'valuable contact'. All these facts were known to the American . . . he pointed out that I had worked against the Soviet Union and in favor of Germany, and on that account it would surely be quite natural that I should now do the same thing for America.[5]

If politely couched, this suggestion was really a threat. Swedish collaboration with Nazi Germany was a sensitive subject in post-war Europe, and refusing the American request could have put Wennerström in some peril. But, by his own account, the prospect of returning to his secret life as a spy was enough motivation for him to agree. On a rail trip across Russia he undertook an initial mission on behalf of the US, mailing a parcel of radio tubes for a clandestine transmitter to an anti-communist group in Leningrad. It would not be the last time that Washington put its trust in a man it knew to have been in the pay of Nazi intelligence.

But Wennerström's ambition to become a fully fledged Cold War spy began in earnest in 1948, when he was elevated to the rank of lieutenant colonel and given orders to return to Moscow for a second stint as air attaché in the Swedish Embassy; here he would be expected to spy on Soviet military forces for his country.

Shortly before he left he was approached and recruited by the GRU: in exchange for a fee of 5,000 krone[6] (delivered in a plain brown wrapper and in used notes), he readily agreed to hand over details of a secret Swedish Air Force base then under construction. Working for both sides simultaneously was decidedly risky, but in Wennerström's mind the GRU deal was too good to pass up: 'In a fashion it was satisfying that I had succeeded in my purpose and got at least a foot, so to speak, into their organization. But on the other hand it was entirely clear that I was setting out on the most dangerous things that one could possibly imagine within [the field of] intelligence service.'[7]

He took up his post in Moscow early in 1949 and quickly began sending military intelligence back to Stockholm. But within weeks he was approached again by the GRU and asked to spy for the Soviet Union on a regular basis. The targets, however, had changed. Moscow was no longer interested in information about Swedish defences; henceforth Wennerström would be required to acquire and deliver to his handler top-secret information about NATO and the United States' military plans for Europe:

> The emergence of NATO . . . was relatively new. He [Wennerström's handler] declared that by reason of this the Soviet Union had been faced with altogether new strategic problems, which made necessary a complete reorganization of military strategy . . .
>
> What was particularly uncomfortable from the Soviet point of view was the fact that hostile-minded states were popping up in practically all directions . . . The great danger was that the large and powerful United States lay in the background . . . The United States was the nucleus, and the . . . main enemy of the Soviet Union. All resources they had at their disposal must be deployed against the United States.[8]

Wennerström, then, had little ideological commitment to either side in the deepening Cold War. By his own account, his motivations were the excitement of a long-term career in espionage and the lure of substantial payment. He happily accepted an initial fee of 10,000 roubles (worth $5,000 then, and equivalent to more than $50,000 today) and a monthly stipend of 5,000 roubles, with unlimited additional funds for expenses. After a luxurious lunch he and his handler toasted their arrangement with vodka and caviar, and the GRU began schooling Wennerström in the tradecraft he would need. Over the next three years he tapped his contacts in the American Embassy, delivering reports on US strategy and capabilities to nine separate dead drops the GRU had set up throughout Moscow.

The GRU was not, however, his only paymaster. He simultaneously sold his services to US intelligence, providing information on the Soviet armed forces to the air attaché at the American Embassy in return for payments made in Italian lire; this haul included photographs he took of strategic sites inside the Soviet Union to be targeted for bombing by NATO in the event of war. By his own account, Wennerström found the task of working for both sides laughably easy: 'It was almost comical. I would get a query from my Soviet contact man that from his point of view was fairly hard to obtain. When, later on, I would meet my American contact man, I would get a direct reply to the question in the form of a report from him, as well as a task from him.'[9]

If Wennerström felt any loyalty, this was now gradually tilting towards his GRU handlers. Near the end of his tour of duty in Moscow, they asked him to supply details of how – and from where – the US and NATO would attack the Soviet Union in the event of war. At the time, the Kremlin's assumption was that any Western assault would be land-based; Wennerström tapped his US intelligence contact for information, and discovered that the Pentagon had drawn up a map of targets which clearly indicated that there would be no invasion, but a lengthy bombing campaign instead. He also found out that the map was shortly to be sent, via special courier, to the American Air Force European headquarters at Wiesbaden in Germany. Wennerström quickly reported this to the GRU, which was then able to intercept the courier and covertly photograph the map of targets.

Wennerström was rewarded with promotion to the honorary rank of a GRU major general and given what Soviet intelligence termed 'top agent's authority': 'I was left with the very strong sense of having accomplished something and of having reached a high level of prestige. And there is no use in denying that thanks to this feeling I experienced a deep inner satisfaction with the results.'[10]

In the spring of 1952, Wennerström received new orders from his official employers in the Swedish Air Force: he was to be posted to the United States, replacing the existing air attaché in Washington DC. The assignment delighted his GRU handlers: 'Their reaction was as though they had just won the big prize in a lottery . . . the Soviets were setting great store on the possibility of my working for them in the United States.'[11]

It also dovetailed with his own full conversion to Moscow's side in the Cold War:

> When I first jumped into international espionage among the big powers, I had a feeling of sympathy for NATO and an antipathy for the Soviet Union [but] during my stay in Moscow there was a progressive change in my sympathies which ended up by swinging completely to the other side . . .
>
> It was entirely obvious that the Soviet intelligence efforts were of a defensive nature and that those of the Americans were offensive.[12]

But Wennerström's celebrations at this fortuitous turn of events were short-lived. As he prepared to leave Moscow as a clandestine Soviet spy, the GRU discovered that he had also been supplying US intelligence with its secrets for more than two years. Almost inevitably, it had done so thanks to American incompetence.

While Soviet intelligence was careful only to use his assigned cryptonym in radio traffic, its US counterparts were rather less assiduous; two separate messages, sent from the American Embassy in Moscow to Washington, referred to Wennerström by his real name. The GRU intercepted both and promptly summoned Agent EAGLE to a meeting in an isolated *dacha*: 'The first thought that went through my head was that it was very possible that they were prepared to liquidate me with a shot in the nape of the neck or something similar. We were a long way from Moscow, and nobody knew where I was.'[13]

But instead of a swift bullet in the back of the head, Wennerström's handler unexpectedly expressed delight. The discovery that American intelligence evidently trusted the duplicitous Swedish air attaché offered an invaluable opportunity: he would travel to Washington not merely as one of the GRU's top spies but as that most prized asset of all – a double agent: 'The net result upon leaving Moscow [was that] . . . instead of being a false agent inside of Soviet intelligence, I am now this same thing within the American organization . . . I looked on my work with the Americans as an excellent way to achieve better results for the Soviet intelligence service.'[14]

It was an opportunity which the GRU – and Wennerström himself – would exploit ruthlessly over the next five years. From the moment he arrived in the United States, together with his wife and family, in April 1952, Washington went out of its way to make him welcome. A US Marine officer – one of his contacts in Moscow – arranged for the rental of an upscale house in a pleasant neighbourhood, and secured a place at a sought-after private school for the couple's daughter. For good measure, the Marine also loaned him a car.

He was quickly accepted in ambassadorial circles, and the Wennerströms found themselves invited to all the best and most interesting receptions. He was, then, forty-five, the official representative of a friendly and technically advanced nation, and his covert activities on behalf of the United States had preceded him on the diplomatic telegraph. He was handsome, charming, and together with his attractive, outgoing wife, an instant hit on the capital's cocktail circuit.

America's growing military-industrial complex – a neat phrase yet to be coined in public, but very much a reality on the ground – also threw open its doors. Sweden was then on the cusp of upgrading its air defences and, with the encouragement of the Pentagon, US companies were eager to cash in on a lucrative new opportunity. Wennerström was invited to tour aircraft and electronics plants across the United States, and manufacturers were only too pleased to press on him top-secret technical details of their latest innovations:

I went on trips within the United States and Canada . . . My lively contacts with the American Air Force resulted in an acquaintance with, or recommendations to, practically every place I went . . . I had [an] entrée everywhere . . . My interest in data [on behalf of the GRU] and their interest in a sale met at the same level . . . I can honestly say that many times very astonishing results were obtained.[15]

Wennerström duly passed these 'astonishing results' back to the GRU using the techniques demonstrated by his handler in Moscow. He became adept at 'brush contacts' – slipping material to a Soviet agent in public, in what would seem like momentary and innocent chance encounters – or leaving it in an overcoat in the cloakroom at an embassy reception to be recovered later, as well as depositing microfilmed documents in a series of dead drops.

The GRU provided him with a miniature camera and film which it alone could develop in a unique solution: should they be intercepted, the tiny celluloid strips would self-destruct in normal photographic chemicals. For these efforts, Wennerström received a monthly salary of $750 plus a series of lump-sum payments of between $4,000 and $5,000.[16] Simultaneously, however, he was pocketing at least $2,000 in cash from US intelligence.

The CIA made contact with him at a lunch at the Pentagon. One of its officers – his identity was redacted from Wennerström's testimony – asked Wennerström to accompany him to a meeting at one of the Agency's scattered offices immediately after the meal. After an initial jolt of panic that his espionage for Moscow had been uncovered, he agreed to go along:

We went in his private car to an out-of-the-way office in Washington with no door plates . . . he had a hard time finding the place . . . The person in question . . . asked me whether I was willing to help them overcome some difficulties they had. My reaction was one of relief, because it was not as I had feared – that they had found out about my activity ... He explained that there was material in the Soviet Embassy that had to be gotten out of there.[17]

The CIA had, its officer explained, a contact either inside or with access to the Soviet Embassy. Wennerström's instructions were to get himself invited to receptions there; the contact would make himself known with a password and then slip him a small package for onward transfer to the Agency. It proved to be an easy task – Wennerström's status with the GRU and his role as Sweden's air attaché ensured invitations were quickly forthcoming – and he took possession of the little parcels on two separate occasions.

It is a measure of the CIA's inexperience – or more probably its desperation – that the Agency again entrusted such delicate missions to a man it knew to have previously worked for at least two other enemy intelligence services. For Wennerström, however, it was a double-windfall; he was paid $1,000 in cash on each occasion, and he was also able to warn Moscow that security at its embassy had sprung a leak.

By the time his tour of duty in Washington ended in June 1957, Stig Wennerström had provided the GRU with a wealth of top-secret US and NATO military documents, including plans for the deployment of nuclear weapons at bases across Europe as well as the locations of Sweden's anti-aircraft missile network and technical data on its new fighter aircraft. He had also gained access to Britain's most important defence secret, handing to his Soviet masters details of the submarine-based Polaris ballistic missile system.

Nor was agent EAGLE planning to retire from the espionage business. He ensured that his next posting, back home in Sweden, would give him continuing access to the West's most sensitive intelligence. After a highly lucrative twenty-year career working for four different spy agencies, often simultaneously – he had bought an expensive house in the Stockholm suburb of Djursholm on the proceeds – Wennerström had little reason to believe his double life was at risk of exposure.

Sniper's report in mid-1959 was the moment when Wennerström's carefully built facade began to crumble. As with LAMBDA 1 and LAMBDA 2 in Britain, the CIA's mysterious Agent in Place didn't know the name of the spy who had burrowed deep into US and Western intelligence and into NATO, but he was able to provide clues which helped pinpoint the prime suspect. There were not many Swedish Air Force officers who had spent time in Moscow as air attaché at the embassy: Wennerström's résumé, added to his unusual personal wealth, were a perfect match.

In November 1959, Swedish Security Police, the Säkerhetspolisen (SÄPO), installed a tap on the phone in Wennerström's villa. But like MI5 in London, with Sniper still in play somewhere behind the Iron Curtain, there was little Stockholm's counter-espionage chiefs could do but sit back and hope that the traitor would incriminate himself. At the same time, Sniper's revelations were causing a seismic shock two thousand miles away in one of the world's newest democracies.

6

Tel Aviv

O N FRIDAY, 14 May 1948 the Jewish People's Council gathered in the Tel Aviv museum to proclaim the birth of a nation. In front of cameras and the world's press, David Ben-Gurion, de facto leader of the Jewish community in Palestine, set out the democratic ambitions of the new state of Israel:

> It will be based on freedom, justice and peace . . . it will ensure complete equality of social and political rights to all its inhabitants irrespective of religion, race or sex; it will guarantee freedom of religion, conscience, language, education and culture; it will safeguard the Holy Places of all religions; and it will be faithful to the principles of the Charter of the United Nations.[1]

The announcement and the hopes it represented were a personal triumph for Ben-Gurion, the culmination of thirty years fighting for the Zionist cause. He had endured the indifference of world leaders to the growing anti-Semitism in the interwar years, lobbied and pleaded for a safe Jewish homeland before, during and immediately after the Holocaust, and tried to curb the excesses of the Zionist paramilitary organizations which fought a bloody campaign against the foreign troops controlling Palestine in the final stages of British rule.

His reward followed swiftly. Within hours of the declaration, the US State Department sent a telegram to its embassies, acknowledging the provisional government 'as the de-facto authority of the new state of Israel'.[2] Three days later the Soviet Union, which had set the whole process in motion at the UN six months earlier,[3] became the first country to announce the more formal, *de jure*, recognition.

On the same day, Ben-Gurion became Israel's first Prime Minister. But the nation he led was already under attack by four neighbouring states; on 15 May troops from Egypt, Syria, Transjordan and Iraq had all crossed the newly declared borders. This first Arab–Israeli war lasted eleven months, entangling Ben-Gurion and his military staff in a succession of hard-fought battles for strategic locations, and for the country's very survival. The Israeli Defence Force, formed from the ranks of one of the Jewish paramilitary groups, the Haganah, bore the brunt of the fighting; among its most senior officers and planners was a highly regarded veteran of European warfare and future close confidant of the Prime Minister. It would be another eleven years before a letter from Sniper would expose him as a secret agent for a country vehemently opposed to the lofty ideals set out in Ben-Gurion's declaration of independence, and one which sought to aid the enemies surrounding Israel.[4]

～

For a spy whose activities would embroil the intelligence services of at least three democratic nations, there are remarkably few cast-iron facts about the life of the young man who arrived before World War II in what was then the British Mandate of Palestine. Neither the CIA nor MI5 – both of which eventually opened investigations into his espionage – has released any part of its files; only the Israeli Security Agency, Shin Bet (also known as Shabak), has publicly disclosed details of his biography and career[5] – and even these are riddled with unsolved mysteries.[6]

The man then calling himself Georg Beer disembarked, at an unnamed port, in October 1938. He told British immigration officials that he had been born in Austria, the son of a Jewish family active in the

Social Democratic Party, SPO. The years between World War I and II were turbulent and often violent; the Social Democrats had traditionally been the strongest Austrian political force, but as the country polarized into radical factions on the left and right, activity moved out onto the streets, where armed groups fought for power.

Beer claimed to have been a youthful member of the SPO's paramilitary organization, the Republikanischer Schutzbund, and to have taken part in the battles it fought with government troops. Despite this, he somehow managed to secure a place at an Austrian military academy, and thereafter to serve as an officer in the national army, rising to the rank of colonel; he also gained a doctorate in modern literature from the University of Vienna. Since Beer's birth date is recorded as October 1912, the young man had evidently crammed an impressive roll call of achievements into a very few adult years. Nor were these the only honours he claimed to have won.

Soon after arriving in Palestine he joined the Hebrew University in Jerusalem as a research student, and made contact with the Haganah, then one of several militia organizations defending Jewish settlements from attacks by local Arab groups. He told its leaders that in addition to his other military accomplishments he had been a volunteer – on the Republican side – in the Spanish Civil War, and that as a member of the Thäimann Battalion[7] he had fought against Franco's fascist forces. It was here that he had first encountered, and been converted to, the Zionist cause.

According to Shin Bet's account, Beer – who had quickly ditched his Aryan-sounding first name and now styled himself 'Yisrael Bar' or 'Be'er' – made a strong impression on Haganah's leaders:

> [He had] first-hand knowledge, theoretical and historical, in many military areas, which made him an expert in these issues . . .
> He was proficient in the details of the battles, names of places, commanders, military units, a proficiency which left no doubt as to his credibility and military experience.[8]

By 1940, Beer was a permanent member of Haganah, regularly taking part in training exercises and helping to plan its paramilitary operations. When the organization was subsumed into the newly formed IDF he was given the rank of lieutenant colonel and appointed to a series of senior roles: some, including head of planning for the Operations Division and Deputy Chief of the General Staff, gave him access to many of Israel's most sensitive secrets. In time, this role would also smooth his path into Ben-Gurion's inner circle, and provide him with a back door into intelligence agencies across Europe and the United States.

Although President Harry Truman's administration had welcomed Israel's birth as a nation and subsequently formally recognized it as an independent state, Washington had been slow to provide more tangible support. In the late 1940s and early 1950s, although it supplied modest loans, primarily to assist the new country's agricultural development, American policy in the Middle East was more closely focused on securing alliances with the oil-rich Arab and Persian states; furthermore, both its diplomats and its intelligence service were suspicious of the political direction piloted by Tel Aviv. 'No one at the State Department or CIA was anxious to have an open relationship with Israel,' one (anonymous) CIA official told the author of a history of the Agency. 'Israel was a country made possible by the Soviet Union . . . [and] was a collectivist socialist state that had a very cozy relationship with the Soviet intelligence services.'[9]

Moscow certainly took a keen interest in Israel from the outset; the country's geographical location and its contacts with Western European governments were strategically important and, at the Kremlin's direction, Czechoslovakia and Yugoslavia provided armaments for Ben-Gurion's forces in addition to training pilots of the nascent Israeli Air Force. At the same time both the KGB and the GRU recruited agents inside the country's political and military establishments, sending experienced handlers to run them. By the early 1950s an estimated half of the sixty employees in the Soviet Embassy in Tel Aviv were spies or spy handlers.[10]

But Israel's own civilian intelligence services – Shin Bet which handled internal security, and Mossad which was responsible for espionage and counter-espionage – were beginning to earn their own formidable international reputation, and in June 1951, Washington and Tel Aviv signed a formal – but secret – cooperation agreement; both countries pledged not to spy on the other, and to share the fruits of their respective intelligence labours.

Inside the CIA, responsibility for what became known as 'The Israeli Account' was given not to the specialists of its Middle East division but personally to James Angleton, who jealously guarded all the resulting information coming into or going out of his office. It is a measure of the sensitivity still surrounding Angleton's stewardship of the Israeli Account that all seven pages devoted to it in the Agency's internal history of the period were completely redacted when the document was declassified; only a solitary photograph of Angleton has escaped the censor's pencil.[11] The effect of the dual intelligence pact, however, was to make the CIA almost entirely reliant on Mossad and Shin Bet for its information – and by extension, uniquely vulnerable should either of those services become penetrated by Moscow's spies.

Israel Beer had, by then, left the Israeli Army and moved into politics. He joined the left-wing Mapam party and for two years ran its internal security department. Despite its pro-Soviet leanings, he retained high-level access to the country's defence secrets and obtained military intelligence information from contacts within the IDF.[12] He also managed to gain the trust of Prime Minister David Ben-Gurion, converting this patronage into unusual admittance to top-secret staff meetings; in them he saw, or was given, Israel's military plans and even blueprints of weapons it had acquired.[13]

In 1954 the former firebrand left-wing socialist moved unexpectedly to the right, and joined Ben-Gurion's Mapai party. The following year, while Ben-Gurion was Minister of Defence, the department awarded Beer a civilian commission to write an official history of the 1947–9 War of Independence. It came with considerable benefits:

The contract with the Ministry of Defense afforded him the rank of colonel and thus he was considered among the ministry's senior administrative officials . . . [and] received various updates, including classified material . . . Despite his civilian status he would often wear the uniform of lieutenant colonel. Furthermore, he had the habit of spending lunch breaks in the General Staff base, where he would meet senior officers and exchange updates and opinions.

Many of them trusted him fully, and given that he presented himself as a close confidant of the Minister of Defense, they even considered him to be a close link to the minister, one who could promote their personal and professional matters. Some even provided him classified documents, including intelligence assessments, for consideration.[14]

Among the documents which passed across Beer's desk in his grace-and-favour IDF office were copies of secret contracts Israel had signed to buy weapons from France and Germany. They would not remain confidential for long.

Isser Harel, Israel's own chief spymaster, was a deceptively unassuming figure. He lived in an unostentatious Tel Aviv apartment, where his neighbours considered him to be a minor government bureaucrat. But behind the bland facade, Harel was an astute operator, who headed both Mossad and Shin Bet simultaneously;[15] and he viewed Beer with growing suspicion.

In part this stemmed from Beer's extravagant lifestyle. Neither the writing contract nor his full-time job as head of the Military History Department at Tel Aviv University provided the funds for his series of volatile sexual affairs, nor for his increasingly heavy drinking. But, according to Shin Bet's official account, although these worried the puritanical Harel, it was Beer's cultivation of relationships with foreign governments which was most troubling:

Bar began to develop close connections in Europe, including Germany, France, UK as well as other Western countries. Furthermore, he embarked on several trips to those countries, while creating the impression that he was on a government mission and thus obtaining the aid of military attachés and Ministry of Defense delegations. His meetings included the German minister of defense . . . and the head of French intelligence, among others.[16]

Nor were these contacts limited to Israel's allies in the West. Shin Bet officers reported that, despite a prohibition against encounters with foreign agents, Beer was in the habit of meeting Soviet officials. Convinced that the man posed a serious security risk, Harel ordered a covert search of Beer's apartment; although this produced no evidence of espionage, the spy chief took his suspicions directly to Ben-Gurion, warning that Beer had been 'gathering military information which is of no concern to him. He has been visiting communist cities on his trips through Europe. He has been too friendly with the Russian diplomats serving in Israel. He meets them frequently . . . [He is also] undergoing some kind of strain – the sort of strain which an agent leading a double life suffers from.'[17]

But Ben-Gurion, now in his second stint as Israel's leader, refused to heed the advice. And given the protection of the Prime Minister, without solid proof against Beer there was nothing more that Shin Bet could do.

In the middle of 1959, Sniper provided the evidence Harel needed. In one of his monthly reports, smuggled to a CIA dead drop, he told US intelligence that the KGB had a mole 'somewhere in the upper levels' of the Israeli Defence Ministry. Unusually, he gave both the man's Soviet cryptonym – KURT – and his name: Israel Beer.[18]

The Agency passed the information to Shin Bet, but as in London and Stockholm, warned the Israelis that it would be best not to move against the spy; with Sniper still risking his life as an Agent in Place somewhere behind the Iron Curtain, an arrest was too dangerous to contemplate. For the time being, the only option was to put Beer under constant surveillance.

Then, in May 1960, Beer's latest international trip raised yet more red flags. He flew out of Tel Aviv, bound for Munich and a highly unusual appointment which had no bearing on, or justification in, his work at the university or with the IDF. Israel Beer, a suspected Soviet spy, had arranged a personal meeting with the man heading the Cold War's most important front-line espionage agency: General Reinhard Gehlen, president of West Germany's Federal Foreign Intelligence Service, the Bundesnachrichtendienst or BND.

7

Munich

THE AUSTERE GREY building in Pullach, a small village south of Munich, was amongst the most secure facilities in Western Europe.

Since its inception in 1957, number 30 Heilmannstrasse had been the formal – if publicly undisclosed – headquarters of the BND, West Germany's embryonic foreign intelligence service. The location in the Bavarian heartland was ideal: the closest border with a Soviet bloc state was 200 kilometres away – a solid territorial buffer against incursions from communist aggression – and within Pullach itself a line of dense trees shielded the offices from prying eyes, while armed guards ensured that potential enemies remained firmly outside the building's gates.

But the most serious problem for the BND was neither an armed attack on its fortress, nor surveillance of the comings and goings of its thousands of staff: the organization had a far more dangerous Achilles heel – and one which it had inflicted upon itself. Moscow's spies were not physically surrounding the Pullach perimeter: they had burrowed deep within the senior ranks of its most sensitive departments. And even before Sniper sounded the alarm, Washington, which relied on the BND as a proxy force in Cold War espionage and counterintelligence against the USSR, as well as paying the vast costs of doing so, knew it.

~

At the end of World War II, Germany ceased to exist. From 7 May 1945, when the remnants of the Nazi High Command unconditionally surrendered to the Allies all the land, armed forces and population formerly belonging to the Third Reich, the country was formally wiped from the map. In its place, the Big Four victorious powers – America, Britain, the USSR and France – divided the territory into separate zones of occupation: America in the south, Britain in the north-west, the USSR in the east and France in the south-west. Henceforth they would be responsible, jointly and individually, for administering law, life and security within these borders.

As the Cold War dawned, and Moscow tightened its grip on the sector it controlled, security became a pressing problem. The Soviet Union's evident intention to create a subservient communist state in the east, and its covert efforts to undermine the democratic ambitions of Washington, London and Paris, highlighted an urgent need for intelligence.

The United States was the de facto senior partner in the West's fight to stop the spread of communism; France, in any event, had little counter-espionage capability and Britain, bankrupted by the war, was beginning a fundamental retrenchment. America, by contrast, had a long-standing and extensive wartime intelligence operation in and around the former Germany, but it was hopelessly diffuse; between forty and fifty separate and often competing units – both military and civilian – occupied a constellation of largely unconnected offices throughout the American zone. And Washington, too, was under pressure – financial and political – to bring its forces home.

The solution to this formidable problem presented itself in the shape and uniform of a decorated lieutenant general of the once-mighty Wehrmacht. In 1945, Reinhard Gehlen was forty-three, an able and ambitious veteran of the Reich's external wars – he had been a staff officer in one of the infantry divisions which attacked Poland in 1939 – and of internal conflicts between the military and the Nazi leaders. In 1941, after a period on the General Staff in Berlin, he had been posted to the Eastern Front, where he took charge of the German Army's intelligence branch, Fremde Heer Ost (FHO). When, in 1944, an Allied victory seemed inevitable, he threw in his lot with the Wehrmacht rebels who attempted to assassinate

Hitler. When this failed, he somehow avoided the fate of his fellow plotters and resumed his duties gathering intelligence on the Red Army and Moscow's inexorable advance towards Berlin. Just weeks before Stalin's forces conquered the capital, Hitler finally dismissed Gehlen for defeatism.

In May 1945, Gehlen surrendered to US forces in Bavaria and offered them a deal: in return for protection from Moscow, which was demanding his extradition for investigations into alleged war crimes,[1] he offered to hand over the FHO's voluminous files, including the identities of its still-active agents at large inside the Soviet Union. After a lengthy interrogation and debriefing, the US Army's Counter-Intelligence Corps (CIC) agreed.

But Gehlen's ambitions extended far beyond saving his own skin. He foresaw the coming fracture between West and East, and spotted opportunity in the tension between America's eagerness to get out of Europe and its leaders' growing understanding that only the United States was in a position to counter Moscow's plans for expansion. He offered his new masters in Washington a way to satisfy both competing demands. His experience, and his network of spies, agents and informers, provided a unique and invaluable resource; and with US blessing – as well as substantial covert funds – he would resurrect his former Nazi intelligence service, and become America's eyes and ears on the front line of the Cold War.

Since Germany itself did not, then, exist, the new unit could not be an official intelligence service and would instead bear his own name. It would also be entirely secret and display no outward sign of being an extension of the US Army. The CIC agreed and, under the code name 'Operation RUSTY', began providing extensive funding for Gehlen's eponymous network.[2] By October 1946 he claimed to have 600 agents working undercover in the Soviet-controlled zone.[3]

When the CIA inherited the arrangement in 1949, the Gehlen Organization had become the de facto intelligence and espionage agency for all western zones in Germany, and was costing American taxpayers $1.5 million a year – the equivalent of almost $16 million today.

Despite this, and its semi-legal trading on the black market, 'the Org' (as it was known in Washington) was in dire financial straits and, due to the Army's hands-off approach, was very badly managed. As a belatedly declassified CIA study recorded,[4] the Agency assumed responsibility for its first satellite intelligence service – now listed under the code name ZIPPER – with substantial misgivings: 'The Central Intelligence Agency found the Gehlen Organization in disarray in the summer of 1949. A deep financial crisis compounded the Army's benign neglect ... [the Organization] was in deep need of reform.'[5]

The first issue was that Gehlen was concentrating on the wrong target, devoting the majority of his staff and resources to domestic operations against Germans in the Soviet zone; in the Agency's view, Moscow, not East Berlin, was the main threat and the Basic Agreement, signed by Gehlen and Washington in June 1949, directed the Organization to begin the 'development of a long-range and effective intelligence organization against Communist Russia and her satellite governments'.[6]

A rather more dangerous hazard, however, was General Gehlen's lackadaisical approach to security:

> Even prior to the Agency's assumption of the Gehlen Organiza-
> tion from the Army in 1949, CIA officers expressed considerable
> concern about the counterintelligence vulnerabilities of the Ger-
> man service. In fact, many American intelligence officers opposed
> the CIA's takeover because the Gehlen Organization exercised
> poor operational tradecraft and had been badly exposed between
> 1946 and 1948.[7]

'Badly exposed' was something of an understatement: from its inception, 'the Org's' operations had been frequently uncovered and dismantled by Soviet counter-espionage units. Nor, as CIA's official history outlined, did this record ever greatly improve; the concerns raised by its own officers 'remained valid' throughout the seven years the Agency was in charge of the Organization.

The fundamental problem lay in the men Gehlen and his staff had recruited. An internal Army memorandum in August 1948 reported that many of the Organization's operatives were suspected war criminals:

> [We] found that some of the agents employed were SS personnel with known Nazi records and, in most cases, undesirable people. Recruiting methods . . . were so loose that former German officers and noncoms were blindly being approached to work for American intelligence in espionage activity directed against the USSR . . .
>
> No attention was paid to the character of the recruits, security, political leanings or quality with the result that many of the agents were blown almost immediately.[8]

A second report that summer, by another senior military officer, confirmed the problem. Gehlen's shoddy security precautions meant that the Organization's existence – and its US ownership – was widely known and discussed throughout the occupied sectors. The secret was so open that a cynical, if accurate, local aphorism had grown up: 'American intelligence is a rich blind man using the Abwehr as a seeing-eye dog. The only trouble is the leash is much too long.'[9]

The CIA did try to control its troublesome protégé, but Gehlen rejected its most important demands. Despite the fact that Washington was paying all the bills, he denied the Agency permission to assess the background of any of his operatives:

> [We] played no role in the vetting of the Organization's staff members or agents because Gehlen refused to reveal the true names of his staff personnel and those of his agents. The Agency simply knew the cover names used by the Organization's officers and the V-numbers[10] for the agents . . .
>
> CIA efforts to introduce polygraph testing in the Organization proved futile; consequently the Agency was never satisfied with the security of the Organization's recruitment procedures and modus operandi.[11]

Because, as it ruefully noted, the CIA could never 'get the Germans to "clean house"', ZIPPER became a safe haven for men who had played active roles within Nazi organizations: 'A CIS staff officer at Pullach estimated in the mid-1950s that some 13 per cent of Gehlen's organization (76 out 600) were known to have been either former SS, SD, SA members, NSDAP members, War Crime offenders and/or a combination of the same.'[12]

This lax approach to security made 'the Org' ripe for penetration by Soviet intelligence. As a subsequent internal Agency analysis reported, Moscow mounted 'a well-targeted, well-developed' campaign to exploit the vulnerability of Gehlen's staff:

> Some of these people might be susceptible to a Soviet approach because of their general sympathies. Others, such as former Elite Guard (SS) and Security Service (SD) members, many of whom were now war criminals able to make their way only by hiding a past which had once put them among the elite, would be vulnerable to blackmail.[13]

Certainly the KGB and its forerunners,[14] in conjunction with the Stasi, remained conspicuously successful in identifying the Organization's spies – though initially the CIA did not know whether this resulted from blackmail, penetration or simply better tradecraft:

> The Soviets and East Germans made a concerted effort to destroy the Gehlen Organization. In late November 1953, the Communists announced that they had rolled up networks of West Germans in the East . . . By the end of 1954, over 200 Organization agents had fled to West Germany to avoid arrest.[15]

By 1954, however, the Agency knew where the problem lay. On 15 February a would-be defector walked into US Military headquarters in Vienna and asked for political asylum; in return he offered detailed information on Soviet espionage and assassination operations in Western Europe.

Petr Sergeevich Deriabin[16] was just thirty-three years old, but a veteran of Moscow's wars, both overt and clandestine. A Communist Party member since childhood, he had fought at Stalingrad before being sent to the Red Army counterintelligence school; after World War II he had joined Soviet State Security and, following a period in the Kremlin Guard Directorate, was posted to Austria. At the time he defected he was the Vienna station chief of internal counterintelligence, and he brought with him a wealth of information about his employers' operations in Western Europe. As he subsequently explained to a Congressional committee, Germany was seen as a key entry point into America and NATO: 'In July or August 1953 . . . instructions [were given] to all intelligence officers and that instruction said . . . It is now very hard to get information from the United States . . . we have to work against the United States from East Germany, from Austria, and other European countries.'[17]

The methods used by Moscow's spies included 'blackmail, bribery and kidnapping'; Deriabin admitted that he had personally taken part in the abductions of two of Moscow's targets, helping to spirit them through the western sectors of Germany and into the Soviet zone. But it was his allegation of Soviet penetration of 'the Org' which was most serious.

Before his arrival in Vienna, Deriabin had served in the German Counter-Espionage section at MGB (later KGB) headquarters; there he had read a file on the Gehlen Organization, and the Soviet's successful infiltration of its staff:

> In the middle of 1952 . . . the KGB had decided . . . that as the creature of the strongest occupation power, it would probably one day become the official German [intelligence] service. From the Soviet point of view, it was no longer simply a vehicle with which to harass and penetrate US operations, but another place to seek a toehold in the future West German Government.[18]

At that point, Moscow had managed to place two spies in Gehlen's local field offices, but not in the upper echelons of the Organization. Within a year, that gap had been amply filled. Two moles had been inserted into the most senior ranks of the Pullach HQ itself and were operating as Soviet double agents. Deriabin was not able to give the CIA their names; all he knew was their KGB cryptonyms – 'PETER' and 'PAUL'.

The revelation was precisely what the Agency had always feared, and should have rung the loudest of alarm bells. Lengthy interrogations and debriefings convinced American intelligence officers that Deriabin was a genuine defector and that his information was reliable; Tennent Bagley, one of those who worked on his material, reported that 'Deriabin never lied and had a fabulously sharp memory.'[19]

Inside the CIA his information was kept securely within James Angleton's Counter-Intelligence Branch and the Soviet Division; both began trawling through old reports and files in the hope of discovering the identities of 'PETER' and 'PAUL'. Moscow, too, was worried: as a detailed Agency analysis recorded, its spy chiefs knew that Deriabin's defection could jeopardize the KGB's most important German espionage operation:

> The KGB was perhaps uncertain of the full extent of Deriabin's knowledge of agent identities . . . Knowing that Deriabin's revelations would prompt another investigation of Gehlen Organization security it became important to the KGB to divert the investigation in a way designed to protect the most important KGB agents.[20]

Throughout 1954 and 1955 the CIA logged a succession of cases in which low-ranking Soviet spies were suspiciously easily caught by 'the Org'. It concluded that all had been deliberately sacrificed – a long-established technique known as 'false victims':

> When an important agent is known to be endangered, the KGB will try to set up a 'false victim' whose arrest takes the heat off the actual agent . . . Documents on State Security training show that this 'false victim' technique was being taught to trainees at least as early as 1939.[21]

Coupled with Deriabin's warnings, this string of unlikely captures should have been enough for the Agency to pause its ongoing relationship with Gehlen. Instead, it did the opposite.

In February 1956 – nine months after the establishment of West Germany as a sovereign country – the Gehlen Organization formally became the new state's intelligence service. Yet although the BND was notionally answerable to the West German Chancellor, its true ownership still lay not in Bonn but in Washington; the CIA paid its bills and ran it as the spearhead of US covert operations in the Cold War with the Soviet Union, and the Agency's then Director, Allen Dulles, sent Gehlen a gushing letter to celebrate the BND's inauguration and the continuation of its earlier marriage to American intelligence: 'You can imagine with what gratification I received this news [of the BND's inauguration] and with what hopefulness I view the future collaboration which I know will continue between our two services.'[22]

The Agency also provided a substantial dowry, supplying Gehlen's new organization with 'large quantities of vehicles, office equipment and buildings', and posted numerous officers to work inside the Pullach compound. Then, in September 1956 it flew six senior BND officials to America, treating them to a lengthy tour of CIA sites in Washington DC, where they were extensively briefed on US plans and intelligence operations.[23]

But if the CIA held the BND's purse strings and theoretically controlled its activities, the cooperation that Dulles predicted seemed remarkably one-sided; Agency intelligence and plans flowed into Gehlen's files, but the material he passed back was more often a trickle than the anticipated flood. The general, and his inner circles, continued to guard their secrets from American oversight.

～

Then, in spring 1959, a new report from Sniper caused consternation within the CIA. He reported that the KGB had a mole in the upper reaches of the BND who had provided Moscow with specific details of 'a joint American-BND office running operations against the Soviet Embassy in Bonn and against the Soviets traveling in the West'. As usual he was not able to give the spy's name, but he gave a vital clue to help discover the man's identity – and that of a second spy in Gehlen's inner circle. His letter accurately described the visit of the six German senior intelligence officials to Washington and said that 'the KGB had had two agents in the BND group'.[24]

The CIA began an urgent investigation and within weeks Sniper's information enabled it to identify the prime suspect: Heinz Felfe, a former Nazi SD and SS officer and post-war British agent who had risen through the ranks of the Gehlen Organization and was now head of the BND's counterintelligence operations. The revelation was potentially devastating: as the Agency recorded, Felfe was in charge of all 'counter-espionage operations against the Soviets' and had access to all 'BND files, including American intelligence information'.[25] If, as Sniper claimed, he was a KGB double agent, many of the Agency's biggest operations were likely to have been betrayed to Moscow.

There were two immediate obstacles to staunching this likely haemorrhage of US secrets. The first was that if Sniper was right – and his growing record of success indicated he was an agent of unprecedented value – then Felfe had an accomplice, a second KGB mole somewhere in the highest echelons of the BND; the CIA was unable to work out who this might be, nor could it now trust Gehlen to root out the spies. The second problem was the same as prevented immediate action against the traitors Sniper had helped identify in London, Stockholm and Tel Aviv: the Agency still had no idea who their mysterious benefactor was, nor how to bring him in from the cold. For as long as he remained an undercover Agent in Place it would be too dangerous to arrest Felfe. Instead, and without informing the BND, it put him under 'unilateral' surveillance and tapped his phone. Until Sniper surfaced, the CIA could only watch and wait while Moscow plundered its secrets.[26]

8

Washington

THE LETTERS KEPT coming. Month after month, as regular as a Swiss watch, Sniper's detailed multi-page reports landed in CIA dead drops across West Berlin. But by January 1960 they were accompanied by even more valuable material; he had acquired a Minox subminiature camera, using it to photograph Soviet bloc intelligence documents, and each package now contained rolls of tiny film. Amongst other secret papers, he had taken pictures of a Polish intelligence report detailing the naval strength of West Germany, Swedish Air Force manoeuvres, 'the production of atom [sic] weapons in France and new American weapons for submarines (NATO)'. All had been sent to Warsaw by Soviet bloc spies operating in the West.[1]

Photographing these pages was no easy or risk-free endeavour. The Minox had been the camera of choice for espionage services for more than a decade; its size – barely bigger than a modern USB memory stick – and its advanced close-focusing lens made it ideal for snapping high-resolution images of secret files very quickly. But although the manufacturer had marketed the product in the West, cashing in on the growing consumer demand for luxury items, its availability behind the Iron Curtain was almost exclusively confined to government agencies. Sniper's acquisition of the little camera, presumably from his own employers since US intelligence had no means of providing him with one, could not have gone unnoticed by Soviet bloc spymasters.

Inside the CIA there were two schools of thought about the

development. One, championed by Soviet Division officers and analysts, was that the letters and films were a rich and continuing seam of vital information about Moscow's operations. Tennent Bagley, shortly to take up his post as the Division's head of counterintelligence in Washington, summed up Sniper's importance in a single pithy phrase: 'His aim was sharp.'[2]

Across town from CIA intelligence, in the shadowed corridors of the counterintelligence branch, the Minox films, the breadth, detail and sheer quality of the material, pointed in the opposite direction: it was all too good to be true, and therefore must be a trap. For its chief, James Angleton – whose hobby was creating elaborate fly-fishing lures – the undoubtedly 'good' information on Houghton, Wennerström, Beer and Felfe was no more than a beguiling camouflage which concealed a lethal hook of disinformation: bogus leads and fake intelligence, designed to tempt the Agency and lead it down a false trail. As Howard Roman, one of the team handling the flow of revelations, recalled, Angleton 'was certain that Sniper was some sort of Communist provocation agent'.[3]

At the heart of the growing conflict within the CIA was Sniper's provenance. Despite his attempts to disguise both his nationality and his position in Soviet bloc intelligence, the Agency was now firmly convinced that he was 'a high-ranking officer of the Polish security service', the UB, and also held a senior position in the KGB.[4]

Although Poland retained some semblance of political independence from Moscow, careful analysis by Bagley and the Soviet Division specialists revealed that its intelligence agencies had been controlled by the Soviet Union for the best part of two decades:

> The invading Soviet forces in World War II had turned Poland into a colony, and created a 'Polish' state security service as a subservient model of the KGB, department by department, function by function, putting KGB men (some of them Russians posing as Poles) in command of these departments. Though by now they

had come to be called mere 'advisors' and 'liaison' officers, their word was still law.[5]

The mixture of Soviet and Polish intelligence documents which Sniper delivered suggested that he was in a unique position: employed by Warsaw while simultaneously sending its secrets to communism's ultimate spymasters in Moscow – a role which gave him access to KGB material.

This assessment was reinforced by an internal Agency evaluation of the pecking order within Iron Curtain espionage agencies: 'Traditionally, the Soviets exploit but do not trust the Satellite [intelligence] services, but within the limits of their basic distrust, they probably trust the Poles more than the East Germans, Hungarians, Czechs, etc.'[6]

Beyond that limited judgement, however, until 1958 the CIA had possessed very little up-to-date information about the various (and often overlapping) branches of Polish espionage and intelligence which operated under the umbrella of the Ministry of Public Security, or of the country's military forces. A February 1954 internal Agency report on the 'Organization and Personnel' of the Ministry managed to identify some of the most senior officials, but below them a number of presumed department heads (the document stresses that its contents were 'unevaluated') are marked 'fnu' – 'full name unknown'.[7] A similar report, four years later, on Poland's military strength and plans is littered with the stark abbreviation 'Unk.' – 'unknown'.[8]

Throughout 1959 and 1960, Sniper's letters rapidly filled in many of those gaps, providing, as the Agency admitted, 'the most complete and detailed charts and organizational description of the Polish Security Service and the Polish Military Intelligence Service received on any Communist Service'.[9]

The only complete Sniper report to have escaped the CIA's determined efforts to keep the correspondence secret reinforces that assessment. Sent from Prague on 15 January 1960, and recovered from a dead drop at Berlin Zoo's railway station three weeks later, it was marked '1/60' – making it the first letter of the new decade – and ran to twenty-one closely typed pages, each one listing the real names, crypto- nyms, job titles, career backgrounds and personal idiosyncrasies of scores of UB and KGB officials:

> The great activity of the KGB is increasing here as well as in War- saw under the direction of the new KGB CE [counter-espionage] representative General Szwyrkov ... It has already been decided to transfer General Huebner from the Ministry of the Interior to Rumania ... Between the 15th and 25th of February of this year, DYBALA will be in Berlin on official business in the company of the Chief of Section 5 of Department I, Major Wojtasik. He is to carry out an important mission meeting with an agent from the US ... FROSCH was recruited after the war and has kidnapped approximately 200 persons in recent years ...[10]

The package also included the latest products of Sniper's spy-camera work – more than a hundred individual pictures of top-secret KGB and UB documents which had evidently been photographed in a hurry – and instructions to contact him via a newspaper lonely hearts column should they prove difficult to develop:

> In the attachment you will receive eight undeveloped Minox films – exposure time 1/20th of a second. For security reasons I was not in a position ... to check whether they are correct and legible. I hope they are good. In case they are not I ask you to put in the next 'Lady Optimist' ad[vert] the codeword *Charmant*, which will mean that the film was not legible and that the pic- tures must be repeated.

But Sniper also included a strong warning about the risks he was taking and a plea that US intelligence should 'exploit my information very cautiously'. Since he was still under the impression that he was reporting directly to the head of the FBI, the appeal was addressed to J. Edgar Hoover:

> Dear Herr Direktor . . . I call to your attention that I will be forcibly included in the ranks of singing angels if there is the <u>slightest</u> [emphasis in original] negligence on your part in . . . maintaining the proper cover . . . As is generally known such a summons is connected with a certain operation called 'Being stood against the wall'.[11]

If Sniper's tone for such a serious threat to his life seemed jocular, it spoke to his unfounded confidence that he was dealing with the single American agency he knew had not been penetrated by Soviet intelligence, and to his fateful ignorance that the CIA had hijacked his correspondence. Nor, under those circumstances, could he have realized that he was about to snag an invisible trip wire within the Agency: Report 1/60 threatened to focus unwanted attention on one of US intelligence's biggest and most closely guarded secrets.

The letter was broken down into sections covering eleven countries and specific Soviet bloc espionage operations, each listed under a code name of Sniper's own choosing. Over three pages he returned to his account of a post-war fascist underground, a sinister network of ex-Nazis recruited as agents for Moscow and currently at large throughout the world. Now he was able to give more details of the organization he called 'Hacke':

> At the end of 1943, in view of the approaching defeat of the Third Reich, the NSDAP [Nazi Party] boss, [Martin] Bormann, began to build up a secret Nazi cadre organization unknown to Hitler and other Nazi bosses. This organization was set up according to the organizational plan of a Freemason lodge in that there were strict 'secret circles'. The highest circle was formed by Bormann with four other unidentified Nazi leaders; the organization was further set up according to the 'V pattern' (five persons). Members of one 'V' became leaders of further 'Vs', and the leadership was anonymous to the lower circles . . .
>
> According to Bormann's plan 'Hacke' was supposed to be very restrictive in the number of its members (allegedly only 35 persons

up to 1944) . . . and above all was to be active through 'inspiration' of others.

For security reasons, 'Hacke' bases were built up abroad in order to be able to operate freely and securely after the defeat. The main bases were set up by the end of 1944, especially in Spain, Portugal, Argentina, Japan and Italy. [They had] enormous organizational capital in gold jewelry and cash (all from concentration camp 'booty') of an approximate total value of half a billion dollars.[12]

Unlike the supposed ODESSA network designed to spirit SS war criminals out of Europe at the end of the war,[13] Bormann's 'Hacke' members were to remain in place and act as a 'stay behind' organization of diehard Nazi spies or covert agitators. But according to Sniper, Viktor Abakumov, head of the Red Army counterintelligence agency SMERSH, learned of its existence in 1944 and instantly spotted the potential to turn these men into double agents and 'false flag' operatives:

As soon as the RIS [Russian intelligence service] got wind of it, it immediately recognized its importance . . . Without waiting for the end of the war, Abakumov recruited a few members of 'Hacke' by blackmail . . . After the war the MGB worked on 'Hacke' [to achieve] the maximum infiltration of MGB agents. Hacke expanded organizationally around 1947–1948 and this opportunity was exploited.

[It] was all the more important to the MGB because 'Hacke' had kept alive the old Nazi slogan, 'Fight the Jews and plutocrats in the USA', and had a goal of the founding of a Fourth Reich, and thus was always hostile to America . . .

In particular Abakumov sought out former Abwehr agents in the United States, turning them into unwitting double agents who, if they were caught, would believe themselves to be neo-Nazi spies but who were, in reality, working for Moscow:

One of the most dangerous methods of Abakumov was the IS [intelligence service] work 'under a foreign flag' which has been brought to the point of perfection today by the KGB . . . It is certain that in 1955–1956 the KGB had a few excellent agents in America who had come from the repertoire of the Nazi CI [counterintelligence] . . .

And Sniper named names. His report provided the identities and cryptonyms of more than a dozen alleged 'Hacke' members at work in the UK, France, Holland, Belgium and, above all, the United States: 'I warn you very seriously about this dangerous conglomeration of brown-red Fascists who unexpectedly one day can cause enormous damage and who are an acute danger to the free world and to peace.'[14]

If all of this sounded like the plot for a pulp novel, the CIA had good reason to take it seriously. From 1944 to the early 1950s it and its Army predecessors had mounted a very similar operation to that undertaken by the Soviet espionage services. Under this scheme some of Washington's most senior intelligence officers had located Nazi officials with knowledge of Moscow's spy networks, and bribed, blackmailed or pressured them to join up on America's side in the Cold War.

These men were protected from war crimes investigations – including those being run by other branches of US or British intelligence – and the Agency even enabled some to emigrate to America. And one of the earliest and key figures in the operation had been James Jesus Angleton, then the chief of counter-espionage in Italy for the Office of Strategic Services (OSS), now the head of counterintelligence for its successor, the CIA.[15]

Unsurprisingly, since the project involved recruiting and pampering some of those responsible for atrocities in a war which cost almost half a million American lives, it was one of Washington's most protected secrets; it would be kept entirely from the US public until the mid-1980s, and even when forced by an Act of Congress to declassify its documents, the CIA, OSS and the Army CIC failed to hand over many of their records.[16] By revealing the existence of 'Hacke', Sniper was accidentally drawing unwanted attention to its American mirror image, and his revelations had the potential to expose Angleton's role within it. At the very least it provided further incentive for the already hostile counterintelligence chief to disparage Sniper's information.

Nor, though he could not know it either, was this the only danger; as his information slowly seeped into the upper reaches of Washington's labyrinthine bureaucracy, a serious threat to his safety was gathering force. Although most of the information in his monthly letters focused on the KGB and UB, naming their senior officers and the network of agents they handled throughout the world, he also highlighted US government officials working – willingly or otherwise – for Moscow.

'Sniper spotted Americans', recalled Tennent Bagley. 'A State Department official ... and ... KGB recruitment targets like the wife of an American Army colonel who was having an affair with a Soviet agent ... "Boxer" was his heading for news of an American military officer recruited and run by Soviet intelligence.'[17]

Sniper had made clear from the outset that the intelligence he provided carried with it the risk of exposing its source – a point he had reinforced with his January warning to Hoover. But although the FBI Director was now seeing at least some of the material, he had not been able to prevent its distribution by the CIA, and the seven-page report that Sniper sent in July 1959, describing 'problems concerning security conditions in the US Embassy in Warsaw', had been seen by three separate services: the Agency, the Bureau and the State Department. Once again, poor American security placed Sniper at risk.

The letter specifically warned that senior US foreign service officers and diplomatic staff, as well as members of the Marine Guard unit stationed there, had been compromised by 'red swallows' – the *femmes fatales* of Polish intelligence, and their male counterparts. Four male staff had been caught in a 'photography-blackmail ambush' in Warsaw itself, while the 'wife of an American foreign service officer had been led to make a solo visit to Moscow where, in a room fitted with hidden cameras and voice recorders, she had been compromised by a KGB gigolo.'[18]

But the key Soviet mole – who had, Sniper claimed, being spying for eighteen years – was one of the most senior officials inside the embassy: a career diplomat just two ranks below the ambassador, Jacob Beam.[19] Since all foreign service officials were employed by the State Department, the CIA sent the information over to its offices in Foggy Bottom; it landed on the desk of Otto Otepka, Deputy Director of the Office of Security, and a veteran of the vicious Washington feuds caused by Senator Joseph McCarthy's 'Red Scare'. The Agency made some attempt to stop the report spreading throughout the State Department's notoriously leaky corridors, sending strict instructions that no action was to be taken on Sniper's leads without written approval from the CIA; but it was an injunction never likely to be fully heeded.

Otepka was then acting head of the office while his boss William O. Boswell was away; as Otepka later told a secret Senate committee hearing, although he was given the Agency's summary of the intelligence he was not let into the origin of the report, much less the code name of the man who had sent it: 'The true identity of the source of the information was not revealed to me ... I was instructed that the Office of Security should not take any action with respect to the principals (employees) named in the document without the express permission of the originating agency ... I adhered to the agency's instructions scrupulously.'[20]

He did, however, immediately recognize the incendiary potential of the information. Unwilling to handle the time bomb alone, he sought the CIA's approval to show the report to Boswell, when he returned to duty. It was an understandable and routine example of governmental buck-passing, but it led to a serious breach of security:

> Mr. Boswell personally briefed a US Ambassador to the country
> where the principals [the diplomatic staff identified by Sniper]

were stationed about the contents of the document. On the
Agency's instructions these principals were permitted to serve
out their normal tours of duty on the ground that it would be to
the net advantage of the United States.[21]

Although Boswell did not know the identity of the CIA's informant,
simply telling the ambassador in Warsaw about the existence of an intelligence source exposing the KGB's control of embassy staff in Poland
put Sniper at significant risk. It was now a question of when, not if, his
Soviet spymasters would hear that their secrets were being betrayed by
a mole within their ranks.

It took less than a year for word to reach Moscow. By the summer of
1960 the KGB knew its operation in Poland had sprung a serious leak; it
didn't know the traitor's name, for the simple reason that its informant
in Washington – whether in the CIA, the FBI or the State Department –
didn't have Sniper's identity. And since, as Bagley later reported, it didn't
know who to trust in the UB, Soviet intelligence instead turned initially
to its own spy in Warsaw – Sniper himself:

> So sensitive was their source that they didn't tell the Polish ser-
> vice through routine channels but came just to [Sniper]. His main
> KGB contact in Warsaw asked him to help them identify a 'pig'
> [traitor] in the UB's foreign intelligence component whom they
> had learned was leaking its secrets to the CIA. [Sniper], of course,
> recognized the 'pig' as himself.[22]

Although he was badly shaken, Sniper initially believed he could handle
the problem and even turn it to American advantage. In a report he sent
in September he explained that the best person to catch a mole was
another mole:

> The KGB is in possession of two of my informations [sic] which
> I sent to [you], and which were intercepted by top KGB source
> (supposedly in US) and that for reason of the importance of said

source and its security the KGB is forced to conduct a most careful clandestine investigations [sic] concerning these informations
and its author . . .

The fact that these independent KGB investigations were
conducted with my participation . . . gave me a control about this
matter . . . I hope to be able to find out who the KGB source was
[and that] said KGB source would flee in panic to the East.[23]

It was a brave, if ultimately doomed, decision. By December 1960 the
KGB had lost faith in its point man in Warsaw and had briefed the UB;
both were now investigating. Sniper's time was running out.

That Christmas, Soviet bloc intelligence mounted an operation
designed both to plunder more secrets from Washington's embassy in
Poland and potentially to flush out the mole who had leaked the existence of its previous penetration. It involved exactly the type of 'red
swallow' entrapment technique that Sniper had advised American
intelligence to watch out for, and before long it would confirm his
warning that the KGB was willing to sacrifice an intelligence pawn to
protect a far more important asset.

9

Warsaw

O N THE EVENING of Thursday, 22 December 1960, Irvin Chambers 'Doc' Scarbeck arrived at a discreet Warsaw apartment anticipating a night of deliciously illicit sex with his lithe young Polish mistress. He found her waiting naked, and quickly stripping off his office clothes and thick horn-rimmed glasses, joined her in bed.

Scarbeck was forty, married and the father of three children. A former Army staff sergeant during World War II, he had joined the State Department in 1956 and two years later, after earning a Meritorious Service Award, had been given his first overseas posting, as Second Secretary in the US Embassy in Warsaw. His wife and their children accompanied him and the family lived together in a government-issue house on the other side of the city; they – and he – became accepted members of the American diplomatic community in Poland.

If it ever occurred to Scarbeck to wonder why a pretty, twenty-two-year-old doe-eyed local girl had so willingly become the mistress of a stocky and unprepossessing toiler in Washington's overseas bureaucracy, such concerns were far from his mind as they began making love. Reality, in the shape of a posse of stern Polish security officials, was about to catch up with him.

The men pushed through the apartment door; flashbulbs popped, illuminating the bed in an unforgiving glare as a camera captured the lovers in what would later be delicately termed 'a compromising situation'.

Irvin Scarbeck's romantic idyll was over: his long night of blackmail and espionage was about to begin.

Scarbeck occupied a relatively lowly tier in diplomatic ranks. His duties involved the generally tedious tasks of managing the embassy building's upkeep, making travel arrangements for more senior officials and procuring living quarters for new staff. But the post also gave him unrestricted access to the embassy's secure File Registry and to the coded signal traffic between the ambassador and the State Department in Washington. That, and his weakness for women, made Scarbeck a very attractive prospect indeed for Soviet bloc intelligence.

Scarbeck first encountered Urszula Discher on the telephone. In September 1959 she phoned the embassy seeking employment, and the Marine Guard manning the switchboard routed her call through to the Second Secretary. Discher told Scarbeck a sob-story, claiming that she was an orphan and desperately needed work. He – by his own subsequent confession – found her 'throaty voice' deeply alluring, and suggested they meet for drinks the same evening.

Drinks led to dinners; dinners led to sex. In April 1960, Scarbeck rented an apartment and installed Discher in it as (in her words) 'a fully kept' woman.[1] For the next eight months he lavished gifts on her and visited her 'almost nightly'; only work trips outside Warsaw kept him away from the delights of their bed.[2]

The men who so rudely interrupted Scarbeck's pleasures three nights before Christmas 1960 claimed to be local Warsaw police – though one was wearing the uniform of Poland's militia; in reality they were members of the state security service. What followed was set out in a subsequent judgement by the US Court of Appeals:

> Miss Discher was then taken to the police station where she was interrogated by Polish Security police (known as the 'UB') and threatened with expulsion from Warsaw, imprisonment for black market dealings, and forced service as a prostitute . . . [Scarbeck]

remained in the apartment and conversed with two other men who arrived to interview him. He was told that Miss Discher would be imprisoned, that his activities with her would have to be reported to the United States Embassy, and that his career would be finished.

Given the circumstances, it was understandable that Scarbeck didn't stop to wonder how the officials had known where to find him, nor how they had managed to gain entry to the apartment. Had he done so, he might have realized that Discher's abrupt removal, the threats to jail her, and the spectre of compromising photographs being sent to his employers were all textbook 'honeytrap' techniques, used by Soviet bloc espionage services. He might also have questioned why his two new interrogators had Russian, not Polish, names. But caught quite literally in the act, he could barely speak – a weakness which the agents standing over him were quick to exploit:

> The men suggested, however, that if [he] furnished information and documents from the Embassy to them, they might be able to quash the report to the Embassy concerning his activities and to procure the release of Miss Discher . . . [He] disclaimed having knowledge of any classified matters and stated that he would not under any circumstances give them any information which would endanger the security of the United States. He agreed, however, to meet with them again. Miss Discher was then returned to her apartment from the police station.[3]

This version of the conversation, which Scarbeck later gave to FBI and State Department investigators, was misleading to say the least. Discher's account makes clear that as soon as the 'police' left, Scarbeck told her that he realized he was being blackmailed by the UB, and that it 'wanted him to get for them the cipher [the top-secret codes used to encrypt embassy signals to the State Department] and then some kind of a plan of work he was receiving from Washington'. He also made clear that he intended to do so.[4] Faced with the choice between disgrace – and likely prosecution – and selling out his country, Irvin 'Doc' Scarbeck chose betrayal. From 22 December onwards he met his handlers regularly, turning over a succession of papers he took from Registry files and smuggled out of the embassy:

> He first gave them unclassified documents and information . . . but the men became insistent that he provide them with more important documents and information . . . About five or six weeks after his first meeting he took to them Despatch No. 344, a document prepared by the Ambassador, classified and marked as 'Secret'. The men photographed and returned this document to him in about fifteen minutes. He also provided them on other occasions with information contained in Despatch No. 518, classified and marked as 'Secret', and in Despatch No. 444, classified and marked as 'Confidential'.[5]

The contents of those documents included Ambassador Jacob Beam's analysis of US policy towards Poland, together with suggestions for future action; an internal US military estimate of the effectiveness of Poland's armed forces; and a secret report, assembled after covert surveillance by embassy staff, on the construction of a new Polish airfield.

Scarbeck's reward – aside from the UB's promise not to deliver the explicit photos to his employers – was the gift of a passport for Urszula Discher. This, in itself, was highly unusual: documents enabling a Polish national to travel beyond the Iron Curtain were rarely given to those outside the regime's politburo or security services. To a man less desperate or naive, the UB's willingness to provide Discher with the means to emigrate would have rung alarm bells: the Soviet bloc was not in the business of allowing its citizens to escape – especially given the relatively low-key secrets received in return. Scarbeck entirely failed to spot the signs; he used his position in the embassy to secure a West German visa for Discher, and rented an apartment for her in Frankfurt am Main, frequently travelling there to resume their interrupted relationship.[6] He even 'borrowed' $400 – the equivalent of at least $3,000 today – from his Soviet bloc handlers to help Discher set up home. There would, before long, be a price to pay.

The KGB and UB had very much larger targets in their sights than Irvin Scarbeck; neither had mounted such a crude sting operation merely to snare a junior American diplomat and the meagre take of low-level documents he could provide. Behind the honeytrap lay two rather more subtle schemes.

The first of these was a textbook distraction strategy from Moscow's counterintelligence playbook. The KGB had a long-term agent several ranks above Scarbeck in the US Embassy in Poland; as Sniper had set out in his letters, this diplomat had been spying for the Soviet Union since the early years of World War II and had repeatedly used his position in the foreign service to feed America's secrets to his Communist handlers. When that warning was leaked back to the KGB it realized the mole was likely to come under scrutiny from the State Department or CIA – or both. It needed a high-profile case to take the heat off its proven and senior asset and Irvin Scarbeck was set up to be the fall guy. When the time was right, Moscow would expose Scarbeck, sacrificing him to distract the CIA and thus safeguard the genuinely valuable spy.

The second part of the scheme was rather more urgent. The investigations to uncover the mole leaking secrets to Washington had, unsurprisingly, stalled. The KGB suspected that he lurked somewhere within – or at least had access to – Department II of the UB in Warsaw. It calculated that he would alert Washington and that its own agent inside the American government would rapidly feed the news back to Moscow.

The Scarbeck honeytrap and blackmail operation was designed to confirm its suspicions; only a handful of Department II officers were briefed on the plan: if it leaked, as expected, back to Washington, the mole would be quickly uncovered.

In other circumstances it might well have worked. But that December, the CIA's undercover agent inside Soviet bloc intelligence knew he was caught in the tightening coils of the KGB's counter-espionage service and was simultaneously facing his own romantic dilemma. The Iron Curtain was inexorably closing around him, and with it his last chance of escaping a rendezvous with a firing squad.

Three days after Scarbeck was hauled from his lover's bed, Sniper grabbed a set of bogus identity papers and a wad of foreign currency. He placed a bundle of documents in three sealed envelopes and handed them to his staff to courier out of the country; they were, he explained, too sensitive and dangerous for him to take across the border personally. Then, after stashing a final cache of files and microfilm inside a tree in a nearby park, he fled Warsaw.

After thirty-three months as an undercover Agent in Place and in fear for his life, on Christmas Day 1960, Sniper went on the run.

10

Berlin

Late on Christmas night a tall, heavy-set man sporting a distinctive cavalry moustache stepped down onto the platform at Friedrichstrasse station in East Berlin.

He carried travel papers showing him to be Roman Tarnowski, a Polish journalist. This, however, was for the benefit of the Vopos, the omnipresent East Berlin people's police; his briefcase held other documents, to be produced if he was stopped by representatives of East Germany's rather more sinister internal security service. These indicated his real occupation – an officer of the Polish intelligence service – and stated that he was on a mission to rendezvous with his undercover agents in Germany; they also recorded that the visit had been sanctioned by the Stasi.

But hidden beneath these documents, sewn into a concealed section of the case's lining, was his Polish military identity card, bearing his real name, rank and serial number, and a small cache of top-secret files which would – should he be subjected to more rigorous enquiries – ensure immediate arrest, deportation and eventual execution.

It was close to midnight. The 500-kilometre journey from Warsaw to East Berlin had taken more than fourteen hours. It was bitterly cold and although there was no snow that Christmas, temperatures had barely risen above freezing.

He walked cautiously past the ubiquitous signs wishing visitors to East Germany 'Greetings from the People's Democracy', scanning the station for tell-tale indications that he was under observation, and slipped out into the night. East Berlin was dark and gloomy. The bright lights and thrill rides of the Christmas fair in Marx-Engels Platz had been switched off and the streets were almost deserted. This, at least, was welcome; in a city of watchful eyes he needed to disappear from sight. He had ten days before he was due to return to Warsaw: ten days in which he needed to meet with the local Polish intelligence *rezidentura*, reclaim the files he had sent ahead by courier, and add to the bundles of foreign currency hidden in his luggage. He also needed to evade Stasi and UB surveillance teams long enough to meet his East German mistress, explain the real reason for his visit, and persuade her to join him on the next and most dangerous step of the journey. It would, he knew, be touch and go.

The next morning he presented himself at the Polish Embassy and asked to speak with Colonel Władysław Michalski – officially a diplomat, but in reality the resident Polish intelligence chief, code-named 'REN' – and requested 15,000 deutschmarks to fund his 'mission' in Berlin.

The two men were not strangers: Michalski had previously supplied his visitor with cash to pay his network of informers. This time, however, he was reluctant. Word had reached him that the UB officer had drawn 11,300 deutschmarks from office funds before leaving Warsaw; this new request, coming so soon afterwards and for such a substantial amount, needed to be cleared by UB headquarters. He told 'Tarnowski' to come back in a few days.[1]

Berlin was then the hottest zone of the Cold War. Spies from America, Britain and France fought – sometimes physically – with those working for Moscow and its satellites, as well as the 'domestic' intelligence services of the rival German states. But although the city was divided there was – as yet – no wall physically separating East from West; all that marked the notional borders were large signs warning travellers they were about to step across the invisible line between the 'people's' Democratic Republic and the capitalist political enclave administered by Bonn. Even for a Polish national with such distinctive facial hair, it was easy to slip from one to the other.

Roman Tarnowski spent the last days of December 1960 tramping the frozen streets. He met with some of the agents he controlled, but missed previously made appointments with others. The constant movement, however, served a much more urgent purpose; it gave him cover and helped him to spot the Stasi and UB 'tails' he knew to be following him.

He dodged them long enough to make two calls from public phones. The first, on 2 January 1961, was to a 'defector hot line' inside the American Consulate on Clayallee in West Berlin; Sniper had been given the number early in his days as an Agent in Place, and with it the code name – 'Herr Kowalski' – he would need to use in an emergency. Speaking quickly, he relayed a brief message that he needed to come in from the cold and arranged to call back in the next forty-eight hours.

The second call was to an apartment in East Berlin. Wollinerstrasse was a tree-lined street in the Mitte district; by East German standards it was a pleasant neighbourhood, a marked contrast to the grim and often ruined housing in other parts of the city. Inside, however, the accommodation was as cramped and crowded as anywhere else; flat number 54 was shared by an elderly couple, Franz and Luize Kampf, and their thirty-one-year-old daughter.

Irmgard Kampf, a pretty but unmarried school secretary, had been waiting for the call. Just before Christmas she had received a telegram, sent from her lover in Warsaw, asking her to take whatever holiday she was due from work, and telling her to expect him around New Year. Briefly – the Stasi was known routinely to tap home phones – he arranged to come to the apartment; he had, he said, important news.

The Kampf family did not know 'Roman Tarnowski'; they were, however, very familiar with Jan Roman, a handsome Polish journalist with an air of weary sadness; he said he was a Jewish, childless widower and had been courting Irmgard for almost two years. He had generously given them hard currency – deutschmarks, US dollars and British pounds – to make life more comfortable, and precious consumer goods to brighten up the apartment.

When he arrived at 54 Wollinerstrasse, Sniper's first task was to apologize for misleading them about his name – a deception he claimed had been necessary to protect them, since his work involved reporting on 'fascists' in West Germany[2] – and to give them his 'true' identity, Roman Tarnowski.

He then dropped a second bombshell. He told the Kampfs that he had decided to defect to the West; he was evasive about exactly how he planned to escape, or where he would go, but they assumed he meant slipping across the unguarded border with West Berlin. He asked permission to take Irmgard with him and, since he had previously promised to marry her, they gave it.

The Stasi, though, posed a problem: Irmgard was an East German citizen and forbidden from leaving the state without official sanction. The secret police invariably learned about defections within days and were known to act in reprisal against the families of those who had escaped. 'Tarnowski' suggested that Franz and Luize should also leave and, until the heat died down, stay with one of their other children who lived in West Berlin; thereafter, he promised, he would ensure they were safely relocated inside the Federal Republic. Remarkably – given the man's highly suspicious behaviour – once again, the Kampfs agreed to go along with whatever he recommended; together they set a date for the flight to freedom – Wednesday, 4 January.

As the Kampf family digested these revelations and prepared themselves for a new life in the West, the US Consulate was on high alert. The heart of the CIA's operation was Berlin Operating Base, generally abbreviated to BOB; its chief, forty-one-year-old David Murphy, was eager to meet the mysterious Sniper at long last. '[His] identity had been a matter of intense speculation in CIA ever since his first letter had been received in the West,' Murphy recalled in his Agency-sanctioned memoir. 'Now it seemed likely that the enigma would finally be resolved. The excitement at BOB was palpable.'[3]

But Murphy, a veteran of World War II who had been with BOB since 1954, knew that the final stages of any defection – especially one in a city where the KGB and the Agency fought for control of the streets – were the most fraught with risk. With so much at stake he was determined to take no chances:

> Because no-one had ever seen Sniper, BOB decided that a clandestine street-corner meeting was out . . . The American Consulate was finally chosen as the site for this crucial meeting . . . An emergency telephone number at the BOB switchboard had been established for Sniper, and the operators had been warned that if they missed his call they would be on the next boat home.[4]

Murphy also sent an urgent flash message to CIA headquarters in Washington. The Agency immediately put two experienced men on a flight to Germany; Howard Roman was dispatched to its secure reception centre at Wiesbaden, while an officer named Trickett[5] flew on to Berlin. He was given instructions to take the lead in bringing the defector in safely – although Director of Operations Richard Helms made it plain he 'thought this was a bunch of crap', and while the team was still in the air James Angleton sent a cable to BOB telling it 'not to waste much time waiting for Sniper'.[6]

Time was one of Sniper's biggest problems. To maintain the appearance that he was fulfilling his UB mission – doing otherwise would risk an abrupt, and firmly enforced, recall to Warsaw – he continued to meet with his agents across Berlin. He also kept in touch with Irmgard, assuaging her conflicting emotions and trying to bolster her courage for the coming escape. In addition, he needed to return to the embassy and secure from the evidently distrusting Michalski the last tranche of funds, and the documents which had been couriered there for him. Throughout, he was uncomfortably aware that his every step was being watched – though he couldn't be sure whether the teams were from Polish or East German intelligence.

On 3 January he arrived at the Polish Embassy to find that UB headquarters had sanctioned only a third of the cash he had requested – just 5,000 deutschmarks. It was another sign that Sniper was under increased suspicion. He stayed long enough to recover the documents and to complain to Michalski about the surveillance – a last throw of the dice which might, if he was lucky, buy him a few more hours.[7]

By the following day, however, the 'tails' were back in place. In late afternoon a Stasi agent, on station at 54 Wollinerstrasse, noted the arrival of his tall, heavily moustached target; at 5 p.m. the door opened again and the man re-emerged, this time with a slim brunette, each carrying a small case. They walked quickly away from the building in the direction of West Berlin, while the watcher remained in place to see who else would leave the apartment. Later that night he noted the departure of Franz and Luize Kampf; they, too, headed towards West Germany.

Mitte was one of the districts closest to the border. It was no more than 150 metres from Wollinerstrasse to the notice signalling the geographic edge of East Berlin; at 5.30 p.m., safely across the otherwise invisible demarcation line, Sniper found a pay phone and called the BOB emergency number. Once again, according to David Murphy's log of the day's events, he spoke in German, gave the code name 'Kowalski' and 'confirmed "delivery of the package in about half an hour"'. But he added an unexpected request: 'Maintaining the V-Mann fiction to the bitter end, Subject . . . [asked for] careful and considerate handling of Mrs. Kowalski.'[8]

The CIA team was puzzled; there had been no previous indication that Sniper was married, much less that he would be bringing his wife with him when he defected. But with little other choice, the BOB operator told the caller that 'all was in readiness and Mrs. Kowalski would be afforded the most humane treatment possible'.[9]

Murphy now moved quickly. Unsure of which of the Consulate's gates Sniper would approach, he placed officers inside both the main and side entrances, and ordered a roving security patrol to liaise between them. Outside, US-plated Chevrolet staff cars moved into position beside the main gate on Clayallee itself and a side road leading to the Berlin Military Compound.

They and the armed guards inside the Consulate grounds were a precaution – but a vital one. The lack of any physical barriers between East and West Berlin meant that Soviet bloc agents could move easily into the surrounding streets and stop Sniper from reaching safety. Since the end of World War II, the CIA and BND had logged hundreds of cases of successful kidnapping and attempted assassination by Stasi or KGB operatives.[10]

Murphy was not authorized to receive the defector. Instead he and his deputy, John Dimmer, walked briskly to a room deep inside the building, where they would listen to the initial debriefing via a secure audio link. Murphy's log recorded the next, tense stages:

> [At] 18.06 hours a West Berlin taxi pulled up in front of the Consulate; a man and a woman, each carrying a small piece of luggage, stepped out and proceeded to the main entrance of the Consulate. [REDACTED] met the couple at the entrance and introduced himself as 'Dr Peter'. In turn [Sniper] muttered something to the effect that he had been sent by Kowalski.

'Dr Peter', a Berlin-based officer, escorted the couple into the building and handed them over to Trickett, the CIA officer sent from Washington; here they were, for the first time, on US territory and, for the moment, safe.

Maintaining the fiction that Sniper had been communicating with the FBI, Trickett formally greeted them on behalf of 'Direktor Hercules' – the cover name the Agency had used for J. Edgar Hoover – and in line with standard CIA operating procedure, also gave himself a false identity. He was about to receive the first in what would become a series of surprises:

> [Trickett] introduced himself as 'Sonderbeauftragter [Special Representative] Mr. Drew' and suggested that the party proceed to an office where necessary discussion could be conducted undisturbed. En route [he] asked if Subject's wife spoke German; Subject's surprising answer: 'Of course she does; she is German.'

By ten past six Trickett and the couple were installed in the secure debriefing room. Concealed microphones captured the conversation and Murphy carefully recorded what transpired:

> [Trickett] opened the business discussion by again welcoming Subject and what was still thought to be his wife; by assuring them that they were now under the protection of the US element West Berlin and hence out of immediate danger; [and] by explaining to them that, in recognition of the somewhat uncomfortable status of West Berlin as an island in the middle of East Germany, a US military plane was standing by to fly them out into even greater safety – hopefully by that very evening.

Washington's man was evidently under orders to put the defector at his ease, assuring him that an American military doctor was also on hand 'in case immediate medical attention was needed by him or his wife'. He remained, though, less than honest about exactly who he was: he kept up the pretence that his name was 'Drew' and repeated the lie that he was the special emissary of FBI Director J. Edgar Hoover.

He told the couple that 'all their demands would be met': they would both be granted asylum, eventual US citizenship and Washington's gratitude. 'They would', Murphy's log recorded, 'receive the full protection of the US government and they would be afforded all the support and assistance necessary to ensure a satisfactory resettlement in the US.' The sole stipulations – which had to be agreed immediately – were that the defector undertook to tell the government everything he knew about Soviet bloc intelligence, 'regardless of how long this might take', and that he fully identified himself. Both conditions were obvious requirements for any defector and Trickett had not expected to encounter any difficulty; he was about to receive the second of the night's surprises:

> It was at this point that Subject, with obvious embarrassment, explained that his companion, although to all practical purposes his wife, really was not his wife and asked if, under these

circumstances, his mistress (hereafter referred to as Irmgard) could still be granted asylum. When assured that this made no difference, [he] suggested that his mistress leave the office since he had a matter of some sensitivity to discuss.

There was an element of farce to what followed. While Irmgard Kampf and another CIA officer paced up and down outside the office – Murphy's log reports that they 'walked the corridor' – the defector led Trickett through the tangled story of his relationship with her:

Subject explained that not only did Irmgard not know that he was an intelligence officer, she did not even know his true name. As far as Irmgard was concerned, he was a Polish journalist named Roman Tarnowski whom she had met during one of his frequent business trips to East Berlin, with whom she had fallen in love and whom she had joined that day in an adventure destined to make it possible for them at long last to live as man and wife in the free West.

Subject repeatedly emphasized that news of what was really involved would have to be broken to Irmgard very slowly, lest she suffer irreparable psychological damage. Trickett . . . agreed to maintain the journalist fiction vis-à-vis Irmgard as long as possible.[11]

Reassured, Sniper then finally agreed to identify himself, and handed over his identity card bearing the name Roman Tarnowski. Only after Trickett had spent some time examining it and making detailed notes did 'the Subject' point out that this 'was a waste of time since this particular document only identified him under his cover name and profession'.[12]

After a lengthy succession of grumbles that he still felt in danger, particularly from assassination, the real ID card was finally unearthed. He 'cut open the inside lining of his briefcase and, after considerable fumbling and pulling, produced the document'. This turned out to be a Polish Army pass, 'Legitymacja oficerska, Seria RW Nr. 0737', identifying him as an employee of Department II of the UB. Trickett studied the identity card; it had a passport-sized photo of the man, embossed with a Polish government stamp, and showed him to be Lieutenant Colonel Michał Goleniewski; the biographical data on the reverse recorded that he had been born in Nieśwież[13] on 16 August 1922 – making him thirty-eight years old.[14]

For absolute clarity, Goleniewski was asked to confirm that he was Sniper and that he was a Polish intelligence officer: 'Subject's answer was a bored "aber sicher" ["of course"].' He then signed a formal request for political asylum.

Finally, a bewildered Irmgard Kampf was led back into the room. Trickett examined her East German identity papers; these showed her to have been born in Berlin on 6 January 1929, making her seven years younger than her 'fiancé', and that she lived with her parents in the apartment at 54 Wollinerstrasse. Goleniewski made a point of securing a promise that her family would also be helped to leave the East, and, stroking her hair and kissing her, reassured Irmgard that 'the worst was now over and they would soon begin a new life in the West'. He then belatedly told her exactly what she had signed up for:

> In answer to Irmgard's question as to where in the West, Subject, apparently for the first time, informed her that they were destined for eventual resettlement in the United States. Irmgard accepted this disclosure with the same stoicism with which she went through the rest of what, by any criterion, must have been the most surprising evening of her life. Her sole comment at this juncture was something to the effect that 'ich tue was immer Du fuer richtig haelst' ['I will do whatever you think is right'].

Kampf's nationality posed a slight problem: she was a citizen of East Germany, the hostile state encircling West Berlin, and since she was not an intelligence asset her defection did not strictly fall within the unofficial rules of clandestine warfare by which the CIA and the Stasi notionally operated. But Trickett and Murphy decided that her arrival with Michał Goleniewski – the long-awaited Sniper – was enough to warrant immediate exfiltration for both of them.

The original plan had been to sneak them out of Berlin in an unmarked vehicle, and drive them 570 kilometres south to Wiesbaden Air Base; here a US Air Force plane was waiting on the runway, booked to fly them out of Germany at 10 p.m. But it was 6.40 p.m. by the time the bizarre initial debriefing finished; too late to make an internal flight to Wiesbaden, much less attempt the alternative – a six-hour drive. Above all, both Goleniewski and Kampf were understandably exhausted. Murphy had them escorted to a safe house within the Consulate compound and rescheduled departure for the morning.[15]

In any event he and Trickett had two immediate tasks to address. Both knew that news of Goleniewski's defection would reach his masters in Soviet bloc intelligence very quickly, and the KGB would move to protect the agents he would expose. The network then under MI5 surveillance in London was the most urgent concern; a secure cable was sent to the Security Service, advising it to make immediate moves to arrest the Portland spies, Harry Houghton and Ethel Gee.[16]

Murphy then composed a flash message for Washington, informing the Agency that its most-prized defector was in the bag and would be flown to America in the coming days.[17] As he later recalled, Murphy and his fellow officers were jubilant: 'Agents in the listening post sighed with relief and smiled with joy . . . Sniper was for real.'

Yet the highly unusual circumstances of Goleniewski's defection – the bizarre and unexpected arrival of his mistress, the farcical business of preventing her from knowing his real name and his arrogantly dismissive replies to standard questioning – should have sounded a faint note of alarm.

The events of 4 January 1961 were a foretaste of what lay in store for the CIA, the FBI and the US government. They could not say – at least, not honestly – that they hadn't been warned.

11

Flight

THE MAN COULD certainly talk.

From the moment Howard Roman met Michał Goleniewski it was clear that the CIA's original plan for an immediate exfiltration to the United States was not likely to survive. Once the burly defector began speaking – pontificating was a more accurate description – it was almost impossible to interrupt him, much less staunch the flow. Hour after hour, barely seeming to pause for breath, he held forth, drowning his listeners in information, all of it apparently urgent.

Roman had been analysing the Sniper letters for thirty-three months. At the initial debriefing session he discovered that their length and exhaustive detail accurately reflected the character and intelligence of the author. Goleniewski had an apparently encyclopaedic knowledge of the KGB and the UB, as well as a photographic memory for the dates, times and places of operations that each had run against the West. The idea of imposing a hiatus of at least twenty-four hours – the time it would take to fly to the United States – was clearly out of the question. Roman made plans for a lengthy stay in Germany.

~

In the early hours of 5 January the BOB team had driven Goleniewski and Kampf to Tempelhof airport and escorted them inside a military aircraft laid on for their benefit alone. At 6 a.m. it took off for a two-hour flight to the Lucius D. Clay Kaserne US Air Force Base at

Wiesbaden, thirty kilometres south-west of Frankfurt am Main.[1] During World War II the CIA's predecessors had used parts of the compound to interrogate captured or surrendering Nazi troops, and when the Cold War began the Agency set up a new, purpose-built Defector Reception Center close by.

The DRC – CABEZONE in US intelligence's endless list of cryptonyms – was secure and discreet: no signs identified it as the first staging post for Soviet bloc intelligence officers who were trading secrets for sanctuary. To further disguise its function and to keep its highly vulnerable inmates away from prying eyes, there were no residential facilities on site.

'The word "Center" was a misnomer,' recalled former counterintelligence officer Ted Shackley. 'The defectors were not kept in one place, but were housed individually in villas scattered widely through the city's environs . . . with only CIA security guards and a cleared German housekeeper for company.'[2] By 10 a.m. that January morning, Goleniewski and Kampf were installed in one of them: their stay would be unexpectedly long.

The CIA's manual for assessing new defectors laid down key tasks for interrogators. Ted Shackley's account spelled out the most urgent:

> One of the first things to be discovered in this process is the matter of motivation. Why did he come over? We want to eliminate the possibility that the defector's underlying motive is to feed us incorrect information and thereby cause us harm. But beyond that, understanding what makes this person tick will be vitally important later if and when we undertake to help him build a new life in the West . . .
>
> Defectors' motivations tend to run to such things as fear for their personal safety, exasperation with their living conditions, hatred for a boss, marital problems, or a life complicated by alcoholism, gambling debts, embezzlement or womanizing. Whatever it may be, once you understand what it is, you take the defector as he is.[3]

Goleniewski made his motivation clear from the outset: he was driven, he said, by a deep-seated hatred for the Communist system he had served, and a determination to help the United States and its allies in the covert war with Moscow. His reports as a volunteer Agent in Place had already exposed KGB, GRU and UB spies in the West: that, it seemed to Roman, argued against the possibility that he was a bogus defector, sent to sow the seeds of disinformation.

But there is rarely a sole impetus for any human action and, as Howard Roman was about to discover, Goleniewski's professional and personal life contained most, if not all, of the less honourable character traits described in the Agency's operating procedure. Rather than expressing gratitude for helping him and Kampf escape, the defector promptly issued his own set of demands.

The first reflected an understandable concern for the safety of the Kampfs. Before discussion of intelligence matters could begin in earnest, he wanted the entire family – Irmgard's parents, Franz and Luize, her widowed sister Margette, and her brother Franz, together with his wife and their children – removed from danger. It was feasible, if expensive – assuming all were willing to abandon their existing lives and be relocated under assumed names – but Roman knew he would have to clear both the principle and the cost with Washington.

Next, Goleniewski insisted that Roman dispatch a CIA agent to Warsaw, to recover the rolls of microfilm he had cached in a tree in the park near his apartment. This, too, was no easy task, and one which exposed the Agency – let alone the individual it selected for the mission – to considerable danger; under normal circumstances, an operation to recover top-secret documents from a dead drop behind the Iron Curtain would require careful planning over several days.

Delays, however, were not acceptable to the imperious defector. The clock, he said, was now ticking fast: the UB expected him to report back for duty in Warsaw on 6 January – now less than twenty-four hours away;[4] when he failed to appear, Polish intelligence would start looking for him, and the Stasi would hunt for Irmgard's relatives. The same time constraints made it imperative to recover the microfilms from the park immediately.

Roman, an experienced and confident officer, conceded the point. He arranged for the Agency's East European Division to send an agent to clear out the Warsaw dead drop, and agreed to have all nine members of the Kampf family exfiltrated from West Berlin. The rescue came just in time. The family reached Frankfurt am Main on 7 January; on the same day Polish intelligence officer Colonel Henryk Sokolac arrived in Berlin and began searching for Goleniewski and Kampf; he found that no one had seen either of them after they had left her apartment three days earlier. The flat itself was empty. When Sokolac realized that the entire family had disappeared, the only explanation was a joint defection.[5]

But Goleniewski's third demand was more problematic: he wanted to know exactly who he was dealing with, and for which of 'Direktor Hercules'' numerous offices his debriefer worked.

Thus far, Roman had maintained the fiction that he, and the American officers at the Consulate, were FBI agents, reporting directly to Hoover. But as Goleniewski turned the tables, refusing to be the subject of questioning and assuming for himself the role of relentless interrogator, the lie became unsustainable; Roman finally admitted that he, at least, belonged to the Central Intelligence Agency, not the Federal Bureau of Investigation. The revelation was not well received. 'After 33 months of my anti-Soviet efforts in the East,' Goleniewski told a subsequent interviewer, 'Howard made the first contact with me by lying and making small distortions.'[6]

Goleniewski's anger was genuine, and grounded in very real fear. He knew that the KGB had penetrated the CIA, and his Sniper letters had repeatedly given leads to the identities of Moscow's spies within it. Now he discovered that he had been dealing with the compromised Agency all along; worse, he was entirely dependent on it for his safety, that of his 'fiancée', their accommodation, food and the secure future they and the entire Kampf family had been promised in the West.

He faced an invidious choice: to gamble his life on working with the organization which had deceived him for almost three years, and which had been infiltrated by Moscow's moles, or to refuse further cooperation and risk being returned to Poland and certain execution. After forty-eight hours of deliberation, he realized he had no option; he sat down with Roman to resume the debriefing.

By Goleniewski's own accounts – there are no corroborating CIA documents or reports – before he began the lengthy process of identifying Soviet bloc intelligence operations in the United States, Roman took possession of his Polish identity papers and carried out routine tests. 'He ordered the making of my fingerprints,' Goleniewski claimed, in characteristically disjointed English. 'Two sets of a special kind were made, including handprints. One set was sent to the United States and one set was sent immediately to London':[7]

> [Then] two days after my arrival in Frankfurt [Wiesbaden], I, in a
> very detailed manner, debriefed the representatives of the CIA
> about all facts and informations fingerpointing the existence of
> KGB penetrations of CIA.[8]

He first handed over the papers that had been couriered to him, care of the Polish Embassy. These turned out to be a complete account of current espionage operations run in the West by the UB, together with the identities of 191 UB agents.

There were thirty-one based in West Germany, twenty in Britain, nineteen in France, with the remainder spread across mainland Europe, North America, Scandinavia, Asia and the Middle East; many were employed in strategic defence and telecommunications companies.[9] The files listed their locations, cryptonyms and real names, and even included some copies of their handwritten reports.[10] It was a unique and stunning 'take': no other defector had ever provided such a complete breakdown of a Soviet bloc intelligence service and its operatives.

But even this was eclipsed by the canisters of microfilms recovered from the Warsaw dead drop. They were flown to Wiesbaden Air Force Base on 9 January and rushed to CABEZONE, where the CIA maintained a lab able to develop the tiny rolls of celluloid.

Their contents reinforced Roman's conviction that Goleniewski was a genuine – and uniquely important – defector; able and apparently willing to give the United States unprecedented insight into Soviet bloc intelligence. According to the CIA officer's subsequent account, the package contained 'three hundred pages of Minox film ... lists of names, tables of organization [and] several hundred names of Polish agents'.[11]

Goleniewski himself claimed the number of pages was rather greater, and provided a fuller description of the material they revealed. This emphasized the enormous volume of KGB and GRU documents – including their file reference codes – he had photographed, and highlighted evidence suggesting the alarming extent to which both US and British intelligence had been penetrated by Soviet spies:

> The 798 microfilm pages of 'Top Secret', 'Secret' or 'Top Secret – Handle as Coded' (the highest level of secrecy in Soviet Bloc) – present a collection of most vital informations [sic] for the national security of the US and its western allies. The microfilmed documentation contained amongst other [sic]:

> CIA file #516: Information re: activities of US Intelligence, edited by Department of Counter-Intelligence, Warsaw 1960.

> CIA file #533: First part of a new instruction of British Staff Gen. (Top Secret – edited 1959) re: principal intelligence and counter-intelligence during the war, its purposes and targets, sources of information ... and of dates & informations from intelligence and counterintelligence services.

> Bulletin of Z-II Pol. Staff Gen. Warsaw, based on informations from GRU also ... 41 pages ... This bulletin was based on original British Top Secret documents from agent of III Head. Dir. KGB.

#535 of CIA file: KGB II Head Directorate (Counter-Intelligence) . . . concerning methods of works [sic] with chiffre [ciphers], and codes as well as collection and transferring of clandestine reports of US intelligence, 4 pages, edited 1960.

#539 of CIA file: KGB I Head Directorate (Intelligence Service): June 1960 intelligence targets and orders appointed by staff of NATO, 6 pages, edited June 1960.

#537 of CIA file: KGB I Head Dir. July 1960 re: Secret Committee of NATO of May 25, 60, during which was discussed a special elaborate [sic] of special committee of NATO re: intelligence activities of Soviet block [sic], 4 pages.

#540 of CIA file: KGB II Head Dir. Copy of memorandum of Committee of Security of NATO in Paris, 1960, 10 pages re: 'Danger to the security of high-classified informations in the diplomatical [sic] mission of NATO in the countries behind the Iron Curtain'.

CIA file #518 & 519: Top Secret, handle as coded matter. Register of agents, co-opted workers and affairs of Independent Branch VI (Scientific & Technical Intelligence) of the Intelligence Department I, on 32 pages, Warsaw, per November 30, 1960 . . . said document contained completed data on 240 agents, co-opted workers and other sources of said branch who were cooperating in the [sic] western Europe (few in USA & in Canada) ie: their names, identifications, assignments, locations & operations from the East to West or directly in the Western countries.

CIA file #562: Bulletin (GRU-ZII). Mil. Intelligence, 70 pages, edited 1958/60 re: Armed Forces of Great Britain (all Forces incl. 'Sea & Air Forces, in all territories in the world').

CIA file #563: Bulletin (GRU-ZII). Mil. Intelligence, 100 pages, edited 1960, re: NATO and its armed forces including atom [sic] weapons.

CIA file #564: Bulletin (GRU-ZII). Mil. Intelligence. Re: Armed Forces of United States, edited 1960 (Part #1) on 80 pages.[12]

By any measure, this was an unprecedented treasure trove of Soviet bloc intelligence material, and one which added immeasurably to the CIA's understanding of Moscow's spies and their tactics. But the devastating sting in the tail was that, according to Goleniewski, most of the documents which the KGB, GRU and UB had used to write these reports had been obtained from their moles inside Western agencies.

The debriefings wore on, hour after hour, day after day. There seemed no end to the information Goleniewski wanted to pass on about the actions and identities of Moscow's spies, and Roman realized that the revelations would occupy the Agency's counterintelligence and Soviet Division analysts for years to come. But one lead was too sensitive and too urgent to wait for Washington's patient scrutiny: it concerned the MI6 mole he had previously code-named LAMBDA 1.

Goleniewski said that the KGB was receiving documents from an agent inside the Secret Intelligence Service, and he gave Roman details of the countries in which the mole had previously served.[13] Roman had been party to the ineffective joint investigation by MI6 and MI5, and he saw that the additional information about LAMBDA 1's previous postings might light a much-needed fire under the apparently complacent British intelligence services. The CIA duly sent an urgent cable to London.

By now Goleniewski's stay in CABEZONE was drawing to an end. As Roman and senior officials in Washington began planning to fly the defector and Irmgard Kampf back to the United States, the Agency prepared a safe house on the east coast, and summoned up a Military Air Transport plane to make the journey.

They had all now been cooped up in CABEZONE for almost a week. With exfiltration to America imminent, Goleniewski faced up to the sensitive and much-delayed task of telling his mistress who he really was, and what she should expect once they touched down on US soil. Irmgard still laboured under the belief that the name her fiancé had belatedly given her and her parents in the apartment on Wollinerstrasse was true; for the second time in less than a week, he had to confess that he had lied to her. Just as Polish journalist Jan Roman had been a fiction, so too was Roman Tarnowski. His real identity, he promised, was Lieutenant Colonel Michał Goleniewski, and, under the protection of American intelligence, they would finally make a new life in the country which epitomized freedom and justice.

If these revelations resulted in the 'irreparable psychological damage' which Goleniewski had predicted to BOB, neither his writings nor those of Irmgard Kampf record it; nor does any CIA document make mention of a breakdown in her mental health. But the new, true, name with which he had revealed himself to her – the one under which, in theory, he would marry her – was destined to last no longer than twenty-four hours. When, on 11 January, the couple, accompanied by Howard Roman, boarded the MATS flight from Wiesbaden, they had become Mr Franz Oldenburg and Miss Irmgard Henschel.

At the exact moment the aircraft took off on the first leg of the 4,000-mile journey to America, identities, names and cover names – real, temporary or entirely fictional – were causing very serious trouble in London. MI5's investigations into LAMBDA 2, the Portland spy Harry Houghton, had unearthed a KGB network far bigger, and far more sinister, than one simply selling Admiralty secrets to Moscow. It had all the makings of yet another major British espionage scandal: one which was certain to embarrass the government, the Security Service and its sister agency, MI6, but one which would also highlight glaring failures by intelligence services in both Canada and the United States.

12

Reverberations

L ONDON, ON SATURDAY, 7 January 1961 was wet and cold. The streets were slick with recent heavy rain, and although occasional shafts of winter sun broke through the leaden skies, they were quickly eclipsed by heavy clouds. Despite the persistent showers, weekend shoppers pressed into the open-air market on East Street in the borough of Southwark; among them was an unremarkable middle-aged couple. Both were in their late forties or early fifties and looked drab; he was stocky and balding, she was pale with black wavy hair.

To the sizeable MI5 and police surveillance teams, however, there were two points which distinguished this otherwise nondescript couple from the crowds around them. The first was that they were not native Londoners but had made a special journey from the south-west of England; the second – which made the trip rather more strange – was that although the woman carried a large shopping basket they made no purchases. After half an hour meandering past stalls selling fresh fruit and vegetables, they left and walked to a nearby bus stop.

They boarded a number 68 bus, a red double-decker heading north towards Waterloo. At 4.15 p.m. they alighted and ducked into Tsaperelli's, an Italian café in a side street across from the railway station; ten minutes later they emerged and began walking towards the Old Vic theatre.

At 4.30 p.m. a smartly suited younger man 'fell into step with them'; he politely offered to carry the woman's basket and 'together they continued walking towards St. George's Circus'. Seconds later, plain-clothes officers from the Metropolitan Police's Special Branch 'plunged forward and . . . a very firm and sure grip was placed on the wrists of all three persons'.[1]

Harry Houghton, Ethel 'Bunty' Gee and their companion, a Canadian businessman known as Gordon Lonsdale, were bundled into separate unmarked cars and driven across the river to New Scotland Yard. Three hours later, police hammered on the door of a bungalow in the West London suburb of Ruislip and led away Peter Kroger, an antiquarian bookseller from New Zealand, together with his wife, Helen.

The arrests marked the end of an exhausting eight-month investigation into the leaking of Navy documents from the Underwater Detection Establishment (UDE) at Portland. It had begun with Sniper's report identifying Houghton as the spy for Polish intelligence he called LAMBDA 2, and whom MI5 had christened REVERBERATE. It had grown inexorably into an operation which consumed unprecedented resources. The Security Service had assigned dozens of round-the-clock surveillance teams, even pressing officers' wives into service when overstretched; it had bugged at least four homes – and burgled one – as well as deploying its latest top-secret radio-detection technology.

As it began interrogating Houghton, Gee, Lonsdale and the Krogers at Canon Row police station, MI5 had – in theory – every reason for satisfaction. In practice there were no celebrations. The case exposed a succession of woeful security lapses which had enabled the KGB to obtain highly sensitive naval secrets with remarkable ease; more to the point, British intelligence had grounds to believe that the suspected spies were far from the only members of the Portland network.

There was a reason for this: of the five men and women safely locked up in the cells, the Security Service knew the real identities of just two.

~

Operation TOW/ROPE – the cryptonym MI5 assigned to its initial investigation – had begun in late Spring 1960. Backed by the legal authority of Home Office warrants, the Security Service tapped Houghton's home phone, intercepted his mail, and started searching for his former wife, Amy, who had previously tried to warn the Admiralty about his espionage activities. It quickly located a copy of the couple's divorce certificate, which showed that the marriage had formally ended in 1958; this cited Houghton's cruelty as the grounds for granting the order[2] – a domestic issue the Navy had seemed entirely content to ignore.

Amy Houghton had since left Britain and remarried. Her second husband was an RAF aircraftman by the name of Johnson, stationed in what was then Malaya. It took several weeks for the new Mrs Johnson to overcome her fear, but she finally agreed to another interview. She said that she was 'not surprised' to be asked about Houghton who, the report noted, 'had bullied her for years'. Nor had the drunken abuse which marred their time in Warsaw ended when the couple returned to England and he bought a semi-detached cottage in Meadow View Road, Weymouth:

> She had lived for years in terror of her previous husband who had repeatedly assaulted her and had threatened on numerous occasions to kill her if she opened her mouth about his activities. She states that he had on different occasions broken her leg, injured her by throwing her over a wall, threatened her with a pair of revolvers and endeavoured to push her over Portland cliffs . . .

Mrs Johnson was also able to provide more information about Houghton's suspicious behaviour and his illicit wealth:

> [She] noticed that REVERBERATE started making trips to London once a month. He told her that he had to visit the Admiralty but she realised that this was untrue since the trips took place at weekends . . . On one occasion when REVERBERATE returned cheerfully tipsy from one of these trips, he pulled a bundle of £1 notes out of his pocket and threw them into the air.

Mrs. Johnson estimated that there was as much as £150[3] in the bundle. She noticed that he kept a piece of chalk in the glove pocket of the car and when asked what he used it for, he said 'to make signs in places'.[4]

Meanwhile, 'watchers' from MI5's A4 Branch reported that Houghton was a serial philanderer. Despite his distinctly unprepossessing appearance, he was conducting simultaneous sexual affairs with at least four women, some of them married. The surveillance teams observed him meeting his lovers in pubs, then taking them to London to catch a show; frequently they spent the night in the expensive West End Cumberland Hotel. This lifestyle explained why he needed so much money: the more troubling question was how he came by it.

The Admiralty, however, maintained its wilfully blind eye to these indiscretions. Although it was on notice that Houghton was a suspected and long-term spy for Soviet bloc intelligence – which should have made his sexual and financial activities a cause for serious concern – the sole action it took was to move him to a new job in the Port Auxiliary Repair Unit. This was still within the Portland Naval Base, and Navy officials made no attempt to restrict his movements; unsurprisingly, he took advantage of the freedom.

Ethel Elizabeth 'Bunty' Gee was forty-four when Harry Houghton found her. She lived with her widowed mother and bedridden aunt in a run-down end-of-terrace cottage on Hambro Road, Portland. She was unmarried, plain and, as a middle-aged spinster, had little prospect for joy in her life – a dull existence reflected in the suburban cryptonym MI5 gave her: TRELLIS. But, as its report in the summer of 1960 recorded, her job at UDE would have made her a very attractive prospect to Houghton:

Miss Gee works in the Drawing Office registry. She shares a room and a telephone with two other employees. The drawings kept in this Registry are those concerned with projects which have

reached the production stage. They are either Unclassified, CON-
FIDENTIAL or SECRET . . .

Miss Gee can visit the Drawing Office where are kept drawings relating to projects which are still in the experimental or
prototype phase. She could fairly easily find out in general what
projects were being undertaken but it would not be possible for
her to take drawings, or copies of drawings, from the Drawing
Office without arousing suspicion . . . It appears that . . . Miss Gee
has access to classified information: this information would relate
to equipment which was being fitted in HM ships or in those of
our NATO allies . . .[5]

Houghton deliberately set out to seduce the lonely filing clerk; they
became lovers and then co-conspirators. He drove her to and from work,
and she stole documents from the drawing-office strong room. 'I put
them into a large official envelope and walked out of the office to go home,'
she later confessed. 'As usual Harry was waiting for me with his car outside the office and I rode with him out through the dockyard gates.'[6]

MI5 knew that Houghton must have a handler. It increased surveillance on his home, following him on the frequent trips he made to
London, and in July 1960 watched as he made what was plainly a covert
delivery of the files Gee had stolen:

On the weekend of 9th/10th July he came to London accompanied
by Miss Gee . . . They shared a room at the Cumberland Hotel. On
the afternoon of 9th July they travelled by underground to Waterloo Station and met a contact outside the Old Vic, who will be
referred to as 'A'. They walked around the streets with 'A' for about
half an hour. During this period 'A' handed to REVERBERATE
two tickets . . . for the Bolshoi Ballet.

They then returned to a bench near where they had recently
met . . . [and] REVERBERATE handed . . . a brown paper container
to 'A'. When they parted 'A', who now appeared to be extremely alert,
made his way by a very circuitous route to a car parked near the
meeting place and drove off.[7]

A4 branch covertly photographed the mysterious 'Mr. A', but his picture did not match any of the known *rezidentura* – spies working under diplomatic cover in the Soviet or Polish embassies. Checks on the number plate of his distinctive imported American car – a Studebaker – revealed that it was registered to a thirty-nine-year-old Canadian businessman. Within a month, MI5 had established his background, and recorded a second suspicious meeting with Houghton:

> We have now firmly identified contact 'A' as a Canadian, Gordon Arnold Lonsdale, who came to this country in 1955, ostensibly as a post-graduate student at London University. He has no security record. His father, Jack Emmanuel Lonsdale, was a labourer and his mother was the former Olga Elena Bousu who received Canadian naturalisation in 1931.
>
> On 6th August 1960, REVERBERATE came to London and again met Lonsdale outside the Old Vic. They went to a café and fragments of their conversation were overheard. These included references to future meetings on the first Saturday of each month . . . REVERBERATE complained about the cost of his hotel (he was again staying at the Cumberland) and Lonsdale said that he would look after that . . .
>
> After they left the café they walked to a telephone kiosk. While Lonsdale held the door open, REVERBERATE concealed a large envelope or package in the newspaper previously carried by Lonsdale and handed it to him. Then they parted.
>
> This incident goes far to strengthen our suspicion that REVERBERATE is still spying and, if so, Lonsdale must be suspected of being an 'illegal' spy. It is possible that Lonsdale is controlling other spies than REVERBERATE and, indeed, more important ones. We have, therefore, embarked on an investigation of Lonsdale.

MI5 mounted an extensive surveillance operation, tailing Lonsdale night and day. 'To all intents and purposes,' recalled Peter Wright, one of the senior officers involved in the case, 'he lived the life of a London playboy, travelling abroad frequently and pursuing a succession of glamorous girls attracted by his easy money and good looks.'[8]

The source of Lonsdale's wealth, however, was something of a mystery. Ostensibly, he was an entrepreneur, cashing in on the craze for jukeboxes and coin-operated vending machines while simultaneously marketing a new range of security products. But the Automatic Merchandising Company which he managed and in which he held shares had collapsed in October 1959; his next venture – the Master Vending Machine Company (its products included 'The Trump – the combined picture card and ball gum vendor that can't lose!') – seemed similarly unsuccessful.

Despite this, he was able to afford the lease on an office in Soho's Wardour Street and a series of flats across London; the latest was in the distinctly upscale White House apartment block in Albany Street, on the edge of Hyde Park. MI5 bugged the flats and set up observation posts to monitor Lonsdale's comings and goings.

By the end of the summer, the Security Service had received a full biography of the thrusting young playboy businessman from its counterparts in Canada. These showed that he held a Canadian driving licence – No: 685329 – and in January 1954 had successfully applied for a passport – number 4-467593 – in order to travel to London from his home in Toronto:

> Lonsdale stated that the purpose of his passport was to travel to the United Kingdom to study, that he had never changed his name, that he did not possess any passport and that he had not applied for one during the last ten years . . . and that he intended to take up post-graduate studies at the University of London.[9]

In February 1955 he had arrived in Southampton, by way of Niagara Falls and New York City, on the SS *America*. For the next six months he was apparently unemployed, though able to lease apartments and pay for frequent trips to Scandinavia and Paris. Finally, in October, he signed up for a course in Mandarin Chinese at the School of Oriental and African Studies (SOAS) in Bloomsbury, claiming to have previously attended two schools in the San Francisco area.

SOAS was then regularly used by both British intelligence services to prepare agents for assignments abroad, and according to MI5's subsequent account, Lonsdale 'obtained useful information from his conversations with these officers. He was able to take photographs of many of them and would send these photographs together with biographical information to Moscow'.[10]

Under closer scrutiny, however, Lonsdale's biography began to crumble. Neither of the California schools had any record of him, and the Royal Canadian Mounted Police (RCMP) discovered that his passport had been issued on the sole strength of his driving licence, which in turn had been obtained when Lonsdale presented his birth certificate – a document freely available to anyone. Regretfully, the RCMP advised MI5, 'though the birth is fully documented in Canadian records, it has not been possible to prove that the child born to Jack and Olga Lonsdale is identical with the subject of this enquiry'.[11]

All of this suggested that 'Gordon Lonsdale' was a 'legend' – a carefully crafted false identity – and that he was a Soviet intelligence officer operating under deep cover: an 'illegal' in spy parlance. MI5 opened a file on him under the twin cryptonyms LAST ACT and TREK.[12]

In early September 1960 phone taps on his White House flat revealed that Lonsdale was about to travel to Belgium, apparently for a rendezvous with one of his mistresses. Shortly before he left, A4 branch followed him to the Midland Bank in Great Portland Street. He arrived carrying a suitcase and a brown paper parcel; when he emerged he had neither.

Roger Hollis, MI5's Director General, made a discreet approach to the Midland's chairman and discovered that Lonsdale rented a safety-deposit box in the bank's strong room; he persuaded the official to allow the Security Service to break into it. What they found proved beyond doubt that the man was a very senior, and very dangerous, intelligence agent – and gave Peter Wright an unprecedented insight into Soviet bloc espionage equipment.

Late on Monday, 5 September, the bank box was emptied and its contents rushed across London to the MI5 laboratory at St Paul's. As the items were laid out on a table and individually examined, Wright realized they had uncovered 'the complete toolbag of the professional spy': in addition to Minox and Praktika miniature cameras, a hardback book – ostensibly a teach-yourself guide to typing – turned out to be part of Lonsdale's 'secret writing' kit: painstaking examination revealed the minute indentations of previous messages.[13]

But the most damning evidence had been hidden in a Ronson table cigarette lighter: its wooden bowl had been hollowed out and used to store two miniature one-time pads – tiny cipher booklets identical to those used by the KGB to encrypt top-secret radio messages. 'As soon as I saw Lonsdale's cipher pads,' Wright later wrote, 'I could identify them as Soviet issue. This was no Polish Intelligence officer – this was a full-blown KGB operation.'[14]

The one-time pads were evidently in current use; that meant MI5 could – in theory – use them to decrypt messages Lonsdale sent to Moscow. There were, however, two immediate problems. The first was how to copy the little booklets without leaving any trace. Wright needed to examine every page, but they were glued together; pulling them apart would break the seal, and the Security Service didn't possess any supplies of Soviet adhesive to repair the damage. The second was that the safety-deposit box contained neither Lonsdale's transmitter nor any schedule of the times and frequencies of his broadcasts.

By good fortune, Swiss intelligence had recently obtained a KGB one-time pad. The Security Service arranged for it to be flown to London for analysis, where Post Office technicians set to work on reproducing the Russian glue. On 17 September, Wright's team returned to the bank, once again 'borrowed' the booklets, and gingerly took them apart to be photographed. They then put the originals in a custom-built frame and stuck them back together with their freshly made gum.

To overcome the second hurdle, MI5 opted for a twin approach of burglary and state-of-the-art surveillance technology. Breaking and entering was, then, routine practice – 'we bugged and burgled our way across London,' Wright recalled.[15] Inside the White House apartment MI5 agents found Lonsdale's transmitter – 'a Bush wireless of a kind well suited for the reception of short-wave messages', with a bogus label on the front used to conceal sheets from the one-time pads.[16]

This knowledge was valuable, but it didn't solve the problem of how to listen in to Lonsdale's broadcasts. The answer was RAFTER, one of Wright's recent innovations which enabled his staff to pick up on the small bursts of radiation produced by short-wave transmissions; careful tuning of RAFTER receivers would then identify the frequency Lonsdale used. The team set up their equipment in the flat next door to Lonsdale's and waited for him to return from Brussels.

By the middle of October, MI5 had begun to worry that Lonsdale had somehow discovered he was under surveillance. It could find no record of him returning to London, and there was no sign of him at the White House flat. It was also under belated pressure from Naval Intelligence to staunch the flow of documents being harvested by Gee and Houghton. A file note by MI5's Deputy Director General, Graham Mitchell, on 17 October recorded a testy meeting with his opposite number:

> DNI [Director of Naval Intelligence] asked me how long the Admiralty would be invited to put up with the situation in which secrets from UDE were being passed out. I said . . . that it was impossible for us at this stage to say how long this situation might last . . . We did not like any better than he the transmission of Admiralty secrets to a hostile intelligence service . . .
>
> I told DNI we now knew it was Russian espionage that was involved and that we had reason to hope that further investigation of the controller of REVERBERATE might lead us to other spies.[17]

Within a fortnight, Mitchell's hopes were realized. A4 finally located Lonsdale and tailed his car across London. He stopped in Ruislip and the surveillance team watched him walk briskly towards a small, detached bungalow at the end of a short residential street.

Number 45 Cranley Drive was owned by a middle-aged antiquarian bookseller. Peter Kroger was from New Zealand, and his wife, Helen, was Canadian. They had arrived in the UK in December 1954 and rented a house in South London; Peter opened a specialist bookshop in the Strand, but when the couple moved to Ruislip in 1958 he closed his London premises and operated the business from home. The Krogers were, according to local police enquiries, quiet and respectable, well liked by their neighbours.

Lonsdale was very clearly staying at the bungalow, but it was just as evident that he didn't want to advertise his presence in Ruislip. A note in MI5's files in November recorded that 'whenever he was seen to approach the neighbourhood of their house the watchers reported that he appeared to be taking pains to see that he was not being followed'. Unsurprisingly the Security Service concluded 'that Kroger is connected in some way with Lonsdale's espionage. Perhaps he is the communications officer?'[18]

MI5 opened yet another file, giving the Krogers the cryptonyms KILL JOY and THE PANGOLINS,[19] and began to investigate their history. Then, on 10 November, Peter Wright's team returned to the White House flat for a second burglary. This time it discovered 'a small Photostat approximately 2cms by 1.5cms which turned out to be a signal plan, giving the dates, times and wavelengths of wireless transmissions'.[20] When Lonsdale moved back into the White House, RAFTER was in business.

He continued to meet Houghton and Gee on the streets around Waterloo station; each time he took away a bundle of papers. Then, shortly before Christmas, the radio detection team picked up one of his short-wave transmissions, indicating that in early January he would take delivery of a package of microdots.

This was a new, and worrying, development: microdots – tiny pieces of paper no bigger than a typewritten punctuation mark but which hold photographs with huge amounts of information – required specialist cameras as well as powerful microscopes to enlarge their contents; MI5's burglars had found no trace of either in Lonsdale's flat. That, in turn, suggested he had an accomplice. Attention turned back to Peter Kroger.

Security Service investigations established that he was a genuine dealer in antiquarian books. His name featured regularly in the trade's directories and magazines, where he placed advertisements seeking 'Americana' with a particular interest in 'fetters, handcuffs, leg irons and instruments of torture'.[21] Soon, however, MI5 found evidence to suggest that the business, while real, was an elaborate cover, and that Peter and Helen Kroger were not merely Lonsdale's 'communications officers' but instead very dangerous spies in their own right.

According to their passports, both issued by the New Zealand government, Peter John Kroger had been born in Gisbourne, a small city on the country's North Island, on 10 July 1910; Helen Joyce Kroger was Canadian and had been born in Boyle, Alberta, on 17 January 1913. But their identity documents had a curious history.

Peter had been issued his first passport – number C323816 – in London on 20 December 1948. Six years later he used it to obtain a new version, with an updated serial number, from the New Zealand Legation in Paris; Helen received her passport on the same day, solely on the basis of her marriage. Those two new documents were the only 'proof' of their identity; both rested on Peter's original 1948 passport.

The problem, however, was that C323816 had – provably – been destroyed by the British Consul General in Shanghai in 1947, at least one year before it was supposed to have been issued in London. It was, therefore, a very clever forgery – and, since there was also no trace of his supposed birth in New Zealand, the names Peter and Helen Kroger were similarly bogus.[22]

By the beginning of the new year, MI5 was dug in for a long-haul investigation into the Portland Spy Ring. Without the real identities of

Lonsdale and the Krogers, it knew that uncovering the full extent of the network would take time and more precious resources. Then the CIA's urgent cable, warning that Sniper/LAVINIA was about to defect, forced its hand. On Thursday, 5 January 1961, the head of C Branch (Security), Martin Furnival Jones, called an emergency meeting in Leconfield House, the Service's Mayfair headquarters:

> I outlined LAVINIA's career in the PIS [Polish Intelligence Service] and concluded that the probability was that sooner or later the Russians would deduce that he had known about REVERBERATE and might consequently withdraw TREK [LAST ACT/Lonsdale] and the PANGOLINS [KILL JOY/Krogers].
>
> It was not certain when the fact that LAVINIA had defected would become apparent to the Russians but there was a possibility that they could learn as early as the evening of the 5th. If they did, there was a possibility that they would warn TREK.[23]

Telephone taps had established that Houghton and Gee planned to travel to London for a new rendezvous with Lonsdale in two days' time. MI5 hoped to catch them in the act of handing over more Admiralty files, and quickly drew up plans to follow and arrest them all. It also increased surveillance on the Krogers, and resolved to seize them as soon as the other three were safely in custody.

At 7.50 a.m. on Saturday, 7 January, surveillance units tailed Houghton's Renault Dauphine car from Weymouth to Salisbury railway station; he bought a pair of day-return tickets to London then, after a convivial pub lunch, he and Gee boarded the 12.32 train to Waterloo.

At the same time, A4's teams covering the White House apartment block and the bungalow in Ruislip reported Lonsdale and Helen Kroger leaving their homes; MI5 assumed (correctly) they were planning to meet but, for fear of inadvertently alerting them to the surveillance, made no attempt to follow them.

Four watchers picked up Houghton and Gee when they arrived at 3.15 p.m. The watchers followed them to East Street market, the café, and then as they strolled towards their meeting with Lonsdale. He was spotted in a nearby street at 4.25 p.m., tailed to the rendezvous and, as soon as he took the shopping basket from Gee, Special Branch officers rushed in and snapped handcuffs on all three.

At New Scotland Yard, MI5 examined the contents of the basket. It found a large bundle of documents, including blueprints for, and test results of, the latest underwater detection technology, ASDIC, and 200 Secret Pages from an Admiralty dossier – 'Particulars of War Vessels, British Commonwealth of Nations'.

At 6.45 p.m. the team at Ruislip banged on the Krogers' door; the couple were arrested immediately and driven across London to join Houghton, Gee and Lonsdale in the cells at Canon Row. Almost a year after Sniper's letter set the investigation in motion, the Portland Spy Ring had been broken.

Over the next two days specialist search teams combed through their respective homes. At the house Gee shared with her elderly mother and aunt, they found further ASDIC test documents, Admiralty charts and plans of Portland Naval Base.

Houghton's cottage yielded more secret papers as well as camera and film-developing equipment and a 'Swan Vesta match box with primitive double bottom containing a scrap of paper with . . . directions for using markings for R/Vs in London'; there was also £650 – equivalent to £10,000 today – hidden in an old paint tin.[24]

If Lonsdale's flat held nothing that MI5 didn't already know about – Wright's team had already comprehensively burgled it twice – number 45 Cranley Drive, Ruislip, proved to be a gold mine. Initially the specialist team from A2 branch failed to locate much more than a Ronson lighter identical to the one in Lonsdale's safety-deposit box; one-time pads and a radio-transmission schedule were stored inside its hollowed-out base. Then over the next three days more rigorous searching uncovered messages in Russian and codes to encrypt them. But the major discovery – hidden in a series of brick-lined compartments which had been dug underneath the kitchen floor – was a complete shortwave radio transmitter, 'a tape recorder/sender for automatic transmission', a Minox camera, and a full set of microdot equipment – the high-resolution lens and a state-of-the-art dot reader. There was also $6,000 – equivalent to $51,000 today – in $20 notes.[25]

None of this, however, brought MI5 any closer to discovering the true identities of Lonsdale or the Krogers. Under interrogation all three refused to talk, and so on 13 January they were charged with espionage under names that British intelligence knew to be false.

It was not until shortly before their trial began that the truth about Peter and Helen Kroger arrived at Leconfield House – and when it did, the news was distinctly embarrassing. Copies of the Krogers' fingerprints, taken at the police station, were examined by the FBI in Washington and quickly produced a match to a pair of notorious American spies who had been on the run for almost a decade: Morris and Lorna Cohen had been part of two major Soviet espionage rings – the first involving the transfer of US nuclear bomb test information to Moscow, the second as key players in a KGB network operated by Colonel Rudolf Abel in New York. After Abel's conviction for espionage in 1957, the Cohens had disappeared, using the bogus Canadian passport acquired for them by the KGB in Shanghai. Although the Bureau had sent a request to London, asking British police to search for the couple and even providing a copy of their fingerprints, nothing appeared to have been done.[26]

None of this information was provided to the court when, on 13 March, the five members of the Portland Spy Ring appeared in the dock at the Old Bailey. After a two-week trial, all were convicted of espionage, and the Lord Chief Justice, Hubert Parker, imposed severe sentences: twenty-five years for Lonsdale, twenty years each for the Krogers, and fifteen years for Houghton and Gee respectively.[27] Only then were the Krogers' true names – and their lengthy history as Soviet spies – disclosed.

But the revelation, and the intelligence failures it implied, made little impact: the judge went out of his way publicly to praise the 'excellent work done by the Naval Security officers and the Police [no reference to the Security Service was then permissible] . . . I think that all those connected with the investigation of the case are to be sincerely congratulated.'[28]

Away from the honeyed words, MI5 knew better. The Service had, in Peter Wright's words, been 'desperately embarrassed' by the case.[29] Prison interviews with Lonsdale – now finally unmasked as Konon Molody, a long-term KGB agent who had used the birth certificate of a dead child to create his alias[30] – indicated that Houghton had given him 350 documents on the Navy's anti-submarine equipment tests, which helped Moscow produce 'a new and more silent generation of Soviet submarines'.[31]

MI5 also realized that it should have caught Houghton very much sooner. 'Looking at it dispassionately now,' the Security Service recorded in a subsequent internal memo, 'I think it is clear that we ought to have carried out some investigation in 1956. If we had done so there is a fair chance that we would have unearthed Houghton's espionage . . . we might also have hit upon Miss Gee. If we had done so we should have stopped a leakage of information from the Admiralty some four years earlier. The consolation is that in the event we have hurt the R.I.S. [Russian Intelligence Service] more.'[32]

Behind this belated navel gazing was the knowledge that had it not been for Sniper's persistence, the entire network might never have been uncovered. This prompted a renewed examination of the information he had sent, while still an Agent in Place behind the Iron Curtain, about LAMBDA 1: the alleged Soviet spy inside MI6. But another fragmentary lead – a reference to 'a middle grade' officer in MI5 itself – caught Peter Wright's attention; it seemed to fit with alarming data from the RAFTER reports, suggesting that the KGB might have known about Operation TOW/ROPE all along. If so, it had deliberately allowed its spies to be caught, and *that* pointed to 'only one explanation': a mole at 'the very summit' of MI5 who had told Moscow about Sniper,[33] and whose identity was so important that the Portland spies had to be sacrificed to protect him. It was the first thread of a worm of worry which would, in time, burrow deeply inside British intelligence.

But for the moment, the hero of the hour – albeit still publicly unsung – was Sniper/LAVINIA, safely in protective custody in America. Michał Goleniewski – or whatever name he might now be using – had helped expose the biggest Soviet espionage ring in Britain for a decade. And, as the CIA was about to discover, he was just getting started.

13

Oldenburg

O N Tuesday, 7 March 1961, Franz Roman Oldenburg married Irmgard Margarete Henschel, in Arlington County, Virginia. The groom declared himself to be a thirty-eight-year-old bachelor, his bride a thirty-two-year-old spinster. Both listed their address as 1201 South Court House Road, an apartment block just across the Potomac River from Washington DC. The wedding was a civil ceremony and no relatives attended; the sole witnesses were two 'US government employees', Peter Skov and Howard Roman.[1]

The circumstances of the marriage were distinctly unusual. The Commonwealth of Virginia obliged prospective spouses to present state or federal documents to prove their identities: a driver's licence, passport or, in the absence of either of those two options, a certified copy of both birth certificates. Mr Oldenburg and Miss Henschel were unable to provide any of the required evidence – for the very good reason that neither person actually existed, much less possessed any official papers.

The application for a marriage licence – issued earlier the same day by the Arlington Circuit Court[2] – was, however, supported by the organization to which Messrs Roman and Skov belonged. The Central Intelligence Agency vouched for the couple's *bona fides*, and backed their sworn attestations that neither was already married. It was a bold decision: by 7 March the Agency had known them for just seven weeks.

Some two months before, at 12 noon on Thursday, 12 January 1961, Franz Oldenburg and Irmgard Henschel – otherwise known as Lieutenant Colonel Michał Goleniewski and Irmgard Kampf – had stepped onto American soil at the Dover Air Force Base in Delaware.[3] It had been a long and exhausting journey: the Military Air Transport flight from Wiesbaden had stopped first at a secure airport in Paris, then again to refuel at a US Air Force base in the Azores. Here, according to Howard Roman's account, Goleniewski/Oldenburg had alleviated the boredom by pumping coins into slot machines in the officers' mess.[4]

At Dover, they bypassed US immigration niceties since their arrival was sponsored by the CIA which, under 'Program PL-110', had the power to import up to 100 valuable assets per year from behind the Iron Curtain.

The Agency was under no obligation to report the numbers – much less the names – of those it chose to bring to America. Under its protective umbrella, 'Mr. Oldenburg' and 'Miss Henschel' were automatically deemed to have landed lawfully, and were swiftly driven to a 'safe house' outside McLean, a pleasant, verdant community in northern Virginia, ten miles from Washington, much favoured by intelligence officials and members of Congress wanting a home outside the capital. This was to be their accommodation for the immediate future; they would be held here in isolation, under armed guard, and closely interrogated.[5] Above all, the CIA was determined to keep their presence completely secret for what it knew could be an extended debriefing.

Establishing a defector's '*bona fides*' – CIA jargon for his exact identity, background and motivation – was usually expected to take 'one to four weeks'; in addition to daily interviews, Goleniewski was to be fingerprinted, medically examined, and required to fill out 'a questionnaire' detailing 'the salient facts of his life history and defection.'[6] Since 1950 the Agency's Interrogation Research Branch had also used polygraph tests to detect 'deception' in a defector's responses;[7] amongst a checklist of red-flag areas, it was particularly designed to uncover 'falsification of vital statistics (age, birthplace, employment, education, etc)'.[8]

Goleniewski was duly strapped into the polygrapher's chair and attached to the lie-detector apparatus; according to his own subsequent accounts, and those of former CIA officers, he passed the test with flying colours. But while the Agency trusted the technology, it placed most faith in the relentless questioning by Roman and his colleagues.

'The first critical phase of an interrogation,' noted a lengthy internal guide by one of its most experienced examiners in the summer of 1960, '[is] that undertaken to determine whether the defector is genuine, an enemy agent, or just a swindler. [It] demands much poise, knowledge, human understanding, dexterity and perseverance.' As lead interviewer, Howard Roman had already established – at least to his own satisfaction – that Goleniewski was sincere. But that alone would not equip him to extract all the information needed by the Agency: he would also need 'inordinate patience and determination.'[9]

The manual laid down three fundamental aims for the daily sessions inside the safe house: to establish the defector's *bona fides*, to obtain 'knowledge useful to intelligence', and to extract 'operational information' about Soviet bloc espionage. To achieve the best results, interrogators were instructed to take advantage of their subject's total reliance on his 'hosts' for shelter, food and, ultimately, money: 'The fact that a defector is dependent on the West's good will for his future well-being is a lever which the interrogator can use to control him; it does not take a defector long to realize that he enjoys favors in direct proportion to his cooperation.'[10] The key to exploiting this vulnerability was the twin approach of 'establishing a personal rapport with the subject' while simultaneously maintaining 'the psychological superiority essential to control'.

The manual's author, Stanley B. Farndon, was 'a senior CIA interrogations supervisor'. It was evident, however, that nowhere in that experience had he come across a defector quite like Goleniewski. In McLean, as in Wiesbaden, Howard Roman found that his subject was utterly unwilling to accept the role of supplicant: he, not the CIA questioner, assumed 'psychological superiority'. While the interviews 'were always strictly business-like, utterly sober and taut run', according to

Roman's subsequent recollection, Goleniewski sat 'behind his desk as if he were in charge of the proceedings'.[11]

Roman also tried to follow Farndon's advice that 'a harmonious atmosphere' would be beneficial, and organized occasional night-time parties for Goleniewski, Kampf 'and one or two of his case officers, at which we drank without much stint to the accompaniment of loud music'. Despite these attempts to recreate some simulacrum of normal life, 'the strain of daily interrogation and the fears for his security and the uncertainty of the future showed in G. in the shape of occasional erratic behavior and somewhat paranoidal [sic] complaints'.[12] It was – or should have been – a warning of what lay in store.

But however imperious and difficult the man might be, for the CIA's analysts in Washington, as well as for the FBI's counterintelligence division, his revelations were invaluable.

Poland, inevitably, was the initial focus of the debriefings. The Agency's own internal assessment credited Goleniewski with handing over the 'names and considerable information on 650 ranking and middle level officers of the PIS [Polish Intelligence Service]. He was able to provide CIA with a complete list of agents and co-opted workers in the field . . .'[13] Additionally, one of the documents Goleniewski had brought with him was a complete internal review by the UB of the infamous WiN deception. It described, in excruciating detail, how easily the UB and the KGB had been able to dupe US and British intelligence into funding and arming a non-existent anti-communist underground movement.

Nor was this of merely historic interest. Goleniewski also explained that the KGB was currently using the WiN deception – an operation it had christened CEZARY – as a template for its continuing disinformation programme. He was 'the first CIA source to report [this programme] in detail', according to analyst Richards Heuer, and he specifically warned that Moscow would, at some stage, send bogus defectors 'to mislead Western Security Services'.[14] That, too, was a lesson the Agency would learn the hard way.

But it was Goleniewski's dual role, spying simultaneously for

Warsaw and Moscow, which, according to the Agency's own internal assessment, yielded the most important intelligence:

> His status as a KGB liaison officer and a KGB penetration of the Polish services made it possible for him to report on KGB operations and personnel ... Goleniewski gave an extensive amount of information on the KGB. He reported on KGB organization and at length on those KGB officers with whom he had been acquainted ... He was extensively debriefed on KGB illegal operations and the KGB Illegal Directorate. The basis for his knowledge was a campaign the KGB undertook to force the Poles to establish illegal *rezidenturas* in North America, where, the KGB stated, the number of Polish immigrants made it relatively simple to build up illegal networks.[15]

Most crucially, he named names. In addition to the roster of UB spies, Goleniewski provided the identities of 110 KGB and GRU officers, as well as thirty of their agents. Nor was this information confined to the United States. When, on 16 January, the Agency allowed a team from British intelligence to interview its star defector, he offered up new details of LAMBDA 1 – the spy operating inside MI6, whom the KGB had code-named DIOMID and who had provided Moscow with lists of SIS assets in Poland.

Investigations in London had foundered on the spurious belief that the documents had been taken during a botched burglary at an MI6 office in Brussels; Goleniewski insisted that the papers had not been stolen, but instead were handed over to the Soviets by a hitherto unknown agent in Berlin. It was a lead which would, eventually, be the crucial factor in uncovering the mole.[16]

The CIA's willingness to share Goleniewski with MI5 – albeit briefly and under controlled conditions in its safe house – indicated its rising level of confidence in his *bona fides*. Since his career in Poland had also encompassed Soviet bloc military secrets, the Agency also extended the courtesy to US Army intelligence. The outcome was spectacular, for both good and ill.

The CIA's internal assessment recorded that Goleniewski provided unique insight into the strength and disposition of Warsaw Pact armed forces, the Polish Order of Battle, technical data on Soviet fighter aircraft, and the location of Surface to Air Missiles which the USSR had deployed throughout its satellite states. But the most vital information he revealed concerned Moscow's deployment of its deadliest arsenal:

> Nuclear weapons: Soviet units of tactical destruction and assault; Soviet nuclear submarines and Soviet deception methods to conceal true submarine strength; bunker for atomic ammunition . . .[17]

No previous defector had delivered anything approaching this level of insight into Moscow's ability to wage war, or the methods by which it planned to do so. He also made plain that this was just the first tranche of military information he intended to disclose. Unfortunately, a combination of US Army hubris and Goleniewski's habitual arrogance stopped the data flow in its tracks:

> The representatives from the Army interviewed Goleniewski alone without a CIA representative present. Goleniewski was extremely antagonistic towards one of the Army debriefers and, if his comments to his CIA debriefer are indicative of his attitude, he was not [thereafter] very cooperative.[18]

For the time being, however, his relationship with Howard Roman progressed well. Although he was curiously evasive about some aspects of his personal history – 'his biography was never completed', the Agency's internal report noted ruefully – he was voluble about KGB operations in Western Europe.

Throughout January and February, he provided more detail about 'Hacke', the alleged false-flag neo-Nazi underground, including the name of his source, which the CIA was able to track back and confirm; and he identified several other Soviet bloc espionage penetrations, particularly inside West Germany's BND.

If James Angleton, the Agency's head of counterintelligence, was as sceptical as ever, the senior officers in the Soviet Bloc Division were delighted with the yield from the debriefings. The question of his identity, however, remained a pressing issue. On 24 February, Roman and Skov drove Goleniewski and Irmgard Kampf to the offices of the US Immigration and Naturalization Service.

According to her account, I&NS staff fingerprinted both of them and promised to issue Alien Registration Cards; these were to be in the 'temporary cover names' of Franz Oldenburg and Irmgard Henschel, and were the first step in regularizing the couple's existence inside the United States. Without them they would not – officially at least – be able to realize their wedding plans, to rent their own home or even buy a car.[19]

A few days passed with no sign of the cards. But the Agency had now decided that it was no longer necessary to confine Goleniewski in the McLean safe house; it helped him find the apartment in Arlington, smoothed over any problems the landlord might have about the couple's lack of documentation, and promised to cover the rent.

It also granted him a monthly stipend of $750,[20] to be paid in cash, and when, on 1 March, they moved in to 1201 South Court House Road, they were able to furnish it courtesy of a $5,000 gift[21] from CIA funds: this was described as a down payment on a substantial future financial aid and salary package, and was shortly supplemented by an ex-gratia payment of $24,000[22] to cover the thirty-three months Goleniewski had worked as an undercover Agent in Place.[23] Six days later, the Agency sponsored the wedding between 'Franz Oldenburg' and 'Irmgard Henschel'.

The marriage and new home did not, however, signal the end of the debriefing sessions, nor of the need for security. Week by week, Oldenburg/Goleniewski divulged ever more detail about Soviet bloc espionage, and gave leads to the identities of agents working undercover in the United States and Europe. The sheer volume of information highlighted the need for secrecy.

The CIA knew that both the UB and the KGB would be working feverishly to discover where Goleniewski had gone; while both services would have realized very quickly that he had defected, neither would – or so Washington hoped – know which country had spirited him away. The longer they remained in the dark, the greater the chance of rolling up the spy networks he exposed: on the strength of his information, the FBI had already arrested two Polish agents operating in the United States, and a third was seized in Canada,[24] but there were plainly many more to locate.

Not for the first – or the last – time, the Agency's incompetence handed Moscow and Warsaw the information they sought. In the middle of March, its Paris station made a crude attempt to persuade the Polish military attaché to defect, thrusting a badly typed letter through the letterbox of his apartment in the sixteenth *arrondissement*; this promised him $50,000 to 'start a new and free life in America', and explicitly stated that 'Goleniewski told us your long history as an agent'. The attaché promptly reported the approach to his masters in Warsaw. Then, at the end of the month, 'two US security service employees' approached a UB officer operating in West Berlin, and – equally unsuccessfully – pressured him to become a double agent; once again, Goleniewski's name was dangled as bait.[25]

Despite these amateurish security breaches, the CIA evidently believed there to be little immediate threat to Goleniewski or his wife. At the beginning of April 1961 it put Irmgard on a military transport plane to Frankfurt am Main, where she was reunited with her mother, father, sister and brother; the Agency provided accommodation for the entire family for six days, then flew her back alone to Washington DC.[26] It also began preparing a full employment and salary package for Goleniewski – one which reflected his continuing importance to US intelligence and its confidence in everything he had disclosed to date.

Had it been able to witness proceedings in the Warsaw District Military Court that same month, the Agency might have been less confident about the honesty of its new star intelligence source – and, simultaneously, rather more concerned for his safety.

14

'Betrayal of the Homeland'

O N TUESDAY, 18 April 1961 the case of *Polish People's Republic v. Michał Goleniewski* opened in the Warsaw District Military Court. The defendant was accused of two offences: stealing substantial quantities of state funds, most of it in hard foreign currency, and the more serious charge of 'betrayal of the Homeland' – treason – under Article 83 of the Army's Penal Code. If convicted, the latter carried an inexorable sentence: death.

Despite the gravity of the indictments, the trial was scheduled to last just one day. Only two witnesses were summoned to give evidence; they, like the prosecutor and the three judges, were both senior officers in the Army or the intelligence service.

Yet this was no Soviet-style show trial. The defendant was not present in the dock, to be photographed and filmed making a damning confession of his crimes; even had he not, by April that year, been beyond the immediate reach of Poland's government or military, there was never any likelihood that he would have been publicly arraigned. The proceedings were also terse and to the point – the entire hearing was concluded well before the day's end – and took place entirely behind closed doors. No report was published in Poland's state-controlled media, and there is no evidence that the CIA, or any other Western intelligence service, was even aware it had taken place.

There was a reason for this deliberate and strict secrecy: the damage Goleniewski had caused to the Urząd Bezpieczeństwa's intelligence operations, as well as to those of Soviet Bloc espionage agencies with which it worked, was devastating. Publicizing his defection, and the secrets he betrayed, would only have deepened the wounds and highlighted the dramatically enfeebled position of the Soviet bloc spy networks to their counterparts in the West.

Hidden from public scrutiny at home, and out of the sight of its international enemies, the Polish Intelligence Service was remarkably frank. The evidence it presented to the Warsaw Court set out the details of Goleniewski's career as a spy, the chronology of his defection, and the UB's desperate efforts to limit the damage it caused. But the trial also revealed his full personal history – one that was significantly at odds with the selectively edited biography he had given to the CIA.

~

Michał Goleniewski was born on 16 August 1922 in Nieśwież,[1] a city in the north-east corner of Poland, close to its border with the Soviet Union. His father, also named Michał, was an accountant; his mother, Janina Turynska, a housewife. During the interwar years, the family moved to Wolsztyn, 800 kilometres to the west and close to the border with Germany; Michał senior worked for a brewery, a job which could not have helped his incipient alcoholism, while his wife ran the home and brought up their son.

Michał attended the local high school, before secondary education at the *gimnazjum*, graduating just before the outbreak of war in 1939. By his own account, given to the US Immigration and Naturalization Service, he spent the years in which Poland was occupied by Hitler's troops studying law at the University of Poznan[2] – although subsequently he also claimed to have been arrested and imprisoned by the Nazi authorities on suspicion of belonging to an illegal organization. The truth, as presented to the Warsaw District Military Court, was somewhat less respectable than either of these alternative histories: 'In the years 1940–1944 he worked as an accountant in agricultural properties at Tloka and

Wroniawa in the Poznań Province,' the prosecutor reported, adding that at all times this employment 'was under German administration.'[3] He had, in short, been a collaborator.

When the war ended Goleniewski applied for membership of the Polish Workers' Party and started work – initially as a sentry, then as a clerk – at the new Communist government's Ministry of Public Security, the MBP, which, under the umbrella of the UB, oversaw the state's domestic and foreign intelligence services.[4]

Over the next twelve years he would rise steadily through the ranks of the MBP/UB. In 1946 he was awarded one of Poland's highest honours – the Cross of Merit – later to be supplemented by the Knight's Cross of the Order of *Polonia Restituta*,[5] cementing his status as a reliable *apparatchik* in the new Communist state's labyrinthine bureaucracy.[6]

He also evidently had powerful patrons within the intelligence service. In 1948 he was promoted to chief of the Counter-Intelligence Division for the district of Poznan, a post he would hold until 1950. Throughout those two years, fellow officers made a succession of formal requests that Goleniewski should be investigated for 'cooperating with the Nazi occupier and acting to the detriment of Polish citizens'. Each attempt was quickly snuffed out: 'cancelled in Warsaw', according to notes on an internal Polish security service report.[7]

By 1955 he was a division head within the MBP's Department 1, which controlled civilian counterintelligence;[8] at least part of his duties involved monitoring members of the fragmented anti-communist resistance – a task which he pursued under the cover identity of 'Dr Roman Tarnowski', an official of the General Prosecutor's Office, and one which earned him a reputation as a relentless and unforgiving interrogator of dissidents.[9]

On 1 February 1955 he was appointed deputy head of the scientific and intelligence branch of Department 1. It would be his final role and, like the positions which preceded it, brought Goleniewski into close contact with all of Poland's military and civilian espionage services.[10] According to the indictment against him:

As the Head of the Department VI Dep. 1 of the Ministry of the Interior, the suspect had access to materials constituting a state secret of special significance. In particular, he was thoroughly oriented in the organization of the work of the intelligence service of the Interior Ministry on the technical and scientific section, and knew the network of secret collaborators of Department VI ... conducted by the Department as well as the structure, tasks, forms and methods of work of Department 1 and cooperating units.[11]

But Goleniewski's responsibilities extended far beyond Poland's borders. During the 1950s he became the KGB's 'point man' in Warsaw, combining an official role as the UB's liaison to the Soviet intelligence service chiefs with a covert remit to brief Moscow on the activities of his colleagues. Both jobs required him to travel throughout the Soviet bloc states and, frequently, into the West.

Despite the extra demands caused by this dual role, the UB found Goleniewski to be a competent and efficient worker on behalf of the Polish secret state. An internal performance review, written by his immediate boss, Colonel Witold Sienkiewicz, on 25 August 1960, reported that:

> The work of the department headed by Comrade Goleniewski is very diverse and besides operational qualifications requires knowledge of technical and economic problems. Despite this specific work, Comrade Goleniewski, having organizational skills and self-denial at work, fulfils it. The contribution of Comrade Goleniewski's work to the department is large ... He [has] gained experience in working with agents and works with them both legally and illegally with good results.[12]

Colonel Sienkiewicz did, however, note that Goleniewski's arrogance and unconcealed ambition had made him unpopular with his fellow spies:

In relations within the office and with colleagues he is conceited. He considers himself the wisest and best on all the issues entrusted to him. He makes judgements about people too hastily, often on the spur of the moment, though he may revise them in the course of his work. He likes to show off his friendships and relate to highly placed personalities.[13]

More tellingly, Sienkiewicz also noted his subordinate's 'difficult and complicated' personal life. It was, Sienkiewicz recorded, a marital problem that adversely affected Goleniewski's work; it would also be one of the motivations for his defection in January 1961.

Anna Diachenko was just one year older than Michał Goleniewski, but her adult life had been rather more difficult than his seemingly effortless rise. She was born in Russia in June 1921, but had come to Poland in the 1930s and been granted citizenship. During the first years of Nazi occupation she was transported to Germany for forced labour, before escaping with a lover she had met in the work camps; from 1943 onwards they survived by marrying under a false identity, then hiding from German troops in, or near, Wolsztyn. In October 1944, Anna gave birth to their daughter, Halina; but at some point before or just after the end of the war – the UB's extensive files do not record an exact date – her husband died, leaving her to bring up the child alone.

That changed in 1945 when she met Goleniewski; the couple were married in March 1946 and Halina was formally registered as his adopted daughter. As his career progressed, the family also grew; Danuta, another daughter, was born in April, and a son, Jerzy, followed in November 1950. Both children were fathered by Goleniewski.

The couple's relationship was, however, deeply troubled. Anna suffered from mental health problems – probably the result of her wartime experiences, but exacerbated by Goleniewski's frequent infidelity. She periodically walked out of their government-provided apartment on Warsaw's Solariego Street, and on at least two occasions she was hospitalized for 'delusional schizophrenia'.[14]

By 1954 the marriage was – according to Goleniewski's own written account for his Polish intelligence employers – 'in complete disintegration'. Anna frequently accused him of 'poisoning' or 'destroying' her, and had come to view her husband as 'Enemy Number One'. When Goleniewski's father died, in an ill-documented industrial accident in 1952, he brought his mother Janina to live with them in the apartment; the move caused yet more turmoil – Anna vehemently objected and eventually 'banished' her mother-in-law from the family home.[15]

By the middle of 1958, Goleniewski decided he could no longer cope with his wife. He asked the UB for permission to apply for a divorce – a bureaucratic sanction necessitated by his senior role in the intelligence service – citing Anna's illness and unreasonable behaviour as justification. But that was only half of the truth: Michał Goleniewski had another, more pressing, reason to rid himself of his unstable spouse – he had embarked on a new and passionate affair.

Irmgard Kampf was twenty-eight years old when she first encountered Goleniewski. She was a secretary in the Thirteenth District Secondary School in Mitte, East Berlin, earning a modest 300 ostmarks a month – a fact which explained why she still lived with her elderly parents in their small apartment at 54 Wollinerstrasse. According to his own account, Goleniewski bumped into her 'accidentally' on one of his missions to East Germany in 1958.[16] Although Poland and the German Democratic Republic were notionally allies within the wider Soviet bloc of nations, their intelligence services maintained a cautious rivalry. When Goleniewski and Kampf first met, across the spartan tables of the Melodie restaurant on Friedrichstrasse,[17] he was initially suspicious, fearing that she might be an agent of the GDR's ubiquitous secret police and that the apparently chance encounter might be 'a provocation' by the Stasi.[18]

He introduced himself as Jan Roman, a Polish journalist 'of Jewish origin',[19] claimed to have been a resistance fighter during the war, and said that his entire family, apart from his mother, had been murdered by the Nazis.[20] If the story was fundamentally untrue, according to his own, internal UB account of the relationship, it evidently found favour with the somewhat impressionable Irmgard:

> She spoke about the tragedy of the Jewish people during the Nazi era and expressed herself in a decidedly anti-fascist way . . . She told me that she liked Jews very much; when her mother worked as a seamstress in a tailor's workshop before the war . . . she [Irmgard] often stayed with a Jewish resident near her, who gave her sweets and treated her like her own child.
>
> I did not hide the fact that I was a communist or the fact that I hate the FRG [West Germany] and fascists of all types. If IK had any worries, it was only due to the fact that she is German and that as a result she might lose me . . .[21]

Soon the friendship blossomed into a clandestine love affair. Goleniewski arranged to see Irmgard whenever he travelled to East Berlin and she introduced him to her parents, Franz, seventy-five, and Luize, sixty-nine. Over time she invited her widowed sister, Margette Mische, and her brother Franz to cross the border from their homes in West Germany and meet her lover over meals at the apartment on Wollinerstrasse.

Irmgard Kampf was falling in love with the older, handsome, powerfully built Polish 'journalist'. But the lies he had told her initially were becoming unsustainable – not least because the documents he carried on missions to the GDR identified him as Roman Tarnowski, not Jan Roman. Goleniewski further embroidered his initial cover legend, telling the Kampf family that after the war he had served in the Polish Army for four years before becoming a journalist, first in China and then in a news agency working with Poland's foreign service.

He said that his work required frequent travel to conferences across the Soviet bloc of countries and involved writing 'propaganda about fascists in the German Federal Republic'. When he came to the GDR, he said he was provided with an office in the Polish Embassy in East Berlin – an entirely bogus detail which could have caused trouble had Irmgard ever tried to contact him there.

Happily, he recorded, 'for the entire period of our acquaintance she never once tried to call me at the Embassy or to ask for my phone number there'. Goleniewski attributed this good fortune to Irmgard's 'incredible discretion' – though naivety and the hard-learned East German survival technique of never asking risky questions probably played a significant part.[22]

Evidently unaware that their affair had been discovered by the Stasi, the couple exchanged a remarkably frank succession of letters and telegrams. These, as the UB files sniffily noted, 'devoted a lot of space to erotic matters', but they also revealed Kampf's insecurity, and Goleniewski's touching attempts to comfort her.

'I have a constant concern and fear that something could happen to you,' Kampf wrote in an early letter to her lover. 'That would be quite bad for me. But I believe that everything will be good and my faith wants to support you in your hard work.' Some months later, she tried to express the frustration and loneliness she felt in the periods when that work prevented Goleniewski coming to see her in Berlin. 'It's hard to be reasonable without knowing you will be back again with me . . . I am getting weak now . . . [but] you know that at the right moment I can never say "no" to you . . .'[23]

For his part Goleniewski tried to reassure her and, as the relationship deepened, he asked Kampf to marry him:

> I firmly believe that everything will be fine. Try, please, once again
> [to] support my proposal. I would like to be with you, give you new
> courage and arrange everything that is only a hindrance. Travelling
> for my work is very complicated and time-consuming, but give me
> a quick reply and I will do whatever you think will be good.[24]

However, he failed to disclose that he was already married, and had three children – a lie he justified to himself on the grounds that he 'did not want to cause her [Irmgard] any worry'.[25] Blissfully unaware, Kampf accepted his proposal and began learning Polish in anticipation of a new life in Warsaw.

That prospect of a rosy future was further burnished by the luxury goods and substantial sums of money which Goleniewski sent to Irmgard and her parents between 1958 and 1960. According to investigations by the UB's finance section, supported by matching entries in the Stasi's files, he drew thousands of West German deutschmarks, US dollars and British pounds from Polish intelligence funds and gave at least half to Irmgard; over two years she stashed 4,000 DM in a bank savings account, plus a further 6,700 DM with the post office.

Since the total was almost three times her gross annual salary, it was only a matter of time before the deposits attracted attention. Similarly her newly acquired stylish outfits and consumer items – she took to wearing 'precious jewellery from Switzerland, an expensive fur coat from Paris and fashionable clothes from England', and the family apartment was suddenly blessed with a Western-made television – were guaranteed to catch the eye of the Stasi.[26]

By October 1960 it had seen and heard enough. Erich Mielke, head of the Ministry for State Security, sent a detailed report to his opposite number in the Polish government, setting out the details of Goleniewski's 'unauthorized contacts' with Irmgard Kampf, a GDR citizen. Rattled, the UB ordered Goleniewski to write an exhaustive account of – and explanation for – his dangerous secret life, and warned him that he would have to end his affair in Berlin.

On 11 November, Goleniewski delivered his response to his immediate boss, Colonel Sienkiewicz. Over nine closely typed pages he attempted to justify himself, complaining about the 'harassment' he had received from his wife and asking once again for permission to divorce Anna and thereafter to marry Irmgard. Above all he stressed that he genuinely felt affection for Kampf, that she had fallen in love with him, and that they had been sexually intimate for quite some time. If the UB insisted on rejecting his pleas, and forced him to break off the relationship, he requested approval to do so in person:

The negative attitude of the Ministry management to my personal plans [has created] an unhealthy climate about a completely human matter, and . . . I am in a very difficult personal situation: how to give up my plans and break my acquaintance with IK. I can do this only in a humane way by personal contact . . . and without causing a 'shocking' situation.

I must inform you that, from telephone conversations with IK, as a result of phenomena and facts incomprehensible to her over the last 2–3 months, she finds herself in a state that equals complete mental imbalance. I don't think anyone is interested in condemning this woman, whose whole fault is confined to the fact that she has human feelings for me, to irreversible or serious illness . . .

That is why I am asking – if it must be so – to help me solve this matter in a human way. I have 14 days of unused vacation for 1960, and I am asking for permission to use it in the GDR on 7 days for the sole purpose of solving my personal matter in accordance with the decision of the Management.[27]

Goleniewski's claims to be in love with Irmgard might have carried more weight had the UB not already discovered that he was simultaneously carrying on an affair with a woman in Poland, and that he had also promised to marry her. Deeply unimpressed, just before Christmas 1960 the UB summoned its amorous spy to a formal meeting, ordered him to break off all contact with Irmgard, and for good measure told him he was to be moved out of his current senior post.[28]

The best Sienkiewicz could do to soften the blow was to grant Goleniewski's request for a final trip to East Berlin at the end of the month – and then only on condition that he combined tying up loose ends with his agents in Germany with giving Irmgard the bad news in person. He told Goleniewski to go, but to make sure he was back in Warsaw on 6 January 1961.[29]

Faced with the likely collapse of his career and the imminent loss of the financial and travel privileges that went with it, Goleniewski realized that time had almost run out. With no other viable route out of his troubles, he made urgent plans to defect. Using the Minox miniature camera, he photographed the remaining documents in his office safe, stashed some of them in the Warsaw park dead drop, and put the remainder in three envelopes to be carried separately by courier to await him in Berlin.

One of the envelopes was sealed – a security measure Goleniewski explained on the grounds that it contained sensitive 'ciphers [which] must not fall into anyone else's hands'.[30] He then drew 11,300 deutschmarks from office funds and sent a telegram to Irmgard, advising her that he would arrive in East Berlin around New Year, and instructing her to book annual holiday from her school between 3 and 8 January.[31]

The rest of the UB's evidence to the court rehearsed the story of his meetings with his controller in East Berlin, his demands for more money, and his complaints about being under surveillance; then it laid out the circumstances of his presumed defection on 4 January and the events which followed.

Much as Goleniewski had predicted to the CIA's Howard Roman, UB headquarters discovered his absence on 6 January. When he failed to make the planned rendezvous with one of his East German agents, and when he could not be found at the Berlin apartment he had rented, alarm bells began ringing inside the corridors of Polish intelligence. Colonel Henryk Sokolac, Deputy Chief of Department 1, was dispatched to track down the missing agent. He discovered that the watchers' last sighting of Goleniewski had been hurrying from Wollinerstrasse with Irmgard Kampf towards the border with West Berlin and came to an unavoidable conclusion: Goleniewski had defected, and must have taken with him the UB 'ciphers'[32] – the cover identities and matching real names of agents operating in the West.[33]

Back in Warsaw, Sienkiewicz ordered an urgent investigation to determine exactly what top-secret material Goleniewski would already have betrayed. UB technical staff broke into the locked safe in Goleniewski's office; they discovered that he had clandestinely amassed a vast range of documents detailing some of the intelligence service's most sensitive information.

This included the 'secret cooperation of the intelligence service of the Ministry of the Interior' with Polish government ministries – both military and civilian. The files also identified the UB's 'network of secret collaborators . . . operating in Western countries'. Worse, Goleniewski's broad responsibilities had given him access to data on Poland's pursuit of nuclear energy, as well as 'secret information about the Polish Army'. As Sienkiewicz recorded, in a sombre initial report to the state prosecutor, the loss of these secrets was the most devastating betrayal ever to hit Polish intelligence:

> Disclosure of the above information to the other side paralyses our activity and will result in the arrest of individual secret collaborators – which, according to our understanding, has already taken place . . . Transfer to the enemy will seriously hinder the fight of security organs against espionage and other hostile activities organized or inspired by foreign centres.[34]

On 13 January the UB flashed urgent cables to its heads of station in London, Paris, Rome, Berlin, Vienna, Washington, Ottawa, New York, Stockholm, Copenhagen, The Hague, Tel Aviv, Mexico, Rio de Janeiro and Buenos Aires, advising them that Goleniewski was missing – presumed defected – and instructing them to warn their agents 'about the need to take precautions in personal and workplace behaviour, in the city and at home . . . Ensure employees do not panic. They should not comment on this matter because it is necessary to avoid leaks.'[35] The UB knew, however, that this amounted to little more than shutting the stable door after its thoroughbred had bolted.

Sienkiewicz and Sokolac were summoned to testify at Goleniewski's trial in absentia on 18 April 1961. Behind the closed doors of the Warsaw District Military Court both men gave sobering evidence, and Sienkiewicz, in particular, left the three military judges in no doubt about the devastation Goleniewski had caused:

> There have been several arrests in the territory of the German Federal Republic and our analysis shows that this was due to the information given by Goleniewski. We also recently had two 'accidents' in the United States; these involved searches and detentions. In Canada, there has currently been one arrest, and we had to withdraw one of our employees from France. All the people who were arrested were on Goleniewski's list.
>
> But . . . our losses may be even greater. At the moment, we are assuming that Goleniewski handed over the material he took with him. But what we know for certain is only the smallest part of what was actually given to the enemy. We now have to start anew and examine everything [to which he had access] for the last 5 years.[36]

At the end of the hearing, the court issued its ruling: Goleniewski, while employed as a senior officer in Poland's intelligence service, had deliberately collected 'a list of secret collaborators' of the UB and after 'escaping into the territory of the Federal Republic of Germany, handed over a secret inventory of Polish agents to the Imperialist Intelligence service' – presumed to be the CIA:

> The Court took into consideration the great damage, conscious and consistent, done to the defence interests of the country, and the accused's willingness to profit from it. This is the most serious crime that a soldier can commit – betrayal of the Homeland – and we do not find any mitigating circumstances.[37]

The judges duly stripped Goleniewski of his medals and of his 'public and civil rights', ordered the forfeiture of all his property, and imposed a two-year jail sentence for stealing money from UB coffers. It then sentenced him to death for his treachery.[38] One month later a superior military court affirmed both the verdict and punishment, and ordered the sentences to be instituted from 14 June 1961.[39]

If the jail term and financial seizures were purely notional – the judges, like the UB, accepted that Goleniewski was never likely to return to Warsaw – the capital sentence was rather less theoretical. Polish intelligence might be a junior partner in the Soviet bloc spy hierarchy, but the Military Court's verdict was certain to be forwarded to Moscow – and Goleniewski's KGB spymasters had a proven history of abducting and killing turncoats.

Petr Deriabin, the KGB officer who fled to the West in 1954, had given graphic testimony to the US Congress House Un-American Activities Committee that 'the foreign section of the Soviet civilian intelligence service is responsible . . . for carrying out occasional assassinations, kidnapping . . . and similar activities', and had freely admitted having taken part in at least one ultimately fatal kidnapping prior to his defection.[40] Nor was he alone.

In one of his 'Sniper' letters, sent while still an undercover Agent in Place, Goleniewski had provided details about Moscow's involvement in the murder of Stepan Bandera, the head of a militant anti-communist Ukrainian independence organization, in a Munich restaurant in October 1959. According to the account 'Sniper' smuggled to the CIA in early 1960: 'Bandera was liquidated by the KGB . . . a drop of poison was squirted into Bandera's coffee cup . . . the poison was not cyanide but a special poison prepared by the KGB for "special purposes" and . . . Bandera was dead the next day.'[41]

But the problem for Polish intelligence chiefs and their ultimate masters in Moscow was that neither knew where Goleniewski had gone. They knew from the bungled approaches to the Polish military attaché and the UB agent in March that the CIA had almost certainly spirited him away; that, in turn, suggested he was now tucked up in a safe house somewhere in America. But until they could trace his exact location, neither had any way to enforce the court's capital sentence.

The UB decided on a dual approach. It opened a case file – code name TELETECHNIK – and assigned officers to two separate investigative strands.

The first and most urgent was to discover where Goleniewski was living. Agents throughout America were tasked with tapping every possible contact within the US government for leads; simultaneously, officers in Warsaw took the first steps in what would turn into a long and grubby undercover operation to target the defector's Achilles heel.

Throughout his troubles with his wife Anna, Goleniewski had relied on and supported his widowed mother; the UB reasoned that while he was unlikely ever to contact his estranged wife or children again, he would, at some stage, telephone or write to Janina. Discreet enquiries revealed that she was sixty-two, lived alone in a small apartment in the city centre, and that she was helpfully vulnerable: she was prone to heavy drinking and, in the UB's opinion, had a surprisingly busy sex life. Polish intelligence began searching for suitable candidates to exploit both perceived weaknesses, and through them to trick her into revealing her son's location; once she did, it reasoned, the court's death sentence could be fulfilled.

The second, parallel strategy was aimed at something less immediately lethal. The UB began planning a careful and subtle programme to discredit the defector in the minds of those who had given him refuge. The weapon it adopted for this was far more powerful than the poison in a KGB syringe: it was the truth.

By abandoning his wife and children in Warsaw – and especially by telling Irmgard he was legally free to marry her – Goleniewski would be living under a self-suspended Damoclean sword. As soon as he surfaced in the United States, the UB would ensure it fell – and very publicly; he would be shown up as a shameless liar and the CIA as credulous dupes.

Neither US intelligence nor its new star informant was aware of the fate that Warsaw planned for them all. That spring of 1961, as Goleniewski and Irmgard celebrated their bigamous wedding and settled into the CIA-funded apartment in Arlington, Operation TELETECHNIK slowly ground on. It would, ultimately, last almost a decade and would eventually play a significant part in destroying Goleniewski's credibility.[42] Meanwhile counter-espionage services throughout Europe and the Middle East began arresting the major Soviet bloc spies he had exposed.

15

LAMBDA 1

G EORGE BLAKE HAD what the British liked to call 'a good war': more precisely – at least by that idiosyncratic standard – he'd had two of them.

He had served bravely in the Dutch resistance, risking his life as a youthful courier during the fight against the Nazi occupation of Holland. Then, after a spell as a sub-lieutenant in the Royal Navy, he had joined Britain's Secret Intelligence Service. In 1948 he was sent east to spy, under diplomatic cover, on North Korea; when that war broke out he was quickly captured and held for more than two years in a remote communist prison camp on the border with China.

When Blake finally got back to Britain in 1953, he was greeted as a returning hero; his years in captivity sealed his reputation as a courageous and extremely promising intelligence officer. MI6 welcomed him back and two years later dispatched him to Berlin, the front line of the deepening conflict between the West and the Soviet bloc.

It was his role in this new Cold War which gave the lie to his reputation for loyalty. For nine years George Blake, war hero, former prisoner of war and trusted British intelligence officer, was a Soviet deep-penetration agent, betraying to the KGB many of America's and Britain's most vital secrets and enabling the capture of hundreds of Western operatives.

In the files of the KGB he was recorded by his cryptonym, DIOMID, but in the reports Sniper had smuggled out from behind the Iron

Curtain he was identified as LAMBDA 1. Fittingly, since his leads had started the mole hunt, it would be Goleniewski's information which finally brought Blake down.

~

It is a measure of the damage George Blake caused, and the profound embarrassment to British intelligence which ensued, that much of the story of his journey from teenage anti-Nazi volunteer to unrepentant KGB spy remains officially secret. Six decades on, MI5's files – as well as those of the Home Office – are still withheld from the National Archives, and the authorized history of MI6 from its inception to 1949 devotes just eight lines in its 800-plus pages to Blake's employment.[1]

The CIA, however, has released at least some of its documentation. This, together with the sanctioned memoirs of its former officers, Blake's own published accounts and that of his KGB handler, as well as Goleniewski's voluminous writings, have filled out the picture; in sum, they reveal just how close Western intelligence services came to letting Agent DIOMID slip through their collective fingers.

He was born George Behar – the anglicized surname came later, by deed poll – in Rotterdam in November 1922. His mother, Catherine, was Dutch, middle class and resolutely Protestant; his father, Albert, was a Sephardic Jew who had served, with distinction, in the British Army during World War I and had been given British citizenship. He died when his son was twelve years old, setting in train the events which, according to Blake's own account, would eventually lead him down the tortuous road to Moscow.

George's widowed mother sent him at the age of thirteen to live with his paternal aunt and her husband in Cairo. The couple had two sons of their own, more than a decade older than Blake; although their family was wealthy, the young men were committed socialists: 'Both of them had very decided left wing views . . . especially the younger of my two cousins who had a great influence on me. He was, by that time, a Communist and he talked a lot with me.'[2]

That cousin, Henri Curiel, was no ordinary communist; repeatedly arrested and imprisoned, he went on to form the Egyptian Movement for National Liberation and would ultimately die at the hands of right-wing assassins in Paris. But although their conversations had 'a great influence' on young George Behar, he returned to Holland still gripped by his mother's fervent Protestant faith and a determination to enter the Church.

Hitler's invasion of Holland in May 1940 ended that ambition. Behar was then staying with his grandmother in Rotterdam; trapped by the rapid German advance he was unable to return to his mother's house in The Hague for several days; when he finally reached home, he found that she and his sisters had been evacuated to England, courtesy of Albert's British passport. After a brief period of internment, and at the age of just eighteen, George joined the Dutch resistance and went underground: 'I was, of course, against Nazis because of my background. I was a British subject; I was half Jewish . . . and the country of my mother had been occupied, brutally occupied. I was very anti-German and had every incentive to do everything I could to resist them.'[3]

Behar's youthful appearance – by his own account he looked no more than fourteen – gave him excellent cover. For almost two years he dodged Wehrmacht patrols to deliver underground papers and intelligence on German Army positions to the resistance; it forwarded the latter on to London.

In July 1942, Behar left Holland and headed for Spain, where he hoped to volunteer his services to British forces. The journey took him half a year, and when he arrived in Madrid he was promptly arrested and interned for another three months. Finally, in the spring of 1943 he was sent to Gibraltar and given a place on a convoy bound for England.

All wartime arrivals were automatically detained for security investigation and Behar was held at the Royal Victoria Patriotic School in Wandsworth, South London; he evidently passed the interrogation since he was thereafter granted British citizenship. In November he changed his surname to the anglicized 'Blake' and joined the Royal Navy. After a short period on coastal minesweepers, followed by an officers' training course, he was commissioned and briefly posted to the submarine branch. Hearing and breathing difficulties meant that sub-lieutenant George Blake was deemed unfit for 'the silent service', but his language skills – he was fluent in Dutch and German – brought him to the attention of the Secret Intelligence Service. He was summoned for an interview at number 54 Broadway and duly accepted into MI6: 'I felt very honoured and very excited, and I thought, well, now I'm going to be sent to Holland as an agent, which is what I so much wanted. It turned out I wasn't, because they only sent Dutch subjects to Holland, not British subjects.'[4]

Instead, for the rest of the war he trained the men and women who were sent undercover to the Netherlands, and worked on the coded material they fed back to London. He earned a reputation as a safe pair of hands and in September 1945, MI6 dispatched him to Berlin for his first taste of espionage in the field. His task was to spy on Soviet forces and he quickly realized that former German officers, many of whom were in dire financial straits, were willing to use their extensive contacts in East Germany as the beginnings of a local intelligence network. The mission was evidently successful; when MI6 brought Blake home it dispatched him to Cambridge University to learn Russian.

Cambridge was both the traditional recruiting ground for MI6 and, as the cases of Burgess, Maclean and Philby showed, a very fruitful source of double agents for the KGB. Like them, Blake came under the influence of a charismatic teacher – an English professor whose mother was Russian. She, he recalled later, 'had a great love not for Communism, but for Russia', and inculcated in her students the country's culture and its Orthodox Church. Under her influence, MI6's fast-rising new star discovered 'a great attraction towards Russia'.[5]

George Blake was gradually drifting towards the country with which he and his employers in SIS were at war. If he was not yet a communist, much less a Soviet spy, neither was far away, and his next posting proved the final stage on his personal journey: in late 1948 he was sent to Korea.

The country had been occupied by Japan in the 1930s and had been savagely treated during World War II. After the war, the peninsula became a proxy battleground for the new ideological battle between East and West and in 1948 it was divided along the 38th Parallel; the Soviet Union supported the former communist resistance fighters in the north, while the United States controlled an aggressively anti-communist regime in the south. Both sides fought bloody guerrilla and intelligence campaigns, backed by their respective masters in Moscow and Washington. It was into this volatile and dangerous new conflict zone that MI6 pitched George Blake, with little but his diplomatic cover for protection.

His task was to establish an agent network inside North Korea – a mission that proved largely impossible. But over the next year he came to view America's puppet administration in Seoul as 'fascists'.

After the Korean War broke out in 1950, he and other British diplomatic staff were captured, taken north, and interned in communist prisoner-of-war camps. Here Blake would complete his transition from British intelligence officer to KGB double agent.

'In the autumn of 1951', MI5's official history records, 'Blake handed his captors a note written in Russian and addressed to the Soviet embassy, saying that he had important information to communicate. At a meeting with Vasily Alekseevich Dozhdalev of the KGB, he identified himself as an SIS officer and volunteered to work as a Soviet agent.'[6]

The Soviet intelligence service was an old hand at the game of espionage and habitually alert to the possibility of a bogus defection. But Blake convinced Dozhdalev that his conversion to the communist cause was genuine; the final catalyst, he said, had been witnessing the damage inflicted on North Korea by the US Air Force:

> I had seen the devastation in Germany after the war, but it was nothing, absolutely nothing, I could assure you, compared with the devastation in North Korea . . . I saw this from my [own] eyes, and it made me feel ashamed. Made me feel ashamed of belonging

to these overpowering, technical[ly] superior countries fighting against what seemed to me quite defenceless people . . .

I was engaged in intelligence work against the Communist world . . . and I felt I was committed on the wrong side. And that's what made me decide to change sides. I felt that it would be better for humanity if the Communist system prevailed, that it would put an end to war, to wars.[7]

By September 1953, when British POWs were released from North Korean captivity, Blake had become Agent DIOMID, a fully signed-up officer of the KGB. Newsreel cameras filmed his return to England, catching the moment he embraced a woman whom the narrator called his 'wife'[8] on the tarmac at RAF Abingdon.[9] She was not, however, the only person waiting for him. Moscow had dispatched a rising young intelligence officer to be his handler.

Sergei Kondrashev had only recently been assigned to the KGB's foreign intelligence directorate – a fact that worked in his favour, since it ensured his photograph was not in MI5's file of known Soviet spies. He was also experienced in surveillance and counter-surveillance tradecraft, and had the skills to operate under his official diplomatic cover, as first secretary for cultural relations inside the Soviet Embassy in London. He – and he alone – was entrusted with running Moscow's mole inside MI6. As MI5's official history noted, 'The Centre [KGB Moscow] considered [Blake] so important that no other member of the London residency was permitted to know either DIOMID's identity or the fact that he was an SIS officer.'[10]

One month after Blake returned to work, he met his handler and began his career as a double agent. '[The] first meeting with DIOMID came in late October,' Kondrashev recalled in a book co-authored with the CIA's David Murphy:

This conference was a chance for [us] to get acquainted, to work out plans for further meetings, and to discuss Blake's need for a camera to photocopy [sic] the many documents passing through his hands. Blake also passed [me] a preliminary list of SIS telephone taps and microphone operations against Soviet installations.[11]

Kondrashev quickly supplied the necessary equipment, and from then onwards Blake handed over a vast collection of top-secret MI6 material. Internal Security Service file notes record that 'he used a Minox camera to take about 200 exposures a month of classified documents which he passed on to his controller. In order not to arouse suspicion, he was careful to limit himself to documents to which he would be expected to have access . . . General information gained through gossip and personal contact was passed briefly and verbally at monthly contact with his RIS [Russian Intelligence Service] case officer.'[12]

Both men successfully evaded the attentions of any watchers from MI5's A4 branch. At least one brief rendezvous took place on the top deck of a London bus – a hurried contact in which Blake delivered details of joint British and American covert missions behind the Iron Curtain. As the CIA later concluded:

> [He] passed to the RIS memoranda dealing with British operation projects affecting the British and American intelligence operations against Russian targets. These projects included a joint British-American telephone tap operation directed against the Polish Military Mission in Berlin, a telephone tap operation directed against the Yugoslav Mission in Berlin, and similar targets.[13]

Blake knew that the consequences of his information could be deadly. In the early 1950s both British and American intelligence covertly worked with an anti-Soviet Russian émigré organization in Berlin; the Popular Labour Alliance of Russian Solidarists (NTS) used German intermediaries to make clandestine approaches to Soviet military officers. The details of these contacts, and those who made them, passed across Blake's desk in London, and he handed them over to Kondrashev.

In 1954, based on his intelligence, the KGB kidnapped the NTS leader in Berlin and attempted to assassinate its chief of operations.[14] But his most devastating betrayal concerned one of the most extraordinarily inventive, and vastly expensive, joint CIA–MI6 operations of the early Cold War.

Schönenfeld Chaussee was an unremarkable, if lengthy, street in the Altglienicke district of East Berlin. Two facts, however, made it of exceptional interest to Western intelligence.

The first was its proximity to the border with the American zone; the second was a shallow trench running beside the road in which three cables converged; they carried phone traffic from the Soviet military headquarters in Zossen, conversations between the Kremlin and its embassy in East Berlin, and messages sent by East German officials to their Soviet counterparts.

In 1952 the CIA developed a plan to dig a long tunnel from scrubland on the US side of the border and to tap into the cable junction from below. Because British intelligence had previously mounted a similar exercise in Vienna, MI6 was brought on board, and from 15 to 18 December 1953 senior officers from both services met in London to work out the details of the scheme. The man SIS chose to take the minutes of what it called Operation Stopwatch, and the Americans code-named Gold, was George Blake. 'I realized,' he recalled later, 'how important this was. When I met Sergei the next time . . . I handed him a copy of the minutes from that meeting and a very small sketch, which I drew myself, of how that tunnel would run . . . As I was the secretary of the meeting and I had to make a certain number of copies anyway, it wasn't very difficult to make an additional copy.'[15]

The plan was certainly ambitious. The tunnel would have to run for 1,480 feet through sandy and unstable soil; even beginning the work in an area of West Berlin which, the Agency acknowledged, was 'a squattersville of shacks and hovels constructed from rubble by refugees from the East German zone', would draw the attention of security patrols on the other side of the border.

Added to that was the sizeable problem of disposing of an anticipated 3,000 tons of spoil. To provide cover for both, US intelligence built
a vast warehouse above the planned entrance. Work began in early September 1954 and by the following February, British engineers had
installed the electronic tapping equipment. The project consumed enormous amounts of energy and resources; according to a 1967 internal
CIA study the final bill, to be borne, unknowingly, by US taxpayers,
exceeded $6.5 million – the equivalent of $62 million today.[16] But to
both the Agency and MI6, the Berlin Tunnel's potential as a window
into Soviet intelligence far outweighed the cost.

For the KGB, Blake's revelation of the scheme's existence and
details – sent by Kondrashev to Moscow in February 1954 – posed a
dilemma. Should it stop sending messages along the cables it now knew
to be compromised or, more profitably, seize the opportunity to feed
disinformation to the West via the tapped lines? The problem with
either option was the risk each posed to their agent inside MI6.

'This . . . highlighted the terrible Catch 22 [we] were in,' Kondrashev
remembered. '[We] knew about the tunnel but were unable to do anything about it immediately for fear of compromising Blake.' The same
concern ruled out disinformation which, if it was detected by the CIA,
would reveal that Operation Gold was blown: '[it] would have involved
too many people and would have risked Blake's security'.[17]

In the end, the KGB decided on the least damaging solution: it
restricted, as far as practicable, the information passing along the
cables,[18] and bided its time to expose the espionage 'provocation' in a
propaganda coup. Finally, on 22 April 1956 – after eleven months and
eleven days of its existence – Moscow directed the East German regime
to 'discover' the tunnel in front of an invited audience of journalists and
photographers.

Blake himself was in Berlin when the stage-managed event took
place. MI6 had posted him to Germany in April 1955 and he would
remain there for the next four years. From the outset he systematically
betrayed every sizeable secret that crossed his desk, and exposed

hundreds of undercover agents working for British and American intelligence. The KGB's own files, parts of which were later smuggled out of Russia, credit Agent DIOMID with enabling 'the elimination of the adversary's network in the GDR [East Germany] in 1953–55'.[19]

In May 1959, Blake's tour of duty in Berlin ended and he returned to 54 Broadway. He had added field experience to his theoretical knowledge and language skills, and was, in the eyes of the SIS, a rising star. As a CIA report noted, 'he was given an important assignment in the British intelligence operation station in London where he was charged with activity directed against Soviet targets'.[20] For the next eighteen months he channelled all the intelligence MI6 gleaned from this project to his KGB handler: 'That was very important information for them, so that they could protect these targets . . . And I gave a lot of information on the Secret Service . . . They got a good inside view how it operated.'[21]

~

Had Michał Goleniewski not intervened, Blake would have continued to betray British and American secrets to Moscow. Ironically, he was in many ways a mirror image of his nemesis, since both were primarily motivated to spy by a genuine ideological conviction. And although Blake survived the first lacklustre joint MI5–MI6 investigation which followed an early Sniper lead, a subsequent letter sent by Sniper in late summer 1960 provided information which reopened the case.

'George Blake was never *named* by "Heckenschuetz" [Sniper],' Tennent Bagley wrote later, '[but] his letters told of one or more British documents (especially a list of MI6 recruitment targets among Poles) that the KGB passed to the Poles, and from there the investigation led eventually to Blake as the source.'[22]

In September 1960, MI6 moved Blake out of active service and away from London, posting him to the Middle East Centre in Beirut; here he was to study Arabic and, ostensibly, prepare for his next position. In reality British intelligence spent the next six months preparing the evidence for a robust interrogation. On 3 April 1961 – with Goleniewski now out of danger in the CIA safe house – SIS summoned Blake back to London.

He was expecting to be interviewed for his forthcoming posting; instead he found himself in front of a grim MI6 tribunal and fighting for survival. Over the next forty-eight hours he was confronted with evidence indicating that he had been spying for the Soviet Union, but he denied each and every accusation and, as the CIA noted, seemed to be winning the battle:

> The encounter with Blake began unsuccessfully. As the hours of his interrogation dragged on, Blake showed no indication of weakening. It began to appear that the effort to break him would be unsuccessful. The carefully prepared ammunition had been largely shot away without breaching his defence. The prospect of his getting away with his denials loomed ominously.[23]

On the third day, the MI6 interrogators played their trump card: the information Sniper had provided which proved that at least one of the SIS documents he had been shown by the KGB and UB could only have come from someone in Berlin station. The only British intelligence officer to have had access to the papers and to have been based in Berlin at the time was Blake. It proved to be the decisive breakthrough.

'When faced with this evidence,' the CIA noted, 'and asked to explain how it had come into the possession of Soviet intelligence, Blake broke. From that moment on, he began to cooperate with the interrogators and seemingly has answered their questions with a remarkable degree of openness.'

Both MI6 and the Agency were convinced that without Goleniewski's lead to deploy as their final weapon, Blake would not have confessed. 'It is the view of the Chief of the British Service that it was not only the nature of the material but the timing of the play which achieved the result', the CIA's memo recorded.[24]

On 3 May 1961, Blake appeared in the dock at the Old Bailey and, behind closed doors, entered guilty pleas to each of five separate charges of spying for the Soviet Union; the Lord Chief Justice, Hubert Parker, then sentenced him to forty-two years in prison.[25]

In the aftermath, the Prime Minister sought to mislead Parliament and the British public about the impact of Blake's treachery. 'He has done serious damage to the interests of this country,' Harold Macmillan told the House of Commons, 'I can, however, assure Hon. Members that Blake's disclosures will not have done irreparable damage.'[26] The truth, as both MI6 and the CIA knew, was very much less comforting. By Blake's own account he betrayed almost 400 Western intelligence operatives working undercover behind the Iron Curtain – though he claimed none had come to any harm.[27] The Secret Intelligence Service knew better: it calculated that at least forty of those agents were executed by the KGB.[28]

For its part the CIA recorded that 'the Blake case represents a most serious and damaging compromise of Allied intelligence activity directed against the Soviet [sic]'.[29]

If there was one bright spot on this otherwise bleak horizon, it was the man settling into married life in Arlington, Virginia. Michał Goleniewski, aka Franz Roman Oldenburg, the agent formerly known as Sniper, had proved his worth once again and his success showed no signs of abating. Six months after George Blake began his prison sentence, the next of Sniper's major targets was arrested and taken into custody.

16

Felfe

F OR A SLIGHT, sickly middle-aged man known to his colleagues by
the distinctly effeminate nickname 'Fiffi', Heinz Felfe put up an
impressive struggle.

On the morning of 5 November 1961, staff at the heavily fortified
Bundesnachrichtendienst headquarters in Pullach were treated to the
extraordinary spectacle of the head of counterintelligence wrestling with
armed West German police on the office floor. As they struggled to subdue
him, Felfe thrust a small piece of paper into his mouth and unsuccessfully
tried to swallow it; finally the federal agents subdued him and marched
him out of the building. Shortly afterwards, additional police squads
picked up two co-conspirators, Hans Clemens and Erwin Tiebel.

The arrests were the culmination of Operation DROWZY – a joint
US–West German investigation which had begun with Goleniewski's
letter in the spring of 1959. They marked the end of Felfe's twenty-year
career as a spy – two decades in which he had been employed by the
espionage services of no fewer than four countries. It also prompted a
painful post-mortem inquiry by the Agency which revealed how much
it owed to agent Sniper, and gave significant credence to his astonishing
claim that the KGB was running a false-flag organization of ex-Nazis at
the very heart of Washington's proxy agency. For good measure, it provided sobering evidence of gross failures by the CIA, German and
British intelligence – and the extensive damage Felfe had caused to the
West's Cold War battle with Moscow.

Heinz Paul Felfe was born in March 1918, the son of a police inspector in Dresden. At the age of thirteen he joined the Hitler Youth and signed up as a volunteer in one of the Third Reich's paramilitary border units; two years later he was inducted into its elite security force, the Schutzstaffel. 'From then on', the CIA's 1969 report noted,[1] 'his schooling, legal training and subsequent assignment to a job in the Criminal Police was guided and fostered by the SS.'[2]

In 1943, Felfe took up a new post in the foreign intelligence section of the Reich Central Security Office (RSHA), serving first in Switzerland, where he helped spread forged British currency, before transferring to Holland with instructions to organize subversive groups behind the advancing Allied lines. By the end of the war he had risen to the rank of Obersturmführer – equivalent to a first lieutenant – in the Waffen-SS, the organization's military arm.[3]

Under Allied post-war regulations, German officials who had belonged to the SS were automatically deemed to have committed a criminal offence. Felfe was arrested by Canadian troops and detained at the Blauw Kappel Interrogation Centre near Utrecht, which handled former Nazi intelligence personnel. On 10 July 1945 he was questioned by British Army specialists about his history and beliefs: his willingness to detail the aims and staffing of his RSHA stations evidently impressed his interviewer, since the subsequent report was extremely positive:

> Felfe is a very intelligent young man and creates a very favourable impression. Is extremely straightforward in all his answers and does NOT [emphasis in original] give any impression of trying to conceal anything. He freely admits to having been an ardent Nazi . . . is perfectly frank and does NOT try to put the blame on anybody else for anything.[4]

Within a few months the Army wrapped up its investigations and Felfe was marked for future release; he was not prosecuted for his SS activities and in November 1946 was set free. More remarkably still, in the summer of 1947 he was hired by British military intelligence, and as the CIA's file reported, set to work in the new war with Moscow:

> His task was to develop information on Communists [sic] student groups at the University of Bonn. Under British instruction he . . . joined the Communist Party. In the course of his work he made several trips to East Berlin and East Germany to observe student rallies.[5]

After three years of generously paid employment, Felfe was sacked by British intelligence for 'serious operational and personal security reasons . . . these included attempts to sell information collected for the British to several other intelligence agencies, two West German news services and to the East German Socialist Unity (ie: Communist) Party'.

Other evidence showed that he had concocted a highly dubious 'double-agent operation with the Soviets', that he had blown his own cover by boasting to anyone who would listen that he was a British spy, and that he had refused orders to cease consorting with his former friends from the SS.[6]

Despite this setback, Felfe soon found other gainful employment, joining one of Germany's regional security offices; he betrayed this organization as promptly as he had his previous masters, sending classified material to a contact in East Germany and then attempting to sell the draft charter of the future counterintelligence agency, the BfV, to a newspaper. Somehow, however, he survived these scandals and, in October 1951, was recruited to the Gehlen Organization, serving first in its field offices before being promoted to the headquarters staff two years later.

Here he earned a reputation as 'a good worker, a valuable addition', and was quickly assigned to counter-espionage operations against Soviet bloc intelligence; before long he became the head of the entire unit. His credentials were further burnished by a succession of astonishingly successful operations against Moscow and its satellites, which uncovered previously unknown KGB espionage rings inside West

Germany. 'Felfe is excellent,' Gehlen reportedly commented, 'he does what others cannot do.'[7]

By necessity, this work involved contact with US intelligence – a task which Felfe accepted with some enthusiasm. After the Org became Germany's first official foreign intelligence agency, those ties grew even closer; in autumn 1956 the CIA's Security Department cleared Felfe – by now given the cryptonym FRIESEN – as one of the small party of senior BND officers to be given a week-long guided tour of the Agency's facilities in Washington DC.[8]

Had the Agency been rather more assiduous in investigating Petr Deriabin's story about PETER and PAUL – the two KGB moles he claimed had burrowed into the BND's Pullach base – it might have been rather less complacent about the remarkably successful Heinz Felfe. Instead, for the next three years, he was given almost unlimited access to operations run by the CIA's Berlin Operating Base against Soviet targets, and saw almost all of the resulting intelligence yield.

Goleniewski's Sniper report, in Spring 1959, should have jarred the Agency out of its complacency. He specifically warned that 'the KGB had two agents in the BND group which visited the US . . . [and] also had an agent who was in [a] position to obtain information on a joint American-BND office running operations against the Soviet Embassy in Bonn and against Soviets travelling in the West. The KGB had guidance papers used by this office and prepared by the Americans in 1956.'[9]

Instead, the CIA moved painfully slowly. It began what its own documents describe as 'a quiet closer investigation of suspect agents in the BND'.[10] Despite this, in July 1959 – a full two months after Sniper's letter – the Agency's Berlin station blithely gave Felfe a very favourable testimonial:

> Personality-wise, Subject can be described as intelligent, competent and inclined to be reserved. He has always been in contact with members of the KUBARK [the CIA's own cryptonym for itself] liaison staff and has uniformly been cooperative . . .

He appears to be a dedicated intelligence officer, keenly interested in his work and one who places a premium on professional
competence . . . He can be reserved, sly, shrewd, imaginative and
energetic. His personality is not a warm one and there are few
endearing traits in his make-up. On the other hand he can be
most pleasant to deal with.[11]

Above all, the (unnamed) author decided, '[FRIESEN/Felfe] is a man
who apparently ties his personal future to the West and has made the
decision to fight Communist ideologies within . . . UPSWING [the
Agency's cryptonym for the BND].'

Although the same report did record two slight concerns about this
star of German counterintelligence, noting that he had an unusually
high standard of living and that a fellow officer had alleged that Felfe
had sold his services to the Stasi, neither was taken seriously.

By February 1960, even after the CIA narrowed its focus and identified Felfe as the prime suspect, a senior case officer in West Germany
grumbled that 'I tend to conclude, at least on the basis of what we now
have to go on, that FRIESEN is not a penetration agent . . .' He reached
this verdict despite simultaneously admitting that Felfe had a habit of
slipping away from his American protectors on visits to Berlin,[12] and
that his lavish lifestyle far exceeded his salary:

The fact that his country house is conveniently close to the Austrian border, that he has a big apartment, that his son attends an
Internat [boarding school] which is no cheap proposition, that he
has a good car, etc etc, could mean he has Eastern contact. They
could [emphasis in original] mean nothing, or that his rich uncle
[Moscow] pays the bills.[13]

Over the next year, surveillance, telephone taps and mail intercepts
answered that question definitively; they also revealed that Felfe was not
a lone mole but an integral part of a substantial network of former Nazi

intelligence officials inside the Gehlen Organization (and later the BND) who had been targeted by Moscow:

> It was especially vulnerable because it was heavily staffed by for-
> mer SD and SS personnel who in order to maintain their jobs
> were obliged at least proforma to conceal their background . . . In
> reaction to this there had gradually developed within [it] a sort of
> mutual aid society of ex-SS and SD personnel for self-protection
> and personal advancement.
>
> This group was particularly susceptible both to simple black-
> mail and to the somewhat more complicated appeals of revenge
> or vindication. It was through this base . . . that one of the most
> able and tenacious of staff penetrations of the Gehlen Organiza-
> tion was launched.[14]

The CIA investigators discovered that Felfe was engaged in regular, clandestine, communications with Hans Clemens, a former Sicherheits-dienst[15] and foreign intelligence officer, now based in one of the BND's field stations. Like Felfe, after the defeat of the Third Reich, Clemens was interned in POW camps, and he had in fact been indicted – though acquitted – in a 1948 war crimes trial.[16]

During this period in Allied captivity he discovered his wife, Gerda, had been sleeping with Soviet troops in Dresden, and after his release, Clemens settled in West Germany – though he remained in contact with Gerda. He also contacted another former SS comrade, Erwin Tie-bel, then a West German lawyer on a Soviet list of wanted war criminals accused of having murdered hostages in Dresden.

By 1949, Gerda Clemens was working for Soviet intelligence, reporting to a Russian colonel known as 'Max' who headed a special office to locate and 'turn' former Nazi police and intelligence officers. At the end of the year, he sent Frau Clemens to West Germany with orders to recruit her ex-husband, Tiebel and Felfe. The proposition was simple: sign on with Moscow – and receive substantial financial rewards – or refuse and face undoubtedly severe consequences. 'Max' also played on the trio's lingering resentment at the destruction Allied bombers had wreaked on Dresden, stressing that if they undertook 'to seek out old police and SD contacts and through them try to penetrate the Gehlen Organization', they would be striking a blow at its ultimate master, the United States. Over the course of the next eighteen months, all three agreed to become KGB agents: Clemens was given the cryptonym PETER, and Felfe became PAUL.[17]

From 1951 onwards, as Felfe and Clemens rose through the ranks of the Org and later the BND, they systematically burrowed into German and then US intelligence. Felfe, who had the more senior role, photographed hundreds of top-secret documents on a Minox camera, and was also able to control almost all joint US–German operations against the KGB's headquarters in Karlshorst, East Berlin. For safety, the two men rarely met, and only spoke on the phone when Felfe was at his country house – a line he (wrongly) believed too difficult to tap. Instead, Tiebel – code name ERICH – acted as their cut-out, couriering microfilms and microdots between them.

The CIA's investigation also revealed that just as Sniper's letters had predicted, Moscow had gone to extraordinary lengths to preserve its spy's cover and to enhance his reputation with Gehlen. The KGB fed Felfe a succession of low-grade Soviet secrets to pass on to his employers in Pullach and – again as Sniper forecast – deliberately sacrificed other agents, giving Felfe their names and ordering him to 'uncover' them. These were the source of Felfe's astonishing 'successes' for the BND, and four apparently profitable BND/CIA counter-espionage operations – code names BALTHASAR, LENA, LILLI MARLENE and BUSCH – also now appeared in a rather less positive light.[18]

The discoveries made for grim reading. The BND was not merely a wholly owned subsidiary of US intelligence, it was its most important front-line weapon in the Cold War; the treachery of Felfe and Clemens – and, the Agency had to assume, an unknown number of other former Nazi officials employed in sensitive posts at Pullach – meant that many of the West's most vital secrets were haemorrhaging to Moscow. Nor, with Sniper still operating somewhere behind the Iron Curtain, could it do anything to staunch the flow.

In February 1961, once Goleniewski was securely in CIA custody, the Agency finally deemed it safe to tell the BND about the moles in its midst; Gehlen's response was, to say the least, surprising: 'He immediately agreed that his heretofore favourite case officer – Felfe – was the major suspect. He set up a small task force to investigate Goleniewski's leads to penetration of the BND.'[19]

If Gehlen's volte-face was unexpected, the records of his organization's previously undisclosed internal inquiries were shocking; they showed that it had ignored evidence which should have unmasked the traitor several years before:

> In February 1956, Felfe was asked 'officer to officer' whether he had been a member of the SD. He replied with a brazen 'No Sir', despite the fact that his SD past was known to a number of Gehlen officers and could have readily been proven by a check of wartime records under Allied control . . . Although the BND's security file on Felfe was kept up in a desultory fashion for the rest of his career . . . by this time his professional reputation was growing, and Felfe's corner was a disheartening place to look for additional treachery.[20]

For the next six months, the CIA and Gehlen's in-house team steadily built a case against the moles. They also discovered evidence which clearly indicated that Felfe was attempting to conceal the true source of his unusual wealth: 'In the summer of 1961 [he] began dropping remarks about having received a large bequest from a recently deceased aunt in the US. CIA checked and found the aunt very much alive, and . . . indeed a few weeks later she applied for a passport to make a trip to Germany to visit Felfe.'[21] A covert examination of his office showed that he had stolen large sums of money from the BND and, more disturbingly, that he had falsified records on at least one of its anti-Soviet counter-espionage operations.

In September surveillance teams followed Felfe and Clemens to Vienna, where they met with a known KGB field officer; then on 5

November phone taps revealed that Clemens was about to send Felfe a coded message from their KGB handler. The joint US–West German team decided it was time to act:

> By 11.30 am the appropriate police officers with BND escort were assembled at the BND headquarters in Pullach; the compound gates were locked, the telephone lines cut. All principals were armed and the BND doctor was standing by for any emergency.
>
> A few minutes later, the arresting officers . . . served their warrant. Felfe's first reaction was to grab for his wallet and attempt to destroy a scrap of paper which was in it. There was a scuffle; the officers retrieved the paper, subdued Felfe.[22]

The paper was the coded KGB message. Exactly eight minutes later, other officers seized Clemens at the BND field office in Cologne. He made no attempt to resist, meekly handing over his collection of KGB-issue one-time pads; Tiebel was picked up the following day, and all three men were charged with espionage.[23] Gehlen and the CIA breathed a sigh of relief: more than a decade after it had begun, the KGB's penetration of West Germany's intelligence service was finally broken.

The celebrations were short-lived – a realism reflected in the ominous telex US intelligence sent to Gehlen: 'Congratulations. You found your Felfe: we're still looking for ours.'[24] Now the inquests began into how the spy ring had been allowed to operate for so long, and how much damage it had inflicted. Both would be profoundly painful.

'Felfe met regularly with members of the CIA liaison staff accredited to BND headquarters and with selected CIA case officers at other bases in Germany', the Agency's sombre post-mortem reported.[25] 'For several years . . . he had received periodic briefings and CIA reports on the Soviet Intelligence Services and their activities in East and West Berlin. He had been privy to several operations on a case by case basis [and] had also been the guest of CIA at Headquarters for a week's briefings.'[26]

The sheer volume of intelligence Felfe passed to the KGB was staggering: during ten years as an active double agent he had photographed more than 15,000 documents and sent innumerable coded messages to Moscow. A search of his apartment unearthed a further 300 microfilms containing 15,660 additional pages of top-secret material:

> Felfe has provided the KGB with information which makes both CIA and the BND vulnerable to intensive attacks from the East . . . The degree of compromise of operations, personnel and facilities in Germany has been very heavy. The details of more than 65 CIA REDCAP and LCIMPROVE operations [the Agency's code names for attempts to attract Soviet defectors and uncover Moscow's worldwide intelligence efforts, respectively] . . . are known to the opposition, as is much of their related M/O . . .
>
> Over 100 CIA staffers were exposed in true name or alias. The damage is not confined to the approximately 15,000 recorded individual items of known or possible compromise, but includes the more difficult to document loss occasioned by Felfe's manipulation of certain operations on behalf of the KGB in either the planning stage or during actual execution.
>
> Berlin Base entered into joint operations with the BND in July 1959 . . . Felfe was able to provide the KGB with such extensive data . . . that in time the Base suffered virtual neutralization of its efforts.[27]

In short, Soviet intelligence saw and heard almost everything that reached the Agency's eyes and ears in Pullach, and was able to nullify it. US intelligence was not simply flying blind in the eye of the Cold War storm: it had also been misled and misdirected down false trails for more than a decade.

What made this catalogue of havoc even more troubling was the humiliating knowledge that it could – and should – have been prevented. 'There are many ways by which Felfe might have been unmasked earlier than he was,' the second of the CIA's internal reports on the debacle concluded: 'Even a thorough name check might have done the trick . . . For almost every year of Felfe's post-war existence an item of derogatory information was entered in the files of some Western agency. Unfortunately no one agency, much less the BND, had it all until shortly before his arrest.'[28]

Badly wounded, the Agency sought scapegoats to shoulder the blame, complaining that British intelligence was at fault for not disclosing its files on Felfe until 1961, and that Gehlen had given dozens of known ex-Nazis a safe home inside the BND.[29] Both criticisms were true and warranted, but they conveniently overlooked the uncomfortable truth that internal CIA memos showed that from 1952 it was fully aware of both the presence and dubious loyalties of the former SS officers.[30]

But the most telling verdict was that Sniper was the sole reason Felfe's espionage ring had been broken. His letters, and his letters alone, had finally forced US intelligence into overdue action.

'Felfe,' the CIA report concluded, 'could have been caught earlier if more weight had been given to analytical evidence which clearly indicated that something was amiss, rather than waiting to be spurred to action by report[s] from our own sensitive penetration source.'[31]

In November 1961 that 'sensitive' source was about to begin the two most productive years of his post-defection career. Governments in Washington and London were ready to reward Michał Goleniewski for his unprecedented successes; and in return he was determined to match their commitment with a slew of further revelations.

17

Glory Days

U S Government Contract Number #B-3972-52/1961 was hand-delivered to the occupant of 1201 South Court House Road, Arlington, on 16 September 1961. It was a bulky, complicated document: twenty separate subject clauses imposed stringent obligations on the proposed signatory – not least the absolute imperative to keep the agreement entirely secret.

Much of the language was impenetrable bureaucratic jargon. Protracted subordinate clauses were peppered with archaic legalese: 'Hereby' and 'herein', 'said subparagraph' and 'pursuant to'. It would have challenged the comprehension of an average American law student, let alone a recently arrived Communist-state defector with only a limited command of conversational English, and who had no access to independent counsel.

Nor was it a contract of employment – one which would confer a right to health coverage, life insurance and the full protection of the state. Instead it was an agreement which bound the recipient to provide his services to the United States for a fixed one-year period: Goleniewski was, in Washington's eyes, still on probation.

Nonetheless, it was the first official documentation which formalized his status and by which the government undertook to pay its newest intelligence consultant $1,000 per month.[1] And its appearance, in the hands of Howard Roman, that early autumn morning marked the start of what both parties intended to be a long and fruitful relationship.

There was one curiosity: the name under which the man was to inscribe his signature. Eight months after Sniper unmasked himself as Michał Goleniewski, only to be re-christened Franz Oldenburg, his identity was unilaterally changed once again. The oddity was not explained, nor in any event did Goleniewski have much choice; he accepted the instruction without argument and duly scrawled 'Martin N. Cherico' in the space provided.

The CIA knew that by the nature of their precarious position, their total dependence on a complex and opaque bureaucracy and the disorientation of being transplanted into an alien environment, defectors were susceptible to depression and doubt; its own manuals specifically advised interrogators to exploit this weakness,[2] and the issue of identity lay at the heart of the vulnerability.

All new arrivals from Soviet bloc intelligence had to relinquish every aspect of their previous lives: their homes, friends, past history and, above all, their names. While this was a vital precaution, protecting them from the very real threat of reprisals, it inevitably had a profoundly destabilizing effect, and, added to his long-standing worries about the Agency's integrity, it was already taking a toll on Goleniewski.

At the end of September, Howard Roman drove him into Washington for an hour-long audience with CIA director Allen Dulles – one of the last major meetings to be held in the Agency's downtown DC headquarters before it moved to purpose-built premises in Langley, Virginia. By his own subsequent account, Goleniewski planned to raise the question of his identity; but like the building itself, the Agency's veteran chief was also on borrowed time[3] and was too distracted to focus:

> I was expecting that Mr. Dulles would have many reasons to speak with me in an open and fair way. But this visit and conversation . . . was empty of results . . . Mr. Dulles took quite a little time . . . discussing his pipe collection and how he expected to have trouble, when he moved into his new office at Langley, finding a place to hang all the pipes he wanted there.[4]

The confusion worsened the following month when the Agency finally presented the Goleniewskis with their Immigration and Naturalization Service documents. Alien Registration Card number A12727330 bore the name of Franz Roman Oldenburg, and A12727331 identified the holder as his wife, Irmgard Oldenburg.[5] There was – for the moment – no mention of 'Martin N. Cherico', and, once again, no explanation.

If the CIA was playing mind games, in a belated attempt to reclaim some of the 'psychological superiority' which had been absent from Goleniewski's initial interrogations, it was being remarkably reckless about the impact on his vulnerable psychological state. Whatever the reason, it was laying the foundations for a future identity crisis.

Materially, at least, life in the West was rather better. If Goleniewski had not yet fully grasped the realities of American-style freedom and democracy, his stock was high inside most of the CIA – though Angleton and his counterintelligence team still harboured doubts – and his successes in London and Berlin had been augmented by the arrest and prosecution of two further Soviet bloc spies.

In March, Shin Bet, Israel's Security Agency, caught Israel Beer in the act of delivering documents to his KGB handler in Tel Aviv. Three months later a closed Israeli court sentenced him to ten years in prison.[6] The same month, after a lengthy debriefing of Goleniewski,[7] FBI agents arrested Irvin Scarbeck, the US Embassy official caught in a Polish security honeytrap; in July, Scarbeck was indicted on three counts of passing US secrets to the UB. The case would, in time, become a problem for both the American government and its new consultant, but that summer it cemented Goleniewski's status as the most important defector US intelligence had ever known.

Tangible evidence of American gratitude arrived every month during the spring and summer, in cash. 'Mr. Howard Roman,' Irmgard wrote in still-fractured English in a sworn 1967 affidavit, '[was] always bringing by hand the monthly salary of my husband ($750 take home pay) deducted of that monthly $184 for the rent, without leaving any receipt.'[8]

A more formal – and more generous – endowment followed in

August 1961, when the CIA opened a checking account for Franz Oldenburg at Riggs Bank, Washington – its regular financial institution of
choice – and paid in the substantial sum of $25,000. The money, equiva-
lent to $210,000 today, was intended as the first instalment of a larger
lump sum to recompense 'Agent Sniper' for his service as an Agent in
Place in Poland.[9]

The Agency also regularly commandeered Military Air Transport
planes to fly Irmgard to Frankfurt for a series of further reunions with
her parents and family; each lasted between eight and ten days, all at US
taxpayers' expense.[10] In addition, the American government picked up
the tab for a belated honeymoon the couple enjoyed in Florida early in
1962.[11]

Goleniewski repaid this generosity with an endless stream of new
leads. Throughout the winter and spring of 1962 a succession of CIA
officers arrived at 1201 South Court House Road for lengthy debriefing
sessions; but if its prized defector was happy to instruct them on the
machinations of Soviet bloc intelligence services, he occasionally chafed
at the conditions and intensity of the Agency's demands.

'I was very often and most unnecessarily treated as a rare animal and
shown to various officials,' he later grumbled. 'At this time the CIA, using
the excuse of my personal security, placed me in more and more an
enforced isolated position.'[12]

But, irritated or not, the information he provided was extraordinarily
rich and exposed a wealth of previously unknown KGB activities across
the globe. In particular, according to the Agency's own assessment of
Goleniewski's 'intelligence product', he provided extensive additional
material on Moscow's worldwide 'MOB' sleeper and sabotage networks:

> According to Goleniewski, the Russian term for the MOB nets is
> 'in storage', and the agents should be exempt from the draft and
> in good standing with the local police. An example of a large
> 'MOB' net was given [to Goleniewski] by General Korczyński[13] . . .
> [who] said that the Chinese had 2,500 MOB agents in Japan . . .

who would remain inactive unless war was declared. Goleniewski stated there was a MOB net in Scandinavia and in Canada.
The Canadian net was created in the early 1930s with the assistance of the Canadian Communist Party. The information . . .
was given to the RCMP.[14]

Day after day, the CIA's debriefers filled their notebooks with revelations
on the UB's cracking of Western cipher codes, the defection in 1960 of
two US National Security Agency officers,[15] the disastrous shooting
down of Gary Powers' U2 spy plane and the implications for US intelligence of Moscow's revolutionary new digital computer.[16]

A heavily redacted supplement in the Agency's files recorded that
Goleniewski also returned to the problem of Moscow's infiltration of
West German intelligence, and revealed the identities of other KGB
double agents at work inside the BND. CIA headquarters at Langley
began a new operation – code-named BEVISION – to investigate
the flood of leads. It proved to be a rewarding, if frustratingly demanding, task.

In the spring of 1962, Howard Roman – by then assigned to a new
post in Munich – wrote to Goleniewski, expressing the CIA's gratitude
and giving an update on the progress of BEVISION:

> First of all I want to tell you that the material you produced the
> last time I saw you was of very great interest and use and has
> repeatedly been studied. It was extremely helpful in giving the
> group working in that area some ideas for their further research
> that I think they otherwise would never have had.
>
> Actually the job was a very tough one, and, as you predicted,
> not too much progress was made in the short period of time we
> had for the project. It is expected now, however, that our research
> group will go back to the same job later, probably in the fall. I might
> try to arrange . . . some further advice and analysis from you, unless
> Tom Miller [Roman's replacement and a veteran Russian expert] is
> keeping you busy with some of the other projects.[17]

Goleniewski was, undoubtedly, busy. By one of his own later accounts, the Agency sent him to Greece – one of Washington's post-war bulwarks against Moscow's ambitions, but increasingly riven by political tension – to report on its 'geo-political situation, tremendous involvement in these areas on the part of CIA and other US Intelligences, and presence of certain "Specialist" types [Soviet spies]'.[18] Polish intelligence files record that he was also present at the interrogation of a UB agent detained by the CIA and BND in West Germany.[19]

Somehow, in the middle of this, Goleniewski also found time to move house. In March 1962 he and Irmgard left Arlington and relocated to New York. They rented an apartment in the Silver Towers block at 125-10 Queens Boulevard, Kew Gardens, close to Idlewild international airport on Long Island.[20]

The new flat was bigger and had space for an office for further debriefings; it was also rather more expensive, but the CIA increased his monthly salary to $1,150 to cover the extra costs involved.[21] Soon a regular procession of Langley's analysts and FBI agents made the journey from Washington to tap into his 'exceptional memory' and 'almost total recall'.[22]

There was, however, an exception to the US government's interest: the State Department was offered, but declined, the opportunity to question Goleniewski.[23] This was odd: he had given the CIA details of what appeared to be a wholesale penetration of the US Embassy in Warsaw, and had made it clear that he had a great deal more information to divulge. In addition to the low-level compromise of American security guards, the activities of the UB's 'red swallows' and their male gigolo counterparts, he claimed to have evidence that a very senior diplomat had been working for the KGB for eighteen years; more pertinently, he insisted that Moscow had deliberately sacrificed Irvin Scarbeck as a diversion to protect its more important agent.

The CIA knew that this was, at the very least, plausible. Scarbeck had been exposed by an anonymous phone call in June 1961, shortly after Goleniewski's defection was confirmed in Warsaw and Moscow. The willingness of his young Polish mistress, Urszula Discher, to testify in person in the US against him was also distinctly unusual.

At the very least, the State Department had substantial reason to pay close attention to the allegations. Yet not only did it spurn the opportunity to question Goleniewski, it also shut down internal attempts to investigate his claims. Otto Otepka, the responsible security department official in Foggy Bottom, was blocked from reviewing the files: 'I wished only to determine the extent of the implication of other State department employees,' he later testified; 'I was rejected on one occasion after another.'[24]

The State Department's absence seemed particularly unusual given the interest of other Western services. Throughout 1962, as well as briefing the FBI and the CIA, Goleniewski worked closely with the BND in West Germany, and MI5 also took advantage of his input on the latest spy scandals to erupt in London.

British intelligence already had good reason to be grateful to him. The arrests of George Blake and the Portland Spy Ring had been made possible by the information he supplied; and just as his lead on Harry Houghton had led to Gordon Lonsdale and his collaborators, Helen and Peter Kroger, material uncovered in the searches of the Krogers' bungalow in the West London suburb of Ruislip had pointed the Security Service to yet another of Moscow's agents.

In 1954, John Vassall, a naval attaché at the British Embassy in Moscow, had been compromised in a gay honeytrap and photographed 'having oral, anal or a complicated series of sexual activities with a number of different men'.[25] Since homosexuality was illegal in both the Soviet Union and Britain, the KGB was able to blackmail him into handing over a substantial volume of Royal Navy technical secrets. In October 1962 he was tried at the Old Bailey and sentenced to eighteen years in prison.[26]

Although some accounts state that a later defector[27] exposed Vassall – and MI5's files on the case remain under lock and key – Goleniewski always claimed the credit, and Allen Dulles went on the record to confirm this: 'Microfilms found in [the Krogers'] apartment eventually led to the apprehension of John Vassall, another Admiralty employee,' the CIA's director wrote in a lengthy valedictory account of his intelligence career in April 1963.[28]

Documents in Goleniewski's own voluminous archives suggest that he also helped the Security Service with the two other British espionage scandals *du jour*: the tangled sex and spy saga of War Minister John Profumo,[29] and the festering sore of former MI6 officer Kim Philby.

In a letter to his handlers in the CIA's East European Division shortly after Philby's escape to Moscow in January 1963, Goleniewski insisted that he had previously identified the KGB's star agent as 'LAMBDA III', and that for 'more than two years I did report about his activities [but] I was told that these information [sic] . . . had been "not entirely correct", or presented "some discrepancies".'[30]

Although his claimed contribution to these exposés is impossible to confirm – MI5 continues to withhold its files on Profumo, Philby and Goleniewski himself – British intelligence unquestionably consulted him extensively. In a letter sent to the CIA in in early 1963, it expressed profound gratitude for his continuing assistance:

> I think that this may be an appropriate moment at which to put on record our appreciation of the services rendered to the British Security Service by [Goleniewski]. Some cases of spies who have been detected and arrested as a result of leads supplied by him received a great deal of publicity and [Goleniewski] must be aware of how the value of his information has been appreciated and what effective action has been taken.
>
> There is, however, a large mass of information which he has provided which is less spectacular and of which he sees no end result. In fact, often where he has indicated agents or operational targets . . . we have been able to take effective preventive action which received no publicity.
>
> The mass of data which he has provided about individual Intelligence Officers and organization and methods of the Polish

Intelligence Service has been of inestimable value. He is still a copious source of information and an invaluable point of reference. We are always impressed by his outstanding expertise, his grasp of detail and his encyclopaedic memory.[31]

MI5 asked the Agency to deliver the letter to Goleniewski 'together with our gratitude for the unvaryingly helpful way in which he replies to the innumerable questions which we have referred to him'. As tangible proof of its gratitude, a gift of an antique silver George III tankard accompanied the note.[32]

British admiration was shared by the CIA's handlers and analysts, but there were growing signs of division between them and James Angleton's counterintelligence staff. In March 1963, Goleniewski complained that it had blocked investigations into the leads he gave which pointed to Soviet penetration of the Agency and numerous other Western intelligence services:

In 1962 and early in 1963 [I] alerted Howard [Roman] Pete [Bagley], Paul [unidentified] and others (including FBI), that the French sector including NATO, presents for the national security of this country extremely important and dangerous complex [sic]. There are reasons – as I alerted – to believe that the French security region is endangered with Soviet penetrations (including Polish Communist Intelligences) not less than the British security region, as the already investigated and tried cases had demonstrate [sic].

I had been assured . . . that [this] would be reviewed with me and . . . co-elaborated [sic] with substantial information and evidence from the French sector which I did collect and supplied the U.S. Government under the conditions of risk of my life [sic].

However, nothing, with the exception of [sic] few minutes conversations in these matters, had been accomplished up to date. This is astonishing . . . I cannot accept various explanations about this or other lack of cooperation inside of the Agency, and that is not my business to clarify the positions of conflict between the Eastern Europe Division, and Chief, Counterintelligence [sic].[33]

The letter was a further indication of Goleniewski's limited tolerance for those who declined to heed his advice, and an omen of future battles – both inside the CIA and between the Agency and its star defector. The following month, in an attempt to restore a measure of calm, an officer from the Eastern Europe Division wrote to him (as Franz Oldenburg):

> Five years ago tomorrow, your original 'bomb' was dropped on the Embassy in Bern. The reverberations are still being felt. A great deal has happened since then and, while you or I might not feel that everything has been done correctly or most efficiently at every turning point, the results have been, and are, impressive and are of the utmost importance to our agency and government.
>
> I can assure you that everyone here recognizes and appreciates this. Those who are aware of our future planning are equally confident of future success. With best wishes to you and Irmgard. 'Paul'.[34]

Goleniewski's unprecedented run of successes prompted him to demand an end to his probationary period. He felt he had proved his worth and now he wanted the recognition he had been promised. At the end of April he wrote to 'the Administration of American Intelligence', asking for a 'definite decision' on a full contract of employment, and to have 'a personal talk with high officials of American Intelligence'. The CIA, however, seemed strangely reluctant to make good on its earlier commitments: according to one of Goleniewski's subsequent affidavits, the letter resulted in little more than vague assurances of future assistance:

> In answer, instead of help, care and the settling of delinquent obligations of American Intelligence in a humane and just manner there arose only pressures on me, by taking advantage of my isolation, my dangerous situation, and favors were granted exclusively on the whim of American Intelligence, with the purpose of

keeping my status quo of illegality and with empty words promise [sic] to settle urgent matters in an indefinite period of time.[35]

The Agency did, however, react to Goleniewski's fears about his
'dangerous situation'. It had good reason to take the couple's personal security seriously, since an inquiry by the Senate Internal
Security Subcommittee (SISS) had determined that the Soviet
Union was in the habit of assassinating its renegade spies, and doing
so on American soil. The SISS report ruled that the apparent sui-
cides of two earlier defectors were instead carefully staged murders
carried out by the KGB.[36]

With this in mind, Langley HQ instructed the New York City Police
Department to issue a handgun licence to Goleniewski, and provided
him with one of its own stock of automatic pistols for protection.[37] It
was, though the Agency could not have known it, a particularly timely
precaution.

In Warsaw, the UB was then stepping up its attempts to locate its
former officer and had tasked an undercover agent in the United
States to track him down and deliver 'a clear signal that his former
colleagues in the department were still interested in him'.[38] Within
weeks, Soviet bloc intelligence had further reason to target Goleniewski when the Swedish security service arrested Colonel Stig
Wennerström in Stockholm, and quickly secured a full confession to
spying for Moscow. As with Houghton, Blake, Beer and Felfe, without
Goleniewski's information the GRU's long-time agent EAGLE would
not have been uncovered.[39]

For the CIA this was – or should have been – additional reinforce-
ment of Goleniewski's remarkable run of success. But in the corridors
of Langley, trouble was brewing between two increasingly antagonistic factions inside the Agency. While one continued to champion
Goleniewski, and set in train Congressional recognition of his contributions to American national security, the Counter-Intelligence

Division under James Angleton was working behind the scenes to bring him down.

The cause was the arrival, almost two years earlier, of a rival Soviet intelligence source: a 'mid-level' KGB officer who insisted that he – and he alone – was a genuine defector. Half of the Agency viewed the man as dangerously insane, but Angleton swallowed the claims completely. During that summer of 1963, Goleniewski's fate hung in the balance as the two antagonistic cliques fought for supremacy at Langley.

18

Monster

A LITTLE AFTER 6 p.m. on Friday, 15 December 1961 a short, thick-set man in his mid-thirties rang the doorbell of a private residence in a quiet Helsinki suburb. He was wearing a heavy coat and fur hat to protect him against the sub-Arctic winter; a similarly dressed woman and young girl waited behind him.

The house in Haapatie Street belonged to Frank Friberg, the CIA's head of station in Finland. When he opened the door, the man introduced himself, in halting and Russian-accented English, as Anatole Klimov; he said the woman was his wife and the child their daughter. He wasted little time on pleasantries, instead quickly demanding asylum for himself and his family.

Friberg knew that his unexpected visitor's name was not Klimov. The Agency kept detailed files on Moscow's officials in Helsinki, and the man in front of him matched the photograph of Major Anatoliy Golitsyn, a mid-level KGB officer based at the Soviet Embassy. Walk-in defections were exceptionally rare – and turning up at a station chief's home was unheard of – but since Russian intelligence officers seeking to change sides remained a precious commodity, Friberg ushered the family into his sitting room to open the first careful stage of the established asylum request negotiations. It did not go to plan.

It was standard CIA practice to ask would-be defectors to postpone their escape and instead to operate undercover, as Goleniewski had done voluntarily, as an Agent in Place. This provided two significant benefits for the Agency: ongoing access to Moscow's secrets, and sufficient time for its counterintelligence specialists to work up a detailed profile of the subject.

Golitsyn pre-empted the suggestion. He insisted that he and his family had to be flown out of Finland within two hours; his KGB masters would shortly begin searching for him, so this timetable was, he stressed, non-negotiable.

Friberg moved remarkably quickly. He booked seats on the eight o'clock commercial flight to Stockholm – all reserved under false names – and arranged for fake travel and identity documents to be couriered over. He also flashed an urgent message to Langley and then rushed the family to the airport; they made the flight just in time for take-off.

The group spent the night in a CIA safe house in Sweden, then flew to the US military airbase at Frankfurt am Main, close to the Defector Reception Centre at Wiesbaden. They did not, however, go there: Golitsyn persuaded Agency officials that his exfiltration was too urgent to be delayed by the sort of lengthy debriefing Goleniewski had undergone in Germany just eleven months earlier.

'He thought that the plane was going to be bombed,' Friberg recalled in 1989. 'He said that the Soviets would stop at nothing to get him if they knew where he was.'[1] Instead, the CIA bought tickets for a commercial flight – an initial attempt to leave on an ancient cargo plane had to be abandoned – bound for the United States via London. But even these emergency arrangements did not satisfy Golitsyn. 'I can't believe you don't have a plane to fly me direct to Washington,' he complained to Friberg. 'Why did you put me on such a *slow* plane?'[2] It was an inauspicious beginning, but one which revealed the defector's arrogance towards his benefactors, and foreshadowed the 'monster' – as the Agency later described it – he would shortly unleash.

What made this all the more remarkable was the paucity of material he brought with him. For a man who would shortly ruin dozens of lives and paralyse at least two intelligence services, Golitsyn arrived bearing just twenty-three KGB documents; none had any real value.[3] This threadbare haul was in contrast to the several hundred Minox frames and reams of Soviet bloc secrets that Goleniewski handed over – let alone the thousands he had sent with the Sniper letters. Despite this, according to an internal analysis of his case, produced by the Agency in 2011 and 'based almost entirely on classified studies and papers written by senior CIA officers', Golitsyn demanded the CIA accept both his motives and his value as a defector. 'As the precipitating factor in his decision, he cited disagreements with the KGB resident in Helsinki. He went on to say that he wanted to fight "the evil inherent in the KGB and Soviet system", and he asked for $10 million[4] for the effort.'[5]

If he failed to prise this substantial sum from Langley's coffers, his treatment over the coming weeks was extraordinarily preferential for a defector who, by his own account, was no more than a mid-ranking KGB officer with little field experience and no real access to Moscow's secrets. In late December the CIA stashed the family Golitsyn in a safe house in rural Virginia and prepared for what it expected to be a lengthy – if standard – debriefing; according to a highly classified Agency investigation into his case in 1976, this was intended to confirm 'His own biographic data, family background and career, and his knowledge of the structure, organization, personalities and operations of the KGB. What he said was checked against CIA files and formed the basis for his acceptance within weeks of arrival into the United States as a bona fide defector.'[6]

The CIA's investigations revealed that Major Anatoliy Mikhailovich Golitsyn had been born in August 1926 to a 'humble Ukraine family'. He joined the Soviet Army at the age of eighteen, and in 1945 was briefly assigned to a military counterintelligence unit.

After the war this was taken over by the KGB, and in 1951, Golitsyn was transferred to the counterintelligence section focused on the United States. A two-year tour of duty at the Soviet Embassy in Vienna was followed in 1955 by a four-year deployment to a KGB school. Finally, in August 1960, he was sent to Helsinki, then an undemanding backwater of the Cold War. He remained there until his defection sixteen months later.[7]

His transition from interrogation to acceptance was, however, far from trouble-free. The CIA found Golitsyn – now given the cryptonym AELADLE – almost impossible to control and, largely at the behest of James Angleton's counterintelligence staff, the Agency broke almost every one of its rules for the handling of defectors.

'Golitsyn was very demanding and very much a prima donna from the beginning,' its 2011 analysis recorded; worse, he exhibited a worrying tendency to embellish his credentials. He told his interrogators that in 1952 he had personally briefed Stalin on recommendations for a reorganization of KGB operations; the Soviet leader's death the following year, Golitsyn claimed, had been the only reason the plan was abandoned. It was an improbable tale, but one which, strangely, passed unchallenged: 'It is not clear whether any independent corroboration of this incident was ever obtained. On the face of it, it seems highly unlikely that Golitsyn, at the time a junior officer in the KGB, would have gotten an audience with Stalin.'[8]

If the volume of KGB documents he brought with him was small, it exceeded the counterintelligence information he had to offer. 'The only substantive CI lead he provided up front was his "knowledge of a penetration of CIA in Germany",' the CIA's report noted. This turned out to be a supposed double agent of Russian origin who had served in US intelligence in West Germany during the early 1950s; Golitsyn called him 'Sasha'. He told the debriefers that although he had seen a document detailing the mole's real name, date and place of birth, and the region in the Soviet Union where his parents had lived, he could not now remember them; all he could offer was that the traitor's name sounded Polish, began with the letter K and ended with the far from unusual suffix '-ski'. 'Unfortunately,' as the Agency analysis ruefully recorded, 'Golitsyn made this the cornerstone of his hypothesis about multiple senior-level penetrations of CIA.'[9] He did so, however, while simultaneously admitting he had no evidence to justify his theory:

During this period Golitsyn made no claim to having information regarding KGB penetrations of CIA beyond Sasha. In his early debriefings he asserted that Western intelligence was well penetrated by the KGB, but said nothing about CIA. In fact, at one point he 'excluded the possibility that the KGB had any agent placed as high as a country desk in CIA.'[10]

Of the few other leads he provided, none 'was new or timely', and one – a KGB penetration of the US Army Security Agency – had been exposed eleven years before with the arrest of the Ukrainian-American cryptanalyst and NKVD agent-handler, William Weisband.[11]

Despite this meagre 'take', Golitsyn was given unusually preferential treatment during his debriefing period. The bizarre circumstances of his lie-detector tests encapsulated the Agency's inexplicable tolerance of his demands. Polygraphs were not simply standard operating practice, but a requirement for all defectors seeking sanctuary in the United States. Golitsyn initially refused point-blank to submit to the examination, and according to the CIA's 1976 report, only agreed to do so after Angleton's counterintelligence division rewrote the long-established test procedures:

> Golitsyn was given two polygraph examinations, on 27 and 28 March 1962, by a polygraph officer of the Office of Security. The tests were administered under special ground rules . . .
>
> It was agreed at that time that Golitsyn was to be regarded as a 'special case'; his 'flap potential' was regarded as high, because high US government officials were aware of Golitsyn's allegations that the US government and CIA were penetrated at a high level, and these allegations had been accepted to that point by CIA without reservations.

The 'unusual manner in which the tests were conducted' included an agreement 'that Golitsyn should be disturbed as little as possible by the questions asked during the polygraph so that he would not feel personally offended and as a result become "sour", unmanageable or uncooperative. Furthermore, that no indication should be given to Golitsyn during testing that there were any doubts as to his reliability.'[12]

The outcome of this wholesale deviation from Agency practice was predictable. At the end of the tests, the polygraph operator told Golitsyn they showed he had been 'substantially truthful'. But since this reflected only the pre-agreed conditions that he should not be told anything which indicated otherwise, the supposed result was meaningless. The conclusion, recorded in files which would remain locked inside the CIA's archives for the next fifty-five years, was that Golitsyn's lie detector tests were completely unreliable:

> A review of the operator's report reflects everything except a clear-cut statement of whether or not Golitsyn lied or did not lie to any of the questions. The report states that the first day's testing was inconclusive. The results [sic] of the second day's testing is not set forth. The report is rather remarkable for this reason.
>
> The conditions and limitations placed on the (polygraph) officer . . . imposed a set of procedures that preclude and make impossible any unequivocal statement that a conclusive (polygraph examination) was conducted.[13]

Despite this fundamental problem, throughout 1962 the Agency continued to handle Golitsyn with the softest of kid gloves. He responded to this indulgence by making a succession of demands for further special treatment; in particular, he railed against the security measures in his safe house, regularly complaining about the presence of the CIA's guards and insisting that he alone should decide how to protect his family from possible KGB retaliation. By the summer he had worn the Agency down:

> In July 1962, when Golitsyn moved into his own house, [he] was given complete personal control of the guards, their hours of duty and their responsibilities. From that point on, Golitsyn was essentially unguarded.

His wife also railed against her 'companions' in the early days. She made frequent trips into Washington to shop or to attend movies, theater or ballet. At these times she would dismiss her chauffeur for lengthy periods. On two occasions she took the bus alone to New York for the day, and Golitsyn also visited New York in November 1962, at which time he roamed the city unescorted.[14]

If Goleniewski had also been demanding, neither he nor any previous defector had been allowed to dictate terms to his benefactors in the way that Golitsyn did. Therefore, coupled with his growing avarice, Soviet Division officers within the CIA were viewing him with increasing suspicion. They reluctantly concluded that someone outside their unit was putting a very heavy thumb on the scales which should have been weighing his value, and they knew the culprit's name: James Angleton.

By then, many officers – frustrated at Angleton's refusal to allow any scrutiny of his allegations of, much less evidence for, wholesale Soviet penetration of their ranks – had come to view Angleton as either a fantasist or a cunning liar. Either conclusion, they reasoned, explained his unwavering support for Golitsyn's wafer-thin theories.

'He [Golitsyn] is a conman,' George Kisevalter, one of the Agency's most experienced agent handlers, said in a 1988 interview. 'He thought "I could bullshit Americans." And he did. And he decided "I'll use Angleton because he is the softest." He's a con artist. And a con artist is always the biggest sucker for another con artist.'[15]

But by the time he began interfering in Golitsyn's case, the forty-five-year-old Angleton had been chief of the Counter-Intelligence Staff for eight years and was well on the way to achieving complete domination of the entire Agency. He had 'no-knock' privileges, allowing him to walk into the CIA Director's office without appointment and, according to its subsequent post-mortem analysis, 'wielded immense authority, particularly on operations against the Soviet Union'.[16]

Remarkably, he had achieved this success despite not speaking a word of Russian and, according to David Robarge, the CIA's chief in-house historian, having no experience of running a KGB spy:

> He was not a Soviet case officer. Notwithstanding Angleton's pro-found knowledge of Soviet intelligence affairs, he never handled a Soviet agent until Anatoli [sic] Golitsyn . . . His CI staff, which at one time had a few hundred employees, was surprisingly thin on Soviet field expertise and had few Russian linguists (Angleton was not one). These weaknesses, combined with the CIA's contin-ual paucity of good Soviet sources during the early Cold War, left Angleton and his shop vulnerable to the manipulations of a use-ful but self-promoting and manipulative defector such as Golitsyn.[17]

Even Robarge's distinctly respectful 2003 account – much of which con-flicts with the damning assessments in the Agency's internal and (then) unpublished documents – records that the CIA's most senior manage-ment knew and accepted this without question, just as they tolerated Angleton's 'unorthodox' and dangerous work practices:

> He arrived at the CI Staff's suite late in the morning and left late in the evening. His curtain-shrouded office was dimly-lit, hazy with cigarette smoke, and full of scattered files and papers. His lunch 'hour' often lasted well into the afternoon, spent at restaurants mainly in Washington with liaison partners, oper-ational contacts and professional colleagues. His capacity for food (despite his wraith like appearance) and liquor was remarkable, and towards the end of his career he was probably an alcoholic . . .
>
> He was secretive and suspicious. Angleton enveloped himself and his staff in an aura of mystery, hinting at knowledge of dark secrets and hidden intrigues too sensitive to share. He often sat silent through operational meetings and shared his information selectively with only a chosen few whom he had indoctrinated personally.

He took standard compartmentation precautions to an extreme, using safes and vaults to hide hundreds of linear feet of files and papers that he never integrated into the regular operations records system ... He often bypassed Agency channels, cultivating private relationships with sources and foreign services independent of the area of divisions.[18]

Worse, according to the CIA's internal 1976 analysis, the truth about Angleton's apparently unchallengeable expertise was that much of it was no more than smoke and mirrors:

In truth, no one *could* compete with him. His analyses, based on fragmentary and often incomplete data, were more imaginative than systematic and therefore neither easily comprehended nor replicated by his interlocutors.

But unlike the Emperor and his imaginary clothes, Chief CI's fantasies were never vulnerable to objective examination, simply because he surrounded such data as existed with a wall of secrecy. His 'facts' were available in full only to a minimum number of trusted apostles; to the rest of the intelligence community, both American and foreign, he doled them out selectively – seldom in written form – to prove whatever point he was trying to make at the time.[19]

By 1962, Angleton's most dominant conviction was that 'the KGB had penetrated the CIA at high levels and that it had taken advantage of these penetrations to run agent provocations against the Agency'. Golitsyn's matching claims – whether supported by evidence or not – were the gospel he had been waiting to hear preached. That the CI chief had previously dismissed Goleniewski's similar and much-better supported warnings seemed not to trouble him in the slightest.

Angleton's problem, however, was that for all his influence he did not have day-to-day control over his new prophet. That autumn Golitsyn was still being handled by the Soviet Division – and it was both deeply disturbed by the defector's mental state and running out of patience with his demands:

> Golitsyn was diagnosed early in 1962 as a 'paranoid personality'. Although account was taken of this psychological problem, it was considered in the light of a threat to the continuity of the debriefing process rather than as a factor reflecting on the validity of the purported intelligence he gave us. It was apparently felt that, if we could maintain his stability, we could depend not only upon the objectively verifiable facts he gave us but also upon his often very theoretical generalizations.[20]

Maintaining that 'stability' was becoming increasingly difficult. Golitsyn demanded audiences with President John Kennedy, FBI chief J. Edgar Hoover and the CIA's recently installed Director, John McCone; he also insisted that he should be given the right to read all counterintelligence dossiers held by the Agency and the Bureau. For the moment, both services held firm against access to their files, and he was refused permission to speak with JFK and Hoover; but he was granted two meetings with Attorney General Robert Kennedy, and several with McCone. He harangued both with a new hypothesis that the United States and its intelligence agencies were being duped by a long-term Soviet deception programme in which the KGB would use 'false defectors to discredit him'; when this warning fell on deaf ears – not least because he could produce little evidence to support it – and when his request for $15 million[21] in US government funding was rebuffed, Golitsyn flounced off.[22]

'By September 1962', the CIA's 2011 analysis recorded, 'things began to go south with Golitsyn. At that point he "went on strike" and refused to be debriefed . . . In February 1963 Golitsyn seemed to have given up helping the United States and moved his family to the UK, officially becoming a defector to the British. At first he appeared to be content with British handling, but he gradually became disenchanted and returned to the United States.'[23]

His stay in London lasted barely more than half a year and yielded little of substance, but when he arrived back in America, Golitsyn found his case was under new and much more tolerant US management. The Soviet Division had been replaced by Angleton and his Counter-Intelligence Staff; they alone would be in full control of his next round of debriefings. It was, in every way, a disastrous outcome. The seven months Golitsyn had spent with MI5 had not diminished his rampant ego, his taste for conspiracy theories or his appetite for money. At Angleton's prompting, a new audience was arranged with McCone, in which Golitsyn told the Director that British Prime Minister Harold Wilson was a KGB agent and that the 1956 Sino–Soviet split – in which Moscow and (then) Peking broke off political relations – was an elaborate KGB disinformation operation. Both claims were entirely without merit, but they fitted neatly into the CIA counterintelligence chief's tortured thinking, and by the Agency's own analysis laid the ground for the next ruinous steps:

> Golitsyn also began to insist that he be accepted as an equal by CIA and FBI, not as a Soviet defector, and be given full access to appropriate CIA and FBI files to uncover high-level penetrations of the US Government and other Western intelligence services . . . He [said he] should have total access to relevant materials (ie: CIA personnel and operational files) [and] he would apply his KGB background and experience to analyse these materials . . . He would [then] provide his analysis and recommendations for action.[24]

Angleton granted these unprecedented demands. He gave Golitsyn an office, complete with secretary and research assistant, in the Langley complex and arranged a 'welcome home gift' of $200,000[25] from Agency funds, as well as the services of a lawyer and a personal stockbroker.[26] He also cheerfully accepted his lodestar's insistence on living in New York City rather than Washington DC – a decision Golitsyn justified by the need 'to have more privacy and separation from CIA.'[27]

But the most damaging development was the counterintelligence chief's decision to allow Golitsyn to comb through hundreds of top-secret files for evidence to support his theory that the Agency had fallen victim to Moscow's devious disinformation schemes. Among those dossiers were the CIA's detailed accounts of Goleniewski's defection and its analyses of his intelligence revelations:

> Angleton looked to Golitsyn to help him unravel these purported KGB operations; he used Golitsyn as a sounding board to weigh the bona fides of other Soviet defectors and volunteers; and predictably, Golitsyn found them all wanting.[28]

Based on these self-proclaimed expert assessments, Angleton concluded that across the entire history of Cold War defectors only Golitsyn was genuine. The others were all Soviet bloc 'provocations' or 'dangles': 'Golitsyn was the only litmus test. Any variation from his information or interpretation – which were not always reliable or accurate, and sometimes were ludicrous – was deemed deception.'[29]

Chief amongst these dangerous deceivers – in Angleton's mind – was Goleniewski. Although he had 'provided CI [counterintelligence] information that was highly damaging to the KGB', the CIA's internal post-mortem reported, 'Angleton never accepted Goleniewski as a bona fide defector.' Worse, he was now convinced that the Agency's former agent was something much worse: a Trojan Horse cunningly dispatched by Moscow to deceive Western intelligence and to lure the CIA in particular down false trails.

The timing of this was telling. The summer of 1963 marked the moment when Goleniewski noticed the first signs that his leads were no longer being vigorously pursued, and the date when he began raising serious concerns about the Counter-Intelligence Staff's attitudes towards him.

Nor was the problem confined to an increasing freeze in his relations with Langley. To enhance his credentials, Golitsyn began borrowing liberally from Goleniewski's information, and claimed credit for some of the major cases he had exposed. A later CIA interview with Donald Deneslya, the 'administrative assistant' Angleton provided to Golitsyn, recorded that he claimed to have 'turned up traitors in many Western countries . . . He told us about Felfe and Klemens [sic] who had penetrated the Gehlen Organization.'[30]

Since Heinz Felfe and Hans Clemens had been arrested more than a month before Golitsyn defected, the claim was palpably false. But his dishonesty went far beyond appropriating the glory of his predecessor's individual case triumphs: he stole, wholesale, the evidence to buttress his overarching hypothesis that the KGB and its satellite intelligence services had duped the CIA with a long-term programme of strategic disinformation.

That information was contained in Goleniewski's files. As the Agency's 1976 analysis recorded, he had been the first defector to provide explicit details of the operation:

> The *dezinformatsiya* [disinformation] concept was first highlighted for CIA by the senior Polish UB officer, Michal Goleniewski . . . The information he provided was of major significance, as he had dealt with the KGB on the subject of *dezinformatsiya* from as early as 1953 and was in fact not only a ranking Polish intelligence officer but also a KGB agent . . . he was the first to bring it to CIA consciousness as a technique to be reckoned with in our analysis of the USSR's foreign policy.
>
> Specifically, Goleniewski stated that one of the many objectives of KGB *dezinformatsiya* was the protection of Soviet agents by means of action designed to mislead Western security services. He listed among specific objectives and types of *dezinformatsiya* operations those designed to confirm unimportant true information, thus establishing in the eyes of the opposition the reliability of a channel through which the KGB passes misleading information to anti-Soviet governments.
>
> Conversely, another type of *dezinformatsiya* operation might be designed to discredit accurate information of significance

received by the opposition through sources not under Soviet control, e.g., defectors, thus casting doubt on the veracity of the source or sources of this true information . . .

Another means might be the provision of 'give away' material, which neither added to information already in the hands of the opposition nor, by the same token, did any particular damage to the KGB. In extreme cases, the KGB would be willing to sacrifice some of their own agent assets in the interest of enhancing the reputation of an agent penetration of the anti-Communist intelligence services.[31]

This was almost word for word the story Golitsyn sold to Angleton as the rule by which everything the KGB did – and everything the CIA had done in response – was to be judged. What they jointly termed Moscow's 'Master Plan' would shortly cause such damage that those outside the Counter-Intelligence Staff referred to it as 'The Monster Plot'. It would paralyse Western intelligence and bring ruin on innocent officers and defectors alike; Goleniewski was the first victim.

If he did not then fully realize the havoc Golitsyn was wreaking – and there is no evidence that he even knew of the man's existence – that autumn Goleniewski had every reason to feel disorientated by the mixed messages emerging from Langley; as Angleton's apostles inside the Agency increasingly treated him as a threat to US national security, a rival faction had been pressing Congress to grant him the right to American citizenship.

19

HR 5507

M ICHAEL FEIGHAN WAS angry.

On Monday, 20 May 1963 a one-page document arrived at his Congressional Office: titled HR (House Resolution) 5507, it pronounced itself to be a 'Private Bill' to give a single individual 'relief' from existing US laws:

> The purpose of this bill is to provide that Michal Goleniewski shall be held and considered to have met the residence and physical presence requirements of section 316(a) of the Immigration and Nationality Act, and that he be exempted from the provisions of section 313 of that act. The beneficiary is a 40-year-old native and citizen of Poland who has been admitted to the United States for permanent residence and is employed by the U.S. Government.

Feighan had never heard of Michał Goleniewski, and HR 5507 contained little to enlighten him. It offered no detail about how, or when, the man had come to the United States nor which government agency now employed him – much less what he had done to earn the unusual privilege of specifically tailored legislation. The only clue as to the reason for its appearance on Feighan's desk that morning was a compliments slip from the chairman of the joint Senate and House Committee on Immigration, asking Feighan to pilot the Bill through the House of Representatives.

Michael Aloysius Feighan was then fifty-eight; a graduate of Princeton and Harvard Law School, for the past twenty-two years he had represented Ohio's 20th District in Congress and had earned a substantial reputation as one of the Democratic Party's most hard-working politicians. He had a lifelong loathing of communism and, in particular, of Moscow's clandestine efforts to undermine the West; at the beginning of May he had been presented with a 'Vigilant Patriot Award' by the All-American Conference to Combat Communism. The certificate, framed and proudly displayed on his office wall, honoured his 'outstanding contribution to public awareness and understanding of the communist menace to the freedoms of our nation'.[1]

Over his years in Congress, Feighan had developed a broad expertise on immigration cases, especially those involving refugees from Eastern Europe; it was this knowledge which earned him the chairmanship of the House Immigration and Nationality Subcommittee where, amongst other responsibilities, he oversaw applications for US citizenship. He had, though, one other distinguishing characteristic – one which sat oddly with his vehement anti-communism. From the moment of its inception, Michael Feighan had nurtured a deep-seated distrust of the organization charged with countering Moscow's espionage intrigues – and in return the CIA viewed him with some trepidation.

It was, perhaps, for this reason that the Agency had never bothered to inculcate Feighan into the cosy arrangements by which it habitually bypassed federal law to obtain US citizenship for Soviet bloc defectors.

The 1952 Immigration and Nationality Act had been passed at the height of the McCarthyite 'Red Scare' – the fear that communist spies had infiltrated almost every major sector of American political and cultural life. It was deliberately regressive, reversing more than 160 years of US immigration policy to exclude a broad swathe of what it termed undesirable 'aliens'. In addition to those 'not of good moral character' because they had committed adultery or had more than one wife, section 313 imposed a specific bar on naturalization applications by 'subversive classes' – those who had, in the previous ten years, belonged to the Communist Party, or a repressive state security organization.[2]

By their very nature, all Soviet bloc spies brought to the United States by the CIA fell into this category, so to circumvent the problem the Agency used tame members of Congress to sponsor private bills which waived the subversive classes impediment and enabled defectors to petition for naturalization.

Feighan, however, was not tame. Worse, according to the CIA's internal history of the period, he had been put in the position of 'sponsoring the citizenship bill without knowing either all the details of the case or the Agency's procedures for dealing with private legislation for defectors'. Unsurprisingly, he was 'irate' at the expectation that he would act as Langley's rubber stamp.[3] He picked up the phone and demanded to speak to the Director, John McCone.

There are no records of the ensuing conversation, but soon a further document landed on Feighan's desk. It was signed – evidently at the CIA's request, and inexplicably dated a week before the Bill was initiated – by the Immigration and Nationalization Service Commissioner, Raymond F. Farrell, and provided a somewhat inaccurate biography of Goleniewski to support HR 5507:

> The Bill would waive the provision of the Immigration and Nationality Act which prohibits the naturalization of aliens who were within the subversive classes during a period of 10 years immediately preceding the filing of a petition for naturalization. The bill would also grant the beneficiary sufficient residence and physical presence in the United States for naturalization and permit him to file a petition in any court having naturalization jurisdiction.
>
> The beneficiary, Michal Goleniewski, a native of Poland, was born August 16, 1922, in Nieswicz [sic]. His wife, Irmgard, is a native of Berlin and a citizen of Germany. They are now living in the United States. The beneficiary's education was all in Poland: in 1939 he graduated from the Gymnasium; he completed 3 years

of law at the University of Poznan, and in 1956 he received a master's degree in political science from the University of Warsaw. He enlisted in the Polish Army in 1945 and was commissioned a lieutenant colonel in 1955, which rank he held until coming to the United States in 1961. He is now employed as a consultant by the U.S. Government.

The beneficiary's one prior marriage terminated in divorce in Poland in 1957. He married Irmgard Kampf in 1961. Both the beneficiary and his present wife are permanent residents of the United States, having been lawfully admitted as of January 12, 1961.

Mr. Goleniewski was a member of the Communist Party of Poland from January 1946 until April 1958, when he defected. Without the enactment of H.R. 5507 the beneficiary will not be eligible for naturalization prior to 1968.

The Immigration and Naturalization Service has been advised that the contributions made by Mr. Goleniewski to the security of the United States are rated by the U.S. Government as truly significant. He has collaborated with the Government in an outstanding manner and under circumstances which have involved grave personal risk.

He continues to make major contributions to the national security of the United States. His primary motivation in offering to work with the Government has been and remains his desire to counter the menace of Soviet communism.

If the letter gave the wrong date for Goleniewski's defection, credited him with a degree he had not earned, and incorrectly asserted that he had been divorced prior to bigamously marrying Irmgard Kampf, it was enough to assuage Feighan's initial irritation. But he insisted that Goleniewski testify on oath; 'I'd like to see the live body,' he explained later. 'The man should make an appearance before all members of the subcommittee.'[4]

The demand provoked a further round of argument. The CIA was a branch of the executive, answerable directly to the President, and was accustomed to deference from the elected representatives on Capitol Hill. It had also, according to its General Counsel John S. Warner, fought previous battles to prevent Congress scrutinizing its importation of Soviet bloc defectors. '[The] head of Senate Judiciary, which has jurisdiction over immigration, said this is an impingement on the immigration authorities. I explained to him that this was not an immigration matter, that this was an operational matter to bring a very important alien into the country without regard to the special provision of the immigration laws.'[5]

Feighan, however, stuck to his guns until the Agency reluctantly gave in. On 27 May, flanked by Warner and officers from both the CIA and the INS, Goleniewski was brought to a closed session of the Subcommittee on Immigration and Nationality. It proved to be a brief hearing.

Although there are no official transcripts – nor even a record of the agenda – in US Congressional archives, according to Goleniewski's subsequent sworn affidavit he spoke only to confirm his name; for the remainder of the twenty-minute hearing, the CIA General Counsel described Agent Sniper's 'voluntary efforts and results on behalf of the national security of the United States, its western allies' and answered all the Committee's questions on his behalf.[6]

The perfunctory hearing satisfied the letter, but not the spirit, of the Agency's commitment, and Feighan left the committee room with a sense of foreboding; something in Goleniewski's strained and silent demeanour hinted at troubles to come. He did not have long to wait.

That summer of 1963 the CIA's changing attitude had begun to affect Goleniewski's equilibrium. The Agency had returned to playing psychological games, constantly switching between his real name and his two alternate identities, Franz Oldenburg and Martin N. Cherico. It had also assigned him a new and strangely hostile handler, whose cover name – 'Clemens' – was the same as that of one of the BND spies Goleniewski had exposed. There was no explanation for these unnecessary ploys, but coupled with the obvious slow progress of investigations into his leads and the rejection of his request to meet McCone, they began to destabilize Goleniewski's mental health.

In the middle of June he decided to bypass the CIA and take his concerns to the head of the US government. The letter he composed was long, rambling and confused, but since it was addressed to President John F. Kennedy at the White House it should have attracted attention:

> Dear Sir. It is very embarrassing for me that I must write this letter to you. I have to bring to your attention an urgent matter, along with my reason for presenting it to you.
>
> Since April 1958, that is without a break for the past five years, I have served, in an undercover status, the American Intelligence Service, and, in effect, the Government of the U.S., in security maters [sic] of the U.S. – and, at the same time, those of its western allies . . .

After setting out – at some length – his biography as a Soviet bloc intelligence agent, the spies he had exposed and the circumstances of his defection, Goleniewski turned to the CIA's failure to keep its promises:

> I voluntarily placed myself at the disposition of American Intelligence and offered to actively help American Intelligence because of patriotic reasons, political reasons, and because . . . I desired to battle the communist system and, at the same time, to insure [sic] the security of the USA and the West against the communist penetrations . . .
>
> In spite of my good intentions, sacrifice, patriotism and political beliefs, along with my great contributions to the security of the USA, the responsible officials of American Intelligence have not fulfilled their obligations to me, to my wife, and to my family . . .
>
> An agreement, reached between me and officials of American Intelligence, in effect a Gentleman's Agreement, concerning various important matters with regard to myself and my family, has been actually consistently broken.

> Instead of help, care and protection, American Intelligence mainly based its relations with me – without the slightest reason for this from my side – on moral and material pressures or problems, along with my enforced existence resulting from threats posed by the Red Intelligence . . .
>
> My wife and I, for the past 16 months, have lived under conditions which guarantee us absolutely no security and which force us into a complete isolation . . . Because of these conditions . . . I find myself on the verge of a dangerous heart condition . . .
>
> I have received none of the promised guarantees for my future existence, and for reasons of continually deteriorating state of health I do not know whether I shall be able to continue working. I do not have the necessary financial resources for the required medical treatment . . . or for helping my family . . .

Since, at the time of writing, HR 5507 was slowly wending its way through Congress, Goleniewski was careful to place on record his gratitude to whichever faction at Langley was supporting it; but he also stressed that until the CIA delivered the long-promised job and accompanying health coverage, he remained in a precarious position:

> In view of the above facts and the arising of a situation over which I had no control, I am forced to turn to you directly in a very urgent request to intervene in . . . satisfactorily settling . . . these extremely important matters for the safety and security of my life. The fact that I am forced to write such a letter to you is a matter of great shame and embarrassment to me.
>
> I hereby sign this letter – for security reason [sic] – with my code-name. I am forced to send this letter by regular mail. I do not know if this letter will come to you directly. I thank you in advance for your humane understanding and help – I remain, with expression of deepest respect, Very sincerely yours. Martin N. Cherico.[7]

The Presidential assistance Goleniewski sought did not materialize; no envelope bearing the White House stamp ever appeared at the apartment on Queens Boulevard. But, according to his own account, the letter provoked an angry response from Langley:

> The representatives of CIA . . . began to threat me [sic] in various ways, additional informing me that these complaint [sic] had been lost by some '. . . niggros [sic] in the White House, in the cellar . . .' and . . . informed me with regard to my complaint also that the US President 'is in no position' to order the CIA to do anything, and additional [sic] tried to threat me [sic] that in case I would make additional complaints to the US President, I would be sorry for such 'self-appointed . . . acts against the CIA'.[8]

The exact nature of those threats soon became apparent. When the temporary consultancy contract expired at the end of June, the Agency failed, without explanation, to renew it. Despite the generous sums he had already received, money once again became a problem and, with funds apparently running low, Goleniewski was forced to sell his second-hand Oldsmobile.[9]

A month later he tried to find a way round the dispute. He wrote to JFK's brother, Attorney General Robert F. Kennedy, pleading with him to put pressure on the CIA; but he also made a panicky phone call to Michael Feighan, claiming that he 'felt he was in grave danger' and asking the Congressman to visit him urgently.[10]

On 2 August, Feighan flew from Washington to New York. He was accompanied by two aides, his chief administrative assistant Dr Edwin O'Connor and Colonel Philip J. Corso, a recently retired Army intelligence officer who worked as an investigator for the Subcommittee; both were Russian specialists and Corso, in particular, had extensive experience of Soviet bloc spy operations.[11]

The meeting lasted a full day. Chain-smoking and pacing the floor, Goleniewski harangued his visitors in broken English about the risks he had taken on behalf of 'the national security of the USA and its western allies', and his frustration at the CIA's sudden change of attitude towards him. Tellingly, he explicitly tied this to the increasing influence wielded

Left: Michał Goleniewski in Polish Army uniform, late 1940s.

Below left: Goleniewski with his mother, Janina, and father, Michał, circa 1944–5.

Below right: Goleniewski with his mother, early 1950s.

Above left: The suave spy. Goleniewski during his employment as a Polish intelligence officer, mid-1950s.

Above right: Goleniewski with the family he abandoned: his mother, Janina, his first wife, Anna Diachenko, and two of their children; early 1950s.

Below: Bahnhoff Zoo, West Berlin. The railway station was close to the Soviet-controlled zone and in 1959 the CIA set up a 'dead drop' in the men's toilets for Goleniewski to leave his 'Sniper' letters and pick up instructions from Washington DC.

Above: The border between East and West Berlin in 1961. That January, Goleniewski spent five days evading East German and Polish intelligence surveillance agents before finally defecting at the US Consulate.

Left: The Silver Towers apartment block in Kew Gardens, Queens, New York City, where Goleniewski lived with Irmgard from 1962 until his death. The CIA reneged on its commitment to protect them and to support their rent.

Below left: Goleniewski in his Queens apartment, New York City, 1964. He sent the picture to his mother in Warsaw. Polish Intelligence intercepted and copied the photo.

Below right: Irmgard Goleniewska (*née* Kampf) in the couple's Queens apartment, New York City, 1964. Goleniewski sent the picture to his mother in Warsaw. Polish Intelligence intercepted and copied the photo.

Above left: The Portland Spies Harry Houghton and Ethel Gee, photographed by an MI5 surveillance team in 1960. Goleniewski's information led to their arrest and the discovery of a major Soviet intelligence network stealing British naval secrets.

Above right: Russian spy Konon Molody used the fictional identity of Gordon Lonsdale to mastermind the Portland Spy Ring. He was exchanged in a spy swap in 1964, and was photographed in East Berlin in 1965.

Right: Portland Spy Ring members Helen and Peter Kroger posed as innocuous book dealers, living in a quiet London suburb. In reality, they were American-born Soviet agents Lorna and Morris Cohen, on the run from the FBI. They were exchanged in a spy swap in 1969 and photographed en route to Heathrow airport.

Left: The Portland spies hid their one-time code pads in the hollowed-out bottoms of cigarette table lighters. The tiny papers contained secret messages to be transmitted to Moscow.

Left: In 1953, MI6 officer George Blake returned to a hero's welcome after two years in a North Korean prison camp. Eight years later, Goleniewski's information exposed Blake as a long-term Soviet spy who had betrayed some of the West's most vital secrets to Moscow. He was jailed for 42 years but escaped from prison and fled to Moscow in 1966.

Above: Goleniewski's information exposed senior German intelligence officers Heinz Felfe (**left**) and Hans Tiebel (**right**) as long-term Soviet spies. In July 1963 they were taken under close guard to court in Karlsruhe and received lengthy prison sentences.

Right: For more than a decade, Swedish Air Force officer Col. Stig Wennerström was a Soviet spy, betraying NATO and US secrets to Moscow. After Goleniewski's information exposed him, he was put on trial in Stockholm in April 1964 and sentenced to life in prison.

Right: The Monster: Anatoliy Golitsyn and his wife Svetlana, enjoying the high life at the Coconut Grove nightclub in the Ambassador Hotel, Los Angeles, in 1961. The CIA's acceptance of Golitsyn's false claim to be the only genuine Soviet Bloc defector paralysed Western intelligence for a decade – and was a major factor in Goleniewski's fall from grace.

Below left: James Jesus Angleton, the CIA's head of counterintelligence, never accepted Goleniewski as a genuine defector. Angleton's disastrous and fruitless search for a mole inside the Agency devastated US intelligence.

Below right: Senior MI5 officer Peter Wright was among the first British intelligence officers to be 'read in' to Goleniewski's revelations. Like his American mentor, James Angleton, Wright led a devastating and unsuccessful hunt for a traitor inside the Security Service.

Right: After a military court sentenced Goleniewski to death in absentia, Polish intelligence mounted a ten-year operation to locate and neutralize him. In 1968 its agents placed his apartment under surveillance, sending sketch maps of the location back to Warsaw.

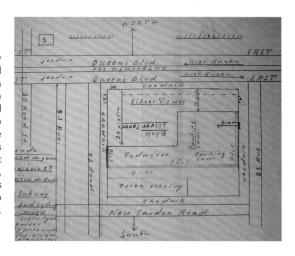

Left: New York City Marriage Registration Certificate for Aleksei N. Romanoff (Goleniewski) and Irmgard M. Kampf, 30 September 1964. Despite their previous wedding in Arlington, and Goleniewski's undissolved marriage in Poland, both he and Kampf swore on oath that this was their first marriage.

A 22146

THE CITY OF NEW YORK
OFFICE OF THE CITY CLERK
MARRIAGE LICENSE BUREAU—BOROUGH OF MANHATTAN

Marriage Register
No. 24955-1964

Certificate of Marriage Registration

This Is To Certify That _Aleksei N. Romanoff_

residing at _Peterhof, Russia_ born _August 12, 1904_

and _Irmgard M. Kampf_

residing at _Kew Gardens NY_ born _January 6, 1929_

at _Berlin Germany_

Were Married

on _September 30, 1964_ at _Kew Gardens, N.Y._

as shown by the duly registered license and certificate of marriage of said persons on file in this office.

Dated at the Municipal Building, Manhattan

October 7 19_64_

City Clerk of the City of New York

VOID IF ALTERED OR SEAL NOT IMPRESSED

Right: The Russian Orthodox Church New York City Parish Register recording the marriage of Aleksei Nicholaevich Romanoff (Goleniewski) and Irmgard M. Kampf, 30 September 1964. The ceremony was conducted by the Church's most senior priest in the United States.

АРХИЕРЕЙСКИЙ СИНОДЪ РУССКОЙ ПРАВОСЛАВНОЙ ЦЕРКВИ ЗАГРАНИЦЕЙ.
SYNOD OF BISHOPS OF THE RUSSIAN ORTHODOX CHURCH OUTSIDE OF RUSSIA.

ВЫПИСЬ ИЗЪ МЕТРИЧЕСКОЙ КНИГИ, ЧАСТИ ВТОРОЙ О БРАКОСОЧЕТАВШИХСЯ ЗА 1964 ГОДА.
EXTRACT FROM THE PARISH REGISTER, PART TWO ON MARRIAGES FOR THE YEAR

Double Eagle versus SS Order Under Death's Head

Left: From 1974 onwards, Goleniewski published his own monthly subscription 'bulletin', *Double Eagle*. The bulletin trumpeted his bogus Romanoff claims and his increasingly wild allegations of an international 'communo-fascist' conspiracy.

Below: Goleniewski in New York City, 1966. He was then approaching the apex of publicity for his claims to be the Tsarevich Aleksei Romanoff.

by Angleton (and therefore, by extension and unbeknownst to him, Golitsyn).

According to an off-the-record briefing given, several months later, by either Corso or O'Connor, Goleniewski also warned that the Agency was ignoring his claims that 'three American scientists with access to defense secrets were on the KGB payroll', and that 'several CIA men actually gave their first loyalty to the KGB or GRU'. Nor was Langley alone in turning a blind eye to alleged penetration of US government departments: Goleniewski complained that the State Department had covered up the activities of Edward Symans, a senior diplomat in Warsaw who 'had been spying for the Reds for 18 years'.[12]

Feighan, Corso and O'Connor carefully noted down the information and, on their return to Washington, each wrote an individual detailed memorandum about the meeting. Two days later Corso returned to New York for a second, lengthy interview; he took with him a subpoena requiring Goleniewski to appear before the Senate Internal Security Subcommittee.

There is, however, a curious gap in the documentation to confirm the details of this account. Michael Feighan was a tireless keeper of records from his years in the House: his official papers run to ninety-four boxes, occupying eighty-five cubic feet in Princeton University's archives, and they include extraordinarily detailed accounts of everything from Congressional battles fought to the recommendation of a new doorman for his apartment block. Yet although several folders contain references to a 'Goleniewski file', there is no trace of it in the collection – only the single-page original HR 5507 Bill.

There is a similar hole in the Congressional archives. The Senate Internal Security Subcommittee subpoena is missing; its interview with Goleniewski never took place. Instead, a one-page agenda sheet for 9 August shows that Corso was summoned to give evidence before SISS about 'Michal Goleniewski (alias Martin Cherico)'.[13] But there are no records of the evidence he gave in room 2300, New Senate Office Building, nor of what the elected representatives did with it.

However, one of the CIA's declassified official histories of the period shows that after the trip to New York, Feighan demanded a meeting with John McCone, and that Langley was sufficiently concerned about the encounter to work up a detailed dossier of 'background information' on Goleniewski for the Director. But before the meeting took place, Robert Kennedy unexpectedly stepped into the fray. On 14 August the Attorney General's office wrote to 'Franz Oldenburg' with a promise to bring the recalcitrant Agency back into line:

> The Attorney General has been informed by representatives of the Central Intelligence Agency of the pertinent aspects of your case and has expressed appreciation for the opportunity to become acquainted with it. The Attorney General has expressed a strong interest in having it settled in a manner equitable to you and the United States Government.
>
> This office has asked the Central Intelligence Agency, as the executive agency of the United States Government responsible for this case, to contact you regarding it. It is the Attorney General's earnest hope that this arrangement will be satisfactory.[14]

There was, initially, little sign of RFK's hopes for an 'equitable' resolution. At their meeting on 23 August 'the DCI [McCone] and other CIA officers persuaded Feighan to encourage Goleniewski to be more cooperative' – an odd exhortation since Langley, not its former star agent, had caused the breakdown in relations.

Five days later, HR 5507 passed its final stages in the House and the Senate, granting Goleniewski the right to apply for American citizenship. But even this positive news was overshadowed by the CIA's confusing behaviour. The Act referred to Michal Goleniewski, but – officially – no such person existed in the United States: it was 'Franz Roman Oldenburg' who had been lawfully admitted to the country in January 1961 and who had been married under Virginia law two months later. Worse, the Alien Registration Card he would need to prove his identity before a naturalization court hearing was in that entirely fictional name. In effect, HR 5507 was meaningless.

There was, though, some progress on the financial front. By the end of the month the pressure, either from Congress or the Kennedy administration, led to a softening in Langley's attitude. 'Agent Clemens' was once again dispatched to New York to reopen discussions about a contract of full employment, as well as what the Agency termed a 'restitution' payment to compensate the couple for the loss of their homes and pension rights in Poland and East Germany respectively.

Goleniewski's calculations for these losses were a strange mix of integrity and greed. Using some remarkably creative accountancy he estimated Irmgard's losses – her 'clothes, linen, furnitures [sic] household goods and electric appliances, china, crystal and silver ware, books, records etc., . . . her rights to retirement and . . . her savings accounts in East Berlin' – at $50,000; when he added in his own 'books, records, clothes, uniforms, rifles, pistols, gold watches, photoapparats [sic] valuable collections etc. and savings accounts' left behind in Warsaw, as well as his UB retirement and health benefits, the total exceeded $440,000 – more than $3.7 million today.

From this startling sum he 'voluntarily deducted' $220,000 – apparently as a gesture of goodwill – plus the $24,000 the CIA had given him in 1961 as payment for his years as an Agent in Place. Even so, the final tally was substantial – $196,000, worth $1.6 million today.

Although it had only Goleniewski's word to support these 'losses', the CIA largely accepted the figures and incorporated them into the long-promised contract of full employment on 7 October. Signed by David Murphy, now relocated from Berlin to Langley, it provided substantial benefits:[15]

> Effective upon the date of this agreement you will be compensated at the rate of $14,565.00[16] per annum (GS-15, Step One).[17] This sum is subject to Federal Income Tax and the income laws of the state of your residence.

You will be entitled to performance of duty death (life insurance) and disability as authorized by Federal Employees Compensation Act as amended. You will be entitled by Federal Employees Compensation Act, to the continuance of pay and allowances in a manner similar to that set forth in the Missing Persons Act[18] . . .

You are herein authorized to apply for enrolment in a health insurance program for certain selected employees, subject to all the terms and conditions of that program . . . You will be entitled to sick and annual leave, subject to the same rules and regulations applicable to Government employees. For the purpose of computing your annual leave entitlement, your length of service shall be presumed to date [from] 2nd April 1958.

The contract committed the CIA to contributing half of the $120 monthly rent for Goleniewski's apartment, and the cost of garaging his car – assuming he chose to buy a new one – since it was vital to his 'personal security'. It also made provision for his eventual retirement from government service:

Upon reaching age 62 you will receive an aggregate sum of $1,200 per month[19] up until you attain age 70. This amount will be comprised of: (1) A monthly payment of $500 which will not be subject to federal and state income taxes. (2) Social Security benefits due to you under the Social Security Act. (3) Any amounts received by you as permanent disability payments under the Federal Employees Compensation Act.

The salary and benefits were, by any standard, generous, but they were dwarfed by two additional lump-sum gratuities. Paragraph 7 provided recompense for the losses Goleniewski and Irmgard had incurred when they defected – though the majority of these were to be invested in an Agency trust fund and would be doled out in monthly dividend payments:

As restitution for the pension and other emoluments to which you and your wife were entitled from your homelands . . . and which were lost by your move to the United States, the Government will pay you the sum of $500 per month from the effective date of this contract until you attain the age 62 . . .

In order to obviate any difficulties caused by lack of documentation regarding your age, the parties to this contract agree to and recognize the fact that for the purposes of this contract you will be considered as having attained age 41 on October 1, 1963 . . .[20]

This amount is not subject to United States Federal and State income taxes. Payment will continue to you in the case of separation from the service for reasons other than health, ie: your resignation or notice of termination served to you by the United States Government . . . In the event of your death such payments will be paid to your surviving wife or children up until the time you would have attained age 62.

More immediately, the Agency agreed to top up this restitution allowance with a substantial tax-free signing-on bonus of $70,000 – equivalent to more than half a million dollars today.

There were also clear guarantees about Goleniewski's employment rights. His job was to be 'for an indefinite period', but although either side had the right to terminate it, he was required to give just thirty days' notice, while the Agency undertook to give him a full year's warning of any intention to end the arrangement.

For good measure it also expressed 'its willingness to provide aid and advice to assist you in obtaining non-governmental employment in the US economy', and recognized the need for Irmgard to earn her own living by promising to pay half of the cost of any 'reasonable training course' in which she chose to enrol.

Understandably, the CIA demanded value for all this expenditure. Goleniewski was required to 'accept assignments and relevant instructions . . . and [to] devote full time and attention to those matters, topics and requirements assigned to you by the Authorized Government Representative and [you] will refrain from engaging in or devoting any work to other problems'. There was also a clause concerning publicity:

> Any publication by you touching upon these matters will require the express approval and clearance of the Central Intelligence Agency . . . The Central Intelligence Agency, on its part, undertakes to apprise you in advance of publication of all information obtained expressly and solely from you and which is intended for public distribution and consumption . . .
>
> The Central Intelligence Agency . . . or the US Government also has the right, with your knowledge and consent (or, in certain cases, with your help), to publish or otherwise make use of material originating solely and exclusively with you . . . If any of your independent publication lies within the interest of the US Government, the Central Intelligence Agency will assist you, insofar as practicable and from the point of view of preserving your cover and security, in the publication of such material.

Publicity was, however, the very last thing Goleniewski wanted. He knew from experience that his former Soviet bloc masters would, at some stage, come looking for him and would not have his welfare in mind; he had no intention of making their job easier by revealing his new name or location, and he was grateful for the Agency's undertaking, specified in Clause 15 of the contract, to 'make every reasonable effort to provide adequate protection and security, which obligation will continue upon termination of this contract for any cause'.

If the question of his legal identity remained unresolved – the contract was issued in the name of Franz Oldenburg – by early December 1963, Goleniewski had reason to feel satisfied with the outcome of the negotiations. True, there had been unpleasant disagreements with the CIA's senior management, but he was now an official US government employee, comfortably provided for and living with his wife in a pleasant home under cover names no one outside Langley knew. As Christmas approached, he and Irmgard felt safe enough to contemplate starting a family of their own.

The Agency also helped him to undertake additional work for other intelligence services. At the beginning of the month, Agent Clemens brought 'a representative of the British government' to the Queens apartment for a consultation 'about information and leads concerning penetration by Soviet KGB of the British Security Service in London' – an occasion he used to hand Goleniewski, belatedly, MI5's letter of appreciation and silver tankard.[21]

But this brief period of calm was deceptive: within just four weeks the Agency would renege on the contract – and almost all of its commitments. It would throw its most productive spy back out into the cold.

20

Downfall

NEW YEAR'S EVE 1963 was surprisingly mild. For the first time in almost a decade, New York temperatures in the holiday season climbed above freezing and began to thaw the heavy snow which had blanketed the city since Christmas.

That morning Goleniewski was preparing to make what promised to be a troublesome trek from Queens to Manhattan. He had arranged an important appointment in midtown for early in the afternoon, but since the streets were slushy and still partially blocked, he anticipated his journey would take at least twice the usual twenty minutes.

Before he could leave, the doorbell rang. He opened the apartment door and, somewhat to his surprise, was confronted by Agent Clemens. He had not seen or heard from his handler since the joint meeting with MI5's envoy at the beginning of the month. In truth, the man's absence had been irritating. With the autumn's hostilities behind them, Goleniewski was anxious to get back to work, developing the intelligence leads he had already provided; so if the CIA officer's unscheduled appearance was unexpected, it was, nonetheless, welcome.

Clemens, however, had not travelled up from Washington to restart the interrupted sessions. Instead, he was the messenger chosen by Langley to deliver a distinctly unseasonal demonstration of the Agency's broken promises.

As an opening gambit he demanded the immediate return of the pistol it had provided as well as the firearms permit issued by NYPD.

Goleniewski refused both requests. The CIA had no right to impound the licence and he insisted that he would only hand over the gun to uniformed police officers. After an uncomfortable stand-off, Clemens moved on to the main reason for his visit: according to Goleniewski's subsequent account, Clemens informed him that the Agency was unhappy with its employee's location and his ability to concentrate fully on working on its behalf:

> As you know Washington DC has been selected as your work location by the Government in accordance with the terms of the agreement and this decision remains in force . . . [Also] other considerations appear to have become so important that it seems impossible for you to concentrate on Governmental work.[1]

Neither claim made any sense. Not only had the CIA helped Goleniewski find the apartment in Queens, the contract it had signed less than three months earlier specifically stipulated the building as his registered address, and committed the Agency to paying half the rent. Nor had it expressed any similar disquiet over Golitsyn's relocation to New York, even though his home was so close to Moscow's embassy that – in the Agency's own words – he was living 'almost under the eaves of the Soviet Mission'.[2]

Similarly, the suggestion that Goleniewski failed to fulfil his responsibilities was absurd; in fact, he had been waiting – more or less patiently – for Clemens to show up for work.

Thoroughly annoyed, Goleniewski told his handler to leave, dismissing the complaints as 'arrogant, stupid and absolutely nonsense'; he then set off for his meeting in midtown Manhattan. Three days later, and true to his word, he handed over the CIA's gun to NYPD and applied for a new licence for a replacement – a smaller-calibre weapon which would be easier for Irmgard to use in an emergency.[3] The response, from Edward J. McCabe, New York Police Deputy Commissioner in Charge of Licences, was revealing; on Langley's advice, the application was refused:

> With reference to your recent enquiry concerning the possible
> issuance of a pistol permit, please be advised that a review of our
> files discloses that the original pistol permit was issued . . . as a
> result of a request by a Federal Agency . . . We have been informed
> by the Federal Agency concerned that they feel there is no longer
> any justification for renewal of such permit.[4]

The implication was stark and unavoidable; the CIA had decided to cast
Goleniewski adrift. On 9 January 1964 it made this explicit, sending formal notice that he was suspended with immediate effect, pending an
internal investigation. The letter, from a 'contracting officer' named
David H. Embinder, also warned that all his salary payments and benefits would cease by the middle of the month:

> Dear Mr. Oldenburg. Reference is made to your agreement
> with the United States Government, as represented by the
> Central Intelligence Agency, effective 7 October 1963. The
> Authorized Government Representative has brought to my
> attention a number of facts which appear to warrant a deter-
> mination that you have failed in a number of respects to fulfill
> your obligations under said agreement with the United States
> Government.
>
> Pending further review and a final determination, the United
> States Government hereby advises you that as of 15 January 1964
> the compensation specified under paragraph 5 of said agreement
> will be suspended until further written notice to you. This action
> is equivalent to placing you, as an employee of the United States
> Government, in a leave without pay (LWOP) status. This action
> does not affect restitution payments of $500.00 per month as
> specified under paragraph 7 of said agreement.
>
> You are reminded of your secrecy obligations under para-
> graph 14 and your obligations with respect to publication of
> writings under paragraph 16 of said agreement with the United
> States Government.[5]

Goleniewski was now seriously frightened. For some reason he could not understand – neither Clemens nor Embinder had explained exactly what transgression he had committed – the Agency was cutting off his financial lifeblood. Until its internal review was completed, he would receive no salary and would have to meet the substantial apartment rent and all living costs either from his savings or the monthly restitution instalments.

The timing, too, was strange. Just a few days later, on 14 January, the latest successful prosecution of one of the spies Goleniewski had exposed took place in Paris; Joseph Bitonski, a Polish journalist working undercover in France on behalf of Polish intelligence was sentenced to four years in prison for espionage.[6] Two weeks later, the Senate Internal Security Subcommittee took up the case of Edward Symans, the US diplomat Goleniewski had identified as a KGB agent. In a closed-doors hearing, SISS counsel Jay Sourwine put on the record allegations that Symans had contacts with 'known agents of the Soviets – that includes the Soviet secret police', and that he had 'been compromised by a Polish female or Polish females'.

But despite vigorous cross-examination, the State Department's witness, Victor H. Dikeos, refused to answer the charges, citing an Executive Order designed to protect national security;[7] the most he would concede was that the claims against Symans had been investigated and, just as Goleniewski had complained, that the diplomat had been allowed to resign.[8]

Something very serious had evidently occurred to sabotage Goleniewski's relationship with the US government. There was no legitimate reason for the CIA's hostility: according to its own internal assessment – kept secret for several decades – at that point the Agency considered him to be 'an accurate and reliable source of intelligence'.[9] But, isolated in his Queens apartment, with no further visits from his handlers, Goleniewski could not guess the most likely – and malign – explanation: that he was the victim of Golitsyn's growing domination inside Langley.

Cowed by the CIA's blunt warning that he remained sworn to secrecy, he agonized over his limited options.

Since he was, effectively, forbidden to speak to anyone outside Langley's closed corridors he realized he could not turn to Michael Feighan or his Congressional aides; in desperation, he fired off a flurry of urgent pleas to John McCone, complaining about the 'arbitrary decisions and phony argumentations [sic]' of Agent Clemens, the failure of Embinder to provide any justification for the suspension, and asking for help. From the middle of January to the end of the month he sent three letters – all by registered mail – to the CIA Director; none were answered.

At the beginning of February, Goleniewski was given extra cause for concern when Irmgard told him that she was pregnant and that their baby was expected in the autumn. Antenatal care – let alone the potentially difficult business of a highly stressed thirty-five-year-old refugee giving birth to her first child without any familial support – would be very expensive, and since the decision to place him on LWOP status also removed his right to Agency health coverage, Goleniewski faced having to shoulder the substantial medical bills alone.

Within a week that impending problem turned into an immediate crisis. A routine medical check revealed that Irmgard had a lump in her breast and needed exploratory surgery to determine whether the tumour was malignant. With nowhere else to turn, Goleniewski wrote again to McCone, asking for assistance and explaining that 'this problem bringing for us not only new complications, since we were already more than 3 years in the United States and still without any health and hospitalization insurance . . . causing in addition tremendous expenses – especially in view of enforced status of employee-leave's [sic] without pay'.

He also reminded the Director that both he and Irmgard had been granted political asylum in the United States, had been promised Washington's support and protection, and that not only 'the life of my exhausted wife was under heavy risk in these circumstances but even the life of the unborn baby'.[10] Once again, McCone chose not to reply.

All Goleniewski could do was to wait for the Agency's internal review to clear him of whatever he was supposed to have done wrong.

On 10 February that hope was dashed. A second letter from David Embinder rejected Goleniewski's complaints and confirmed the original suspension:

> Your letter of January 24, 64 has been thoroughly reviewed. You are advised that the United States Government decision conveyed to you by letter on 9 January 1964 is hereby reaffirmed. Effective 15 January 1964 the compensation specified under paragraph 5 of your agreement with the United States Government effective 7 October 1963 has been suspended pending a final determination and until further notice to you.
>
> You are again reminded of your secrecy obligations under paragraph 14 [of the contract] and your obligation with respect to publication of writings under paragraph 16 of the above agreement with the United States Government.[11]

Two days later, a Treasury Department cheque for $500.50 landed on the mat in the Queens apartment. A brief accompanying note explained that this was the entirety of his outstanding salary for January 1964, and reminded him that, since he was deemed to be on 'Leave Without Pay' (LWOP), no further sums would be sent.

Goleniewski promptly sent the money back to Langley, angrily rejecting both the payment and disputing the legality of the LWOP decision. The CIA accepted the former and ignored the latter; from then on the Agency would hold no further debriefing sessions with its former star defector.

Nor is there any evidence that the internal review was ever concluded; instead Goleniewski was simply abandoned on a notional LWOP status, apparently indefinitely. Deprived of his salary and having to pay the full apartment rent, while his pregnant wife needed emotional support as well as expensive surgical and post-operative care, Goleniewski's already-fraying mental state was being pushed dangerously towards a crisis.

But there was an additional effect of Langley's behaviour – and one which would shortly affect his own physical safety. Until it abandoned him, the Agency had allowed Goleniewski to send letters to his mother in Warsaw via a secure CIA operative in Rome. With that cut-out route now closed, he was forced to find a replacement and much more open channel; with few options available, he appears to have reverted to the contacts he made as a Soviet bloc spy, choosing a business acquaintance in Lausanne, Switzerland.

Polish intelligence was then actively searching for its deserter, with a view to carrying out the death sentence imposed by the Military Court. It knew that he was likely to contact his mother, and in February broke into Janina Goleniewska's apartment while she was away on holiday. UB agents rifled through her mail and found letters sent from the new cut-out and in which – unlike those forwarded by his CIA predecessor – his name was spelled out; discovering the go-between's identity brought Warsaw's vengeful espionage service one step closer to locating Goleniewski himself.[12]

By the end of February the one small consolation that Goleniewski could cling to was that no news of his survival – much less his whereabouts – had leaked out. Although HR 5507 was, in theory, a public document available for inspection in Congressional records, neither Feighan nor any of his committee had spoken about the Bill, and the case of America's most prized intelligence asset had not attracted any press coverage.

Then, at the beginning of March 1964, after three years of carefully guarded secrecy, his cover was blown in a single afternoon.

21

Exposed

THE HEADLINE, IN two-inch-high, double-decked text, stretched across all eight columns of the *New York Journal-American*: 'US Secret Agencies Penetrated by Reds'. The story beneath – and continued over two full broadsheet pages inside – ran to more than 2,000 words. It was Monday, 2 March 1964; from the moment the first edition hit the news stands, Goleniewski was out in the open and dangerously exposed.

The *New York Journal-American* was then one of the city's most widely read newspapers, publishing several daily editions from noon to late evening.[1] More importantly, it had extensive syndication deals which ensured that its major articles were picked up by other papers across the country, as well as by international wire services. Written by its city editor, Guy Richards, that afternoon's splash story was the first to reveal Goleniewski's existence to the American public, and gave a breathless account of his years of service to US intelligence, his defection and an indication of where he now lived:

> A defector from the Soviet Secret Police has informed U.S. officials that Moscow has placed active cells in the Central Intelligence Agency and the State Department in Washington and overseas.
>
> The Red defector, a high-ranking operative in Russia's KGB, is sure that they are still operative in the two highly sensitive Government agencies.

He and his wife have been living in a modest apartment not more than 30 minutes from Times Square. He has been given a new name and identity especially fabricated to blot out his past and help him blend into the American scenery.

He has named names. He has provided Washington with details of what looms as a greater scandal than the famous Alger Hiss case. Here are some of his shattering disclosures:

Approximately $1.2 million of CIA funds in Vienna recently was passed secretly along to the Communists – one-third to KGB (the Soviet Secret Police), one-third to the Italian Communist Party and one-third to the American Communist Party.

Three American scientists with access to defense secrets are working for the KGB. They have ties to others in the same category whose identities are unknown to him. But he has clues to a number of them.

KGB has been able to infiltrate all American embassies in important cities abroad and 'every U.S. agency except the FBI'.

Little, if anything, has been done to run down or clean out the KGB men on American payrolls though he fed the facts and exposures on them to the CIA starting as far back as 1960.

Instead of having his information used for the clean-out job he came here for, he charges, he has been thwarted by amateurs and 'Stalinists' in the CIA and even kept from communicating his plight to responsible higher officials there.

He is Michal Goleniewski, a husky and handsome Polish-born agent who resembles the Hollywood prototype of the suave lady-killing spy. He's credited with breaking the Irwin [sic] N. Scarbeck spy case in Warsaw in 1961. The CIA is on record in Congress as endorsing these observations.[2]

Despite the colourful prose style, the *Journal* was not a sensation-seeking tabloid and Richards was a veteran reporter with a long and respectable career. After graduating from Yale in 1927 he signed on with a scientific expedition to the South Pacific and spent two years collecting ornithological specimens in New Guinea and the Solomon Islands before joining the *New York Daily News* as a reporter.

During World War II he fought with the US Marines at Guadalcanal and was briefly considered for an intelligence job by the CIA's predecessor, the Office of Strategic Services (OSS).[3] He ended the war as a lieutenant colonel in the Marine Reserves, joined the *New York Journal-American*, and soon earned a series of Newspaper Guild awards for his work.

Richards had been chasing the Goleniewski story for six months. One of Michael Feighan's aides – probably Colonel Philip Corso – had tipped him off about HR 5507 and provided him with a detailed account of their meetings in the Queens apartment the previous August; he also alleged that the CIA had obstructed attempts to bring the defector before the Senate Internal Security Subcommittee:

> Though he [Goleniewski] has yet to testify on espionage . . . which he wants to do, and which many legislators want him to do, his case has become the center of one of the biggest behind-the-scenes battles ever to rear up in the jurisdictional area between the legislative and executive branches of the Government.
>
> In the tussle over him things have happened which seem incredible in a democratic nation. A Congressional subpoena was virtually smuggled to him – then mysteriously quashed . . . A date and time was set for Goleniewski's appearances before the Congressional committee . . . but instead of that appearance, a man from the CIA arranged to have a key member of the committee involved vacate the subpoena and cancel the date.
>
> Another CIA man is reliably reported to have pressured the Army to investigate the subpoena server [Corso] with a view toward charging him with making use of information gained on active duty (he was then on inactive duty), and for masquerading as an intelligence officer.[4]

For several months Richards had tried, unsuccessfully, to speak with Goleniewski and he found the Agency equally reluctant to make any comment – at least on the record. But it was willing to hint – unattributably – that there might be a problem with its most successful defector's credibility: 'Word was quietly passed from somewhere that Mr. Goleniewski had "flipped his lid" and was becoming unreliable – so CIA doesn't think it "worthwhile" for him to appear before the legislative branch.'

The insinuation – the first hint of how Langley planned to deal with the problem – drew an angry on-the-record response from Feighan: 'That's utterly ridiculous. The man seemed worried, and even excited, but his mind is in excellent shape. I was impressed by everything he had to say.'[5]

Had Richards' scoop been limited to that day's news cycle alone, the CIA might have been able to contain the damage. But he had only just started to unveil Goleniewski's disclosures. On 3 March the *New York Journal-American* broke a second, equally damning, story; under the banner headline '4 U.S. Envoys Linked to Red Spy Sex Net', it spelled out his claims of honeytraps, blackmail and betrayal in the Warsaw Embassy, and boasted that the previous day's story had already forced action on Capitol Hill:

> Four American diplomats came under new and hastily organized Congressional probes today after a high Soviet defector named them as Russian collaborators lured by beautiful Polish girls into a classic fall from grace. The four, along with a fifth diplomat later allowed to resign, were drawn into the Soviet net in the espionage hotbed at Warsaw, the defector charged . . .
>
> While the diplomats were being blackmailed by the Polish girls, a handsome Soviet secret service agent, bent on collecting information, managed to seduce the wife of an American foreign service officer . . .
>
> The disclosures came from the Soviet defector, 41-year-old Michael [sic] Goleniewski, who bared the existence of 'cells' of the KGB – the Soviet secret police – in [the] Central Intelligence Agency and the State Dept., both in Washington and in US embassies overseas.[6]

To a country still mired in fears of Moscow's machinations – the Cuban Missile Crisis less than eighteen months earlier was still fresh in the nation's collective mind – the allegations were politically incendiary. Nor was Richards' claim of new Congressional oversight mere journalistic hyperbole: within hours an influential Republican politician read both stories into the record and demanded that the CIA produce Goleniewski for questioning.

Representative John Ashbrook was 'an ardent conservative and one of the most articulate anti-Communists in Congress';[7] more pertinently, he was a leading member of the House Un-American Activities Committee (HUAC) and despite the unsavoury reputation it had earned during the McCarthyite 'Red Scare', remained an unrepentantly vehement hunter of 'subversives' within the US government. That afternoon he used Richards' revelations in the *New York Journal-American* to flay the executive branch over the failures they exposed:

> It is no secret that the State Department has been working hard to conjure up the picture of Soviet Communists as 'maturing' and 'responsible' world leaders . . . The *Journal-American* article presents a direct contrast to the pie-in-the-sky approach of the State Department and it should be thoroughly investigated by a Congressional committee . . .
>
> Michal Goleniewski, a defector from the Soviet secret police, who has been proven a valuable informer in the past . . . has many further stories to tell concerning Red penetration of our State Department and even the Central Intelligence Agency . . .
>
> No wonder the public is concerned about . . . the laxity of our internal security. Testimony of Michal Goleniewski is the part of the iceberg that is below the surface and judging how bad the exposed part is, it is high time that we delve into the recesses and see what is going on.[8]

The following day Ashbrook and the *New York Journal-American* stepped up the pressure. Beneath a headline denouncing Langley for obstructing legislators – 'CIA Hiding Red Defector, Probers Seek to Quiz Him' – the

Congressman insisted the Agency must allow Goleniewski to testify before HUAC:

> I want to get every particle of evidence of information I can about Goleniewski's charges . . . It is vitally important that Goleniewski appear before my committee . . . The State Department . . . has consistently lied about such communist penetration as those made in Warsaw, Washington and elsewhere.[9]

If the charges provoked some action in Foggy Bottom – the *Chicago Herald* reported that the State Department had, reluctantly 'begun a review of the security status of some of its most trusted employees'[10] – Langley remained obdurate, refusing either to comment on, or to accede to, Ashbrook's demands.

On 5 March the pressure increased again. The *New York Journal-American* published a follow-up story by Richards, revealing that Goleniewski had given Feighan and his aides:

> . . . the names of 19 Americans accused of being agents of the Soviet Secret Police – 12 of whom are in the State Department, and four in the Central Intelligence Agency . . . Of the four KGB agents Lt. Col. Goleniewski named in the CIA, two fall into the category of 'definite and disciplined products of the other sides'. The other two are home-grown theoreticians, he said, who have allowed themselves to be pulled across the line by others.[11]

The same day, the chairman of the Senate Internal Security Subcommittee, James Eastland – a right-wing 'Southern Democrat' and veteran anti-communist – sent Goleniewski a new subpoena to testify on the Hill in just under a week's time.

It was delivered to the Queens apartment the following day and coincided with a visit from a 'representative of the CIA Director', calling himself 'Mr. Williams'.[12] He told Goleniewski to 'clarify publicly' that the stories in the *New York Journal-American* were baseless and warned him against cooperating with Richards.[13]

Both demands were confusing. Goleniewski had assiduously heeded the CIA's warnings about his obligation to maintain secrecy; he had not spoken to any journalist and could not understand how he was supposed to correct the record without doing so. But since the instruction was delivered at the same time as the SISS subpoena, he came to the conclusion that the Agency was in some way pressurizing him not to give evidence on Capitol Hill.

He was, in any event, rather more immediately worried about Irmgard's health: she was still in the first delicate trimester of her pregnancy, and was shortly to go into hospital to have the tumour removed from her breast. Leaving her alone while he travelled to Washington was the last thing either of them needed, so he sent a polite note back to SISS, asking for a postponement. Eastland grudgingly agreed, and the delay gave Goleniewski a brief respite from the growing strain. It was not to last.

On 11 March, the day he had been due to testify before SISS, the *New York Journal-American* ran another lengthy story by Richards detailing the alleged treachery of diplomat Edward Symans, and denouncing the continuing absence from Congressional hearings of the man who had exposed him:

> The hope of keeping buried forever the story of the high-level American turncoat and his Polish mistress, who worked in the Warsaw embassy, is one of the prime motives behind the almost desperate attempts of the State Department and Central Intelligence Agency to keep Goleniewski from testifying before the Senate Internal Security Subcommittee.
>
> Other reasons behind these attempts are fear of his disclosures of 19 Americans working for the KGB (Soviet Secret Police), 12 in the State Department, four in the CIA and three in the US scientific laboratories.[14]

The story prompted Eastland to reissue the subpoena, but it also led the CIA to increase its efforts to silence Goleniewski. According to his subsequent affidavit, 'an official of CIA, named "John" appeared in my apartment, trying to investigate why I had supplied to the press the published informations [sic], which were damaging to the "national security of the United States"'. He tried, unsuccessfully, to protest his innocence, insisting that Richards' articles were 'absolutely nothing to do [with me]' and – worse – they were damaging to his safety and Irmgard's health.

'John', however, was evidently less concerned with the couple's welfare than with preventing damaging testimony on Capitol Hill. He 'admitted, that to his knowledge, the publication of said articles had deconstructed the cover-legend used by us in the neighbourhood', and said the Agency had decided the Goleniewskis should be moved immediately to a nearby hotel: 'He informed me that some US Senators had an interest in informations being in my possession, and if I wished to avoid subpoenas of the Internal Security Subcommittee of the US Senate, I had to move out immediately from the apartment with my (pregnant and expecting difficult operation) wife ...' Goleniewski refused, point-blank, to go, dismissing the Agency's order as 'an attempt of extortion against me and especially against my wife, being exhausted and in needing help condition'.[15]

On 16 March, Goleniewski enjoyed the first good news since the *New York Journal-American* had exposed him a fortnight earlier; surgeons successfully removed Irmgard's breast tumour and established that it was unlikely to be cancerous. But – at least according to his own account – the couple were immediately subjected to harassment and threats:

> After my wife underwent an operation in a hospital in New York City ... unknown individuals began to invade her room ... and unknown individuals from a surveillance team threatened me that if I were to try to appear before the Senate Committee ... I would be murdered, or deported from the United States, or put in

jail without trial or my wife would die, together with the unborn
baby, in hospital.[16]

There is no official record to support Goleniewski's claims, much less to
prove his allegation that the CIA was behind the intimidation, but as the
month wore on a steady drumbeat of Congressional and media pressure
built up. Senator Eastland sent the first of a succession of new subpoenas, summoning Goleniewski to testify before SISS; once again, he
pleaded to be excused, citing the need to safeguard Irmgard's recovery.
Then, on 18 March, Richards and Ashbrook returned to the fray, char-
ging in a new *New York Journal-American* exclusive that the government
was obstructing investigations into State Department penetration, and
revealing that Langley was dragging its heels over a promise McCone
had made to Feighan to bring Goleniewski before Congress.[17] Two days
later the *Journal* claimed that the government was concealing 'a list of
847 grave security risks in the State Department', and demanded that
Goleniewski – being held 'tightly under the wing of the Central Intelligence Agency' – should testify about his knowledge of the alleged
traitors.[18]

The allegations about the Agency's handling of its former star agent
were also picked up, amplified and distorted by right-wing anti-
communist campaigners. Red-baiting organizations then wielded
significant influence and enjoyed considerable popular support; although
their official memberships were low and the circulation of their publications much smaller than those of mainstream newspapers like the
Journal, these groups reached deep into America's heartland and its
psyche.

On 23 March, Dan Smoot, a former FBI agent who claimed to have
worked for the Bureau 'for three and a half years on communist investigations' before turning to independent journalism and publishing his
own bi-weekly newsletter, made a new – and largely unsourced – claim
that the CIA's earliest debriefings of Goleniewski had been undermined
by KGB penetration:

Shortly after the defector Goleniewski was brought to the United States, he was taken to a room for his first secret conference with CIA agents. When he walked into the room, he recognized an undercover communist in the group of American investigators who were to query him. Scared, Goleniewski feigned illness and departed. Later, he reported the fact to a CIA agent whom he trusted. The undercover communist whom he had seen among the CIA agents disappeared. Goleniewski never saw him again, and does not know his real name.[19]

Around 30,000 subscribers paid to receive 'The Smoot Report' in their mailboxes every two weeks, but its footprint extended far beyond this relatively small circulation. Smoot was a regular speaker for the much larger and more powerful John Birch Society, wrote for its widely disseminated magazine, *American Opinion*, and also hosted his own deeply conservative radio show. If the production values of his home-produced newsletter were less than impressive, the FBI viewed him as sufficiently dangerous to justify opening a file on his activities.

By the end of the month the combined pressure from Congress, the media and anti-communist activists finally provoked the US government into action. It did not, despite repeated requests and its own undertakings, deliver Goleniewski to any one of the Congressional committees seeking his testimony; instead, and less than six months after promising to 'make every reasonable effort to provide adequate protection and security', it deliberately set out to discredit the man who, according to its own internal assessment, had made 'an unparalleled contribution' to Western security and who had been 'an accurate and reliable source of intelligence'.[20]

What made this even more shameful was that at exactly the same time, 5,000 miles away behind the Iron Curtain, Goleniewski's former masters in Soviet bloc intelligence were plotting to kill him.

22

Dirty Tricks

'THE GENTLEMAN FROM Illinois is recognized for 20 minutes.'

On Thursday, 26 March 1964 the Speaker of the House of Representatives granted permission for a veteran Republican politician to make an unscheduled speech on the floor of Congress.

Leslie Cornelius Arends was sixty-eight; a former World War I naval officer, farmer, banker and a right-wing conservative, he had represented a largely rural Illinois constituency since 1935. As one of the Republican Party's most steadfast loyalists,[1] he had risen to become one of the senior members of a Committee which – notionally, at least – scrutinized the activities of the CIA. That afternoon, however, he rose to his feet to defend the Agency against its critics and to denounce Goleniewski:

> Mr. Speaker, one of the most important agencies of our government, particularly during this period of international uncertainties and anxieties, is our Central Intelligence Agency. The time has long since arrived when someone should take cognizance of the baseless criticism that has been and continues to be heaped upon it.
>
> That is my purpose here today, as a member of the CIA subcommittee of the Committee on Armed Services since its establishment. I do not purport to speak as an authority on all the functions and activities of the CIA. But I do presume to speak with some factual knowledge about the CIA as an organization and how it functions.

If Arends gave the impression that his speech was an impromptu reaction to the previous three weeks of uncomfortable press coverage, it was, in fact, a carefully planned counter-attack by the CIA, delivered by one of its 'tame' lawmakers. Arends had discussed the speech with Langley and, according to a memo by the Agency's Office of Legal Counsel, he sent over an initial outline with a request to 'strengthen' its contents. The Director and his staff duly redrafted it, and returned the revised document for the Congressman to read out.[2]

The timing, too, was deliberate: 26 March was Maundy Thursday and Congress was about to break for a ten-day Easter recess. Arends' speech was timed to be just early enough to ensure coverage in the following day's newspapers, but too late to attract opposing voices from the Agency's critics who would already have left the House and headed home.

After a brief, boilerplate recognition that the CIA should not be above criticism, Arends launched into a whole-hearted defence of its recent actions:

> Much of the criticism directed at the CIA is not constructive. It cannot possibly be, as it is not based on facts. It is based on half-truths and distortions. Indeed, some of it constitutes complete untruths, with no foundation whatever in fact or reason. This is what concerns me. Something once said, however false, is readily oft repeated and in time is accepted as a fact although an outright falsehood. And we know there are those who would, if they could, discredit the CIA. Others of us, having no such intention, unwittingly become their victims.
>
> Let me present one illustration. I refer to the much publicized, much discussed case of the Polish defector, Michal Goleniewski. I refer to the irresponsible series of articles that has been recently published in the New York Journal American.
>
> Amongst these wild accusations is that the CIA has attempted to prevent Michal Goleniewski from appearing before the Senate Internal Security Subcommittee. They go so far as to charge that the CIA has quashed subpoenas. That simply is not true . . . the

executive branch of the government has been cooperative with the Senate subcommittee throughout.

Contrary to what has been reported in the press, the post-ponements of Michal Goleniewski's appearance before the Senate subcommittee were at the request of the man himself. And the subcommittee agreed to his request.

If most of this stayed – just about – within the bounds of accuracy, what followed was shamelessly false:

I might add that the CIA subcommittee, of which I am a member, went into every aspect of this case. I am personally satisfied that the publicized statements purported to come from Michal Gole-niewski are not correct. The information as reported in the press is not in agreement with the information Michal Goleniewski has made available to many departments of Government.

Stories such as have been circulated on this case display a reckless regard of [sic] the truth. They can be harmful, and those who circulate them do a great deal of disservice to maintaining public confidence in the CIA.

No-one, except members of the subcommittee itself, has any knowledge of just how extensively and intensively we inquire into the activities of this intelligence agency. We hold no public hearings. We issue no reports. We cannot do otherwise and pre-serve the effectiveness of the CIA as a secret fact-gathering agency on an international scale.

We can only hope that the House has sufficient confidence in our subcommittee, as individuals and as a committee, to accept our assurances that we are kept well informed and we have no hesitancy of [sic] keeping a close eye and ear on CIA operations.[3]

Neither Arends nor his subcommittee had ever spoken to – much less heard sworn testimony from – Goleniewski, and his rosy picture of Congressional oversight was arrant nonsense, and he knew it. Nine months earlier, Walter Norblad, a lawyer and nine-term Republican

Representative who had served on the CIA subcommittee, denounced it on the floor of the House: 'I was a member of that committee for either 2 or 4 years. We met annually – one time a year for a period of two hours in which we accomplished virtually nothing.'

The Agency's plans for Arends' ringing endorsement to stand, unchallenged, on the public record were, however, doomed to failure. Two veteran CIA critics got wind of his speech and quickly returned to the Chamber to take him – and Langley – to task. Representative John Lindsay quickly read Norblad's withering assessment into the record, then castigated Langley for its failures and its aversion to scrutiny. Minutes later, Michael Feighan took up the cudgels on behalf of Goleniewski:

> I listened with great interest to his [Arends'] analysis of the Michal Goleniewski case, his charge of irresponsible journalism placed against the New York Journal American for its series of articles on this case, and his statement that the CIA subcommittee of which he is a member went into every aspect of this case . . . By his statements the impression is created that my colleague and other members of the CIA subcommittee are completely informed on all the facets and implications of the Goleniewski case.
>
> I question the accuracy of that statement, not because I question the integrity of my colleague and friend, but because I am convinced that if he and the other members of his subcommittee were completely informed on all the facets and implications of this case he would not have delivered the remarks he has made today . . .
>
> My colleague . . . discusses the Goleniewski case, but what he leaves out is far more important than what he has said. In an earnest effort to assist him and the other members of the House CIA subcommittee, I present the following questions . . .
>
> First: have the members of the subcommittee personally interviewed Michal Goleniewski and if they have had that opportunity, how much time was spent with him and to what extent was he questioned with respect to political intelligence and Russian KGB agent infiltration into the vital organs of our Government?

Second: if members of the House CIA Subcommittee have probed deeply into KGB agent penetration of the vital organs of our Government, are the members satisfied that everything that needs to be done has been done by the security arms of our Government to ferret out and prosecute the guilty?

Feighan knew the answer to both questions. The subcommittee had done little or nothing to investigate Goleniewski's allegations, and it had never sought evidence to support them. Deliberately and forensically, Feighan turned the screw on Arends and the CIA:

Is it not true that Goleniewski, who defected to the United States in 1961, has revealed deep penetration of the CIA by Russian KGB agents?

Is it not true that Goleniewski has told how over $1 million of CIA funds fell into the hands of the Russian KGB and about $400,000 of this money was pumped back into the Communist Party, USA, to pay for their operations and destroy this country?

Is it not true that Michal Goleniewski has been discouraged by certain CIA officials in his efforts to present what he calls political intelligence and which he regards as essential to the defeat of international communism?

Did Goleniewski name Russian KGB agents in both the State Department and CIA and state that to date none of these agents have been arrested or prosecuted? . . .

The American people have a right to hear forthright answers to those questions. I hope they will be answered . . . These are not only critical times, but these times are decisive for our country, for the cause of universal freedom, for the cause of a just and lasting world peace. It is time that Congress faces up to its responsibility and obtains answers – the full story of agent penetration of our Government.

Mr. Speaker, as a man who believes in the message of Holy Week, I am an optimist. But I also believe that it is high time we weeded out of our Government all those who wear the cloak of Judas so that we can freely spread the great message of American liberties, freedoms and individual dignity throughout the world.[4]

It was a brave hope, but one which failed to grasp the government's determination to discredit Goleniewski. Two weeks earlier the State Department had attempted to put the Senate Internal Security Subcommittee off the scent, sending Senator Eastland a private letter in which – according to a subsequent SISS report – 'the information supplied by Goleniewski [was] belittled'.[5] It followed that at the start of April with a lengthy briefing memo to Congressmen and Senators. Like the speech crafted by Langley for Arends, this was profoundly – and deliberately – misleading:

> In December 1958, the Department learned that Michal Goleniewski, a Polish intelligence agent, had accused an officer of the U.S. Embassy in Poland of cooperating with Polish and Russian intelligence services. Subsequently, Goleniewski also alleged that some other members of the Embassy staff had behaved in such a way as to make themselves potential victims of blackmail by Communist agents.
>
> At the time of the original allegation the Polish agent was of unknown reliability. His information and motives were evaluated as quickly as possible. While the evaluation was being made, the Ambassador in Warsaw inaugurated additional security measures in the Embassy designed to isolate the accused member of the staff from classified information.
>
> Only in the single case noted above was there reason to believe that an officer of the Embassy staff may have been implicated in espionage. The individual was discharged, and action has been taken which will preclude his future employment in any position where a security clearance is required. Despite intensive investigation by Federal agencies there was insufficient legal evidence to support criminal proceedings against the suspected individual.

That the State Department's claims were distinctly misleading became clear some years later when the embassy staff officer identified by Goleniewski was named, on the floor of the House of Representatives, as Edward Symans; rather than being fired, he had in fact been 'permitted to resign' and had retained his government pension.[6] The rest of the memo was equally slippery:

> As a result of investigations, the Embassy Marine guards who were guilty of unacceptable conduct (but which in no case involved treason or espionage) were disciplined and returned to the United States. In the case of the other civilian members of the Embassy accused by Goleniewski, investigations indicated that no espionage activities had taken place. However, the behavior of some of these employees was sufficiently questionable to warrant letters of reprimand which will seriously impair their future in the U.S. Government.
>
> The executive branch of the Government has cooperated fully with the Senate Internal Security Subcommittee since that subcommittee served the first subpoena on Michal Goleniewski in August 1963 . . .
>
> At no time have there been efforts by any executive department or agency to quash the subpoena or to prevent Michal Goleniewski from testifying before the Senate Internal Security Subcommittee.[7]

As the subsequent SISS report noted caustically, this document was 'so worded as to indicate to someone receiving it from an official State Department source that the Department had serious doubts as to the authenticity and reliability of Michal Goleniewski and the information he supplied'.[8] More to the point, the executive branch knew that to be completely untrue.

Throughout the spring and early summer of 1964, investigations by SISS systematically unpicked the government's attempts to discredit Goleniewski and the information he had supplied. On 8 May, Eastland dispatched the committee's chief counsel to Queens. Jay Sourwine, a journalist who had become a relentless pursuer of alleged communist subversion during the Red Scare years, took with him a new subpoena, but found Goleniewski angry and in no mood to testify; instead he demanded the Senator's help to rein in the Agency:

> During several hours I informed Mr. J. G. Sourwine about my and my wife's situation, about our difficulties created by the breach of US contracts on the part of CIA [and] about our health conditions . . .
>
> This conversation included my request directed to the Chairman of the Committee on the Judiciary & Internal Security . . . to intervene on the part of the powerful Judiciary and Internal Security Committee of the US Senate, [with the] CIA concerning the breach of US contract and of the US governmental guarantees given to us . . . He promised to present all these problems to the US Senator Eastland and left my apartment assuring me to do his best in order to correct our situation as soon as possible.[9]

However, Goleniewski was also becoming increasingly paranoid. He claimed – without evidence – that the CIA had instigated Guy Richards' articles in the *New York Journal-American*, as part of a deliberate campaign to discredit him:

> The provocation against me arranged by CIA via the NY Journal American [was a] violation of the US guarantees concerning publications . . . of the US contract of October 7, 1963. But also the question automatically arises why the Internal Security Subcommittee tried to subpoena me during my and my wife's most difficult situation . . . well informed that I was not a source for any exposures widely promoted by the NY Journal American, and in other papers in the US and in western Europe.
>
> The answer to this question is . . . that the CIA through the Internal Security Subcommittee arranged against me a channel of pressure – to put it mildly – and in order to be able to put such

pressure into action, the libeling articles by Guy Richards based
on many lies were, amongst other [sic], most necessary. This is
rounding the picture of a well prepared, cynical and most damaging provocation, constructed by CIA, without any respect to
the real interest of the national security of the United States, and
against any US governmental guarantees given to me by its government at several occasions.[10]

Goleniewski's syntactically challenged claims that the Agency instigated
the Richards stories – despite the fact these were deeply hostile to
Langley – were absurd; they were both a sign of his disintegrating mental state and a harbinger of problems to come. Similarly, his demand for
SISS to intercede with the CIA failed to understand the constitutional
divisions of power which governed politics in America. When Eastland
replied at the end of March, explaining that 'the Subcommittee has no
authority over any organization within the Executive Branch'[11] and that
the Agency's breach of contract fell outside his jurisdiction, the Senator's name was added to the growing list of enemies – perceived or
real – in Goleniewski's mind.

This was hardly rational. If Eastland was a deeply conservative and
racist Southern Democrat – he vehemently opposed desegregation and
the growing civil rights movement, and had denounced African-
Americans as 'inferior' to whites[12] – he was also implacably hostile to
Soviet communism, and led opposition to the nuclear test ban treaty
Washington had negotiated with Moscow. For all his faults, the Goleniewski case and the antics of both the CIA and the State Department
plainly troubled him; although he was still unable to force the man to
testify, throughout that summer he held hearings which confirmed the
truth and importance of Goleniewski's revelations.

On 24 July SISS summoned John R. Norpel, then employed by the
State Department but who had been a senior FBI counterintelligence
officer until late 1959, and who had been tasked by the Bureau with eval-
uating Goleniewski's Sniper letters. Under questioning from Sourwine,

Norpel confirmed that he had personally examined much of the correspondence, and that he had knowledge of what had been done with it; a Senate stenographer recorded the exchange, verbatim:

> MR SOURWINE: Do you know of any information ever furnished to the U.S. Government by Goleniewski which turned out to be untrue or inaccurate?
>
> MR NORPEL: I do not; no, sir.
>
> MR SOURWINE: Do you know whether the information which has been furnished by him has been checked out in all or in a substantial part?
>
> MR NORPEL: Yes, sir; it was checked out.
>
> MR SOURWINE: And it proved true in every case?
>
> MR NORPEL: Every case that I am aware of . . .
>
> MR SOURWINE: Did it ever go to the State Department before . . . the Bureau had checked it out?
>
> MR NORPEL: No, sir. It would go in a report . . . after corroborative evidence had been developed to either dispute the claim or establish it.

Sourwine then read Norpel the State Department's briefing note which denounced Goleniewski's allegations of Soviet penetration of the Warsaw Embassy and claimed that 'only in a single case' was there any evidence to implicate an official in espionage:

> MR SOURWINE: Do you have knowledge which would put you in a position to say whether that statement is, or is not, accurate?
>
> MR NORPEL: I would say it was not accurate. There were a number of others implicated in espionage . . . he didn't name just one person . . .

MR SOURWINE: Do you know of any individuals who were civilian members of our Embassy staff in Warsaw, concerning
whom it was established that they had been implicated in
espionage? . . .

MR NORPEL: Yes, sir; I know that there was at least one, and very
likely two cases . . . I know of one instance, for sure, and another
one that is so closely paralleled that, from my experience, I would
say that there would be sufficient grounds to suspect espionage
on that person's part . . .

Norpel then confirmed that all of the individuals identified by
Goleniewski – including Symans – posed a security risk, but that none
had been fired:

MR SOURWINE: In your judgment . . . were persons allowed to
continue in the employment of our diplomatic service or in the
Embassy in Warsaw who . . . should have been removed from
these posts?

MR NORPEL: Yes, sir . . .

MR SOURWINE: Do you know of any case of an officer who
was discharged as a result of the information supplied by
Mr Goleniewski?

MR NORPEL: No, I do not.[13]

The testimony was clear and unequivocal. It excoriated the government
and exonerated Goleniewski of the slurs put out by the State Department and the CIA. Unfortunately, the public remained entirely unaware
of this; SISS proceedings were conducted entirely *in camera* and the
transcripts of its hearings were not even printed, let alone publicized,
until a year later.

There was, in fairness, good reason for this caution. If Goleniewski's
name and work for Western intelligence were now in the public domain,

his security remained an issue, and since Soviet bloc intelligence was presumed still to be searching for him, Eastland and his colleagues remained anxious about raising his profile.

For that, at least, Goleniewski was grateful. Though his contract with the CIA remained suspended, he had stuck scrupulously to its prohibition on talking to the press. He was, however, increasingly worried that his home address would be discovered. Although no photograph of him had been published, and his Queens apartment was rented in the cover name of Franz Oldenburg, the combination of the strong hints about its location in the *New York Journal-American* ('He and his wife have been living in a modest apartment not more than 30 minutes from Times Square') and the steady stream of Congressmen arriving at Silver Towers was beginning to attract attention from his neighbours. It was only a matter of time before the secret leaked out.

He was right to worry. For more than two years the UB had put substantial time and money into locating its former spy. The exhaustive records of what it called Operation TELETECHNIK – they run to more than 1,100 individual pages – show that it deployed agents across Europe and inside the United States; each was tasked with a single goal – to track down Goleniewski. And there was only one reason for this: the as yet unexecuted death sentence imposed for his treachery.

The first and most direct line of attack focused on Goleniewski's mother, Janina – now assigned the cryptonym PRZEKUPKA ('Shopper'). Mail intercepts revealed that she continued to receive letters from him as well as photographs showing him with Irmgard (code-named MIMOZY). Concealed in other packages he sent thousands of dollars – cash which she used to support Goleniewski's abandoned children, trade on the black market, and purchase a few small luxuries to improve the quality of her life:

> According to agent data [PRZEKUPKA] currently has approximately USD 7,000. This is a 65-year-old woman. She has a lot of friends but does not talk about TELETECHNIK with most of

them. She quickly trusts people and . . . is gullible and uncritical. People cling to her, because they are attracted to the glow of her money. She likes the company of young people, especially men, and loves sex. She pretends to be a great worldly lady, which [is] in contrast to her mental level . . .[14]

Possessing Western currency – let alone exchanging it on the black market – was a serious offence in Communist Poland. By exploiting her vanity and her weakness for attractive male company, the UB saw an opportunity to trick Janina into revealing her son's address. It recruited a new agent and ordered him to court and – if necessary – seduce her. This sad and tawdry operation to exploit a lonely and vulnerable old woman began in the early summer of 1964; it would drag on for almost six years.

But in the wake of Guy Richards' *Journal* stories, the most urgent task fell to Polish intelligence agents in the United States. Warsaw's tentacles reached remarkably deep into American political life: a TELETECHNIK report in December 1961 recorded that a Polish agent had met with a prominent German industrialist who was a regular guest at the White House, and who had been pressing his contacts for leads.[15] Although this proved ultimately unsuccessful, the UB was undeterred. From the spring of 1964 onwards it stepped up the search for information about Goleniewski's whereabouts, ordering its *rezidentura* in New York, Washington and Chicago to develop contacts inside Congress and the Immigration Service, as well as courting friendly journalists.[16]

Like the parallel targeting of Janina, the UB's American-based efforts were sanctioned at the highest levels within Poland's Ministry of the Interior and were lavishly financed. Both were organized as long-term operations and would occupy at least two departments within the intelligence service for several years to come.

The UB also had a fall-back plan should neither operation produce results sufficiently quickly: if Warsaw decided Goleniewski had to be urgently discredited rather than eventually killed, the contacts its agents made within American political and media circles would be fed the damaging personal information he had concealed from the CIA – most notably the fact that he had never divorced his Polish wife and was therefore a bigamist. But before it could put this dirty-tricks campaign into action, Goleniewski fatally sabotaged his own credibility. Throwing caution to the gathering winds, he very publicly claimed an entirely different identity – one which was guaranteed to place him in the eye of an international storm.

23

Romanoff

A T 8.15 P.M. on Monday, 10 August 1964 listeners tuning into the nightly current affairs talk show on WOR Radio New York were greeted with a distinctly unusual warning:

> This is Barry Farber and what you're about to hear is not a radio drama. I haven't got that much imagination. I may have to come back tomorrow night and apologize for everything my guest says tonight. I will take that chance. I expect a lot between now and nine o'clock, but I promise nothing except one challenging history lesson.

After pausing briefly for a commercial, Farber introduced his guest for the evening: 'Colonel Goleniewski, the famous Polish spy and a member of Poland's espionage service who came across to our side and helped the CIA and FBI pinpoint top communist agents who had infiltrated into top spots in our intelligence network'.

It was Goleniewski's first ever public appearance. He should have been in Washington DC that day, testifying in secret before SISS, but once again he had asked Eastland for a postponement, claiming Irmgard's fragile health made it impossible for him to leave her side.[1]

That concern did not, however, prevent him from driving to WOR's studio in Manhattan; after seven months of suspension, and with no sign of the CIA rescinding his 'Leave Without Pay' status, he had decided that he was no longer bound by his contractual vow of silence.

But he did not want to discuss the spies he had exposed, Guy Richards' revelations in the *New York Journal-American*, or his troubled relationship with the Agency. 'Colonel Goleniewski is across the microphone right now,' Farber announced, 'but he is not here to talk about espionage only. He has got a disclosure which, if true, is the most sensational disclosure I have ever gotten next to as a journalist . . . Colonel Goleniewski, would you care to take this microphone and tell the listeners who you say you really are?'

Without missing a beat, Goleniewski responded: 'Well, my real name is Aleksei Nicholaevich Romanoff.'

Farber was an experienced reporter and popular radio host. As the show's transcript makes clear, he wanted to make sure his audience understood the gravity of what it had just heard:

> FARBER: Aleksei Nicholaevich Romanoff . . . I wonder how many people realize what you are claiming, that you are the son of the Czar of Russia.
>
> COL. GOLENIEWSKI: That's correct.
>
> FARBER: Who, history says, was murdered in Ekaterinburg by the communists after your father's regime fell.
>
> COL. GOLENIEWSKI: Yes.[2]

For more than four decades the fate of the Imperial Russian Family – Tsar Nicholas Romanoff, his wife Alexandra and their five children: Olga, Tatiana, Maria, Anastasia and thirteen-year-old Aleksei – had been largely settled history. In March 1917 the Tsar[3] was deposed and the Romanoff family, together with a small entourage of retainers, was imprisoned in Tobolsk, Siberia; the following year, in April 1918, they were moved to Ekaterinburg and confined in a substantial mansion, seized from a local mining engineer. Ipatiev House – redesignated 'The House of Special Purpose' by the Ural Regional Soviet which held the

Romanoffs – was sealed off behind high wooden fences and the family was closely guarded.

Around midnight on 16–17 July the Tsar, Tsarina, their five children and four servants were herded into a basement room and executed by a poorly organized firing squad; those who did not die immediately were finished off with bayonets. None of the family or their retainers survived.

Their bodies were then loaded onto a truck, taken to a remote wooded area and, after a succession of failed burial attempts, the guards dumped them in shallow graves before covering them with quicklime and railway sleepers. The Romanoff corpses would remain there, undisturbed, for more than half a century.

The execution of the Russian Royal Family was widely – if not always coherently – reported at the time, and though a semi-official inquiry by a lawyer working for White Russian forces during the country's civil war was deeply flawed,[4] in the ensuing years its conclusion that the Romanoffs had been assassinated became accepted as an historical fact. But the continuing absence of bodies encouraged rumours that at least some had escaped, and beginning in the early 1930s a handful of pretenders emerged. In particular, Anna Anderson, a German woman, made widely publicized – if entirely bogus – claims to be Anastasia, and her story was turned into a highly successful 1956 Hollywood movie for which Ingrid Bergman won an Oscar as the eponymous heroine. Forty years after their deaths, the Romanoffs became big box-office business.

But if the Russian Imperial Family retained an entirely misplaced glamour in the minds of Americans made fearful by the grim Cold War reality of the Soviet Union, no one in any Western government seriously doubted the fact of their murder. This went some way towards explaining the impact caused by one of the CIA's most successful spies when he declared that history to be bunk.

Over the course of his forty-five minutes on WOR, Goleniewski gave the audience a halting and somewhat fragmentary account of what he claimed had really happened in 1918: the Romanoffs, he said, had not been assassinated, and he had been spirited away through Siberia to Poland, where he became one of the leaders of a secret worldwide anti-communist resistance movement.

It was a wholesale rewriting of the record, with Goleniewski claiming a central role in the drama. As Farber drily noted: 'OK – the cat is out of the bag and the questions and the answers . . . and the allegations and accusations and insinuations can take over the field from now on.' He was not wrong. Goleniewski was only just getting started.

One week later, under the banner headline 'Russia's Czar Lives!', the *Manchester Union-Leader* published a 2,000-word interview with the newly declared pretender to the Russian throne. Beside a photograph of 'Grand Duke Alexei [sic]' – the first picture of Goleniewski to be published – a statement from the paper's editor declared:

> A Tsarevich mysteriously escapes a firing squad that was supposed to have wiped out the Russian royal family – a life of intrigue fighting communists – and now a claim for a $200 million dollar fortune, all revealed in a thrilling story by Philippa Schuyler.[5]

Both Schuyler and the *Union-Leader* were strategic choices. The paper's influence extended beyond New Hampshire's borders and deep into American politics; driven by its owner's virulently conservative views, it had earned a national reputation as a champion of right-wing ideology. The reporter, too, was something of a celebrity. A mixed-race child prodigy on the piano, from the 1930s to the 1950s Schuyler had performed on concert stages throughout Europe and South America, drawing huge audiences and garnering rave reviews. But impresarios in the still-segregated United States largely refused to sponsor her until, finally, Schuyler tired of the racism and turned to journalism, writing prolifically for newspapers as well as publishing three well-received books.[6] If the writing style was breathless and gushing, her imprimatur lent weight to Goleniewski's claims.

The most sensational revelation of the past 50 years has just come to light. One of the cleverest lies in history has just been exploded. The world believes that the entire imperial family of Russia perished in a massacre at Ekaterinburg, Siberia, at the orders of Trotsky and Lenin, on the night of July 16–17, 1918.

Except for various claimants of the identity of Anastasia, youngest of Czar Nicholas II's daughters, the massacre itself has never been disputed. The whole world has believed this story, though it was based on the barest of circumstantial evidence . . . now it has become a myth.

The rightful heir of Russia, the Tsarevich Alexei Nicholaevich Romanov, still lives. On the eve of his 60th birthday last week, Grand Duke Alexei tore the veil of silence . . . the following is the first private interview the grand duke has given a journalist since his amazing declaration . . .

Goleniewski's claim to be sixty years old was something of a problem. While the real Aleksei Romanoff had been born in August 1904, Goleniewski was – and very definitely looked – forty-two. Happily, he had an explanation for his remarkably youthful appearance: it was, he explained, a by-product of his miraculous escape from the Bolsheviks:

> I was terribly sick with malaria and other illnesses at the time. My mother, Empress Alexandra, gave me a sleeping draught to calm me and I was smuggled out in a trunk . . . It was a gruelling trip, for I was continuously ill and could not breathe easily . . .

This ordeal had lifelong consequences. 'I didn't grow for ten years after leaving Siberia,' he told Schuyler, and he had worn braces on his 'crippled legs'. She assured her readers that the effects were still visible: 'The indentation left by the constant wearing of the braces can still be seen on his legs. He still walks stiffly, often using a cane. But he is tall and well-built now, and his vigorous personality commands your unquestioning respect.'

If this was hardly rigorous investigative journalism, other parts of Schuyler's enthusiastic story were even less questioning. In the space of just seven days, Goleniewski's story of his escape had changed substantially; having told Farber's WOR audience that he was taken across Siberia and then into Poland, *Union-Leader* readers discovered that he had instead travelled via Turkey and Greece before ending up in Warsaw; Schuyler failed to challenge the discrepancy, preferring to dwell on the 'Grand Duke's' compelling presence:

> He wore a well-cut navy blue suit and a maroon and silver tie. He has forceful, commanding features, a strong nose, and a leonine masterful personality. He looks imperious yet kind – a born leader of men. Despite the frail health of his early youth, Alexei exudes the vital force of an unconquerable spirit . . .
>
> Alexei's eyes are wise, shrewd and penetrating. There is a frank openness there, but also a haunting mystery. I could not decide whether his eyes were hazel, green or blue for they seemed to change with the light.

Beyond Schuyler's uncomfortable school-girl crush, her story also put flesh on the bones of Goleniewski's grandiose claims to have headed a secret anti-communist resistance movement behind the Iron Curtain. From 1930 onwards, he and the Tsar allegedly worked for 'the Russian National Underground' – an organization which was otherwise strangely unknown to anyone in the West:

> They suffered greatly under the Gestapo occupation of Poland. They worked 14 hours a day, and continued with their difficult and dangerous underground activities. Alexei was ordered to enter the Polish Army in 1945; at this time it was not required for him to be a Communist. He never went through the formal proceedings to become a Communist, but later membership in the Party was automatically conferred on him.

> In 1952 . . . his father, Czar Nicholas, died in a village near Posen [Poznan]. At this time Alexei had already worked for four years in the [Polish] Army Counterintelligence, to find out who the West's spies were . . . Ostensibly a Communist, Alexei was still secretly working for the underground biding his time till he could defect.

Not only was this fanciful version of events at odds with his biography in still-secret Polish intelligence files, it was also contradicted by the publicly available account of his life and career issued by the US Immigration and Naturalization Service in support of HR 5507. Untroubled by this fundamental discrepancy, Schuyler then relayed Goleniewski's claims that the CIA knew he was the Tsarevich, but had reneged on an agreement to support his royal claims:

> He says that the American government promised to reveal his true identity when he agreed to come here to help them. He is sad and angry that they have let him down in this, for he is bitterly tired of the decades of concealment.
>
> Alexei says that Allan [sic] Dulles was one of the officials who knew his true identity. He claims that Dulles said to him: 'if you wore a beard you'd look just like your father, the Czar'. We phoned Allan Dulles at his home to check on this. Dulles [then long-retired as Director of Central Intelligence] was courteous but understandably non-committal. Dulles said: 'This story may all be true, or it may not be.' But he did not make a definitive denial.

For her part, Schuyler had no doubts about the remarkable transformation of Michał Goleniewski into Grand Duke Aleksei Romanoff, heir to the Russian throne: 'Looking at Alexei's commanding and imperial presence, I for one, was convinced of the truth of his story.'[7]

Others were less impressed. To the Agency, the *Union-Leader* interview was ample proof of its current Director's assessment that Goleniewski 'was a psychopathic case' – a view now shared by Michael

Feighan; after defending 'the Polish defector' for more than a year, the Congressman accepted that the man had lost his mind.[8]

Curiously, however, neither Langley nor any of Goleniewski's erstwhile champions on Capitol Hill seems to have wondered how, or exactly when, this dramatic decline in his mental health came about. Had they done so they might have discovered it had its roots in something rather more prosaic than madness: a fabled and long-lost Romanoff fortune. And they might also have questioned the influence of a man who would play a central role in the genuine insanity which followed.

Robert Speller & Sons, Publishers, occupied a small office in midtown, Manhattan; the ground floor of number 33 West 42nd Street was home to a popular local coffee shop bearing the unfortunate name 'Chock Full O'Nuts', and an elderly service elevator haltingly hoisted visitors to Speller's fifth-floor rooms.

But though the location was somewhat distanced from the traditional New York publishing powerhouses, the company did steady business, and had earned a respectable reputation for releasing non-fiction books on Russian history and Soviet communism.

Its driving force, Robert Speller Snr, was an amateur historian and something of a Romanoff buff, and in February 1963 a sixty-two-year-old woman, then going by the name Eugenia Smith, brought him a manuscript purporting to be the autobiography of Anastasia; it included a dramatic account of her escape from the massacre at Ekaterinburg.

Smith had arrived in the United States from Holland in July 1922; the passenger manifest for SS *Nieuw Amsterdam* recorded her name as Evgenia Smetisko, a Yugoslavian citizen of German descent. Six years later, now living in Chicago, she applied – in that name – to become a naturalized American citizen.

Over the next three decades she told friends and members of the Russian aristocratic diaspora that her real name was Anastasia Romanoffa, the youngest daughter of Tsar Nicholas. She did not, however, do anything to advance her claims publicly and, as a sizeable cover story in *Life* magazine later reported, when she arrived at 33 West 42nd Street she informed Speller that she was no more than the fortunate custodian of Anastasia's memoirs: 'She said that she had been a friend of the Grand Duchess in Russia and, after her escape from Ekaterinburg, in Romania. Before her death many years ago, Anastasia had entrusted her with notes on which the manuscript was based.'[9]

Although Smith was strangely vague about the date and location of Anastasia's alleged post-execution death, she seemed to know a great deal about the minutiae of Romanoff life; to Speller – 'an expert on royal genealogy' – the manuscript looked convincing. A second meeting, one month later, confirmed his initial assessment:

> The author did have an astonishing familiarity with her subject. In details so minute as to include colors of wallpaper, this Anastasia reported conversations, trips, incidents both previously known and unknown, and altogether displayed a staggering inside knowledge ... She reflected the royal prejudices of the House of Romanov. Her account of the family's imprisonment, of the terrible final moments and the escape was told with emotion and conviction.[10]

Speller began to suspect that Smith was no mere friend of the Grand Duchess but was instead Anastasia herself. If so, he knew that her manuscript would be a publishing sensation.

The records of exactly what followed are a little unclear – the firm collapsed in the 1980s and its once-extensive archive has been scattered[11] – but Smith seems to have confirmed Speller's deduction, and he appears to have sought the advice of two experts: Gleb Botkin, the son of the Romanoff family doctor, who had been a childhood friend of Anastasia, and Cleve Backster, a former senior CIA polygrapher who now ran his own lie-detector company. Botkin allegedly denounced Smith as a fraud,[12] but Backster was convinced she was the genuine article.

Cleve Backster was unquestionably qualified. After serving in the US Army Counter-Intelligence Corps during World War II, he joined the

CIA as 'an interrogation specialist' and was trained in polygraphy; in 1949 he set up and headed the Agency's lie-detector programme and, according to a Congressional report, after moving into private practice, 'conducted classes heavily attended by military, Government agency [and] . . . law enforcement personnel'. Nor, this 'biographical sketch' noted, was his expertise solely academic: 'since 1949 Cleve Backster has at some time served as a polygraphy consultant to most every Government agency who [sic] has made use of polygraph'.[13]

At Speller's request he connected Smith to his table-sized lie-detector equipment. Over several sessions lasting more than thirty hours, she sat in a dowdy hat and coat while he asked a succession of questions and recorded changes in her pulse, blood pressure and breathing. Although some responses indicated she was lying, overall Backster concluded that her story of the Romanoffs' miraculous escape and her claim to be Anastasia were true. In a subsequent statement, published by a New York Russian émigré newspaper, he argued that the inconsistencies in her account and strange behaviour did not invalidate his forensic conclusions:

> I hereby state that, as the result of my committee's research on the fate of the Romanoffs, the evidence uncovered is preponderant that the Russian Imperial Family was not murdered on the night of July 16/17, 1918 in Ekaterinburg and that they all subsequently took refuge in Poland.
>
> Our committee states without reservation that Eugenie Drabek Smetisko, alias Eugenia Smith, is in actuality the Grand Duchess Anastasia Nicholaevna of Russia. In reference to her identity it is undeniable that she has not genuinely co-operated in steps, which she herself initiated, taken to prove her identity and that she has made contradictory and untrue statements.[14]

Backster also roped in some of his former colleagues at Langley. In September he persuaded one of the Agency's specialists to examine a sample of Smith's handwriting. The unnamed officer duly sent back 'a report regarding psychological aspects in the development of the hand-writing'; its conclusions have never been released, but the material was evidently sufficiently interesting for her to recommend further analysis.[15]

Encouraged by this, in October, Speller published Smith's book – *Anastasia, the Autobiography of the Grand Duchess of Russia*. It did not prove to be the runaway success he had hoped for: her claims were roundly denounced by leading anthropologists and forensic experts, commissioned by *Life* to examine the story. But they attracted rather more positive interest from the occupant of the Silver Towers apartment in Queens; to Goleniewski, Eugenia Smith represented an opportunity to get very rich indeed.

For more than forty years newspapers had published rumours about vast, unclaimed Romanoff funds, sitting in the vaults of Western banks. The earliest stories, in the *New York Times* in the summer of 1929, estimated that at the point he was executed the Tsar owned money and jewellery inside Russia worth at least $10 million,[16] as well as a global fortune which could exceed $1 billion.

'Although some of it was invested or held in trust in the Tsar's name,' the *Times* reported, 'a large proportion of it is believed to have been secreted during the war period to avoid the Tsar's enemies.' For good measure, the paper noted[17] that a report recently received from Paris suggested American banks alone held millions of dollars belonging to the Romanoff dynasty.[18]

By 1963 estimates of the value of this supposed hoard ranged from $200 million to $400 million. The only reason – at least, in theory – that it remained unclaimed was the absence of a true Romanoff heir; Goleniewski saw an opportunity to fill that void, and that Eugenia Smith's bogus claim to be Anastasia could provide a direct route to crowning himself as the Tsarevich. On 28 December he phoned Robert Speller.

Announcing himself as 'Mr. Burg', he claimed to have information which might help Smith prove her claim; two days later, he met the publisher at his office, asking him 'to transfer to Grand Duchess Anastasia

Nicholaevna a letter with New Year wishes, and expressing willingness to meet with her as a friend of the Russian Imperial Family'.[19]

Although Goleniewski had not – then – claimed to be Aleksei Romanoff, Speller decided that he was 'one of the few people who wanted to talk to Anastasia . . . whom she should meet', and brokered a meeting with Smith for New Year's Eve.[20] Goleniewski's plans were briefly interrupted by the arrival of Agent Clemens that morning, but by early afternoon he arrived at the midtown office to find the publisher had set up recording equipment.

'It was quite an occasion for our firm,' Speller later told Guy Richards. 'We had all worked with Mrs. Smith for ten months and we sensed this meeting might be important somehow . . . I asked Cleve Backster to bring over a tape recorder and take charge of it. My wife came over too [and] our sons were there.'[21]

The conversation between Goleniewski and Smith began somewhat stiffly, and for the most part was conducted in Russian. The Spellers didn't understand all of it, but managed to follow its general drift:

> We caught the part about the fact that she was recognizing this man as her brother and she was very much affected. I remember at one point the sound of her weeping brought tears to our eyes . . . At the end of about an hour she cried out . . . and then introduced Mr. Backster to him as her brother.

According to Backster's statement the recording of this touching encounter was later fully transcribed, but no copy of it exists in any of the archives holding Goleniewski documents. The only surviving fragment was subsequently published by Richards; this reveals Goleniewski to have asked leading questions, giving Smith carefully tailored snippets from his own biography, then asking her to confirm them. He prompted her to 'remember' that she had 'escaped' from Ekaterinburg using the pseudonym Turynska – in reality, the maiden name of Goleniewski's distinctly non-aristocratic mother, Janina; similarly, he fed her details of an incident which supposedly occurred during their flight to freedom.

'MR BURG' [GOLENIEWSKI]: Do you know who was brought through the Red borders in a washbasket?

'ANASTASIA' [SMITH]: Yes, I know. My father wanted me to forget it. He said so.

'MR BURG': Do you remember Father said: *Neskim*?

'ANASTASIA': (*She cries out*). He knows. He is my brother, Alexei. (*Crying*) My darling, my darling . . .[22]

To a less credulous observer it should have been obvious that this was little more than a tawdry performance by a pair of opportunist imposters. But, with the prospect of global fame and the mythical Romanoff fortune before him, Speller chose to take it as proof positive that Smith was Anastasia and Goleniewski the Tsarevich – a gullibility which, remarkably, survived Smith withdrawing from the charade three weeks later on the grounds that she had 'serious difficulties connected with [Goleniewski's] appearance'.[23] Despite this setback, from January 1964 the publisher became 'Aleksei's' foremost advocate, setting up both the Farber and Schuyler interviews that summer.

At this stage Goleniewski plainly knew his royal pretence was bogus. Three weeks before he revealed his 'true' identity to WOR listeners, Polish intelligence intercepted a letter he had sent to Janina in Warsaw. According to the UB's files, he told his mother that he would shortly claim to be 'the last of the Romanoffs', and, exactly as he had done with Eugenia Smith, tried to feed her the information she would need to play her role: 'The subject, referring to the memory of various allegedly real situations, tries in this way to let his mother understand that he wants her to believe in it and repeat it if necessary as experiences and episodes confirming the truthfulness of his "Tsarist comedy".'[24]

That money, not madness, was his prime motive emerged clearly in the two August interviews. Speller, sitting next to the self-declared Tsarevich, told Farber that the Romanoff fortune was worth 'a few hundred million dollars . . . two or three hundred million, four hundred million . . . all we know is what we hear, but we did understand that the Czar, Nicholas II, was the single wealthiest man in the world prior to the Russian revolution'; then Goleniewski was asked what he planned to do about his 'inheritance':

> FARBER: Colonel Goleniewski, are you going to take this case to the American courts and claim the Romanoff fortune?

> GOLENIEWSKI: Sure . . . If I have legalization of my real identity . . . I am pretty old man, I don't need very big money for myself [but] I think . . . my sisters, the child[ren] of my sisters . . . the Russian Orthodox Church . . . [and] my relatives . . . has the right to have something from that money.[25]

To Philippa Schuyler, one week later, he pronounced himself 'not motivated by greed' and now maintained he had more altruistic plans for the $200 million, plus interest, supposedly sitting in Western banks. 'I do not wish to keep the money for myself. I would want to use it to help the people who helped us through the years, and to fight communism.'[26]

If, at this point, Goleniewski was probably more avaricious than deranged, the next act in his 'Tsarist comedy' locked him, irrevocably, into his royal pretensions: he decided to remarry Irmgard, this time under the auspices of the Russian Orthodox Church, and in his new, 'true' identity.

New York City marriage licence number 24955 was issued by the City Clerk, Borough of Manhattan, on the morning of 29 September 1964. Valid for sixty days it recorded the would-be groom's name as Aleksei N. Romanoff, a 'retired Colonel', born on 12 August 1904, in Peterhoff, Russia; his parents were listed as 'Nicholas A. Romanoff and Aleksandra F. von Hesse', born in Russia and Germany respectively. Both he and his bride-to-be had, the form stated, given 'a full and true abstract of all the facts' and these had been recorded in 'affidavits or verified statements presented to me upon application for this license'. In doing so the happy couple swore on oath that neither had been married previously; since it was just four years since they had celebrated their wedding in Virginia this was a barefaced lie and, on Goleniewski's part, managed the remarkable feat of adding a second offence of bigamy to the felony of perjury.[27]

Shortly before noon the next day, the bridal party rushed to the Orthodox Cathedral of Our Lady of the Sign on East 93rd Street, Manhattan. The reason for their haste was Irmgard's condition; early that morning she had felt the first stabs of labour pains, and seemed likely to give birth within the coming hours. Fortunately, Robert Speller and his sons quickly rounded up witnesses from the Russian émigré community, and summoned the priest to meet them at the altar.

The man who was to conduct the ceremony was not, however, a lowly prelate. The Very Reverend Count Georgi P. Grabbe was Archpriest and Protopresbyter of the Synod of Bishops of the Russian Orthodox Church Outside Russia – in essence, one of the most senior clerics in the exiled official faith – and his close relatives had served in the Imperial household prior to the Revolution. Nor was his presence an accident: one day after the *Union-Leader* appeared, the energetic Robert Speller Snr had brought him to Goleniewski's apartment and stressed the occupant's true identity.

'Before our first meeting,' Goleniewski wrote in a lengthy statement published three months later in the *Journal-American*, 'Father Georgi was informed by Mr. Speller that, based on his investigations, he believed my claim to being the Tsarevich was correct.' Between 18 August and 29 September, Grabbe had five further meetings with the groom- and bride-to-be; they discussed 'the problems of my life and my real identity' as he prepared the couple for the forthcoming ceremony.[28]

Those rites were particularly important. Traditionally, the Tsar was the head of the Russian Orthodox Church, and ever since the assassination the faithful had regularly prayed for him and his family; so fervent was this dedication to the Romanoffs that there had been suggestions the family should be made saints. According to an account by Robert Speller Jnr, present as a witness and photographer, the nuptials seemed to recognize Goleniewski's claimed royal status: 'I'll never forget it as long as I live . . . There are times in the ceremony when the bride and the groom have to walk around and around the altar, with persons holding crowns over their heads. I was holding a crown over the bride, and my father [held] a crown over the groom.'[29]

A little over an hour later the marriage of Alexei Nicholaevich and Irmgard Margareta Romanoff was entered on the Parish Register and Grabbe inscribed his signature, confirming the legality of the wedding. After a brief round of celebratory drinks, the couple dashed across town to a hospital in Manhasset on Long Island, and later that evening Irmgard delivered the couple's daughter. Two days later, Goleniewski registered the birth with the New York State Department of Health; Certificate number 1700 recorded her name as Tatiana Alekseievna Romanoff.[30]

From that moment on, there was no going back. Whatever his official documentation might state, Michał Goleniewski, alias Franz Oldenburg, alias Martin Cherico, was now trapped forever in his self-declared identity as the rightful heir to the Russian Imperial throne. If his former employers in Warsaw and Langley found the pretence absurd and palpable evidence of the man's growing insanity, his claims were shortly to receive very public endorsements – including sworn affidavits from several ostensibly rational sources.

24

Support

'NATURALLY,' GOLENIEWSKI INFORMED the reporter sitting opposite him, 'a man makes enemies when he exposes secret agents. It's a dangerous game . . .':

> But what I didn't expect is the new canard that I'm going out of
> my mind since I did such great work for your country – that I am,
> as you say, becoming a kook. I find a neat communist twist to that
> rumor. If people believe it they will not only forgive all blunders
> in dealing with my case, but they'll please the Russians. If poten-
> tial defectors see what can happen to a man with my record, see
> that he'll be taken for a nut, you can bet they won't defect.

A fortnight before the Russian Orthodox Church wedding, Robert Speller brought Guy Richards to the apartment on Queens Boulevard for the latest of Goleniewski's 'exclusive' interviews. Six months earlier Goleniewski had accused Richards and his paper of 'libel' for reporting his existence and key revelations; now the *soi-disant* Grand Duke Aleksei Romanoff, Tsarevich and heir to the Imperial Russian throne, welcomed the *New York Journal-American* into his home:

> [I] was greeted by a handsome medium-build figure with a
> 'Guardsman' moustache, an urbane manner and a slightly Oxon-
> ian accent. 'Are you really Grand Duke Alexei, the Tsarevich?'
> I asked. 'Yes,' he replied.

'Why have you waited all these years to say so?'

'While Stalin and my father were both alive we were in constant danger and we all followed my father's orders to remain underground in peril of being killed if our identity became known.'

Richards felt obliged to ask why, since Stalin had died in 1953, His Imperial Highness had waited more than a decade to disclose his real identity. The answer, Goleniewski claimed, was security:

> Believe me, in those ten [sic] years I have thought of little else. But I had to give grave consideration to the safety of those Russian and Polish patriots who had risked their lives to protect me and my family. That is still an urgent matter. It governs every move I make.

Strangely, given his frequent warnings that the CIA was deeply penetrated by the KGB, he repeated his account of having revealed himself to its officials shortly after arriving in America, and accused Langley of a 'conspiracy' to deprive him of his rightful inheritance. The claim seemed improbable; if, as he alleged, the Agency was overrun with Moscow's spies, they would, surely, have quickly reported the Tsarevich's presence on US soil. Nor is there evidence in any of the declassified files to support the story; none of the documents released by the FBI or the CIA contain even a hint of it, and it first appears in the largely unredacted Polish intelligence dossier on TEL-ETECHNIK after the Farber and Schuyler publicity.

But Speller, who according to the UB's reports had some previous contact with the CIA, added a tantalizing detail: the Agency had not only known about the Romanoff claims, but had initially suspected they could be part of a Machiavellian financial scam by Moscow:

> Officials of the US Government were on alert to the possibility that Goleniewski's defection could be part of a slick Communist plot to back Goleniewski's claim to the Czar's fortune in cash and jewels in the West – a fortune estimated to be around $400 million.

> If Goleniewski, with the tacit assistance of the Kremlin, could win legal claim to that fortune, then the United States . . . could not deduct such huge governmental debts as Russia has run up on lend-lease. In other words, Goleniewski, as an individual, could get the whole pile – then divvy it up with the Kremlin as per prior secret agreement.

Happily, the publisher was able to reassure Richards' readers that both he and US intelligence had decided this theory 'doesn't hold water', and that Goleniewski had 'been secretly working against the Communists his whole life long'.[1]

If there was surprisingly little other media coverage that autumn, Goleniewski's allegations and pretensions found support in the ranks of the influential and Congressionally authorized US war veterans association. On 19 and 20 October 1964 the National Executive Commission of the American Legion met in Indianapolis to consider requests from several regional branches to take up the case. Fortunately for Washington, FBI files show that it had a mole inside the NEC who, on behalf of the US government, was able to defuse the demands:

> Special Agent Hanning[2] attended captioned meetings and deliberated with the National Americanism Commission,[3] of which he is a member . . . Four resolutions dealt with the Michal Goleniewski case and called for Congressional investigation of Goleniewski's charges that all branches of the Government with the exception of the FBI have been penetrated by Soviet intelligence. On S. A. Hanning's confidential recommendation these four resolutions were rejected.[4]

It would not be the last time federal agents attempted to starve Goleniewski's case of the oxygen of publicity. But, as the end of 1964 approached, it was clear that his claims were gaining unwelcome attention.

In early December, Father Georgi Grabbe attempted to retract his endorsement of Goleniewski's royal pretensions. 'I have never recognized

Mr. Goleniewski-Romanoff as the Tsarevich,' he told *Novoye Russkoye Slovo*, adding the improbable explanation for his willingness to conduct the marriage and sign the Parish Register that 'in Russia there were as many Romanoffs as in the United States there are Smiths . . .'[5]

Whether or not, as Goleniewski claimed three weeks later, this volte-face was instigated by mysterious forces who 'for political, financial and other reasons, have been and are interested in the exile, isolation and prevention of the reappearance of my family . . . and in my Father's inheritance in the West,'[6] Grabbe swiftly asked the Synod of Bishops to change the name in the Parish Register. This provoked an angry letter to the Church from the Speller family:

> As witnesses to the marriage of the Tsarevich and Grand Duke of Russia, Aleksei Nicholaevich Romanoff, to Irmgard M. Kampf . . . we categorically reject any attempt by you to change the record of the marriage record without our consent, which we decline to give.
>
> The marriage was performed by the representative of your Synod . . . who was given documents in our presence before performing the ceremony which clearly and unmistakably stated that he was to perform the marriage of Aleksei Nicholaevich Romanoff, born August 12, 1904 in Peterhoff, Russia, the son of Nicholas A. Romanoff . . . and of Aleksandra F. von Hesse . . . There was at no time any mention of any other name being used by the Tsarevich.[7]

Ever since the revolution, the worldwide White Russian émigré community had been riven by disputes between rival factions, each claiming to be the legitimate heirs to the Imperial legacy. In January 1965, Goleniewski's cause received a welcome boost when an influential figure in one of the warring cliques bestowed his blessing: Colonel Alexis I. Toultzeff, Cossack member of the Supreme Monarchist Front, headed by Grand Duke Vladimir Kirrilovich, the leading claimant to the Romanoff throne,[8] announced that he was switching his loyalty to the new pretender.

'I have seen the Czarevich Alexei myself,' Toultzeff told UPI, 'and can affirm that he deserves respect. The Czarevich had already expressed his desire to liberate Russia from the Bolshevik yoke . . . there is a great opportunity to restore the soul of Russia.'[9]

The internecine squabbles of the Russian aristocratic diaspora were commonplace and did not generally attract much press attention. But the Goleniewski-Romanoff saga proved irresistible, largely due to the allegations of CIA chicanery. Another UPI story, quoting complaints by the Agency's former polygraph chief Cleve Backster that his erstwhile employers were suppressing evidence, was picked up and run by newspapers across America:

> Cleve Backster, an identification expert who has been an advisor to the FBI, said recently that fingerprints and dental comparisons indicated that Goleniewski is the Czarevich. The fingerprints were allegedly obtained from documents found in England which had been handled by the Czar's son.[10]

Nor was Backster the only former officer to come out in support of Goleniewski's claims. On 19 January 1965, beneath the headline 'CIA Challenged to Bare Data on Czarevich Case', the *Journal* announced the entry of a new champion in the battle:

> A former Central Intelligence official challenged the Agency to disclose evidence that a defector Polish spy is actually the son of the last Russian Czar, according to a United Press International report today . . . Herman Kimsey, former chief of analysis and research for the CIA and lately assistant chief of security for the Republican National Committee, said the CIA has made exhaustive tests to establish the true identity of the mysterious Pole, Col. Michael [sic] Goleniewski . . .

Kimsey stressed that he had been employed by the Agency at the time of these alleged investigations, and that he was therefore speaking with first-hand knowledge of their outcome:

During the months of 1961 when Col. Goleniewski's antecedents were under CIA scrutiny with the aid of information gained from the files of British intelligence, Mr. Kimsey was head of the CIA research station . . . [he] said he had knowledge of comparisons of fingerprints, sole [foot] prints and dental charts of Col. Goleniewski and the Czarevich . . .

'On the basis of what I know [about] the CIA's investigation of Goleniewski's identity, I believe he is the Czarevich Alexei,' Mr Kimsey said. 'I do not know why the CIA has withheld the necessary proof of identity from a person who has done so much for this country and who only wishes to live under his own name and claim what is rightfully his.'[11]

Kimsey followed this statement with a sworn affidavit in which he detailed the tests that, he claimed, the CIA had performed and which had provided 'affirmative results' proving that Goleniewski was Aleksei Romanoff:

A. Fingerprint comparison with those of the Tsarevich taken during his visit to London in 1909 and later from other sources in possession of the British Government.

B. Sole prints comparisons with those of birth records and later medical records in possession of British Government, German Government and Synod of Russian Orthodox Church in New York City.

C. Dental charts comparisons with those on file with the late Dr. Kostrycki of Paris, France and formerly the Dentist of the Russian Imperial Family.

D. Anthropometrical test compared with material from sister and other relatives.

E. Face print test comparison with photos taken in childhood, and parents and grandparents.

F. Blood test compared with previous medical records and those of family.

G. Medical records compared for purpose of checking scars and
marks with special attention to legs.

H. Handwriting compared with childhood writing.[12]

As with many of the allegations in the Goleniewski drama, there was
some basic evidential foundation for Kimsey's claims. The Tsar and
Tsarina had indeed travelled to England in August 1909, to spend Cowes
Week with their royal cousin, King Edward VII. The visit attracted a hostile public response and the Romanoffs were closely guarded by British
police. But although photographs show that Aleksei and his sisters
accompanied their parents,[13] there is no evidence that any member of
the Imperial Family was fingerprinted, much less required to provide
prints of their soles.

Similarly, there was documentary support for Kimsey's claim that
blood samples taken from Goleniewski showed he, like the Tsarevich,
suffered from haemophilia. A letter Kimsey secured from Dr Alexander
Wiener – one of the world's leading experts on Serology and Forensic
Medicine[14] – recorded the results of tests carried out the previous
summer:

> I saw [Goleniewski] in consultation in June 1964 . . . My examin-
> ation, and blood tests which I ran on Col. Goleniewski, proved
> that he suffered from hereditary blood disease, giving rise to
> problems in blood coagulation and bleeding . . .
>
> This tend[s] to support very strongly the belief that Col.
> Goleniewski is in fact the Tsarevich and Grand Duke Aleksei
> Nicholaevich Romanoff.[15]

Herman Kimsey's intervention was significant since his credentials
were genuine and impressive: a wartime US Army Intelligence officer,
he had been employed by the CIA from 1954 to 1962, rising through its
forensic section to become Chief of Research and Analysis, and his personnel records contained no complaints concerning his performance or

his honesty. When he left Langley, aged forty-seven, he did so on good terms under the 701 programme, the reorganization and redundancies that followed in the wake of the Bay of Pigs fiasco. The Agency plainly recognized the importance of an apparently responsible former intelligence officer publicly supporting the 'Tsarevich's' case; from December 1964, when he began acting as an intermediary between Goleniewski and Langley, its files filled up with increasingly anxious internal memos. A report of an early meeting, by Ralph E. Tobiassen, one of its senior officials, set the tone:

> By direction of the Director of Security . . . a former Agency Staff Employee, Herman E. Kimsey, was interviewed by Mr. Eugene Winters from 10.20 to 11.30am on 8 December 1964 . . . Mr. Winters used the alias of Gene Williams and Tobiassen used the alias of Ralph Thomas during this interview with Kimsey . . .
>
> Kimsey claims to have the confidence of [02] VISION [one of the Agency's cryptonyms for Goleniewski] and it finally evolved [sic] late in the interview that Kimsey was in fact acting as an emissary for him in attempting to swing a deal with the Agency whereby the Agency would give to [02] VISION some documents which [02] VISION claims to need to establish his true identity as the Tsarevich.
>
> Specifically these documents are: a passport, some dental records (on file somewhere in Europe) and a fingerprint card. Kimsey, throughout the interview, referred to [02] VISION as 'the Tsarevich' and appears to be convinced that [02] VISION's claims are true and also that Eugenia Smith is in fact the real Anastasia and therefore [02] VISION's sister.
>
> Kimsey stated that [02] VISION's sole intentions are to establish his name and claim his rightful inheritance for the benefit of his newborn son [sic]. He said [02] VISION still wields influence within White Russian circles all over the world and has much information which he has not yet divulged which would be of benefit to this Agency. Kimsey further stated that if [02] VISION fails to obtain his goals, there will never be another defector out of Poland.[16]

From early January 1965 onwards, Kimsey had a succession of interviews with CIA staff. At each he stressed that he was acting as Goleniewski's representative and pressed them to meet 'Aleksei's' needs. At first, the Agency was determined to keep its distance, repeatedly insisting that Goleniewski should go through 'established channels' – a demand which, since it had cut off all contact with its former agent, was hardly realistic; when, on Kimsey's recommendation, Goleniewski sent letters asking for a meeting, the Agency simply ignored them.

But by the end of the month senior officers at Langley realized that Kimsey could offer useful insight into Goleniewski's future plans, as well as any activities which could cause problems for the Agency. The meetings resumed and would continue for the next two years. Unaware that he was being played, Kimsey provided a steady stream of information, much of it revolving around Goleniewski's increasingly fantastic claims to the Russian throne and to the presumed Romanoff fortune.

'Kimsey stated that there is an international conspiracy at the highest levels,' one memo recorded:

> ... and named Lord Mountbatten and the 'French premier' as part of this conspiracy to deny [02] VISION's and Anastasia's claims so that the $400,000,000 lodged in banks in England and France and in the United States will stay there.
>
> Kimsey said he and Baxter [sic] and Speller at the moment are not getting any money from [02] VISION, however, should [02] VISION's claims be established he will no doubt pay them at a later date.[17]

But Kimsey also provided intelligence which reinforced Langley's conviction that Goleniewski had lost his mind. On 28 January he met an Assistant Director of the Security Division to pass on 'some highly sensitive information...that could possibly be a source of great embarrassment to the Agency'. This turned out to be a rambling and extraordinarily paranoid story in which Goleniewski claimed that the CIA had attempted to kill him:

At the time that Goleniewski move[d] to New York City, an Agency doctor recommended to him a physician in New York City. Subject contacted the physician and received medication for the treatment of his haemophilia. After taking the medicine for an unspecified period of time, Subject's health appeared to get worse instead of better. A friend of Goleniewski's, who was also known to Kimsey (Kimsey said he could not identify the friend at this time) suggested that Goleniewski go to his (the friend's) physician. Goleniewski did this roughly about nine months ago.

Shortly after Goleniewski had visited the doctor, the friend received a call from the doctor who told him something as follows. The doctor said he would deny this to anyone else but, since he and the friend had known each other for about 25 years, he felt that he could tell his friend that the medicine Goleniewski was taking was actually a slow poison, and that if Goleniewski had continued on this medication he would be dead in 30 days. The physician gave him some other medicine, and Goleniewski's health improved rapidly . . .

Now, whether the doctor or the friend told Goleniewski about this Kimsey did not know, but Kimsey felt that it was important that we know about this since it accounted for Goleniewski's sudden distrust of the people from the Agency with whom he had been dealing and his great reluctance to come to Washington. Kimsey said he did not know the doctors' names but possibly could get them for me.[18]

Since Goleniewski had never complained of being poisoned to any of his handlers, in any of his conversations with Congressional officials or in his lengthy letters to successive CIA Directors, the Agency filed the ridiculous story away as evidence of his descent into full-blown madness.

However, it paid rather more attention to news that he had signed formal agreements for a book about his life; Guy Richards was to be his co-author, and Robert Speller Snr the publisher. Neither contract would survive the summer, but the news caused the CIA some disquiet. It pumped Kimsey for information on progress of the manuscript[19] and quietly began monitoring Richards.[20]

That spring, as his supporters lobbied the CIA and championed his Romanoff claims in the press, Goleniewski himself was preoccupied with the continuing problem of his legal identity in the United States. The Alien Registration Cards issued by the Immigration and Natural-ization Service, as well as the record of his first marriage in Arlington, were in the names of Franz and Irmgard Oldenburg; so, too, was his now suspended second contract with the Agency. HR 5507, however, bestowed the right to apply for American citizenship on Michał Goleni-ewski: the two identities were completely incompatible, and thanks to his insistence on calling himself Aleksei Romanoff for the purposes of his second wedding (and on his daughter's birth certificate) the ques-tion of who was actually entitled to live and – theoretically – work in the country had become a bureaucratic Gordian knot. At the end of March, backed by letters of endorsement from Speller, Backster and Kimsey, he and Irmgard applied for replacement Alien Registration Cards in their new Imperial Russian names.

Unsurprisingly, the immigration service was not willing to provide official recognition of Goleniewski's Romanoff pretence. It sent a terse note, advising the couple that 'after careful consideration of the evidence submitted, the applications were denied'.[21] To Irmgard, plainly bewil-dered by the turn of events, the rejection was inexplicable. 'What kind of law in the United States and of the New York State,' she wrote in a plan-gent open letter to President Lyndon Johnson, 'does forbid me the use of my surname under which I married my husband in a lawful ceremony solemnized by the authorized and competent clergyman, after a legal and rightful Marriage License of the City Clerk of the City of New York was issued? This marriage was and is lawful and documented by issue of the extract from The Parish Register on Marriages by the Synod of Bishops of the Church as well as by issue of Certificate of Marriage Registration of the City Clerk of the City of NY as the lawful and authorized representa-tive of the State New York, and consequently recorded forever.'[22]

If she had a legitimate grievance – the various branches of State and federal government seemed unable or unwilling to work together – she overlooked the fact that much of the problem was of Goleniewski's own creation; as far as Washington was concerned he had made his Imperial bed and it was up to him to find a way of surviving in it.

For his part, this latest rebuff pushed Goleniewski deeper into his already advanced paranoia. Convinced that US intelligence was determined to bring him down, and had somehow turned his allies against him, he publicly fired his most diligent collaborators via a paid advertisement in the *New York Herald Tribune*:

> I, Aleksei Nicholaevich Romanoff, Heir Apparent, Tsarevich, Grand Duke of Russia also known as Colonel Michael Goleniewski hereby discharge Robert Speller and Sons Publishers Inc . . . as my publisher and representative . . . Therefore all rights of said firm used with reference to any publication about my person, activity and appointments, such as . . . Guy Richards from the *New York Journal-American* . . . are automatically cancelled and revoked.[23]

In the autumn of 1965, the CIA lost any lingering patience with Goleniewski and his antics. On 5 October it unilaterally ended his employment, explaining that 'the United States regards your continued nonperformance under the contract as breach of contract by you, and the Government hereby terminates that contract effective this date'. From then on the only payment or benefit he would receive was a monthly $500 dividend from the restitution trust fund.[24]

Four years and nine months after it had given him asylum and the promise of a new life in America, the United States government abandoned any responsibility for its most celebrated agent. The best spy the West had ever known was pushed, firmly and irrevocably, back out into the cold.

25

Wilderness

H E DID NOT go without a fight. If his mental health was disintegrating and if he had yet fully to grasp the complications of Western democracy, Goleniewski had learned enough about America to grasp its instinctive response to any problem: in December 1965 he hired a lawyer.

Vincent P. Brevetti had been practising law in New York for more than two decades; the only interruption in his otherwise successful career was a two-year suspension of his licence for financial misconduct.[1] When he signed on to represent Goleniewski, he had been back in business for four years and anticipated a profitable relationship. His client signed their contract in the names 'Franz R. Oldenburg *aka* Michael Goleniewski' and instructed him to sue the United States government for the sum of $186,500 – the equivalent of $1.5 million today; Brevetti's share was to be 10 per cent.[2]

On 3 December the lawyer sent formal notice of the claim to Langley. He was confident that the law was on his side, stressing that the CIA had improperly terminated Goleniewski's employment:

> This claim is made upon a contract signed between Mr. Franz R. Oldenburg and the Central Intelligence Agency and/or the United States of America, which became effective on October 7, 1963. One of the provisions of said contract was that it could not be terminated unless Mr. Oldenburg was given one year's notice

in writing. Since said notice was given on October 5, 1965, the
contract would in fact be terminated on October 6, 1966.

Of the total figure demanded, $50,000 was the salary withheld since
Goleniewski had been placed on 'Leave Without Pay'; the balance, however, was for the full value of the restitution awarded to both him and
Irmgard, which the Agency was then drip-feeding to the couple at the
rate of $500 per month. Brevetti signed off the letter with a lawyerly
flourish: 'As Mr. Oldenburg's attorney, I strongly recommend that you
wire me for the purpose of setting up an appointment to discuss this
entire matter. If I do not hear from you or your representative within 10
days, further action will be taken in this matter.'[3]

Brevetti had, unfortunately, not anticipated the Agency's determination to punish its wayward former employee. On 16 December the
attorney had a lengthy meeting with CIA General Counsel, John
S. Warner. It did not go well: 'Mr. Warner rejected both claims,' Brevetti
reported. '[He] acknowledged and agreed that there are monies due to
Mr. Oldenburg and his wife, but he refuses to recommend payment.'[4]

For all their bravado, the attorney and his client did not relish the
prospect of taking the Agency to court. Litigation was guaranteed to be
slow and extremely expensive, and Goleniewski could afford neither the
delay nor the lawyer's fees. After issuing a stern warning to Warner that
he would be held 'responsible for Goleniewski's "personal safety" ',[5] they
decided to try their luck again on Capitol Hill.

Goleniewski fired off another impassioned plea to Michael Feighan,
and Brevetti sought support from one of the Congressmen representing
New York, Joseph P. Addabbo. Neither proved willing to help; Feighan
simply ignored the letter while Addabbo replied saying that since Goleniewski wasn't his constituent 'much as I would like to assist you . . . all
Congressional protocol dictates against it.'[6] Nor were they alone in turning their backs. From February to April, lawyer and client approached
more than forty other lawmakers in both the House and Senate; none
responded.[7] Like the agencies of the Executive Branch, the elected

members of the Legislature found Goleniewski's royal pretensions simply too much to swallow.

He met a similarly obdurate – if slightly more polite – response from the British government. On 16 March, on stationery proclaiming himself to be 'Heir Apparent, Tsarevich and Grand Duke of Russia, Hetman of All The Cossacks, Head of The Imperial Russian House etc. etc.', the self-styled Aleksei Romanoff wrote to the British Consul in New York. The letter was long and rambling and contained no explanation of what the writer actually wanted London to do; unsurprisingly, it was met with some scepticism.

'It would be easy,' Consul-General Charles A. Thompson wrote to his superiors in Whitehall, 'to dismiss Mr. Romanoff as a mental case and to ignore any further correspondence. But it bears many of the marks of the beginning of a correspondence which could be taken up by the press and become a nuisance . . . I imagine there is already an ample dossier in London on "Mr. Romanoff" (alias Colonel Michael Goleniewski) and his allegations, and I should be grateful if we could be given some hint as to how to deal with him if he should continue the correspondence.'[8]

Two weeks later, J. E. Jackson, a London-based official, responded with the outcome of the Foreign Office's internal enquiries:

> I understand from . . . the Soviet Research Department that 'Alexsei [sic] Nicholaevitch Romanoff' is an impostor who has been pushing his unfounded claims for some time. There are no other Foreign Office papers about him . . . [and] there is no trace of Mr. Goleniewski on any Foreign Office files . . . I think we can simply reply to New York that we have taken note of the letter and that we do not think anything further needs to be done for the moment.[9]

Jackson's note was technically correct, if slightly misleading. There was, in fact, an extensive file on Goleniewski in London, but this was held by MI5 which reported exclusively to the Home Office;[10] whether the Foreign Office's failure to discover it resulted from the archaic Whitehall practice of maintaining a Chinese wall between departments, or a convenient bureaucratic blindness, it was very clear that the British wanted nothing to do with the supposed heir to the Romanoff throne.

But if the governments in London and Washington had no further use for Goleniewski and his increasingly unhinged pretensions, the militant subculture of American anti-communist organizations had no such scruples; early in 1966 they eagerly adopted him to advance their cause.

Although Senator Joe McCarthy had long since fallen into disgrace, away from the rarefied air on Capitol Hill the 'Red Scare' he inflamed had never died. In late 1961, FBI Director J. Edgar Hoover had felt the need to call his fellow citizens to arms, warning in a speech in December that 'we are at war with the Communists, and the sooner each red-blooded American realizes that the better and safer we will be',[11] and in the mid-1960s across the country's heartlands conservative fears of Soviet influence in domestic affairs were reignited by the Civil Rights movement, demands for desegregation, and the stirrings of youthful revolt against the Vietnam War.

In this climate grass-roots extreme conservative groups flourished, pumping out a steady flow of newsletters, pamphlets and books promoting a broad swathe of conspiracy theories. If some were amateurish in content presentation – the typewritten equivalent of today's web blogs or Twitter feeds – others were professionally printed and attracted sizeable support.

The biggest, most powerful and most virulently right-wing group, the John Birch Society, was formed in 1958 by Robert Welch Jnr, a wealthy retired candy manufacturer from Massachusetts. In the wake of the assassination of John F. Kennedy by Lee Harvey Oswald, it purchased recruitment advertisements in newspapers across the country:

> For five years the John Birch Society has said that, regardless of the external threat, Communism was a serious internal menace in the United States. And we were right . . . We believe that the president of the United States has been murdered by a Communist within

the United States ... The time has come for ... good Americans to join us in this fight against the powerfully organized 'masters of deceit'.[12]

The Society begat, and was the lynchpin of, an assortment of other extreme right-wing groups across America. Most were unrepentantly racist and viciously anti-Semitic, but, with nowhere else to turn, Goleniewski accepted them as allies in his ongoing battles with the CIA and the US government; all he required was the platform they provided – and their unquestioning acceptance of his claim to be the Tsarevich.

The first of these new champions operated from a Post Office box in Zarepath, New Jersey. Frank A. Capel described himself as a pre-war 'Chief of Investigations' for Westchester County Sheriff's Department, and claimed to have run its 'Bureau of Investigation and Subversive Activities'.[13]

His proven history during World War II was rather less distinguished: as a member of the War Production Board he had acquired a criminal record for demanding – and receiving – bribes from companies bidding for contracts.[14] Untroubled by this conviction, Welch hired Capel to write a column on intelligence for the John Birch Society news magazines, *The New American* and *American Opinion*.

In the early 1960s, Capel branched out and set up his own bi-monthly publication, *The Herald of Freedom*. It churned out a familiar diet of conspiracy theories, anti-communist propaganda and claims that the US government was riddled with Soviet spies; it was, then, perfectly suited to Goleniewski's needs.

In February and March 1966 two separate issues were devoted to 'The Strange Case of "Col. Goleniewski"'. These relayed, unfiltered by fact checking, his own version of his life, his service for American intelligence, the treatment he received from the CIA, and the US government's failure to investigate the spies he had identified inside the Agency and the State Department. *The Herald of Freedom* also repeated, without challenge or caveat, Goleniewski's claims to be Aleksei Romanoff, and

Capel castigated Washington's allegedly pro-communist bureaucracy for obstructing the Tsarevich's attempts to claim his rightful inheritance:

> We urge our fellow anti-communists, whether they accept him as Alexei Nicholaevich Romanoff, heir to the throne of Russia, or 'Col. Goleniewski', a Polish defector who tried to help the people and government of the United States by giving information concerning those who are plotting against them in and out of their own government, to insist that justice be done . . .
>
> The CIA must be held responsible for its actions; its secret archives must be made to disgorge the information needed to solve 'the strange case of Col. Goleniewski'.[15]

Capel was a rabid Red pursuer, but his anti-communist passion – and his place within the would-be Tsarevich's new circle of supporters – was soon eclipsed in Goleniewski's favours by Edward Hunter, a former intelligence officer who claimed, in testimony to the House Un-American Activities Committee in March 1958, to have invented the phrase 'brainwashing' as a description for the alleged use of hypnosis by Chinese forces in Korea.[16] Despite the fact that a US Defense Department investigation categorically rejected these theories,[17] Goleniewski was attracted by the potential to advance his case in the pages of Hunter's magazine, *Tactics*, and began sending him lengthy and largely incoherent screeds for publication.

Hunter was initially willing to tolerate the imperious commands issued from the Queens apartment, but not unreasonably insisted on editing the content to make it comprehensible; he was also reluctant to endorse the Romanoff claims without rather more than the would-be Tsarevich's own word to support them.

It was a sign of Goleniewski's deteriorating sanity that he could not tolerate any challenge to his expertise or self-declared authority, and he bombarded Hunter with vitriolic telegrams and letters. 'You operate with phony promises,' he fumed in one characteristically unhinged diatribe. 'You supported the British-Bolshevik conspiracy against me, brainwashing the Americans with my assumed identity of Michael Goleniewski . . . My attorneys know a case in Philadelphia where a reporter got 10 years in jail just for threatening some people with publication of such kind which you already printed concerning my person & activities. I hope . . . it will not be necessary to use aforementioned tactics by court against you.'[18]

Hunter pleaded – sometimes successfully, but often in vain – for Goleniewski to be reasonable. 'You should appreciate [my] sincerity instead of hurling brimstone and fire at me,' he complained:

> You express anger because I do not come right out and refer to you as Romanoff, or Romanov, son of the Czar. If I did, all it would do would be without effect, because I am in no position to do any investigating and confirming in depth, and people know it . . . I cannot determine it myself and neither can any other person without investigatory facilities. I did say, several times, that I would write a special article just on your status, as you declare it to be. I am still willing to do so. But it is impossible, on so complicated a matter, for me to take notes and clippings you send me, and write just from them.[19]

Goleniewski's other choice of champion was immeasurably worse than either Capel or Hunter. Richard Cotten, another John Birch Society alumnus, boasted a résumé which combined fervent anti-communism with rancid anti-Semitism. From his home in Bakersfield, California, Cotten broadcast a daily 'talk' on WGCB radio, *Conservative Viewpoint*, and published an accompanying newsletter; according to the State Controller of California, both were liberally laced with dramatic allegations of a sinister conspiracy involving the federal government and a supposed cabal of influential Jewish-Americans.[20]

None of this apparently mattered to Goleniewski; in the summer of 1966 he welcomed Cotten into the Queens apartment and, flanked by

Herman Kimsey and Cleve Backster, gave a recorded interview to advance his claims that both British and American intelligence had verified his claim to the Romanoff throne:

> My father, his Imperial Majesty Imperator of all Russia, Nicholas II, placed in the British Trust, prior to our going into exile . . . fingerprints, sole prints, pictures and some medical records for necessary identification . . . It is a fact that the CIA conducted all necessary lawful verification tests regarding my person with the aid of the British Secret Service . . .

This alleged 'Trust' also supervised the supposed vast fortune the Tsar had smuggled out of Russia into the safekeeping of three banks in London, two in Paris and Germany, and at least one in New York; and the value of this hoard had, according to Goleniewski, dramatically increased since 1918:

> Any money in deposit belongs to me or, in part, to my sisters but you have to understand that there was approximately $400 million that was deposited a long, long time ago; so consequently it is now probably some billion dollars which could, in my opinion, be used to support people who are fighting for their freedom and are fighting the Bolsheviks.[21]

On the most charitable interpretation, Goleniewski's involvement with these outriders of the extreme right wing stemmed from a mistaken calculation that the enemies of his enemies could be counted on as friends, but it did nothing to enhance his dwindling reputation in Washington. His association with two other groups, however, had no such excuse: it was motivated entirely by his delusions of grandeur.

The Sovereign Order of the Knights of St John had existed, in various countries and incarnations, for more than six hundred years. Originally a fellowship of 'Knights Hospitaller', its genuine iterations were – and are – charitable organizations which carefully guard their reputation.

In 1958, Charles Pichel, a conman, Nazi sympathizer and former convict founded a new, unauthorized outpost in the United States; by 1966 it was based in the tiny Pennsylvania town of Shickshinny, and he had taken to styling himself Baron de Thourot and Lord of Estagel. Both titles were as bogus as the corporation he set up to profit from the honours his Order bestowed on those willing to pay for its imprimatur, and the Shickshinny group is listed by the Australian government as 'a false Order of St John', whose sole claim to fame is selling 'worthless "Knighthoods".'[22]

To Pichel and his adherents, 'Tsarevich Aleksei' was a gift from heaven: Goleniewski was offered – and graciously accepted – a succession of impressive-sounding ranks, in return for granting them the right to use his name and Romanoff title on marketing material. It was a mutually beneficial scam and quickly attracted a copycat scheme in New York, where another fraudster, calling himself – variously – Robert Bassaraba von Brancovan and Prince Khimchiachvili, established a rival Order in an unprepossessing corner of Flatbush. Bassaraba also duly recognized Goleniewski as the Tsarevich[23] and, with his blessing, set about using these credentials to sell more honorary memberships and bogus passports.[24]

The spectacle of the self-proclaimed heir to the Imperial Russian throne – and once America's most valuable Cold War spy – selling his endorsement to these rag-tag outfits of 'chivalric' con artists was hardly edifying; nor was his standing in Washington improved by the regularity with which 'Aleksei Romanoff' very publicly quarrelled with his Knightly backers, generally on the basis of some perceived slight.

As the months and years of his isolation dragged on, Goleniewski fought with almost every individual or organization which offered support. He denounced Capel, railed against Speller, threatened the *New York Journal-American*[25] and fired Brevetti for 'negligence' in failing to bring suit against the CIA.[26]

Cut off from any other channel, he and Irmgard composed verbose 'Open Letters' to the Directors of the CIA and FBI respectively, the

Attorney General and President Lyndon Johnson.[27] They paid for these to be published as advertisements – often covering a full broadsheet page – in newspapers and magazines in Washington and New York. The diatribes were barely coherent and rehearsed Goleniewski's now-familiar litany of grievances:

> Prior to our arrival in the United States, governmental help, support and protection was promised to us in the name of Mr. J. Edgar Hoover, Director of the FBI . . . Since 1961, authorized representatives of the CIA – especially Dulles, Angleton, Helms and [Chief of the Office of Security, Howard] Osborne – have never de-facto realized the promises of the US Department of Justice.
>
> Even disregarded to date have been our most limited rights . . . the CIA . . . is approximately $50,000 in arrears with my salary payment and . . . is forcing us to live in poor and inhuman [sic] status . . .
>
> These circumstances, serving the interest of some foreign agents and private persons, have reached a point of national, religious, political and personal persecution, and of malicious imprisonment; my wife and little daughter are also victims of said persecution.[28]

Unsurprisingly, the only response these rants elicited was a half-hearted visit from the Secret Service, mildly asking Goleniewski for an assurance that he meant no harm to the nation's chief executive.[29]

The CIA initially viewed his antics with a mixture of exasperation and irritation. It tolerated yet more visits from Kimsey and listened to the stream of complaints he relayed on behalf of 'the Tsarevich'. Since these included the unhinged claims that 'Colonel Goleniewski is living in an apartment house in New York owned by Martin Bormann' and 'that he has seen Heinrich Himmler in Washington,'[30] Agency staff simply noted them without recommending any action.

But by the summer of 1967, Langley's patience was running out. An internal report, filed on 3 August, recommended 'that a final stand be

taken with Goleniewski; that no further efforts be made to placate him'
and observed that 'the news media is no longer listening to his pretension to be the Crown Prince Alexei Romanoff.'[31]

The CIA was, however, rather more exercised by the threat its former
employee posed than this memo suggested. It was particularly concerned about the first book to be published on his involvement with
Western intelligence and the US government.

Although Goleniewski had cancelled their contract – and threatened
to sue his erstwhile collaborator – Guy Richards had been labouring on
a manuscript for two years. With Robert Speller also out of favour, he
signed up with Devin-Adair, a small conservative-leaning publisher with
a strong commitment to the anti-communist cause; it began preparing a
nationwide promotional campaign.

The Agency was first alerted to the manuscript's existence by the FBI
in November 1965. A note from the Bureau reported that 'Guy Richards
of the New York Journal American is writing a book on GOLIENSKI
[sic] and alleges to have ready access to classified reports on that individual.' Langley began scouring its files for information about the
reporter, but other than an internal record suggesting he had been considered for a role in its wartime predecessor, found nothing which
might provide useful leverage.[32]

The FBI's efforts were rather more productive. It had 'a long time
contact and supporter' on the staff of *Reader's Digest*. John Barron, a former US intelligence officer turned journalist, worked on the magazine's
editorial floor and intercepted a pre-publication copy of the manuscript
submitted for possible serialization. According to an internal FBI memo,
he knew immediately where his duty lay:

> [Barron] has been asked to see if the 'Digest' people would be
> interested in carrying a condensation of it in one of their future
> issues. [His] first reaction is not to review the book based on what
> he already knows about Goleniewski and Guy Richards, the
> author, without even reading it.

He states that even if part of Goleniewski's story is true, and he did, in fact, furnish some valuable information to United States Governmental agencies, such as the CIA and the FBI, he does not want to do a disservice to the country by having the 'Digest' with its tremendous circulation review the book and thereby imply approval of the entire story. For this reason he would like to discredit it as strongly as possible.

Barron has made available a copy of the manuscript for reproduction and specifically requested that one copy be made available through liaison channels to the CIA. He pointed out that CIA is in a quandary about Goleniewski; they don't know how to handle the book and, in fact, won't comment on it at all. Consequently Barron doubts that CIA has even obtained a copy of the book and feels they are even too embarrassed to admit it although they have much at stake because of the criticism in the book.[33]

The Bureau duly sent the manuscript to Langley, but on its own initiative resolved to help Barron discredit its contents.[34] Since no serialization appeared in *Reader's Digest*, this was evidently successful.

Deprived of this valuable platform, in November 1966, Devin-Adair mounted a determined publicity campaign for *Imperial Agent – The Goleniewski-Romanov Case*, proclaiming the book to be 'one of the most extraordinary documents in the history of espionage'.[35] The accompanying press release went much further, and denounced the CIA for the multiple failures Richards had exposed:

> For 33 months the CIA never knew what a big fish it had on the end of the line. All it knew was that it was getting priceless information from behind the Iron Curtain . . . Colonel Goleniewski said he represented a powerful and secret anti-Bolshevik organization in the communist states who wanted to do business with the one man it trusted in the United States . . . It could offer . . . information about the nearly two score of Americans in government agencies and defense industries who were working for the KGB.

What went wrong with the Goleniewski Case thereafter is the story of how the CIA missed the chance of a lifetime to maintain an enduring 'inside look' at the military and political secrets of the Soviet Union and her allies . . .

Of all the Cold War's hidden battles, this fascinating story deals with the one whose stakes were the highest of all in money, lives, reputations, exposés – and lost opportunities in the great global chess game.[36]

In truth, this rather oversold the book, which was largely comprised of Richards' *New York Journal-American* articles, framed within an excitable first-person account of the 'detective story' undertaken by the reporter, and an unchallenged retelling of Goleniewski's claim to be Aleksei Romanoff. It did not attract a large readership and the one man who might have been expected to approve of it was moved to denounce the publication as a 'provocation', covertly directed by the US government; true to form, the would-be Tsarevich paid for a new advertisement in the *New York Times*, threatening legal action on the unlikely grounds that the book's purpose was 'to confuse the public opinion and bar me and my family from the Constitutional rights of the US granted to me and my wife by right of political asylum and to cover up some manipulations against me, as well as also [sic] to cover up certain actions re: Romanoff Hereditary.'[37]

CIA staff – particularly those who had dealt with Goleniewski first-hand – were by now largely indifferent to his regular raging against enemies, real or imagined. But the Agency saw beyond the man to the damage that he, and *Imperial Agent*, could cause.

An internal memo in December, prepared for the Director of Central Intelligence, warned that the book contained 'several vicious attacks on CIA' and that Richards was using it 'to drive a wedge between CIA and the FBI [by claiming] that the Bureau "had served only as a patsy for the CIA in the case"'. More seriously, the report noted that the journalist 'charges CIA with being infiltrated by Communist agents' and 'names several CIA officials [who] are believed not to have been publicly identified with CIA previously'.[38]

Whether it considered him mad or not, the CIA knew that Goleniewski's tortured mind held secrets that Langley would rather not have betrayed, and that his lengthy association with US intelligence could be used by the nation's enemies as a weapon in the deepening Cold War. It was not alone in reaching that conclusion.

Had the Agency been able to see what its opponents behind the Iron Curtain were planning – an impossibility since, as Goleniewski correctly predicted, the flow of intelligence from Warsaw Pact countries had completely dried up – that concern would have been very much more acute.

26

TELETECHNIK

CAPTAIN JÓZEF MĘDRZYCKI had a plan. It was cynical, complex and unquestionably expensive, but it was calculated to achieve the Urząd Bezpieczeństwa's unrealized goal of finding Goleniewski – presumably with the aim of implementing the death sentence imposed by the Military Court in Warsaw. It also sought to exploit his bogus claims to the Russian Imperial throne, and use his evident insanity to discredit the Western intelligence services which had accepted and harboured him.

By February 1966, Operation TELETECHNIK – the code name for both the defector and the intelligence mission to find him – had been running for more than three years, but despite the best efforts of its *rezidentura* in the United States, and extensive enquiries made by dozens of covert agents in Europe and America, the UB had been unable to discover the defector's address. Given the relatively primitive nature of contemporary information technology this was hardly surprising: Goleniewski lived in an anonymous – and very large – CIA-supported apartment block in an unfavoured New York suburb and neither this nor any of his cover names was known outside a closed circle of selected lawmakers, the Agency and the FBI; there had been no leakage of information about his exact location.

Mędrzycki was a senior officer in Department III of the Ministry of Internal Affairs, the umbrella department for all Polish espionage services, and headed one of the two units tasked with tracking down the missing spy. After thirty-six largely fruitless months, he decided that the insuperable problem demanded a more radical approach: 'Until now operations did not affect directly TELETECHNIK and . . . did not force him to go public,' Mędrzycki wrote in a lengthy memo for his superiors on 4 February:

> I propose that we put out a hoax report announcing the death of TELETECHNIK in car accident. We should call daily [American] newspapers from a public phone and inform them about this death; when editors receive the hoax they may publish the information as a sensation. Further dissemination of the news of TELETECHNIK's death should be done via newspapers in Vienna, Paris, London and Rome once it has been published in the New York press.
>
> The goal of the operation is to force him to go public – at the least he would have to make an appearance on TV. . . All of these actions would reverberate in Congress as well as in the media, and would mean that people other than the CIA would gain access to TELETECHNIK.
>
> That creates new operational opportunities for us and as a result our *rezidentura* in Washington and New York could find individuals through whom we will be able to get to TELETECHNIK.[1]

Nor would the anticipated impact of this elaborate scheme be confined to the United States; once news of the 'death' reached Poland, Janina Goleniewska would almost certainly try to contact either her son or Irmgard; 'The rumour would shock people in Warsaw and it would especially astonish PRZEKUPKA [the UB's in-house code name for Janina] and should help create new opportunities to operate against TELETECHNIK.'

Mędrzycki's plan was evidently deemed impractical by his masters – not least because one of the UB's undercover agents in America was then reporting some progress in the hunt for Goleniewski; the car-crash hoax idea rapidly disappeared from the bulging Polish intelligence case files. His second proposal, however, was received rather more favourably since it exploited Goleniewski's bogus biography and bigamous marriages to discredit the CIA by association. The stark contrast between his real past in Poland – wartime Nazi collaborator, Soviet espionage service *apparatchik* and never-divorced father of three abandoned children – and his self-proclaimed reinvention as Aleksei Romanoff, lifelong anti-communist fighter and loyal husband to Irmgard, was too good to pass up:

> Recently Congressional Committees made an effort to undertake control of the CIA . . . The main complaints relate to CIA assessments of scandals blown by this agency. A group of Congressmen is criticizing CIA for tendentiousness and intentional misguiding of public opinion, government and Congress.
>
> I propose that we keep this discussion on the CIA going, by giving information on TELETECHNIK to a few influential people and especially critics of the CIA in Congress. I also suggest that we pass the information and documents to some newspapers.
>
> The content of this information challenges public opinion of TELETECHNIK as an educated man and shows him in a bad light . . . The CIA will be criticized by public opinion and its critics in Congress will be activated.[2]

Mędrzycki's suggestion took several months to pass upward through the layers of UB bureaucracy, but by early summer his masters decided that recent events on Capitol Hill showed the time was ripe to strike. On 13 June an American-based covert agent, code-named SFINKS, sent letters to senior US politicians – among them Republican Senator James Fulbright, who headed the powerful Foreign Relations Committee, and Senator Eugene McCarthy, its ranking Democratic member – as well as journalists including Guy Richards and David Wise, the *New York Herald Tribune* Washington bureau chief who specialized in reporting on intelligence issues.[3] These provided a truthful account of Goleniewski's life and career behind the Iron Curtain and 'portrayed [him] as an impostor, anti-Semite, bigamist and a person with incomplete secondary education'. They also stressed the CIA's culpability for his descent into insanity.[4]

One month later – according to Polish intelligence files – this campaign produced excellent results. 'On July 27, 1966,[5] a discussion was held in the US Senate about the proposal to extend control to CIA activities by Congress,' Mędrzycki reported to his superiors:

> The discussions were described . . . as very stormy and strongly criticized the CIA. During Fulbright's speech, guests and the press were asked to leave and further deliberations were held *in camera*. To what extent the material contained in our inspiration was used by Fulbright and McCarthy . . . we do not yet have complete data. The minutes of the meeting have all secret matters deleted. There is, however, evidence that our material was used by the above-mentioned persons. I consider this to be the first official outcome of our operation, criticizing the reckless involvement of the CIA in the Tsarevich case . . . I suggest further incitement against American intelligence, exposing the impostor character traits of the Subject [Goleniewski].[6]

Moscow also put its weight behind the UB's determination to hang the 'Tsarist comedy' round the CIA's neck. On 27 August a brief article in *Komsomolskaya Pravda*, the official daily organ of the Communist Party youth wing, denounced Goleniewski and his Romanoff pretence: 'The pretender emigrated to the United States . . . and registered with the US authorities as Aleksei Nicholaevich Romanoff,' the paper thundered, while in reality 'this self-appointed man is nothing less than a sinister creation of American intelligence.'[7]

While Langley's embarrassment was a welcome success in the ongoing war of Soviet bloc intelligence with the CIA, it did not bring the UB any closer to locating Goleniewski. The key to achieving that, Mędrzycki concluded, lay in persuading Janina to reveal his address; but winning her confidence would require the particular skills of a very colourful undercover operative.

Leopold Dende was then fifty-nine and, according to his substantial Polish intelligence files, was officially a journalist for Polish-American publications. Before World War II he had co-edited the avowedly procommunist *Głos Ludowny* ('People's Voice') journal in Detroit. In the same period, however, he accumulated arrest warrants in Chicago for manslaughter, robbery and illegal possession of firearms; in 1936 he was convicted on most of the charges and sentenced to between nine and eighteen years in prison.

Shortly after his release on parole in 1945, Dende became the co-owner and news editor of a respected English-language weekly paper, the *Polish-American Journal*, which held to a firm anti-communist policy. Despite this, he managed to get himself recruited as an agent by Warsaw's espionage service; it provided him with a monthly salary of $450 (the equivalent of $4,700 today), paid out clandestinely by its embassy in Washington DC.[8]

The job, and the paper's reputation, provided excellent cover for the new spy. Throughout the 1950s and early 1960s he travelled to Western Europe, and behind the Iron Curtain, on behalf of both his employers. The trips also presented him with the chance to trade on Warsaw's black market – an opportunity he cheerfully accepted, but which did not go unnoticed by Polish intelligence. It decided that Dende was feckless, amoral and a proven liar: he was, in short, perfectly suited to advancing Operation TELETECHNIK.

Janina Goleniewska was, in the UB's eyes, a promising target, and the one person who could be fooled into exposing her son's location in the United States. For more than two years it had tapped her phone and intercepted letters to and from her Warsaw apartment; it had also inserted one of its informants – an agent code-named 'SZCZEPAN' (Stephen) – into her circle of friends.

This, together with at least one burglary of her home, revealed that she was in touch with Goleniewski via a series of 'cut-outs' in Western Europe, and that he had persuaded her to support his Romanoff pretence by falsely adopting the identity of his Imperial sister, Maria. But Agent 'SZCZEPAN' lived more than 100 miles away and could only visit Warsaw once a month; he had also found the meetings increasingly stressful, since Janina repeatedly demanded that he take her to bed.[9]

There was an additional and rather more fundamental problem: Janina did not know her son's address, but always communicated via the cut-outs. While Polish intelligence officers read every letter she sent to the couriers who delivered them, these men and women lived in the West and were outside the UB's control; to track Goleniewski down, the UB needed to replace her existing messengers with one of its own – someone who could travel freely between Poland and America. Dende, already on the payroll and vulnerable to pressure through his black-market activities, was the obvious choice.

Janina was avaricious and, to Mędrzycki's puritan mind, uncomfortably sexually active, but she was not stupid: to win her confidence, Dende would need an introduction from someone she knew to be one of Goleniewski's American supporters. Happily, the UB had recently established contact with Robert Speller and had been 'developing' him as a source.[10] Dende – now given the cryptonym POLA – was ordered to make use of the new asset.[11]

By the early spring of 1967 the scheme was up and running; at Dende's request, Speller sent word to Janina about a trustworthy new ally, and to expect a visit from his personal courier, who would bring a letter and photographs from Goleniewski; on 14 March, Mędrzycki, posing as Dende's agent, duly presented himself at number 7a Marszałkowska, her apartment in Warsaw.

'Goleniewska at first distrusted me, but that was dispelled after I handed her the referral business card from POLA,' he recorded in a memo for the growing TELETECHNIK file. 'She asked me if I would be able to forward a letter and a package to [Goleniewski] and whether this route is safe. I promised her that the little packet could be picked up next week, and I reassured her about the security of the channel.'

Mędrzycki also noted that Janina was determined to play her part in Goleniewski's Romanoff fantasy; more importantly, she suggested a plan by which she could escape from Warsaw and join him in his Imperial exile in the United States:

> She regretted that she had not received any direct message from 'Aleksander' [and] expressed surprise that he had not yet come up with the idea of taking her out of Poland through a fictitious marriage with an American citizen who could come as a tourist to Poland . . . She mentioned the sum of 300,000 dollars, which she is ready to pay for such a marriage. She claimed that here in Poland she had considerable wealth in the form of gold and fur and jewels. She hinted that she would reward me generously for help in this matter, and even offered to me to be a witness to her at any wedding.[12]

This was an idea which had not previously entered the UB's tortuous thinking, but Mędrzycki immediately grasped its potential. He left Janina's apartment after a convivial one and a half hours, pleased to have duped a foolish and evidently infirm elderly woman: 'To say the least, I think that Goleniewska has gained complete trust in me. She offered me tea, vodka and cakes. She created a warm atmosphere – she played records. She is an older woman and it is likely that sclerosis is already well under way . . . but she probably realizes that she has "crossed the Rubicon".'[13]

A few days later, another UB major called to pick up the parcel for 'Aleksei', and found Janina waiting eagerly for him:

> I was welcomed. She prepared a sumptuous dinner. She was dressed provocatively, hung with jewellery [including] two big bracelets, four rings, a necklace, a large brooch set with stones and pearls . . . I got the impression that Goleniewska is an

erotomaniac because she gave me some clear hints several times by pulling her dress above her knees, saying that everybody was impressed by her legs.

The officer also noted that Janina was sufficiently confident of her courier's supposed anti-communist credentials to boast about Goleniewski's success as a Western agent, and to support his Tsarevich pretence:

She praised his cleverness and intelligence. She said 'please, sir, how many Russians did he expose when he was in Warsaw' . . . She said that the ID card he currently has is 'foolish' [and that] Aleksei is currently 65, but he doesn't look that old.[14]

The package was duly shipped on to Dende, who took it to Speller for delivery to Goleniewski. Agent POLA found the publisher gloomy about the prospects for advancing the Tsarevich's cause:

According to Speller, G. 's condition is 'regrettable' . . . the guy is very nervous, restless, too sensitive, arrogant, surly, distrustful, suspicious, etc. He has grown very old. He constantly quarrels with friends and accuses them of 'conspiring' against him and being interested mainly in order to make money from him.

He is furious that the book about him has not become popular, because it has only sold 7,000 copies so far. He throws himself about like a lion in a cage because he wants to be heard all over the world. His thirst for exposure is so great that he is ready to appear in front of every journalist, just so long as his case becomes public. His wife has the greatest influence on him: by the way, no one likes her. Speller and his companions describe her as a 'nasty German'.

According to Dende's report, 'an unofficial committee . . . of a dozen or so people' was masterminding the campaign to promote the Romanoff story. This team included Speller and his son, Herman Kimsey, Guy Richards, two priests, 'several' lawyers, 'someone' in London and 'some people from the US government'. Its motivation, however, owed less to advancing Goleniewski's claims than to the lure of financial reward:

> Speller and his clique generally dislike G., especially his erratic behaviour, because he wants to manage everything and often doesn't pay attention to their advice. They are not interested in G. as a human being, but only the so-called historical [aspect] – is he or is not the one he claims to be – as well as the financial side, because if his claim is not fiction, it is worth a lot of money; and if he is an impostor they are ready to expose him, because that too could be a good earner.

Janina Goleniewska was, the committee decided, the key to solving the mystery, one way or another, and Speller drew up a long list of questions for 'Maria' about her supposed life as a Romanoff princess; Dende agreed to deliver them on his next trip to Warsaw. The publisher was also enthusiastic about the plot to smuggle Janina to America: 'Therefore, the decision is to bring her as soon as possible, regardless of how she answers the 90 questions I have to ask her. The marriage proposal was considered very good. I gave them a choice – either let them choose the candidate themselves or I will try to find someone. I was given a free hand.'[15]

Dende approached a local Catholic clergyman to help him find a potential husband for Janina, and reported promising news to his UB handler. 'Father Jan Jakubik from the National Church, pastor of the Pánsk Resurrection parish in Brooklyn ... has several candidates for "spouses".' Better still, the priest had agreed to accompany the spy to Warsaw and meet the bride-to-be. 'I am to introduce [Jakubik] to the Spellers upon our return.'[16]

The unlikely duo arrived in Poland in early July 1967. Dende and Father Jakubik had two meetings with Janina, recording her answers to Speller's questions on tape, and collecting a letter and clothing to take to Goleniewski; the priest also agreed to shoulder all the visa and financial requirements for the bogus marriage.[17] On his return to New York, Jakubik handed over the package to Speller and, in return, the publisher gave him Goleniewski's phone number: for the first time since Operation TELETECHNIK began, Polish intelligence had firm evidence of where its errant former agent was living.

It is not clear from the UB's files whether Jakubik realized he was being played by Polish intelligence, but on Dende's instructions he phoned the apartment in Queens. The conversation did not go as planned. 'J. told him that he had seen his sister, whom he met through a journalist friend,' a memo from Major Zielinski noted. '[Goleniewski] was surprised and simply did not want to believe this, but when J. described his sister's appearance he accepted [the account], but declared that no one should contact his "sister" without his knowledge and consent.' Undeterred, the priest phoned again a few days later but once again found Goleniewski in truculent mood; he denounced Speller as 'a charlatan' and insisted that all wedding plans for Janina should be put on hold:

> There was a conversation about his 'sister's' arrival in the USA. Goleniewski declared that he did not wish this to happen at the moment, because his sister was too old, she would be lost and alone, without friends . . . and that he needed to discuss the matter with the relevant American people. When J. asked him what to say to his sister, Goleniewski replied that it would be better if he did not contact her now, but if he sees her, let him tell her to wait for his decision.[18]

Further attempts to speak to both Irmgard and Goleniewski were met with angry letters and phone calls, followed by wild accusations that Jakubik was part of a 'pro-Bolshevik and pro-fascist' conspiracy by 'US government representatives and organized by criminals including some German, British and Russian relatives, banking corporations, Bolshevik agents, hiding mass murderers of the SS, private financial organizations and many other so-called Christians.'[19]

Speller was now increasingly sure that the imperious 'Tsarevich' was an impostor, and his alleged sister a willing – if gullible – collaborator; her tape-recorded responses to his questions were, unsurprisingly, vacuous and unconvincing. According to Dende's account, transcribed by the tireless Major Mędrzycki, the publisher and his committee 'decided that if "Maria" did not give clearer answers, she was either hiding something or not the person she claimed to be. [But] no matter who Maria really is, Speller thinks it advisable to bring her to the US for a confrontation and a final resolution. He stated that the CIA and other US people involved were of the same opinion and that he had been given a free hand in the matter.'[20]

All of this was music to Warsaw's ears. Just as it had helped its 'red swallow', Urszula Discher, give evidence against Irvin Scarbeck in America, it was very happy to allow Goleniewski's mother to emigrate to the United States; the story that Janina was his 'sister', Maria Romanoffa, was so riddled with inconsistencies that it would not survive even the most cursory examination by Western journalists.

The following summer the UB received yet more welcome news. Speller gave Dende the address of Irmgard's mother, Luize, and sister, Margette, in Frankfurt; Goleniewski had recently announced that they were, in reality, two of the other surviving daughters of Tsar Nicholas and therefore his long-lost sisters. On 17 May 1968, Dende turned up at their apartment:

> I introduced myself as a friend of Robert, whom they had met during a visit to the USA, so the conversation went easily . . . They denied that they were Goleniewski's sisters. The older one, who he claims to be Olga, said she was the mother of Goleniewski's wife, Irmgard, and the younger, who he claims to be Tatiana, said she was Irmgard's sister. But they . . . made it clear that they did not really blame him [for making up the story].[21]

Speller proved less forgiving. Exasperated by the lies and erratic behaviour, he finally revealed Goleniewski's cover identity and gave Dende the address of his home: Silver Towers Apartments, 125-10 Queens Boulevard, Kew Gardens, Long Island, flat 2308 or 1801 'depending on where he currently lives – Goleniewski is registered as Franz Roman Oldenberg'

[sic]. He also warned that the building was 'a "safe house" of the CIA, in which a number of people similar to Goleniewski live. The building is guarded by CIA agents.'[22]

Whether or not the Agency had stashed other defectors in the apartment block, there was some evidence that it assumed responsibility for it. In April the company which owned the building had issued court proceedings against Goleniewski for failing to pay the rent – an omission he blamed on Langley's refusal to pay him. The case was scheduled for a hearing in the New York Civil Court on 2 May, but the CIA quietly stepped in and paid the outstanding arrears; when the Silver Towers Management Company failed to appear, the judge dismissed its suit.[23] Inevitably, Goleniewski was not grateful: in a sworn affidavit subsequently filed at New York City Register Office, he claimed that Howard Osborne, head of the Office of Security, had come to the apartment and 'threatened me in a vaguely manner with a murder on the street in the presence of my wife'.[24] This allegation was, at best, highly improbable. Whatever its faults, the CIA was hardly likely to take such draconian retribution over the trivial cost of a few months' rent – let alone assassinate a high-profile defector on American soil.

Its counterparts behind the Iron Curtain, however, had a proven record of doing just that, and promptly sent New York-based operatives to scope out the property. At the end of June a Polish agent code-named JERZYM took the subway to Queens and spent the morning monitoring security arrangements and drawing a detailed map of the building and its surroundings. Deterred by the uniformed doormen on duty at the entrance, he decided against venturing inside.[25] But on 8 July a second agent – LESNY – proved rather more courageous:

> After arrival at the destination I established that the building is a big block located between 82 Road, Queens Blvd and 83 Avenue. This block has 24 floors; as the name says . . . it is silver in colour. It is the highest block in this locality . . . The entry driveway to the

garage, from which car owners go by elevators to their flats, is located on the side of 83 Avenue.

After this external viewing of the block, I went inside . . . In the corridor, on the right-hand side, there is a board with the list of tenants. I counted 150 of them, including 31 solicitors and 6 doctors. The name Franz Roman Oldenberg [sic] is missing from this list of tenants. My 'studies' at this board took about 5 minutes.

Unsurprisingly, LESNY's behaviour attracted attention from the security guard – 'a black man, dressed in a navy suit with a white and red hat' – but the arrival of two residents and an old lady, who struggled with an overflowing shopping trolley, provided a timely distraction:

I lifted the bag, and helped the lady to enter the elevator. The men . . . were stopped by the security guard who asked, 'May I help you?', and then he pressed a button on the telephone board. Meantime, my lift, with the lady, closed the doors. The lady got off on the 4th floor thanking me for the help, while I went to the 23rd floor.

Here, I walked around the whole corridor and I established that on the doors to the flats are only numbers without the surnames. Under the number [of apartment] 2308 there was no surname. Then I took the elevator to the 18th floor. Here I also walked around the whole corridor and I established that some flats had only numbers and some had numbers and surnames. Under the number 1801, the one that we are interested in, the surname 'H. Landisberg' was written.

After establishing this fact, I took the elevator and I went down to the entrance where the security guard was standing . . . I looked on the tenants' board and I found that the surname H. Landisberg is not on it . . . [but] I established that the flat number 1801 . . . can also be reached by the side lift without the need of meeting the security guard.[26]

Until it could be sure exactly which flat Goleniewski occupied, the UB knew that its operatives stood little chance of carrying out his death sentence. A file note by Agent SFINKS recorded its decision to put the building under observation 'for a few days between the hours of 8–9 am and possibly around 4–6 pm . . . perhaps this will bring some results'.[27]

Warsaw was not alone in sending spies to keep watch on Silver Towers. Over the coming months two Russian intelligence agents sent surveillance reports back to the KGB, advising Moscow that 'Goleniewski is in critical psychological state' and that because he was becoming 'more and more troublesome for CIA (demands compensations that they should pay him, and what is more he is messing them about) they don't protect his address very well'.[28]

Guarded or not, none of the Soviet bloc intelligence operatives were ever able to identify exactly which apartment contained their quarry, and the plans for Goleniewski's assassination subsequently disappeared from the UB's copious TELETECHNIK files.

The other half of its scheme, however, was progressing rapidly. By the summer of 1968, Dende and Jakubik had settled on a short-list of suitable husbands for Janina, and purchased an engagement ring for the bride. Speller, meanwhile, promised to cover the cost of bringing her to the United States and offered a $5,000 inducement[29] to answer yet more questions about her supposed Romanoff history. All of this was delivered to her, along with a new security precaution – one half of a card that had been cut in two: when the time came to smuggle Janina out of Poland, her rescuer would show her the matching piece to prove his credentials.[30]

In January 1969, Dende and Mędrzycki had all the logistics in place. They had selected a putative husband, and the UB had crafted a counterfeit passport for the bride-to-be. Another agent, posing as the representative of Speller's American committee, knocked on the door of number 7a Marszałkowska. He found Janina in a volatile state.

After handing over the second half of the card he asked her if she was ready to leave immediately. 'She was surprised by the suddenness of what was to happen,' he noted in a report on the afternoon's events. 'In turn, she began to ask me about her "brother", if I knew how he felt, because she had not been told anything about him for a long time, but had heard that he was sick':

> The second series of questions concerned her matrimonial plans. She said she knew everything was arranged so that she was to marry a rich American whom Leopold [Dende] was to present to her, and that she was ready for it. Anyway, in America she has plenty candidates for husband – at least 25.

But it became clear that Janina was having second thoughts about her escape, the phony marriage arrangements and, in particular, the future problems these would cause:

> She added that she did not quite understand the necessity of leaving on a 'dodgy' passport because it closes off her return to the country. She explained to me that people [who emigrate] miss Poland very much. She did not want to be in such a situation, but instead to leave legally as an American wife who after three years could come back to Poland.

'Grand Duchess Maria' – putative Russian princess and part-heir to the fabled Romanoff fortune – also proved unexpectedly reluctant to abandon her modest Warsaw flat, her few possessions and the cradle-to-grave security of life in a Communist state:

> She began asking to postpone the departure until after the sale of furniture, bedding and clothes . . . She also emphasized the fact that in Poland she receives a pension . . . and has free medical treatment and advice, whilst in the US she would have to pay big dollars for everything she does not have, and she does not know what fate awaits her there, and she would not like to be a burden to anyone.[31]

After several agonizing hours of argument, she finally dug her heels in. Despite the prospect of marriage to a rich American, the promise of

Romanoff wealth, and the lure of an Imperial title in the land of the free, Janina Goleniewska refused, point-blank, to leave Poland.

Her decision marked the effective end of Operation TELETECH-NIK. After six years and the expenditure of vast sums – documents detailing the costs incurred by the scores of officers and undercover agents were quickly, and conveniently, lost[32] – Józef Mędrzycki had to accept that all his elaborate scheming had come to nothing.

But if he was crestfallen, the Polish Intelligence Service and its ultimate masters in Moscow were rather less concerned. By the end of 1969 they knew that the ultimate targets of the operation were tearing themselves apart; in Washington and in London, driven by the toxic combination of Anatoliy Golitsyn and James Angleton, the CIA and MI5 were lost in a counterintelligence wilderness of mirrors.

Their fevered hunt for phantom traitors in their midst was destroying lives, wrecking careers and paralysing Western security. But in the process, both agencies also stopped searching for the very real moles that Goleniewski had identified and who had burrowed deep within their ranks.

27

Mole Hunts

T HE CELL WAS exactly ten feet long by ten feet wide. Constructed entirely in concrete, it had no window and was illuminated by a single naked overhead bulb; behind a cross-hatched gate of heavy steel bars, a second solid metal door excluded any other light. It held only a small bed bolted to the floor, covered by a thin mattress; there were neither sheets nor blankets, and no pillow.

Food, cigarettes and the weekly ration of a single book were arbitrarily withheld. The guards who delivered them were under instructions to remain mute, and aside from the interrogators who appeared at seemingly random intervals, the prisoner spoke to no one in his solitary confinement.

He had no access to lawyers, no right to appeal against his imprisonment; officially, he did not exist and his location was unknown to anyone outside the secretive organization which held him captive. He had not appeared before any court, or been convicted of any offence. His sole 'crime' – if that's what it was – had been to defect from his country's intelligence service to that of its enemy. And yet he was held, without trial, in this tiny, airless cell from 4 April 1964 to 13 August 1965 – a total of 496 consecutive days.

This cruel and extrajudicial punishment – his second period of imprisonment since that defection – was typical of a closed and despotic Communist regime, and the United States had frequently denounced the Soviet Union for its gross abuses of human rights.

But Yuri Ivanovich Nosenko was not confined in a remote Russian gulag; he was incarcerated by the CIA in a covert training facility on American soil. Known colloquially as The Farm, and housed at Camp Peary near Williamsburg, Virginia, according to one of its alumni this 'black site' used sleep deprivation, mock executions and contaminated food to soften up its inmates.[1] Nosenko's plight would – at least within the confines of Langley – become both the symbol of, and the lightning rod for, a bitter war which would tear the Agency apart and paralyse Western intelligence for more than a decade.

The story began on 9 June 1962, when Nosenko approached the CIA in Switzerland. He was thirty-five, a long-term KGB officer whose father had been a Soviet government minister. While on a security assignment, guarding the Soviet delegation to the International Disarmament Conference in Geneva, he made contact with a senior CIA officer, Tennent 'Pete' Bagley.

The tale Nosenko told was, admittedly, strange. He said he had recently slept with a Swiss woman who had taken the opportunity to steal a large quantity of Swiss francs from him; since this hard currency belonged to his masters in Moscow he would have either to repay the money or account for it – and he could do neither. According to the internal CIA report titled 'The Monster Plot', the most detailed account of the case and its disastrous impact, he offered to sell KGB secrets to the Agency to make up the shortfall:

> In exchange for 2,000 Swiss Francs, he therefore proposed that he provide us with two items of information. These items, subsequently verified, related to KGB recruitment of a US Army sergeant while he was serving in the American embassy in Moscow . . . [and] a Soviet official whom the Agency had ostensibly recruited but who was being run against us under KGB control.[2]

Bagley knew a bargain when he saw one. The money Nosenko needed was pocket change – little more than $500 at 1962 exchange rates.[3] The intelligence he traded looked good, and once the deal was done the CIA would have him on a permanent hook. Better still, although the KGB officer refused to meet any Agency representative once he returned to Russia, he promised to do so the next time he was given an assignment in the West.

On 11 June, Bagley sent a cable to Langley, advising that Nosenko had 'conclusively proved his bona fides. Provided info of importance and sensitivity, Subject now completely co-operative.' Ten days later, Bagley flew back to Washington, proudly bearing the tapes of the encounter and briefed the chief of counterintelligence on this new coup.[4]

James Angleton, however, was signally unimpressed. He found the story of Nosenko and the lost francs preposterous and told the rapidly deflating Bagley that he was being played. To prove his point, he inculcated him into the great secret of the Agency's Counter-Intelligence Staff: the transcripts, running to between ten and fifteen volumes, of Anatoliy Golitsyn's recent debriefing sessions. After a weekend studying the files, Bagley emerged shaken.

'Alone, Nosenko looked good to me,' he testified to Congress more than sixteen years later. '[But] seen alongside Golitsyn, whose reporting I had not seen before coming to headquarters . . . he looked very odd indeed . . . Nosenko's information tended to negate or deflect leads from Golitsyn.'[5]

Bagley had just encountered the new logic pervading all CIA counterintelligence efforts: Golitsyn was Angleton's guru, and any intelligence which ran contrary to the opinions of the counterintelligence chief – or failed to meet with his approval – was, automatically, false; worse, as Nosenko would soon discover, the defector providing this material must, by definition, be a KGB 'provocation'.

What followed was an unprecedented breach of all Agency procedure. The transcripts of Nosenko's debriefing tapes were turned over to Golitsyn for analysis; he, however, was not told their source but led to believe that they emanated from letters sent by an anonymous Soviet bloc undercover agent. Since there was only one source who matched this profile – Goleniewski – Golitsyn had to assume that all the material had been provided by his immediate predecessor and nearest rival for the CIA's favour.[6] He promptly denounced it as bogus.

This marked the beginning of Golitsyn's hegemony over the Agency, the entrenchment as unchallengeable fact that he – and only he – was genuine, and that all defectors to the United States before or after him were fakes, dispatched by Moscow to mislead and distract Western intelligence. As the 'Monster Plot' report explained:

> During the remainder of 1962 and 1963, SR [Soviet Russia] Division continued to build up a case against Nosenko. Virtually any information provided by Nosenko, or action taken by him, was interpreted as part of a KGB 'provocation'. If his information was in accord with that from other sources, this fact not only confirmed our suspicion of Nosenko but was interpreted as casting doubt on the other sources as well.[7]

In January 1964, Nosenko reappeared in Geneva and told the CIA that he wanted – urgently – to defect. Bagley, now installed as deputy chief of the SR Division, was once again the 'principal case officer' assigned to handle the KGB man, now code-named AEFOXTROT.[8] Following standard operating procedure he tried to persuade him to remain in Russia as an Agent in Place; Nosenko refused, claiming that Moscow had already sent a cable, summoning him back to what he feared was interrogation and execution as an American spy. This forced the CIA's hand, and on 4 February it arranged for an emergency exfiltration.

After a week's debriefing in Frankfurt, the Agency flew Nosenko to the US and installed him in the attic of a safe house just outside Washington DC. Unlike Goleniewski or Golitsyn he was not promised asylum, and his legal status – technically he was a CIA 'parolee' – was ambiguous and conferred few, if any, rights.[9]

There was a reason for this: the Agency had long since decided that he was not a genuine defector, and every element of his treatment from the moment he arrived in America on 12 February was predicated on this presumption. A memo by David Murphy, now head of the Soviet Division (SR) and like Bagley a true believer in the Golitsyn thesis, laid out the CIA's plans in the starkest of language:

> While admitting that Subject is here on a KGB directed mission . . .
> he still possesses valid information which we would like to obtain.
> At the same time, we . . . believe that Subject must be broken at
> some point if we are to learn something of the full scope of the
> KGB plan . . . Clearly, the big problem is one of timing . . . how long
> will it take us to assemble the kind of brief we will need to initiate
> a hostile interrogation in conditions of maximum control.[10]

Nosenko's most troublesome claims, and ones which the CIA was determined to defuse, were that he had been the 'case officer' who handled Lee Harvey Oswald during his sojourn in the Soviet Union between 1959 and 1962, and that the assassination of President John F. Kennedy in November 1963 had not been directed or approved by the KGB.

To Angleton and his acolytes, this comforting reassurance seemed 'contrived' and was further evidence that Nosenko had been sent to mislead American intelligence.[11] By contrast, Hoover's counterintelligence team at FBI headquarters told Langley that 'AEFOXTROT production . . . looks very good' and that it 'believe[d] Subject to be a genuine KGB defector'.[12] Under the malign twin-axis of Golitsyn and Angleton, the CIA Director Richard Helms, Murphy and Bagley ignored the Bureau's advice and set about trying to break Nosenko. His repeated polygraph tests were deliberately skewed by the assumption he was lying and the SR officers discounted every answer he gave. When he vehemently denied being a dispatched KGB plant, the sessions degenerated into shouting matches.

For sixteen months, Bagley and Murphy worked assiduously to induce a confession; none of their efforts succeeded and they eventually decided Nosenko's treatment in the safe house was altogether too gentle. With the backing of Langley's senior management, they ordered the construction of a concrete cell – code-named LOBLOLLY – and planned a very much harsher regimen. In August 1965, AEFOXTROT was blindfolded and roughly manhandled into his new prison. None of this was disclosed to Congress or the American taxpayers who were paying for this ill-treatment: Yuri Nosenko was simply disappeared – an unperson in Soviet jargon – into the CIA's private gulag.

As the months of fruitless interrogation dragged on, Bagley became concerned. He did not yet doubt the Golitsyn-Angleton credo, nor did he change his opinion that Nosenko was a KGB plant, but he worried that no matter what suffering the Agency inflicted – food and sleep deprivation, the alleged use of psychotropic drugs[13] and near-continuous hostile interrogation – there seemed little prospect of a breakthrough. In the pages of a personal notebook, Bagley contemplated a succession of increasingly desperate options; one – at least – had an uncomfortable similarity to the CIA's contemporaneous treatment of Goleniewski:

> To liquidate and insofar as possible to clean up traces of a situation in which CIA could be accused of illegally holding Nosenko ... liquidate the man ... render him incapable of giving coherent story (special dose of drug, et cetera). Possible aim, commitment to loony bin ... [or] Commitment to loony bin without making him nuts.[14]

Bagley later said that these notes were no more than 'theoretical' possibilities, born out of intense frustration, and that he had never shown them to anyone else. But as 1966 dawned, the first stirrings of unease were beginning to emerge about the human-rights abuses meted out inside LOBLOLLY, and by Angleton's increasingly rabid hunt for supposed moles within the Agency.

The two were inextricably linked. According to a memo by Bagley, Golitsyn's assessment of Nosenko 'had opened our eyes not only to security threats in our own midst and within the US government, but had also revealed that many other important sources were in fact KGB provocations and ... that our entire counterintelligence effort, double-agents and all, may be contaminated and useless'.[15]

Inevitably, Goleniewski was the first to fall victim to this theory and to the hardcore group of CIA staff – known by the cryptonym AESAWDUST – who believed in it. Although he had been the first to warn of bogus defectors bearing false intelligence, in the 'mirror thinking' of Angleton and Golitsyn's logic, Nosenko was a dispatched agent; because he reinforced some of Goleniewski's information, Goleniewski too must be a KGB provocation. Worse, any CIA officers who had believed either of these two 'plants' were themselves automatically presumed to be part of Moscow's Master Plan, and likely KGB moles.

But inside Langley a group of senior officers within the Soviet Division were increasingly appalled by the effects of this conspiracy theory. One former true believer later wrote an account of the damage that Angleton and Golitsyn were inflicting on the Agency:

> Convinced participating AESAWDUST members were terribly concerned and motivated by fear that until this vast deception complex was exposed and countered, we would be in bad trouble which could get worse at any moment.
>
> So the number of cases tossed into the boiling pot grew and grew, until outsiders simply could no longer swallow the idea that all of them [Soviet defectors] were bad. Most people could have accepted that Nosenko might be dispatched, and perhaps could even have assimilated the material used to prove it, but sooner or later those not bound up in the mission said 'Hold it, Wait a minute! Maybe Nosenko, maybe some DA [double agent] cases, maybe even a few more, but almost *all*? Too much.'[16]

According to Richards Heuer, one of the CIA's most experienced analysts, as the mole hunt expanded, the Agency split into two feuding factions, and officer after officer found themselves under investigation:

> The conviction that Nosenko was under Soviet control led to this case becoming the touchstone for evaluating other sources on Soviet intelligence. Sources who provided information supporting Nosenko's story were themselves deemed suspect. The theory

of a 'master plot' developed . . . this theory led to an extensive search for the KGB penetration.

CIA officers with Slavic backgrounds and the most experience in dealing with the Soviets were among the initial suspects; the careers of several innocent officers were permanently damaged.[17]

This paranoia was not confined to the lower or even middle reaches of the Agency's staff. Over time, the most senior officers in the Soviet Division, David Murphy and Tennent Bagley, were suspected of being KGB agents. Furthermore, Clare Edward Petty, a veteran officer who had been one of Angleton's disciples, produced an incendiary internal report which denounced the counterintelligence chief himself as Moscow's most senior and long-serving mole inside the CIA, controlled by the defector who had sparked the mole hunts.[18]

'I decided I'd been looking at it all wrong by assuming Golitsyn was as good as gold,' Petty explained to the intelligence author David Wise:

> I began rethinking everything. If you turned the flip side it all made sense. Golitsyn was sent to exploit Angleton . . . [He was] the perfect man to manipulate Angleton or provide Angleton with material on the basis of which he could penetrate and control other services. The penetration had to be at a high and sensitive level, and long-term . . . All the operation cables went through Angleton . . . Angleton had to be the person.[19]

This was the ultimate irony, and the inevitable outcome of the madness which Golitsyn had unleashed. Angleton had spent so long in the counterintelligence hall of mirrors, staring not at the true image but its reflection in the wilderness of fractured glass, that ineluctably he became both the watcher and the watched.

But since he and his *éminence grise* remained in effective control of the entire Agency, Petty's thesis was ignored and the mole hunts dragged on. Peter Wright, then a senior MI5 officer who had been one of Golitsyn's British disciples, was appalled by what he observed inside Langley:

'Angleton swallowed the "methodology" hook, line and sinker and allowed Golitsyn to range freely across the CIA's files, picking traitors apparently at random, and often unable to justify his decisions on anything other than the flimsiest of grounds.'[20]

Ultimately, according to the CIA's chief in-house historian, 'forty Agency officers were put on the suspect list and fourteen were thoroughly investigated. Although innocent, they had their careers damaged by the "security stigma".'[21]

But Angleton's fixation on moles damaged more than the lives and livelihoods of individual officers: it stopped any effective efforts against Moscow's very real spies in the most dangerous years of the Cold War. 'In the end', according to the Agency's own rueful history of the debacle, 'Angleton took the position that virtually every major Soviet defector or volunteer was a KGB provocation. This position adversely affected CIA operational efforts against the Soviet Union for almost two decades – veterans of the period say it paralyzed operations.'[22]

Nor was this catastrophic paralysis confined to the United States. The dangerous instability afflicting the CIA, caused by the same false premise and by the same two proponents, was mirrored in London. Its outcome, too, was identical. Over a ten-year period, almost two dozen spy hunters searched obsessively for traitors hidden in their midst, and three separate internal inquiries investigated whether Britain's most senior intelligence officials were KGB agents; these mole hunts led to what MI5 itself terms one of 'the most traumatic episodes in the Cold War history of the Security Service.'[23]

Much of the detail of that trauma remains secret. Unlike the United States, none of the British files have ever been disclosed. As a result there are only two direct published sources on the investigation:[24] MI5's official history and the autobiography of one of the most determined 'spycatchers', Peter Wright. Each offers a radically different conclusion on the mole hunts, but both agree that the Security Service was consumed and fractured by their fallout.

Wright, then a senior and well-regarded officer, had been one of the

MI5 team briefed by the CIA on Goleniewski's letters from behind the Iron Curtain in April 1959. He had played a central role in the Portland Spy Ring investigations which Sniper's intelligence had revealed, and it was that, ostensibly successful, case which first sparked concerns about a traitor inside MI5.

In May 1961, Wright was putting the finishing touches to a detailed post-mortem report on the activities of Gordon Lonsdale, the leader of the Portland Spy Ring. He was disturbed by two unexplained details. Why had Lonsdale disappeared abroad and then unexpectedly returned to England in the weeks leading up to his arrest; and why, on the day itself, had the Soviet Embassy in London suddenly changed the pattern and frequency of its radio transmissions?

The latter suggested that the KGB's resident agents were aware of the impending round-up, but if so, Moscow had deliberately allowed one of its most senior spies to be captured. Profoundly troubled, Wright began examining every dot and comma of the case and comparing them to the transcripts of Goleniewski's post-defection debriefing.

As often in espionage analysis, the devil lay in the tiniest of details – in this case, the precise timescale of the Sniper and Lonsdale stories and the points where they intersected. MI5 first observed Lonsdale meeting Houghton on 2 July 1960; his cover name was identified nine days later, and A4 surveillance teams began to tail him on 17 July.

Approximately one week later, according to Goleniewski's account to the CIA, the KGB discovered it had a traitor in its ranks. To Wright's mind, the timing was no coincidence. His experience of Soviet bloc spy services told him that seven to nine days would be the time needed for news that Lonsdale had been blown to filter through to Moscow and Warsaw; the inexorable conclusion was that the KGB had a mole inside the Security Service:

> The Lonsdale report was the most painful document I have ever written. I remember going off sailing in the Blackwater estuary, near my home in Essex . . . but no matter how I turned the boat, no

matter how I adjusted the rigging, I came to the same conclusion. The Russians knew we were on to Lonsdale from the beginning; they had withdrawn him, and then sent him back. But why?[25]

There was only one explanation which made sense of all the inconsistencies: Moscow had deliberately allowed Lonsdale's arrest in order to divert attention from a bigger prize: a senior mole inside MI5. Wright reluctantly spelled this out in his report on the case: 'The Russians would never sacrifice anyone as valuable as Lonsdale for a low-level source. The evidence . . . pointed much higher up – to the very summit of the organisation.'[26]

However, the Security Service's Deputy Director General, Graham Mitchell, was unwilling to heed Wright's advice; the Portland Spy Ring case was closed and marked down as a triumph for British intelligence, and for the next two years the question of whether MI5 was being betrayed from within was forgotten.

In November 1963, MI5 again met Goleniewski face to face, and over several days conducted a thorough debriefing in his Queens apartment. During the course of what became extended interviews, he provided what Wright called 'extraordinarily detailed' evidence of Soviet penetration of the Security Service. He had not, he explained, divulged this previously because 'the British had made such a mess of detecting [George] Blake'. The alleged mole was, Goleniewski claimed, 'a middling-grade agent', whose existence had been revealed to him in the mid-1950s during a discussion with colleagues about the relative merits of defecting to Britain or the United States:

> All three agreed that Britain was the better place to live because of the large Polish émigré community, but MI6 was obviously impossible to approach because of Lambda 1 [Blake]. Goleniewski suggested to the other two that they try to contact MI5 through the émigré community in London . . . [but] Goleniewski's chief said that this plan was equally dangerous because he knew the

> Russians also had a spy in MI5. The spy had been recruited by the
> Third Directorate of the KGB, responsible for the armed services . . .
> The agent had served in the British Army, and held rank as a British
> officer when he was recruited.

Goleniewski's story could have been no more than an effort to dangle an
alluring morsel of intelligence in the hope of keeping MI5's interest;
certainly, there was no way to confirm a clandestine conversation from
nearly a decade before.

But he was able to provide some details which lent credence to his
account. He pinpointed Eastern Europe as the location of the traitor's
recruitment and gave the name of a known KGB colonel as the officer
who had carried it out; more importantly, he revealed that the mole had
subsequently furnished Moscow with 'valuable Polish counterintelligence', which suggested he worked in the Security Service's dedicated
Polish section.[27]

Seven currently serving officers had career histories which, at least
partially, matched Goleniewski's description of the 'middle-ranking'
agent. An eighth, however, 'fitted every single part of it exactly': Michael
Hanley, then Director of C Branch, and tipped to rise to the very top of
the Service. The information should have rung immediate alarm bells,
but amid what Wright termed 'the overload in Counterintelligence from
late 1963 onward', it was overlooked. That 'overload' had a single cause:
Anatoliy Golitsyn.

During his five-month stay in London in 1963, Golitsyn had made a
powerful impression on Arthur Martin, head of MI5's Soviet counter-
espionage section. According to the Service's official history, the
temperamental defector indoctrinated Martin into the theory he was
then peddling in Washington, and 'sought with messianic zeal to try to
persuade both the American and British intelligence communities that
they were falling victim to a vast KGB deception from which only he
could save them.' Neither man was, apparently, troubled by the lack of
evidence to support this contention:

Martin . . . later acknowledged that it was Golitsyn who had 'crys-
tallised' his long-standing suspicion that there was a Soviet mole
within the Service. Yet, as Martin also acknowledged, Golitsyn
could offer only 'circumstantial evidence' with 'no precise information' to back up his theories.[28]

Martin's first choice of suspect was Graham Mitchell, the Deputy Director General who had dismissed the warnings in Wright's Lonsdale
report. In mid-May the two mole hunters joined forces and from then
until his retirement that September, Mitchell was kept under observation by a specialist surveillance team; his home phone was bugged and
his office in Leconfield House was wired for sound and fitted with hidden cameras. The results were mixed: Mitchell had a curious habit of
mumbling to himself and at times seemed to make potentially incrim-
inating remarks, but since the technical quality of the recordings was
poor, the transcripts were often unintelligible.

Martin and Wright asked Director General Roger Hollis for permission to interrogate their suspect; their pleas were refused and by the late
spring of 1964 the atmosphere inside MI5 was becoming poisonous.
Hollis gave Martin a succession of warnings that 'he was a focal point
for dissention in the Service' and suspended him from duty for a
fortnight.

Undeterred, the dedicated mole hunter continued to lobby for a formal investigation and in November the Director General again
summoned him to his office. He bluntly told Martin that 'he was at the
centre of all the unrest in the office', and risked dismissal; instead Hollis
rusticated him to a different branch of British intelligence.[29]

The campaign did, however, produce a concrete outcome: the same
month a joint MI5–MI6 committee – code-named FLUENCY – was set
up to examine all the available evidence of Soviet penetration; Peter
Wright was one of its leaders and, although Martin had been removed
from Leconfield House, the two men worked closely on the investigation.
In May 1965, FLUENCY reported its interim conclusions to MI5 and

MI6, declaring 'not merely that both Services had been penetrated but that the penetration continued'.[30] Influenced by Golitsyn's conspiracy theories, it had also fastened on a new candidate for the mole: Hollis was formally notified that he was now under suspicion, making him the first British intelligence chief in modern times to be investigated for treason. That December he retired with the allegations against him unresolved.

In January 1966 the Committee's full report widened the net slightly: the most likely penetration agent inside MI5, it now pronounced, was either Hollis or Goleniewski's 'middle-grade spy'.

The new Director General, Martin Furnival Jones, a veteran intelligence officer who had spent twenty-five years inside the Security Service, dismissed the idea that Hollis was a traitor and ordered FLUENCY to concentrate on Goleniewski's leads.

After many more months of mole hunting, suspicion fell again on Michael 'Jumbo' Hanley, the affable head of C Branch (and a future Director General), whom Wright had initially identified as a 100 per cent match for 'the middling-grade agent'; but that accusation, like the claim against Hollis, failed to stick, and when Hanley was cleared, Wright turned his sights on another popular officer who was 'a 60% fit'.

The man – whose identity has never been disclosed, but to whom Wright gave the pseudonym 'Gregory Stevens' – was placed under surveillance and his office covertly searched; neither effort produced any evidence of treachery. The only faintly worrying information unearthed was that Stevens had been treated for psychiatric problems by a private Harley Street doctor. Despite this, he was brought in for an intensive interrogation.

For three days he was alternately truculent and defensive; then on the fourth morning he suddenly announced that he was ready to confess. 'I've been wanting to tell someone about it for years. You're right . . . I'm the spy you're looking for.'

Stunned, Wright asked him to repeat the admission, at which point Stevens said he had not been serious and that his confession was a prank; according to Wright's subsequent account of the conversation,

Stevens jeered: 'You really believed me, didn't you? . . . You wanted a spy, didn't you . . . I thought I'd give you one. I was going to get chopped anyway. I know that!'[31]

If this investigation bordered on farce, its results were debilitating. Stevens accused his interrogators of being worse than the KGB, and, as MI5's authorized version of events recorded, soon afterwards he resigned: 'He never fully recovered from the trauma of having his unblemished loyalty to the Security Service called into question. His position became even more invidious when news leaked out to his colleagues that he had been grilled by Wright.'[32]

Morale within MI5 was now becoming a serious problem. The chief spycatcher found himself shunned and his obsessive mole hunt deeply resented: 'There was talk of the Gestapo. Younger officers began to avoid me in the canteen. Casual conversation with many of my colleagues became a rarity. Those of us involved in the penetration issue were set apart, feared and distrusted in equal measure.'[33]

In part this was fuelled by the realization that the trauma was not self-inflicted but instead driven by Angleton and Golitsyn. To reinforce the point, in March 1966 both men appeared in London, suddenly and without invitation, to press home the message that British intelligence should search ever harder for the traitor in its ranks; they lectured both MI5 and MI6 without providing anything in the way of concrete information and then abruptly departed.

By now even Peter Wright was having doubts about the path down which his American counterparts were pushing the Security Service. 'The vast majority of Golitsyn's material was tantalizingly imprecise,' he noted:

> It often appeared true as far as it went, but then faded into ambiguity . . . Where he stuck to what he saw and what he heard, he was impressive and believable . . . But where Golitsyn extrapolated from what he knew to develop broad theories . . . he was disastrous. Most of the Golitsyn acolytes in MI5, of which I was one, soon broke with Golitsyn's wider theories.[34]

And yet the FLUENCY mole hunts dragged on. In September 1967 the investigations into Hollis and Mitchell were relaunched, and for almost three years they undermined MI5's foundations and eroded its ability to combat genuine KGB threats. In February 1970, Hollis was formally, but fruitlessly, interrogated and, in desperation, Wright and his colleagues turned once again to the self-declared saviour of Western intelligence for help.

Although the CIA had now come to realize that Golitsyn was toxic and had started to limit his influence, the Security Service once again allowed him to drive its inquiries. In May 1970 it brought him to England, put him up in a safe house in the quiet Dorset town of Christchurch and gave him free access to its most sensitive files 'in order to identify the penetrations which he claimed to be able to uncover'.[35] The outcome followed swiftly. In June, FLUENCY submitted its final report, identifying Hollis as 'the most likely candidate' for the KGB mole.

The paper was not welcomed by MI5's management: it was, according to the Service's own account, 'a shocking document ... [with] threadbare evidence',[36] and both Hollis and Mitchell were formally cleared – a decision which later met with approval from the man whose original revelations had fired the starting gun on the investigations. 'If the KGB had had a mole at the head of MI5,' Goleniewski told journalist Edward J. Epstein, after listing the Soviet agents he had exposed in London, 'you can be sure all these men would somehow have escaped.'[37]

For the moment, the mole hunts were over – though Wright's insistence that Hollis was a traitor would simmer for more than a decade, and would play a significant part in the British government's doomed court battles during the 1980s to prevent him publishing his memoirs. As MI5 mournfully admitted, however, the harm they caused was long-lasting: 'The damage done to the reputation of the Service in the eyes of the four Prime Ministers privy to the charges against Hollis or Mitchell or both – Macmillan, Wilson, Heath and Callaghan – was inevitably substantial.'[38]

But the Service's history glosses over the other, less immediately obvious problem caused by the failed cases against Hollis and Mitchell; in the rush to identify Golitsyn's seemingly mythical spy at the very top of MI5, the mole hunters forgot Goleniewski's far more detailed intelligence about the 'middle-ranking' officer betraying its secrets to Moscow.

If, as the CIA's Clare Edward Petty believed, Golitsyn was a bogus defector, dispatched by Moscow to spread chaos and divert attention away from genuine Soviet agents, his efforts in Britain had succeeded spectacularly.

And as in London, so in Langley. After 1,277 days of incarceration – at least half in solitary confinement – and 292 days of interrogation, in 1969 the Agency finally and formally concluded that Yuri Nosenko was exactly what he claimed to be; while there were inconsistencies in his statements, he had never wavered from his essential story and the CIA apologetically pronounced him to be a genuine defector. He was freed, given a new identity, home and a lucrative consultancy contract.[39]

But the bitter internal battles over his *bona fides* would continue for another decade and, amid the clouds of paranoia and rancour created by Golitsyn's wild claims, American intelligence would, like its British counterparts, overlook the solid information provided by Goleniewski which pointed to KGB penetration dating back to the 1950s.

If Nosenko's ordeal had a happy ending, and Tennent Bagley's tentative plans to send him mad had not borne fruit, there was no such comfort for the once-prized defector holed up in his Silver Towers apartment; his psyche had proved less able to withstand the CIA's relentless assaults and he was now unquestionably mad. In the early 1970s the CIA accurately – but without admitting its own culpability – denounced him as hopelessly and dangerously insane.

28

Double Eagle

O N 14 JUNE 1973 the CIA prepared a list of Soviet bloc defectors to be placed under surveillance. The immediate reason for the six-page document was the impending arrival in Washington of Leonid Brezhnev, General Secretary of the Soviet Communist Party, for a week of meetings with President Richard Nixon; in preparation, the Agency's counterintelligence officers met with their colleagues in the Psychiatric Staff 'to discuss and decide which of those defectors for whom we have a legal responsibility should be watched during Brezhnev's visit'.

Many of the names were marked as posing no threat. In Langley's estimation several were habitual drunks or passers of bad cheques, but were unlikely to disrupt the summit; others, it noted approvingly, had become solid law-abiding American citizens. However, the Agency offered a very much less benign assessment of Goleniewski: 'He is a real nut who aspires to the Romanoff Crown. Notify Secret Service . . . Absolutely nutty. Put him at the top of the list. He hates the Soviet Government because it's depriving him of the Romanov crown jewels [sic].'[1]

Since this bold assertion managed to be both true and false simultaneously it was symptomatic of the fundamental paradox running throughout the Goleniewski saga. By the summer of 1973 his royal pretensions, coupled with a profound paranoia, had certainly become a debilitating derangement; yet this was not all-consuming, for at the same time as the CIA dismissed him as 'nutty', British intelligence again sought his advice on covert KGB operations, while Moscow took him sufficiently seriously to send one of its diplomatic staff scurrying around Washington to locate his Congressional testimony.

~

In the early 1970s, Romanoff fever was a global phenomenon. The craze for stories about the last Russian dynasty started in 1967 when Robert K. Massie, an American journalist and academic, published the first authoritative biography of the doomed Imperial Family. Drawn entirely from available Western sources, *Nicholas and Alexandra* told a conventional version of the story, ending inevitably with the assassination in the cellar of Ipatiev House; as Cold War fever began to abate, and previously implacable Western hostility to everything Russian gradually faded, the book's combination of glamour, romance and tragedy made it a bestseller.

But the continuing absence of any royal bodies also proved fertile ground for conspiracy theorists on both sides of the Atlantic, and Goleniewski was a central figure in their fantasies. In May 1970, Peter Bessell, a colourful British Liberal MP close to party leader Jeremy Thorpe, lit the fuse for a new twist to the theories, suggesting that for more than half a century governments on both sides of the Atlantic had covered up intelligence suggesting that the Romanoffs had been rescued.

Bessell, a keen amateur historian, lodged a slew of written questions in Parliament; three demanded that the Foreign Office disclose any papers it held which would help Goleniewski prove his claim to the Russian throne and the alleged Romanoff fortune, while the fourth question was more specific. It asked 'the Prime Minister whether Her Majesty's Government has any evidence to suggest that the former Czar Nicholas II or any of the members of the former Russian Imperial Family, who were presumed to have been killed at Ekaterinburg . . . have survived'.[2]

The questions should have been easily answered. The British government had long since made clear that it accepted the assassination as established fact, but for unexplained reasons Bessell's enquiries were rebuffed, and the Romanoff escape conspiracy theories were reignited.

'The four Parliamentary Questions were accepted by the Table Office but rejected by the Clerk of the House,' he explained in a sworn affidavit six years later. 'This is not unusual. But in this instance I had gone over the questions with an experienced official in the Table Office . . . I re-tabled. Again they were rejected.'[3]

This apparent obstruction led Bessell to take to his feet at Prime Minister's Questions, castigating the government for withholding official papers on the assassination, in defiance of the 'thirty-year rule' which required their publication. It was something of a blunder; Harold Wilson brusquely replied that all the documents held by any department had been released to the Public Records Office four years earlier.[4]

Undeterred, Bessell decided to table an Early Day Motion – one of Parliament's more arcane procedures which rarely produces meaningful debate – to place on the official record his support for Goleniewski's campaign for recognition as the legitimate Romanoff heir. EDM 291 of 1970 was duly printed on the Commons' order of business:

> In view of the assistance rendered to the Intelligence Services of the United Kingdom by Colonel Michal Goleniewski, and the evidence he provided in the Philby case, this House calls upon Her Majesty's Government to investigate the claim by Colonel Goleniewski that he is the former Czarevich Alexei of Russia, and that he and other members of the Imperial Family were not assassinated in July 1918 or at any other time.[5]

The Motion was, however, never laid before the House; before it could be debated Wilson called a general election and, since he had decided not to stand again as an MP, Bessell decided 'it would be in bad taste . . . to institute a debate'.[6] It did, however, produce tangible results. The first was an approach by an unnamed Foreign Office official who, according to Bessell's account, showed him previously unpublished papers which purported to record plans to facilitate the Romanoffs' escape from captivity. Although these alleged documents have never surfaced, the copies he made would play a part in the next act of the Goleniewski drama.

Bessell made contact with Guy Richards, then about to publish a second book on the Romanoff case. If *The Hunt for the Czar* was more cautious than its predecessor in supporting Goleniewski's claimed provenance, the author was happy to broker discussions between the former MP and the *soi disant* Tsarevich.

On 28 July 1970 they met in the Silver Towers apartment and Bessell handed over copies of the Foreign Office papers to the man whom he deferentially addressed as 'Your Royal and Imperial Highness'.[7] It was an ill-fated decision. Goleniewski promptly used the documents to forge an entirely fraudulent version which appeared to show British officials endorsing his claimed lineage. Bessell, whose own track record did not display an unswerving respect for honesty, was furious.

'This is a matter of the utmost gravity and could have the most serious and far-reaching consequences,' he complained to Goleniewski the following January. 'It is a major offence to tamper with official papers, or copies of official papers, whether they be Government Records of the United Kingdom or of the United States. I will do what I can to protect you against any action by the Foreign Office in London, but nevertheless I have felt it my duty to report the matter.'

Goleniewski's bogus version of the letter – 'a particularly clumsy forgery' in Bessell's considered opinion – had also led the former MP to reconsider his previous support for the demands of 'His Royal and Imperial Highness':

> For some months I was persuaded that your claim to be the Grand Duke Alexei was well founded. Partly to assist you in substantiating that claim and partly to satisfy my own curiosity I researched the whole question of whether the Imperial Family escaped in depth, and with the cooperation of British officials. I

am now satisfied that while it is highly probable that the Imperial Family escaped, and to that limited extent your story may be correct, I am equally satisfied that your claim to be the original Grand Duke is without foundation.

Also you must know that the United States Department of State and the United Kingdom Foreign Office have fully documented and irrefutable evidence as to your origins, country and date of birth and parentage . . .

Therefore you are putting yourself in a position where, by your insistence that you are the original Grand Duke, you must eventually be subjected to ridicule and disgrace. Nevertheless, you still have time to avoid the worst of this. Even at this late stage, by stating openly and honestly the real facts, you can save a good deal from the wreckage that may otherwise engulf you and your family.[8]

It was good advice. Characteristically, Goleniewski not only rejected it, but added Bessell to the growing list of enemies on whom he planned to exact revenge.

The release in December 1971 of a lavish film adaptation of Massie's *Nicholas and Alexandra* – it would be nominated for six Academy Awards and won two – prompted a resurgence in the public appetite for the Romanoff saga. Hollywood studios opened tentative negotiations to adapt Richards' book and some approached the self-anointed heir to the Russian throne; most, however, quickly retreated, disturbed by Goleniewski's unhinged conspiracy theories and wild rants. By early 1972 the only would-be producer still willing to tolerate his overweening arrogance ran a boutique outfit based in small rented offices in Manhattan's theatre district.

Marshall H. Ward treated 'His Imperial Majesty' with the requisite deference and offered to 'form a partnership' which encompassed brokering a publishing deal for the Tsarevich's putative autobiography and writing the screenplay for a movie based on his life.[9] Neither of these two enticing propositions ever bore fruit, but the initial research uncovered a troubling incident which seemed to suggest that others were less keen on Goleniewski's claims reaching a wider audience.

At the end of January 1972, Ward went to the Queens County Register Office on Long Island, where Goleniewski and Irmgard had lodged all their affidavits together with copies of letters from CIA and Congressional officials; these had been transferred on to archival microfilm reels, open to inspection by anyone who requested them.

The key document was Goleniewski's sworn 1969 statement which, with accompanying exhibits, ran to 142 pages, but Ward discovered that the original paper copy had mysteriously disappeared, and when he examined microfilm reel 359 he found it had been crudely vandalized to remove the entire affidavit.

'As I was about to inspect the reel (with operator assistance), the reel "broke",' he complained to the Register Office supervisor. 'The operator inspected the reel and discovered that the pages in question had been removed. In my opinion as a filmmaker, this microfilm was cut with a razor blade and removed, stolen, or whatever you want to call it.'[10]

An internal City Register investigation confirmed Ward's story. The original document was absent and the reel had, as Ward claimed, been 'cut as if with a razor blade, and all page numbers relating to the document in question were missing'.[11] Fortunately, whoever had removed the material was unaware that the Queens County office kept a back-up duplicate of the original microfilm, and Goleniewski's exhaustive account of his life, career and litany of official correspondence was swiftly reinstated. No culprit was ever identified and no motive established – and given Goleniewski's own crude tampering with Bessell's Foreign Office documents, it is entirely possible that he vandalized his own documents to support his claims of persecution.

Whatever the truth, the incident fed into his rampant paranoia and provoked further claims of intimidation. Some of these strained credulity and appeared to justify the CIA's verdict of his loosening grip on sanity; a barely coherent complaint to the FBI involving Bessell was all too typical:

Returning from food store . . . about PM: 6.45, I had been contacted in the subway by unknown to me young man, medium size, pale, nervous, clothed in elegant manner, blond, who being very excited . . . informed me that . . . a serie [sic] of articles in European magazine by Peter Bessell, former Member of British Parliament . . . would be published in case [presumably 'unless'] I would return the original of the threatening letter by Peter Bessell of January 11, 1971, to his office in the area of Fifth Avenue, and make tape-recorded, in my voice, promise that I will stop to make trouble by the Federal Bureau of Investigations [sic] in New York City.

Furthermore, the young man told me that in such case . . . I would receive in Peter Bessell's office, as reimbursement for the 'damages' done to me by his letter, $500,000[12] in cash and consequently I would have just to forget the all [sic] matter. I told the young man also to forget his proposition, to buy a lollipop and to disappear before I would lose my temper, and he immediately left the subway station in the direction of the street. No other events and/or persons connected with this incident could be observed.[13]

This was undoubtedly unhinged, yet simultaneously there was some real evidence that Goleniewski remained of interest to his genuine enemies. On 4 May 1973, Valeriy P. Butrin, Third Secretary and Vice-Consul at the Soviet Embassy in Washington, appeared unannounced in the offices of the Senate Internal Security Subcommittee seeking a copy of Goleniewski's evidence to Congress. Butrin returned twice over the following days, pestering the staff repeatedly for sight of whatever information it had on the case and, according to the receptionist, 'appeared nervous and frightened'. When he was told that no transcript existed of Goleniewski's 1963 testimony to the House Immigration and Nationality Subcommittee – his sole appearance before Congress – the diplomat scurried away.[14]

At the same time, a more friendly intelligence service also rekindled its relationship with the once 'invaluable' spy. In July 1973, MI5 dispatched one of its assistant directors, Christopher Grose-Hodge, to seek

Goleniewski's advice on KGB operations in Britain and Europe; he graciously agreed to provide the Security Service with 'consultations, actual comments and evaluations of informations [sic] received from other sources', at the rate of $150[15] per four-hour day.

Evidently, Her Majesty's government agreed to pay for this consultancy, since from summer to the end of January the following year, LAVINIA, as the Security Service had originally named Goleniewski, supplied lengthy reports on public protests against the US-backed dictatorship in Greece and the leadership of the military coup which eventually overthrew it, the suicide of a high-ranking BND officer in West Germany, and the mysterious disappearance of a senior British intelligence officer from his house in South London.[16]

MI5 forwarded much of this intelligence to the CIA, where it received a surprisingly warm response from Goleniewski's former nemesis, James Angleton. On 25 January 1974 the counterintelligence chief wrote to Cecil Shipp, the Security Service's liaison officer in Washington DC, recognizing the validity of at least some of the information:

> It seems fair to say that we have so far found aspects of LAVINIA's recent statements which are demonstrably and remarkably accurate, within the bounds of his knowledgeability. On the other hand there is evidence that some of his offerings are tainted if not inspired by his reading of the press. No amount of research is likely to provide a definitive answer as to the overall mix between fact and invention.
>
> Still, the potential of important information in LAVINIA's mind precludes dismissing what he may say. Based upon his impressive record of production, assessment of the reliability of any given LAVINIA lead should perhaps be made only on the specific terms of the individual lead seen after investigation and in the light of LAVINIA's access.
>
> Whether he is now mad, or given to telling us what he thinks may pique our interest, may be for practical purposes beside the point, or at least not susceptible to our control.[17]

Since he had spent more than a decade denouncing Goleniewski as an entirely bogus defector, a 'provocation' sent by Moscow to mislead Western intelligence services, Angleton's qualified volte-face was remarkable.[18] But it was also a day late and a dollar – or rather tens of thousands of dollars – short. Goleniewski's brain was now fatally fractured by anger over what he viewed – with at least some justification – as a betrayal by the CIA, and paranoia about its failure to heed his warnings of a vast 'communo-fascist' underground network orchestrated by the KGB.

By now his original claims that Soviet intelligence had created a covert 'stay behind' group of former Nazi intelligence officials to penetrate the West had metastasized into a much larger global conspiracy. The relatively small network he previously called 'Hacke' was rechristened ODRA, and was, in this new telling, a vast spider's web whose reach stretched from Moscow to the inner sanctums of the White House:

> The complex known under the code-name of 'ODRA' is connected with illegal network of Agents and Sub-Agents as well as their Chiefs of the Third Main Directorate of MVD/KGB, dealing since last approximately 35 years with military security and counter-intelligence services, including Special Counter-Intelligence outside of Soviet Union . . .
>
> After the end of W.W. 2nd, in 1945/46, 'ODRA' had been re-organized and turned into most selected and special illegal group of III M.D. operating from Poland, and using independently from other MVD/KGB Agencies.[19]

Goleniewski claimed to have seen '1,500 pages' of documents about this sinister organization in the course of his work for the UB and the KGB during the 1950s. These allegedly listed 'the code names and short data concerning the principal agents of ODRA' and their locations inside British, West German and American intelligence.

Although he had curiously not provided any of this information in his extensive original debriefings, fully ten years later he was suddenly able to recall the cryptonyms and real identities of some of the most prominent sleeper agents; some were highly improbable, while others were the stuff of madness.

According to Goleniewski, Stalin's son Yakov Dzhugashvili had not, as the West believed, died fighting for Mother Russia during World War II, but instead was brought into the ODRA conspiracy and reinvented as 'Colonel Kujun'; thereafter, however, he was smuggled to the United States, had changed his name to Dodd and had gone on to become a long-serving US Senator. Since Senator Thomas Dodd – the only person to match the latter part of this description – had a well-documented history which included fifteen months as one of the American prosecutors at the Nuremberg War Crimes trials, the story was preposterous. But it was dwarfed in absurdity by the names that followed.

Two old foes were now 'exposed' as secret members of the 'Red Nazi' organization. Peter Bessell was denounced as 'the mass murderer and Chief of Stalin's NKVD Nicholai Yeshov', who in reality had been executed in a basement near the Lubyanka Prison in 1940. Guy Richards fared even worse.

Goleniewski claimed that far from being a mild-mannered and award-winning New York reporter, he was in fact SS Obergruppen-führer Reinhard Heydrich, Chief of the Reich Main Security Office and one of the architects of the Holocaust; since the real Heydrich had been very publicly mortally wounded by Czech agents in June 1942 near Prague, the allegation was ample evidence of Goleniewski's rampant insanity.

But the most bizarre claim involved Henry Kissinger, then President Nixon's National Security Advisor and Secretary of State. Kissinger had – provably – arrived in New York in 1938, aged fifteen, a refugee from Hitler's anti-Semitic purges, and had gone on to serve as an NCO with the US Counter-Intelligence Corps during World War II. All of this, Goleniewski solemnly informed MI5, was a devious ruse to disguise his 'real' identity as a member of the 'Communo-Fascist' underground, which he claimed had been recorded in the cache of secret ODRA files:

Under the code-name of 'BOR' was described as agent of 'ODRA', US Sargant [sic] and later Captain Kissinger, counterintelligence interrogator of US Army, and instructor of military intelligence school in Oberammergau . . . In 1954 it was notified in the investigation's memorandum that Kissinger was in the United States at Harvard University, having contact with United States Intelligence (CIA) . . .

'BOR' is identical with present national security's [sic] advisor of the President, Henry Kissinger . . . who beyond any reasonable doubt was in touch with [Soviet intelligence] during his military service in Germany . . . if he is . . . still in service of KGB, ie: in position without precedence [sic] in history of Secret Service's deeds in the United States, Kissinger [is] endangering not only the national security of the USA but also of its western Allies including the United Kingdom.[20]

There was much more in this deranged vein. The KGB, he claimed, had smuggled into strategic US locations 'small nuclear devices, power of . . . more than 150 Megatons' which could be remotely detonated by its sleeper 'MOB networks' across the country at very short notice.

Unsurprisingly, by the middle of 1974, MI5 decided it had heard enough, and once more abandoned attempts to sift genuine intelligence from the fantasies which haunted Goleniewski's tortured mind. A brief dalliance with Herbert Romerstein, a former communist who abandoned the party and became Chief Investigator for the House Committee on Internal Security, likewise wilted amid an onslaught of wild allegations issued from the Silver Towers apartment.

Cut off from his daily British retainers, Goleniewski was soon running seriously short of money – a problem made much worse when his daughter, Tatiana, fell ill and needed urgent surgery; with no medical insurance, the hospital bills were crippling and the self-proclaimed heir to the Romanoff fortune was reduced to petitioning the CIA for the release of some of the money it held in trust for the family, and to a humiliating public appeal for charity by one of his dwindling army of supporters.

'Late word from His Imperial Highness Aleksei Nicholaevich Romanoff,' conservative talk radio host Allen Mann Jnr informed readers of the *Manchester Union-Leader* on 1 August, 'is that after much foot-dragging the United States government has finally gotten round to releasing to him some moneys from his and his wife's account.' Unfortunately, according to Mann, this had arrived too late and was, in any event, not enough to pay the surgical bills:

> Lack of sufficient funds, caused by the criminal conspiracy against the Russian Imperial Family, and the government's slowness in making some of Aleksei's OWN MONEY [emphasis in original] available to him, resulted in Tatiana being prematurely released from the hospital and subsequent medical complications that aggravated her condition and in a very real way endangered her life. While the condition of the little Grand Duchess seems to have stabilized to some degree, her convalescence is expected to require a long time. During this period, medical expenses, including the fees of specialists, will continue, and the money released by the government from Aleksei's account is insufficient to pay them.
>
> We cannot permit Aleksei's concern over his daughter's serious illness to be further compounded by an inability, through no fault of his own, to pay for her medical expenses . . . I urge you to join in aiding Aleksei by sending what money you can.[21]

There is no record of how much money Mann raised from those still faithful to Goleniewski's Romanoff fantasy, but many of his erstwhile supporters in America's rabid right-wing movements had already cut him off. Even Edward Hunter, the veteran anti-communist and publisher of *Tactics* magazine, had long since despaired of coaxing reason from his ramblings. 'I told him that nothing can satisfy him, ever,' Hunter wrote in a memo to himself after one lengthy harangue. 'He said he has sent long statements. I said they're useless: nobody can make head or tail out of them.'[22]

Deprived of any other forum, in January 1975, Goleniewski launched his own monthly newsletter; available via mail-order for a modest annual subscription of $24.[23] *Double Eagle* proudly proclaimed the author's credentials:

> It is the only self-edited publication issued under the auspices of H.I.H. the Heir to the All-Russian Imperial Throne, Tsarevich and Grand Duke Aleksei Nicholaevich Romanoff of Russia, the August Ataman and Head of the Russian Imperial House of Romanoff, also known under the cover identity of Colonel Michal M. Goleniewski, renowned for his support of the national security of the United States and its western allies.

Despite these grandiose claims and the prominent display of the traditional Romanoff coat of arms – a double-headed eagle clutching the imperial sceptre and orb in its outstretched claws – the newsletter's pages were little more than a professionally printed rendering of Goleniewski's previous jeremiads, filled with near-incoherent recitations of his familiar complaints, together with further fact-free denunciations of Richards – 'the SS mass murderer Heydrich' – and Bessell, who had apparently managed the remarkable feat of being both 'an agent of the British Secret Intelligence Service' and Stalin's deceased intelligence chief Nicholai Yeshov.

'In this issue,' Goleniewski thundered in August 1976, 'the true story of US Government betrayal of a loyal friend . . . and years of CIA and British inspired direct threats, intimidation and conspiracy against the Editor, his wife and little daughter, outlined point by point. The shocking truth behind the myriad of falsifications [sic] and forgeries. A matter involving billions of dollars! Unmasked are the forces at work to keep the Editor in economic bondage and deprive him from his rightful Russian Imperial Inheritance.'[24]

Over two dozen excruciatingly repetitious pages, Goleniewski denounced this 'conspiracy' by US and British intelligence – who had somehow entered into a pact with the KGB and Western banks – involving 'embezzlement, fraud, concealment of assets and other criminal machinations . . . to deprive me of the Russian Imperial Inheritance without due process of law'. He also catalogued, at interminable length, the repeated threats he allegedly endured in the streets and stores around his home; the paranoid absurdity of these claims simply reinforced the diagnosis of a man who had lost all touch with reality:

> I was threatened by a surveillance team, which followed me daily from 1971–1972 . . . the members of which from time to time tried to intimidate and threaten me with murder, with the murder of my little daughter . . . with the murder of my wife, with kidnapping, with bodily injury . . . not to mention my deportation from the United States . . .
>
> On January 20, 1975, during my presence in a supermarket with my little daughter, an aged woman approached me and, amongst other things informed me that it would be much better for my family and myself to [make] . . . a deal on my part with the Soviet Union . . .
>
> On March 23, 1976 . . . I was approached by a man unknown to me . . . who threatened that the SS leaders would not permit me to expose them . . . [and] that I may die in jail or may be murdered [or] that my little daughter will be kidnapped.[25]

Further issues of *Double Eagle* repeated yet again the nonsensical claim that Guy Richards was SS war criminal Reinhard Heydrich, and displayed photos purporting to demonstrate facial similarities between the Nazi and the reporter.[26] Worse, according to a complaint Richards filed with the New York Criminal Court, Goleniewski had followed up the libel with a deliberate campaign of intimidation:

> He has called on US and N.Y. City officials to arrest me and deport me as 'Heydrich' . . . He has called on publishers of my books . . . to advance the same idea and to try to persuade them

to withdraw my works from publication . . . He has harassed me at home with phone calls at all hours of the day and night, delivering epithets in Polish and German.

He has become a personal scourge as well as a financial and physical drain. His malicious actions are all the more outrageous since he was imported to this country by the CIA and, as far as I know, has no status whatsoever as a US citizen.[27]

The complaint did Richards no good; lawyers counselled that since Goleniewski was broke, there was little chance of recovering any damages and therefore filing suit was not financially viable.

The two other public figures defamed in *Double Eagle* also proved unwilling to sue. Henry Kissinger simply shrugged off the allegation that he was ODRA agent BOR, while Peter Bessell – Stalin's supposed former spy chief – was preoccupied with the failure, in somewhat murky circumstances, of his finance brokerage business and was about to become embroiled in the unsuccessful prosecution of Liberal leader Jeremy Thorpe for attempted murder. Spared the prospect of libel litigation, Goleniewski ploughed on with his ever-widening conspiracy theories.

'When this Editor arrived into this country in 1961,' he informed his readership in October 1977, 'it was almost a mission impossible to debrief properly the representatives of the counterintelligence staff of the CIA with the many informations [sic] and leads concerning Soviet and other satellite intelligence penetrations . . . It was obvious that sinister hidden forces inside of the CIA tried to ignore this and . . . the British high representatives offered this Editor . . . certain silence's "reimbursement" [sic].'[28]

But no one was listening. The Cold War was slowly thawing, an anti-ballistic missile treaty had lowered fears of nuclear Armageddon, and the era of *glasnost* and *perestroika* was a few short years away. At the same time, Goleniewski's 'Tsarist comedy' had finally destroyed his last shreds of credibility. After one last hurrah – a lengthy ovation to his Romanoff pretence and espionage credentials[29] – even the John Birch

Society's diehard anti-communists slunk away from the man they had once so feverishly championed.

In November 1979 he, briefly and with characteristic drama, caused international headlines by issuing a statement denouncing Ayatollah Khomeini, recently installed as supreme leader of the new Islamic Republic of Iran, as a long-time KGB asset. 'The Soviets penetrated the Shiite Moslem [sic] sect as early as the 1950s,' he informed UPI, 'and Khomeini was a Russian agent at that time.'[30] But press interest was short-lived and as the news cycle moved on, Goleniewski slipped back into obscurity. 'From then,' Polish intelligence noted in its files, 'no information was received regarding the Subject's behaviour.'

The UB, like the CIA and MI5, now viewed the man once condemned to death for 'betrayal of the Homeland' as an irrelevance. In February 1983 it shut down Operation TELETECHNIK,[31] and three years later a Polish military court formally rescinded his sentence.[32]

The UB also ceased monitoring and harassing the family Goleniewski had abandoned in Warsaw, and issued a long-delayed passport and international travel permit to his son, Jerzy, who had achieved his own measure of celebrity as the bass player in a moderately successful post-punk rock band.[33]

Quite how Goleniewski survived financially in this emerging post-Cold War world remains unclear. *Double Eagle* seems to have ceased publication in the mid-1980s and if the CIA finally relented and paid him, or Irmgard, the money it had promised, that information remains secret, locked in Langley's vaults despite repeated requests for release. His death, too, is shrouded in some mystery.

No press obituaries were published, but three accounts – by American historian Robert Massie,[34] British financial writer William Clarke,[35] and Polish academic Leszek Pawlikowicz[36] – suggest he died in July 1993, in Lenox Hill Hospital, New York, after a short illness. There are, however, no public documents to confirm this date, nor the cause of death. Medical records are confidential, and under New York State law death certificates are available only to family members.

The only national public register of deaths uses social security numbers as the key identifier; since Goleniewski never attained the US citizenship promised by Congress – not least because his Alien Registration Card was in a different name to that on HR 5507, the Bill which opened the door to his naturalization, let alone his Romanoff marriage licence – his details would not have fulfilled this fundamental requirement. Nor is the location of his grave publicly recorded anywhere in the United States, under any of the multiple identities he used throughout his three post-defection decades in the West.

Fittingly, in death as in life Michał Goleniewski remained an enigma.

29

Who *Really* Was Michał Goleniewski?

O N 11 MARCH 2009 an international consortium of scientists published the peer-reviewed results of forensic examinations of a
collection of human remains unearthed two years earlier from a small
grave site near Ekaterinburg in the Urals region of the Russian Federation. Led by Michael D. Coble, Director of Research at the US Armed
Forces Institute of Pathology, the team had spent months performing
state-of-the-art DNA tests on what were clearly the bones of two teenage children which had been in the ground for many decades; these
yielded the solution for what Coble and his colleagues termed 'one of
the greatest mysteries of the twentieth century':

> We have virtually irrefutable evidence that the two individuals
> recovered from the 2007 grave are the two missing children of the
> Romanov family: The Tsarevich Alexei and one of his sisters.[1]

The tests performed by Coble and his colleagues were not the first to
examine remains dug up near Ekaterinburg. Ten years earlier three
teams of scientists in Russia, Britain and the United States had independ-
ently examined a larger collection of equally ancient bones removed
from another grave site in the same area. DNA testing conclusively
established that they belonged to the Tsar, Tsarina and three of their
children.

Added to the findings of the 2009 report, the conventional history of the Romanoff assassination was now scientifically proven: every single member of the Imperial Russian Family died, just as the Bolsheviks had claimed, in July 1918. The DNA results also removed any lingering doubts about the identity claimed by Michał Goleniewski: whoever else he might have been, he was unquestionably not Aleksei Nicholaevich Romanoff.

It is, however, rather less easy to reach a clear-cut conclusion about what – as opposed to who – he really was.

For more than sixty years his life and achievements have been distorted by a toxic combination of misinformation, official secrecy and his own bogus or exaggerated claims, while American and British intelligence services have sought to erase Goleniewski from the history of Cold War espionage.

The continuing suppression of the vast bulk of his once-substantial CIA and MI5 files has added to the miasma of confusion surrounding the very real contribution Goleniewski made to Western security during one of the most dangerous periods of the Cold War. Even by the close-mouthed standards of intelligence services, this is unusual. Other defectors from behind the Iron Curtain have been permitted – often helped – to write books and articles. Many of the CIA officers who dealt with Goleniewski's material, or who handled him as an asset, have also received official blessing to publish their stories.

In the same period the Agency further muddied the waters by assigning credit for his exposure of some of the high-profile spies to James Angleton's favoured defector, Anatoliy Golitsyn. It also floated, anonymously, a baseless theory that Goleniewski was a Soviet provocation – that, wittingly or otherwise, towards the end of his time in Warsaw he was being used to feed KGB disinformation to the West.

'He had been dropped as an agent by the Soviets,' one unnamed Agency officer told intelligence writer David C. Martin in the late 1970s, 'and this was one thing that was eating at him when he turned to us. He was out of favour, but in fairly short order after he began writing to us, they picked him up again, and the content turned around to things the Soviets were telling him.'[2]

There was then – and there is now – no factual basis for that allegation which, according to one of the CIA's first officers to work on the case, emanated from Angleton's wilderness of mirrors. 'I am convinced,' Tennent Bagley, himself once one of Angleton's disciples, wrote of Goleniewski to a fellow intelligence historian in March 1996, 'that he was a genuine source of ours (contrary to theories developed by Angleton even before the defection) and [I] doubt that either the KGB or the UB were manipulating his access to information at any time. So beware the CI Staff's . . . wisdom on this case.'[3]

Goleniewski's declassified Polish intelligence files confirm Bagley's view. They clearly show the unprecedented damage his revelations caused to both the Urząd Bezpieczeństwa and to its ultimate masters in Moscow. Whatever he might have become in the years after the CIA abandoned him, the UB's vast dossier on the agent it called TELETECH-NIK shows that it knew him to be a genuine and uniquely dangerous defector.

The death sentence imposed by the Military Court, and the protracted efforts of both Polish and Soviet intelligence services to locate, assassinate or discredit their rogue agent also give the lie to Angleton's attempt to miscast Goleniewski as a KGB provocation. Neither Moscow nor Warsaw would have wasted their intelligence assets for more than a decade – let alone spending huge sums of precious hard currency – in pursuit of an agent they had created themselves to distract or mislead the West.

There is a painful irony in the CIA's campaign to smear the man who was once 'the best defector the US ever had'.[4] Goleniewski had been the first former Soviet bloc spy to warn the Agency of Moscow's long-term strategic plan to blind it, and its allies, with misinformation and misdirection. He could hardly have imagined that while accepting the principle of the debilitating intelligence disease of *dezinformatsiya*, James Angleton and his disciples would so twist the details that they denounced the messenger himself as the carrier of the virus.

This is not merely long-cold history. The Goleniewski saga might have played out more than six decades ago, but there is a troubling echo today of the lesson he attempted to teach Western intelligence. Moscow has not abandoned the techniques it used to dupe Washington and London from the earliest years of the Soviet Union's existence: instead it has refined the mechanics of disinformation. As the 2016 US Presidential election and the British referendum on Brexit showed, the KGB's successors have become adept at manipulating the anonymity of the internet to sow false information and create dissent. So-called 'troll farms' and a constantly expanding network of 'bots' may have replaced the more personal approaches of The Trust or WiN, but the intention – and the end result – is identical.

For this reason, if no other, this long, strange story of Michał Goleniewski is as relevant today as it was during the dangerous years of the Cold War, and uncovering the shameful treatment he received from the countries he had risked his life to help is just as important. On its own evidence the CIA was substantially responsible for driving its most valuable intelligence source down the rabbit hole of insanity: unless or until that history is understood, the Agency – and its allies in the West – remain at risk of repeating their mistakes.

Yet this picture is not a simple monochrome, nor are its contours and borders easily delineated and discernible. Goleniewski, too, bears some blame for his fate. His conceit, paranoia and avarice, as well as his baseless pretension to the Romanoff throne, all contributed to his downfall.

The truth about Michał Goleniewski is not binary. He played the role of both victim and villain in his own tragedy, a confused and confusing mixture of the good and the bad. He was a courageous anti-communist agent for the West, whose information led to the exposure of some of the most damaging Soviet spies of the Cold War, and a genuine defector, who risked his life to betray his country from principle, rather than for financial benefit.

Yet he was also – and simultaneously – an arrogant, greedy fantasist, who could, and did, play fast and loose with the truth. In his private life, he was a devoted husband to Irmgard Kampf – whom he seems to have genuinely loved – and doting father to their daughter. Yet he was also a bigamist who casually abandoned his first wife and three children in Poland when he defected.

He trapped himself in the hubristic pretence to be Aleksei Romanoff; was abandoned in James Angleton's infamous 'wilderness of mirrors'; and was ultimately driven into insanity by a combination of CIA incompetence and harassment, as well as his own profound personal flaws.

Forty-six years after Agent Sniper defected, Tennent Bagley summed up the inherent contradictions in Goleniewski's complicated story: 'He was an experienced counterintelligence officer of rare sharpness and professionalism . . . It was a great loss to our side when . . . this sharpest of minds slipped into delusion and his information became confused and misleading.'[5]

The Agency's own, internal, verdict – unaccountably withheld from public view for many decades – reinforces Bagley's assessment. Although it fails to acknowledge its own discreditable role in the downfall of its most valuable defector, it is a clear-sighted summary of Goleniewski's importance and what was lost when madness consumed him. It offers a fitting epitaph to his life and career:

> It is unfair to Goleniewski's tremendous contribution to the Western intelligence services to allow the man's exasperating paranoid personality to obscure his value. A review must emphasize the almost total recall with which he was endowed and which enabled him to give the names and details of 1,693 [Soviet bloc] intelligence personalities, including officers, co-opted workers and agents, and his initiative in sending successfully to the West 1,000 pages of classified Polish documents . . . and in caching another 750 Minox film frames of classified documents when he defected . . . It is most important to note that until approximately early 1964, Goleniewski was an accurate and reliable source of information . . .

The Goleniewski tragedy lies in his unparalleled contribution to Western intelligence and his hopelessly paranoid personality which blocked long-term cooperation with any Western intelligence service.

On the basis of his exceptional memory, his experience as an operational intelligence officer and his intimate association with UB and KGB officers, he should have been one of the most enduring and valuable defector assets in the West. His mental illness has made that impossible, which is a loss for the Western services and a tragedy for the man himself.[6]

Afterword

In December 2019, just before I began writing the manuscript for this book, one of my editors posed an unexpected question: given the chance to meet and talk with him, would I have liked Michał Goleniewski?

I had by then spent two solid years researching his history and had been immersed in the man's own voluminous writings, as well as the documents extracted – with varying degrees of willingness – from governmental agencies and private archives. I felt that I knew Goleniewski as well as anyone who had not actually sat face to face with him; but the question of whether I would have liked him had never crossed my mind.

The answer I gave then rather followed the logic of the research. The vast haul of material I had harvested – many thousands of individual pages – painted the picture of a man whose fierce intelligence I would have admired, and whose dedication to countering the activities of Soviet bloc agencies I would have respected. The evidence they contained – often spelled out in his own words – revealed a brave man with a brilliant mind, fractured by the CIA's shameful behaviour as well as his own paranoia, greed and fantasies; unquestionably this was tragic and, at times, poignant.

But would I have actually liked him? I didn't know then, and I'm not sure now.

Goleniewski died long before I first put pen to paper. Although I first came across his story in the mid-1970s, and had brief conversations then with Jeremy Thorpe and Guy Richards, I never came close to speaking with – much less meeting – the man himself. As a result I have to rely on the impressions of those who did to form a less factual, more personal view of his character.

Almost without exception, the dozens of people who did meet, and initially support, him – other spies, Congressmen, Senators, journalists and those on the wilder fringes of right-wing anti-communist agitation – fell foul of his arrogance, impatience, temper and bogus Romanoff pretensions. Very few lasted the course, and even those who backed him throughout his years of insanity frequently despaired at his greed, imperious demands and eye-wateringly prolix denunciations of their imperfections or perceived perfidy. If that was the fundamental nature of the man, then – no: I don't think I would have found him agreeable company.

But was it? If this book (and an earlier one I wrote examining the British men and women who betrayed their country to Nazi Germany during World War II) has taught me anything it is that spying is a grubby, sordid business. As fiction readers and cinemagoers we have, I suspect, been misled into expecting espionage stories to bear at least some resemblance to the tropes of a Bond movie: fast cars, beautiful women, heroic derring-do and monochromatically wicked villains.

Michał Goleniewski was a spy – and a very important one – but his activities did not float on a sea of dry Martinis, nor did his sexual adventures involve svelte sirens, draped across the decks of super-yachts or languidly watching the roulette wheel in glamorous locations. His lovers were steeped in the drabness of Communist states, and his own gambling required stakes rather more viscerally dangerous than a plastic casino chip. Just as the blacksmith's hammer shapes his hand, so was Goleniewski's undoubtedly difficult character consolidated in the crucible of Cold War Warsaw, Berlin and Washington.

There is, today, one person alive who could flesh out Goleniewski the man, rather than Sniper the spy or Aleksei Romanoff, pretender to the lost Imperial Russian throne. His daughter, Tatiana, still lives in New York, although she has discarded the Romanoff name in which her birth was registered.

After some searching, I tracked down her addresses – both physical and electronic – and her phone number. I asked her – repeatedly – to speak with me, to share her experience of Goleniewski as a family man, a father. Over several months, letters and e-mails met no response and when, finally, she answered her cell phone it was only to refuse, emphatically, any further contact.

I respect her right to privacy and her decision, but I wish it were otherwise. Because, years after this project began, I still cannot adequately answer my editor's question. I still do not really know if I would have liked, not merely respected, Michał Goleniewski.

Notes

1. 'Sniper'

1 Affidavit of Aleksei Nicholaevich Romanoff [Michał Goleniewski], 21 October 1969. Register Office, Queens, New York.
2 Tennent H. ('Pete') Bagley [CIA agent handler], 'Ghosts of the Spy Wars', *International Journal of Intelligence & Counter-Intelligence*, vol. 28, no. 1, 2015.
3 Ibid.
4 'Your Land and Mine', NBC Radio, 1945–56.
5 Tennent H. ('Pete') Bagley, email to Col. Dick Blair, 8 March 1996. Tennent H. Bagley Collection, Howard Gottlieb Archival Research Center, Boston University.
6 Bagley, 'Ghosts of the Spy Wars', op. cit.
7 William C. Sullivan, *The Bureau: My Thirty Years in Hoover's FBI*, Norton & Co., 1979, pp. 39–40.
8 Guy Richards, *Imperial Agent*, Devin-Adair, 1966, pp. 134–5.
9 Bagley, 'Ghosts of the Spy Wars', op. cit., pp. 47–8.
10 Ibid.
11 Ted Shackley, *Spymaster: My Life in the CIA*, Potomac Books, 2005, p. 26.
12 Howard E. Roman, CIA officer. Quoted in David C. Martin, *Wilderness of Mirrors*, HarperCollins, 1980, pp. 96–7.
13 Ibid.
14 In Memoriam: Richards J. Heuer. 'Studies in Intelligence' [CIA internal publication], CIA Library, 2018.
15 Heuer spent forty-five years inside the CIA, working in intelligence, counterintelligence and security. He became the Agency's most eminent authority on intelligence analysis.
16 Richards J. Heuer, *Psychology of Intelligence Analysis*, Globalytica/Pherson Publications [private publication], 2018.
17 Bagley, 'Ghosts of the Spy Wars', op. cit.
18 Heuer, *Psychology of Intelligence Analysis*, op. cit.

2. The Intelligence Gap

1 *Sketches from the History of Russian Foreign Intelligence* (Ocherki Istorii Rossii Vneshney Razvedki), Mezhdunarodnye Otnosheniya, Moscow, 1996.

2 As late as 1967, senior CIA counterintelligence staff authored a 125-page internal study, *The Soviet Penchant for Provocation*, which concluded that The Trust had been the model for all subsequent KGB penetration efforts against American intelligence. 'James Angleton and the Monster Plot', *Studies in Intelligence*. CIA Library. Declassified in 2013.

3 George Kennan, 'The Long Telegram', 22 February 1946. National Security Archive, George Washington University, Washington DC.

4 Ibid.

5 'Bedell Smith is Sure the Reds Infiltrated Top Intelligence Unit', *New York Herald Tribune*, 30 September 1952.

6 Equivalent to approximately $5 billion today.

7 *Intelligence on the Soviet Bloc*, CIA internal report, 31 March 1953. Declassified in September 1999.

8 Tim Weiner, *Legacy of Ashes: The History of the CIA*, Allen Lane, 2005, p. 77.

9 Shackley, *Spymaster*, op. cit., p. 20.

10 Lt. Gen. James Doolittle, *Report on the Covert Activities of the Central Intelligence Agency*, 30 September 1954. Released to the US Senate in 1976. US National Archives.

11 Ibid.

12 *A Review of Congressional Oversight*, CIA Center for the Study of Intelligence, 14 April 2007. CIA Library.

13 Congressional Record, 23 April 1956.

14 Congressional Record, 15 May 1958.

15 S. 8, *Central Intelligence Agency Act* (Public Law 110), 20 June 1949.

16 Józef Światło (Polish intelligence, 1953), Yuri Rastvorov (MVD, 1954) and Petr Deriabin (KGB, 1954). Other Western countries had successfully attracted rather more defections and offers of intelligence.

17 Report on the Covert Activities of the Central Intelligence Agency, 30 September 1954. Released to the US Senate in 1976.

18 Pyotr Semyonovich Popov first approached US intelligence in 1952. From then until 1957 he provided a wealth of information about Soviet military capabilities and the GRU's activities. Popov came under KGB suspicion in late 1957, was arrested in October 1959 and executed the following year. The CIA never formally established how he was caught, but Tennent Bagley came to believe he had been betrayed by a Washington DC-based CIA officer.

19 The charts were released in the 1980s in response to FOIA requests and can now be viewed at https://archive.org/details/CIA-Organization-Charts

20 'The Monster Plot', 1976. This 172-page report was the result of a six-month inquiry, commissioned by the then CIA Director and directed by John Hart, a former CIA station chief in Vietnam. US National Archives: www.archives. gov/files/research/jfk/releases/104-10534-10205.pdf

21 Ibid.

22 'James Angleton and the Monster Plot', *CIA Studies in Intelligence*, vol. 55, no. 4, December 2011. CIA Library. Declassified in May 2013.

23 Ibid.

24 Martin, *Wilderness of Mirrors*, op. cit., p. 16.

25 'James Angleton and the Monster Plot', op. cit.

3. 'Dear Mr Director'

1 Tennent Bagley, e-mail to Col. Dick Blair, 8 March 1996. Tennent H. Bagley Collection, Howard Gottlieb Archival Research Center, Boston University.

2 Translation included in a letter from Michał Goleniewski to the *Government Employees' Exchange* newspaper [undated, but probably 1968], US Legislative Archives, Washington DC.

3 Ibid.

4 Ibid.

5 Heuer, *Psychology of Intelligence Analysis*, op. cit.

6 Bagley, 'Ghosts of the Spy Wars', op. cit., pp. 48–9.

7 Document contained in the Tennent H. Bagley Collection, Howard Gottlieb Archival Research Center, Boston University.

8 Richards J. Heuer, 'Nosenko – Five Paths to Judgment', *CIA Studies in Intelligence*, vol. 31, no. 3, pp. 71–101. Originally classified 'Secret', Heuer's analysis was released in 1995. CIA Library.

9 Tennent Bagley, e-mail to Col. Dick Blair, 8 March 1996, op. cit.

10 'Goleniewski's Work with the Soviets'. [Undated] CIA internal report, released to the author in December 2019 following FOIA requests.

11 Ibid.

12 Ibid.

13 Ibid.

14 Howard E. Roman, quoted in Martin, *Wilderness of Mirrors*, op. cit., p. 95.

15 John R. Norpel testimony to the Senate Internal Security Subcommittee hearings on State Department Security, 24 July 1964. US Legislative Archives, Washington DC.

16 Ibid.

17 Bagley, 'Ghosts of the Spy Wars', op. cit.

18 Howard E. Roman, quoted in Martin, *Wilderness of Mirrors*, op. cit., pp. 96–7.

4. London

1 Minimax Ltd was a genuine and well-established company. It produced fire extinguishers for more than fifty years before being taken over by a rival in 1955. The firm had, however, never occupied offices in the Broadway building.

2 Keith Jeffery, *MI6: The History of the Secret Intelligence Service, 1909–1949*, Bloomsbury, 2010, p. 478.

3 Peter Wright, *Spycatcher*, Heinemann Australia, 1987, p. 128.

4 Christopher Andrew, *Defence of the Realm: The Authorized History of MI5*, Allen Lane, 2009, p. 427.

5 *Hansard*, 25 October 1955.

6 Wright, *Spycatcher*, op. cit., p. 98.

7 Ibid., pp. 128–9.

8 Ibid.

9 'Extract from letter from LAVINIA': file note and Appendices, 28 April 1960. MI5 files on Harry Frederick Houghton, KV 2/4380, National Archives. Declassified in November 2017.

10 Ibid.

11 Letter from MI6 to the CIA [sent via the US Embassy, London], 12 May 1960. MI5 files on Harry Frederick Houghton, KV 2/4380, op. cit.

12 D. H. Whyte, MI5: Letter to Security Liaison Officer, Malaya, 17 June 1960. MI5 files on Harry Frederick Houghton, KV 2/4380, op. cit.

13 Ibid.

14 'History of Houghton's Espionage', 1 May 1961. MI5 files on Harry Frederick Houghton, KV 2/4478, op. cit.

15 Ibid.

16 'Secrets Trial: Some Questions'. Admiralty file note, 7 March 1961. MI5 files on Harry Frederick Houghton, KV 2/4476, op. cit.

17 MI5 interview with Captain Austen, 31 May 1960. MI5 files on Harry Frederick Houghton, KV 2/4380, op. cit.

18 'Note on Houghton's Finances'. MI5 files on Harry Frederick Houghton, KV 2/4477, op. cit.

19 'Summary of Security Information about Harry Houghton available before receipt of the LAVINIA report'. Arthur Martin, MI5 officer, 6 March 1961. MI5 files on Harry Frederick Houghton, KV 2/4476, op. cit.

20 File note by Captain Pollock, Underwater Detection Establishment, Portland, to Department of Naval Intelligence, June 1956. MI5 files on Harry Frederick Houghton, KV 2/4476, op. cit.

21 'History of Houghton's Espionage', 1 May 1961. MI5 files on Harry Frederick Houghton, KV 2/4478, op. cit.

22 'Summary of Security Information about Harry Houghton available before receipt of the LAVINIA report'. Arthur Martin, MI5 officer, 6 March 1961. MI5 files on Harry Frederick Houghton, KV 2/4476, op. cit.

23 Ibid.

24 Letter from MI6 to CIA, 12 May 1960. MI5 files on Harry Frederick Houghton, KV 2/4380, op. cit.

25 Internal MI5 letter from D. H. Whyte, 28 July 1960. MI5 files on Harry Frederick Houghton, KV 2/4381, op. cit.

5. Stockholm

1 Congressional Record (Senate), 'Reported Cases of Soviet Espionage', 18 May 1960.

2 Wennerström was interrogated by Sweden's security service over several weeks between June 1963 and February 1964. His testimony and confessions provide an exhaustive account of his career as a spy for the USSR and several rival countries. They were provided to the US Senate Internal Security Subcommittee (SISS), which produced a 168-page report in 1964. 'The Wennestroem [sic] Spy Case: How it Touched the United States and NATO', US Legislative Archives, Washington DC.

3 Interrogation of Col. Stig Wennestroem [sic], 14 January 1964. 'The Wennestroem [sic] Spy Case: How it Touched the United States and NATO', op. cit.

4 Ibid.

5 Ibid.

6 The equivalent of £8,000 today.

7 Interrogation of Col. Stig Wennestroem [sic], 16 January 1964. 'The Wennestroem [sic] Spy Case: How it Touched the United States and NATO', op. cit.

8 Ibid., 17 January 1964.

9 Ibid., 22 January 1964.

10 Ibid.

11 Ibid., 24 January 1964.

12 Ibid.

13 Ibid.

14 Ibid.

15 Ibid., 22 June 1963.

16 Ibid., 5 February 1964.

17 Ibid., 22 June and 5 July 1963.

6. Tel Aviv

1 *Declaration of the Establishment of the State of Israel*, 14 May 1948. Ministry of Foreign Affairs, Tel Aviv.

2 US State Department Telegram, 14 May 1948. US National Archives.

3 United Nations Resolution 181, introduced by the USSR and passed on 29 November 1947, called for the partition of Palestine into separate Arab and Jewish states.

4 Bagley, 'Ghosts of the Spy Wars', op. cit.

5 'Yisrael Bar', Shin Bet biography. https://www.shabak.gov.il/english/heritage/affairs/Pages/YisraelBar.aspx

6 Beer's own book, posthumously published in Israel (*Israel's Security: Yesterday, Today, and Tomorrow*, Amikam, 1966), concentrated on a critique of the country's military strategy, arguing for a closer alliance with the Soviet Union, but gave no insight into his own history.

7 Named after the jailed German communist leader Ernst Thäimann, the 1,500-strong Battalion was primarily formed of German, Austrian, Swiss and Scandinavian volunteers.

8 'Yisrael Bar', Shin Bet biography, op. cit.

9 Joseph J. Trento, *The Secret History of the CIA*, MJF Books, 2001, pp. 80–81.

10 Dan Raviv and Yossi Melman, *Every Spy a Prince: The Complete History of Israel's Intelligence Community*, Houghton Mifflin, 1990, p. 100.

11 *Richard Helms as Director of Central Intelligence*, pp. 131–8. History Staff, Center for the Study of Intelligence, 1993. CIA Library. Declassified in December 2008.

12 'Yisrael Bar', Shin Bet biography, op. cit.

13 'Israel Beer', *Jewish Virtual Library*. American-Israeli Cooperative Enterprise (AICE), Chevy Chase, Maryland.

14 'Yisrael Bar', Shin Bet biography, op. cit.

15 In 1960, Harel masterminded the operation to locate, capture and kidnap Adolf Eichmann, one of the masterminds of the Holocaust who had escaped to Argentina. Harel's agents secretly brought him back to Israel for a public trial.

16 'Yisrael Bar', Shin Bet biography, op. cit.

17 'Israel Beer', *Jewish Virtual Library*, op. cit.

18 Letter from Tennent H. Bagley to Pierre de Villemarest, Centre Européen d'Information, Paris, 18 March 1999. Tennent H. Bagley Collection, Boston University.

7. Munich

1 'America's Seeing-Eye Dog on a Long Leash', draft internal CIA working paper; 'CIA and Nazi War Criminals', Chapter 9, undated, but declassified in 2007. CIA Library.

2 Although they shared the same code name, this Operation RUSTY had no connection to a US Air Force reconnaissance programme over Africa in 1942.

3 'America's Seeing-Eye Dog on a Long Leash', draft internal CIA working paper; 'CIA and Nazi War Criminals', Chapter 9, op. cit.

4 The CIA did not volunteer to declassify this report. It was made public only after Congress passed and enforced legislation – the Nazi War Crimes Disclosure Act – forcing the Agency to hand over thousands of previously secret documents.

5 Kevin C. Ruffner, ed., *Forging an Intelligence Partnership: CIA and the Origins of the BND 1949–1956*, vol. 1, CIA Historical Staff, 2006. CIA Library. Declassified in 2007.

6 Ibid.

7 Ibid.

8 'RUSTY', Chief of Station, Karlsruhe, to Chief, FBM, 19 August 1948. Quoted in 'America's Seeing-Eye Dog on a Long Leash', draft internal CIA working paper; 'CIA and Nazi War Criminals', Chapter 9, op. cit.

9 'RUSTY', Chief Munich Operations Base to Acting Chief of Station, Karlsruhe, 7 July 1948. Quoted in 'America's Seeing-Eye Dog on a Long Leash', draft internal CIA working paper; 'CIA and Nazi War Criminals', Chapter 9, op. cit.

10 *Vertrauensmann* ('trusted man'), or *V-Mann*, was the term Gehlen used for his agents.

11 Ruffner, ed., *Forging an Intelligence Partnership: CIA and the Origins of the BND 1949–1956*, vol. 1, op. cit.

12 'Former Nazi and SS Membership in ZIPPER circa 1954', unsigned and undated CIA memo. Quoted in 'America's Seeing-Eye Dog on a Long Leash', draft internal CIA working paper; 'CIA and Nazi War Criminals', Chapter 9, op. cit.

13 'KGB Exploitation of Heinz Felfe', CIA report, March 1969. CIA Library. Declassified in 2005.

14 Until 1953 the Soviet Union's two civilian intelligence agencies were the MVD and the MGB. The KGB was created in 1954.

15 'KGB Exploitation of Heinz Felfe', op. cit.

16 Sometimes spelled Petyr or Piotr Deriabin.

17 Testimony of Petr S. Deriabin, House Un-American Activities Committee (HUAC). Undated, but printed for internal committee use on 17 March 1959. US Congressional Archives.

18 'KGB Exploitation of Heinz Felfe', CIA report, March 1969, op. cit.

19 Letter from Tennent H. Bagley to Pierre de Villemarest, Centre Européen d'Information, Paris, 18 March 1999, op. cit.

20 'KGB Exploitation of Heinz Felfe', CIA report, March 1969, op. cit.

21 Ibid.

22 Ruffner, ed., *Forging an Intelligence Partnership: CIA and the Origins of the BND 1949–1956*, vol. 1, op. cit.

23 Ibid.

24 Ibid.

25 Heinz Felfe: Damage Assessment Report; CIA internal document, 1 April 1963.

26 Ibid.

8. Washington

1 Letter from Michał Goleniewski to the *Government Employees' Exchange* newspaper [undated, but probably 1968], op. cit.

2 Bagley, 'Ghosts of the Spy Wars', op. cit.

3 Howard Roman, quoted in Martin, *Wilderness of Mirrors*, pp. 97–8, op. cit.

4 Bagley, 'Ghosts of the Spy Wars', op. cit.

5 Ibid.

6 'Goleniewski's Work with the Soviets', op. cit.

7 Information Report: Organization and Personnel of the Ministry of Public Security, Poland, 2 February 1954. CIA Library. Declassified in January 2009.

8 Polish Order of Battle, 1 May 1958. CIA Library. Declassified in August 2010.

9 'Goleniewski's Work with the Soviets', op. cit.

10 SNIPER Report No: 1/60, 15 January 1960, recovered by the CIA from the Berlin Zoo station dead drop, 5 February 1960. CIA files on Heinrich Mueller, vol. 1, 0025. CIA Library. Declassified in 2008.

11 Ibid.

12 Approximately $7.3 billion today.

13 The name ODESSA appears first to have been used in a US Army Counter-Intelligence Corps memo on 3 July 1946 which stated that SS prisoners held in an internment camp at Bensheim-Auerbach used it as the code for attempts to gain food privileges from the Red Cross; other rumours, amplified by Nazi hunter Simon Wiesenthal, suggested it was the cryptonym for a 'ratline' to smuggle war criminals to safety. However, no definitive proof of its existence has ever been found. See Guy Walters, *Hunting Evil*, Bantam Press, 2009, pp. 200–205.

14 Sniper Report No: 1/60, 15 January 1960, op. cit.

15 Angleton played a central role in 'Operation Sunrise': negotiations with senior SS officers in 1944 to arrange a German surrender in return for American protection. See 'Eagle and Swastika', Draft Working Paper, Kevin Conley Ruffner, CIA History Staff, April 2003. CIA Library. Declassified in 2007.

16 The Nazi War Crimes Disclosure Act was passed in 2000. It took five years for US intelligence agencies to send their files to the National Archives, and the official committee tasked with organizing the material complained that these were significantly incomplete. 'Nazi War Crimes & Japanese Imperial Government Records': Interagency Working Group, Final Report to the US Congress, April 2007. US National Archives.

17 Bagley, 'Ghosts of the Spy Wars', op. cit.

18 Sniper Report No: 4–6, July 1959. Translation included in a letter from Michał Goleniewski to the *Government Employees' Exchange* newspaper [undated, but probably 1968], op. cit.

19 Richards, *Imperial Agent*, op. cit., p. 20.

20 Otto Otepka: Testimony to the Senate Internal Security Subcommittee hearings on State Department Security, 24 August 1964. US Legislative Archives, Washington DC.

21 Ibid., 17 August 1964.

22 Bagley, 'Ghosts of the Spy Wars', op. cit.

23 Letter from Michał Goleniewski to the *Government Employees' Exchange* newspaper [undated, but probably 1968], op. cit.

9. Warsaw

1 'The Gal Who Gave Her All Says Doc Gave the Reds Just Trifles', *New York Daily News*, 6 October 1961.

2 *Irvin C. Scarbeck v. United States of America*, US Court of Appeals, District of Columbia. Ruling issued on 12 March 1963.

3 Ibid.

4 Ibid.

5 Ibid.

6 'Polish Girl Tells Court Scarbeck Urged Secrecy', UPI, 10 August 1961.

10. Berlin

1 Indictment of Col. Michał Goleniewski, 7 April 1961. Warsaw District Military Court. Institute of National Remembrance archives, Warsaw.

2 Col. Michał Goleniewski: nine-page report on his relationship with Irmgard Kampf. Submitted to the Polish Ministry of Interior/UB, 11 November 1960. Warsaw District Military Court; Institute of National Remembrance archives, Warsaw.

3 David E. Murphy, Sergei A. Kondrashev and George Bailey, *Battleground Berlin*, Yale University Press, 1997, pp. 343–4.

4 Ibid.

5 The CIA has redacted almost all references to the officer's identity from its log of events for 4 January 1960. However, a clerical error ensured that Trickett's surname slipped through the Agency's censoring pencil.

6 Howard Roman, quoted in Martin, *Wilderness of Mirrors*, op. cit., pp. 97–8.

7 Indictment of Col. Michał Goleniewski, 7 April 1961. Warsaw District Military Court. Institute of National Remembrance archives, Warsaw.

8 *Activities of 4 and 5 January and BOB*, CIA Dispatch, 15 February 1961. Released to the author by the CIA following FOIA requests, September 2019.

9 Ibid.

10 Intelligence report [undated] in Tennent H. Bagley Collection, Howard Gottlieb Archival Research Center, Boston University.

11 *Activities of 4 and 5 January and BOB*, CIA Dispatch, 15 February 1961. Released to the author by the CIA following FOIA requests, September 2019.

12 Ibid.

13 Nieśwież, a small city 460 kilometres north-east of Warsaw, was then in Poland. From 1939 it was subsumed into the new Byelorussian Soviet Socialist Republic, was occupied by Germany during World War II, and then returned to Byelorussia. After the fall of communism in 1989, the country became Belarus, and the city's name was changed to Nesvizh.

14 A copy of this ID card was filed as Exhibit D attached to Irmgard Kampf's affidavit sworn on 11 July 1967. New York City Register Office, Queens. An identical copy is contained in Goleniewski's UB files in the archives of the Institute of National Remembrance, Warsaw.

15 Cable from BOB to CIA HQ, 4 January 1961. Released to the author by the CIA following FOIA requests, September 2019.

16 Wright, *Spycatcher*, op. cit., p. 135.

17 Cable from BOB to CIA HQ, 4 January 1961. Released to the author by the CIA following FOIA requests, September 2019.

11. Flight

1 Ibid.

2 Shackley, *Spymaster*, op. cit., p. 80.

3 Ibid., pp. 80–81.

4 Col. Witold Sienkiewicz, Director, Department I, Ministry of Interior (Intelligence), Warsaw: *Report to Prosecutor re: Michał Goleniewski* [undated], Warsaw District Military Court.

5 Testimony of Col. Henryk Sokolac, UB. Trial of Col. Michał Goleniewski, 18 April 1961, Warsaw District Military Court.

6 Richards, *Imperial Agent*, op. cit., p. 170.

7 Ibid., p. 171.

8 Michał Goleniewski: 'Selected Examples of Dissemination of Soviet Disinformation through Western Publications', 1 April 1985. FBI file on Michał Goleniewski, released in response to an FOIA request by Ernie Lazar, June 2008.

9 'Agents and cases run by Department VI Dept. 1, as of November 30, 1960'. TELETECHNIK files BU_0_1911_97_1. Institute of National Remembrance archives, Warsaw.

10 Indictment of Col. Michał Goleniewski, 7 April 1961. Warsaw District Military Court. Institute of National Remembrance archives, Warsaw.

11 Howard Roman, quoted in Martin, *Wilderness of Mirrors*, op. cit., p. 98.

12 Michał Goleniewski, 'Open Letter to the *Government Employees' Exchange newspaper*, February 1968'. US Legislative Archives.

13 Trento, *The Secret History of the CIA*, op. cit., p. 161.

12. Reverberations

1 MI5 A4 Branch Surveillance Report, 6–8 January 1961. MI5 files on Harry Frederick Houghton, KV 2/4384, op. cit.

2 MI5 files on Harry Frederick Houghton, KV 2/4382, op. cit.

3 Equivalent to more than £3,000 today.

4 Letter from D. H. Whyte, MI5, to Col. R. A. Pigot, Intelligence Division, Admiralty, 22 July 1960. MI5 files on Harry Frederick Houghton, KV 2/4381, op. cit.

5 Letter from D. H. Whyte, MI5, to Col. R. A. Pigot, Intelligence Division, Admiralty, 2 August 1960. MI5 files on Harry Frederick Houghton, KV 2/4381, op. cit.

6 Statement of Ethel Elizabeth Gee, 10 January 1961. MI5 files on Harry Frederick Houghton, KV 2/4385, op. cit.

7 Letter from D. H. Whyte, MI5, to Col. R. A. Pigot, Intelligence Division, Admiralty, 3 August 1960. MI5 files on Harry Frederick Houghton, KV 2/4381, op. cit.

8 Wright, *Spycatcher*, op. cit., p. 130.

9 Gordon Arnold Lonsdale: Biography. MI5 report, 18 October 1960. MI5 files on Harry Frederick Houghton, KV 2/4383, op. cit.

10 Note on Interviews with Lonsdale, the Krogers, Houghton and Miss Gee, 7 July 1961. MI5 files on Harry Frederick Houghton, KV 2/4478, op. cit.

11 Gordon Arnold Lonsdale: Biography. MI5 report, 18 October 1960. MI5 files on Harry Frederick Houghton, KV 2/4383, op. cit.

12 For no apparent reason, different branches within the Security Service simultaneously gave their targets different code names.

13 Wright, *Spycatcher*, op. cit., pp. 130–31.

14 Ibid.

15 Ibid., p. 54.

16 Gordon Arnold Lonsdale: Biography. MI5 report, 18 October 1960. MI5 files on Harry Frederick Houghton, KV 2/4383, op. cit.

17 G. R. Mitchell, Memo to DG [Hollis], 17 October 1960. MI5 files on Harry Frederick Houghton, KV 2/4383, op. cit.

18 Note on 'serial' sheet, 7 November 1960. MI5 files on Peter and Helen Kroger, KV 2/4487. UK National Archives. Declassified in September 2019.

19 As with Lonsdale, A4 branch reports referred to them as 'The Pangolins'.

20 Letter from Charles Elwell, MI5, to Deputy Commander, Special Branch, 16 November 1960. MI5 files on Harry Frederick Houghton, KV 2/4383, op. cit.

21 A4 Brief for the Surveillance of 'KILL JOY' and contacts, 16 November 1960. MI5 files on Peter and Helen Kroger, KV 2/4487, op. cit.

22 Telegram from Charles Elwell to SLO New Zealand, 10 January 1961. MI5 files on Peter and Helen Kroger, KV 2/4487, op. cit.

23 File note by E. M. Furnival Jones, 5 January 1961. MI5 files on Harry Frederick Houghton, KV 2/4384, op. cit.

24 Report on the searches of Gee's and Houghton's houses, 10 January 1961. MI5 files on Harry Frederick Houghton, KV 2/4384, op. cit.

25 Search for transmitter at Ruislip; A2 Branch, 13 January 1961. MI5 files on Peter and Helen Kroger, KV 2/4488, op. cit.

26 MI5 files on Peter and Helen Kroger, KV 2/4484, op. cit.

27 In April 1964, Molody and the Cohens were returned to the Soviet Union in exchange for British businessman Greville Wynne, who had been spying for MI6. Houghton and Gee served nine years in prison; they married in 1971, one year after their release.

28 Statement of Lord Chief Justice, Lord Parker, *R. v. Houghton, Gee, Krogers and Lonsdale*, 23 March 1961. MI5 files on Peter and Helen Kroger, KV 2/4477, op. cit.

29 Wright, *Spycatcher*, op. cit., p. 129.

30 The official history of MI5 (Christopher Andrew, *Defence of the Realm*, Allen Lane, 2009) claims that the Security Service did not establish

Lonsdale's true identity until 1963. In fact, MI5's files show that Washington confirmed Lonsdale was Molody in July 1961.

31 https://www.mi5.gov.uk/portland-spy-ring
32 Report from E. M. [Martin] Furnival Jones to DG, MI5, 6 March 1961. MI5 files on Harry Frederick Houghton, KV 2/4476, op. cit.
33 Wright, *Spycatcher*, op. cit., pp. 142–3.

13. Oldenburg

1 Irmgard M. Romanoff [Kampf], Affidavit, 11 July 1967. New York City Register Office, Queens.
2 Irmgard M. Romanoff [Kampf], Exhibit G, Affidavit, 11 July 1967, op. cit.
3 Irmgard M. Romanoff [Kampf], Affidavit, 11 July 1967, op. cit.
4 Martin, *Wilderness of Mirrors*, op. cit., p. 99.
5 Affidavit of Aleksei Nicholaevich Romanoff [Michał Goleniewski], 21 October 1969, op. cit.
6 Stanley B. Farndon, 'The Interrogation of Defectors', *CIA Studies in Intelligence*, vol. 4, no. 3, Summer 1960. CIA Library. Declassified in March 2005.
7 John F. Sullivan, *Gatekeeper: Memoirs of a CIA Polygraph Examiner*, Potomac Books, 2007, pp. 1–3.
8 Chester C. Crawford [head of the CIA's polygraph testing programme], 'The Polygraph in Agent Interrogation', *CIA Studies in Intelligence*, Summer 1960. CIA Library. Declassified in March 2005; Sullivan, *Gatekeeper*, op. cit., pp. 1–3.
9 Farndon, 'The Interrogation of Defectors', op. cit.
10 Ibid.
11 Howard Roman, Letter to David C. Martin, 14 July 1980. Edward J. Epstein Papers, Boston University. Roman's letter was written to correct Martin's assertion that 'Goleniewski . . . used to play Victrola records of old European songs at top volume and drink booze.' Martin, *Wilderness of Mirrors*, op. cit., p. 108.
12 Ibid.
13 'Goleniewski's Work with the Soviets', op. cit.
14 Heuer, 'Nosenko – Five Paths to Judgment', op. cit.
15 'Goleniewski's Work with the Soviets', op. cit.
16 Martin, *Wilderness of Mirrors*, op. cit., p. 99.
17 'Goleniewski's Work with the Soviets', op. cit.
18 Ibid.
19 Irmgard M. Romanoff [Kampf]: Affidavit, 11 July 1967, op. cit.
20 Equivalent to approximately $6,500 today.

21 Equivalent to approximately $43,000 today.

22 Equivalent to approximately $215,000 today.

23 Affidavit of Aleksei Nicholaevich Romanoff [Michał Goleniewski], 21 October 1969, op. cit.

24 Testimony of Col. Witold Sienkiewicz, UB. Trial of Col. Michał Goleniewski, 18 April 1961. Warsaw District Military Court.

25 Internal UB reports, 13 March and 5 April 1961. TELETECHNIK files BU_0_1911_97_1. Institute of National Remembrance, Warsaw.

26 Irmgard M. Romanoff [Kampf]: Affidavit, 11 July 1967, op. cit.

14. 'Betrayal of the Homeland'

1 See above, Chapter 10, note 13.

2 Memorandum of Information from Immigration & Naturalization Service files re: HR 5507, 15 May 1963. US Congressional Archives, Washington DC.

3 Report on the Desertion of Michał Goleniewski, 24 January 1961. TELETECHNIK files BU_0_1911_97_1. Institute of National Remembrance, Warsaw.

4 Ibid.

5 Goleniewski was given this award in 1959.

6 Personnel Records of the Ministry of the Interior. Warsaw District Military Court. TELETECHNIK files BU_0_1911_97_1. Institute of National Remembrance, Warsaw.

7 Report by Major Józef Mędrzycki, Dept. III, MSW [Ministry of the Interior, successor to the MBP], 23 January 1967. TELETECHNIK files BU_0_1911_97_2. Institute of National Remembrance, Warsaw.

8 Personnel Records of the Ministry of the Interior. Warsaw District Military Court. UB files, TELETECHNIK files BU_0_1911_97_2. Institute of National Remembrance, Warsaw.

9 Jaromir Kwiatkowski, '*Wywiad PRL nękał wybitnego naukowca z Godowej koło Strzyżowa*' ['Polish Intelligence Harassed an Eminent Scientist from Godowa'], 22 February 2009, *Nowiny 24* [Polish regional daily newspaper].

10 *Indictment against Michał Goleniewski*, 7 April 1961. Warsaw District Military Court, TELETECHNIK files BU_0_1911_97_1. Institute of National Remembrance archives, Warsaw.

11 Ibid.

12 Col. Witold Sienkiewicz, *Service Opinion – Col. Michał Goleniewski*, 25 August 1960. Warsaw District Military Court. TELETECHNIK files BU_0_1911_97_1. Institute of National Remembrance, Warsaw.

13 Ibid.

14 Personal Statement of Michał Goleniewski to Col. Witold Sienkiewicz, Dept. 1, Ministry of the Interior, 11 November 1960. Warsaw District Military Court. TELETECHNIK files BU_0_1911_97_1. Institute of National Remembrance, Warsaw.

15 Ibid.

16 Stasi records show this first meeting as having taken place in 1957.

17 Report by Erich Mielke, Minister for State Security, German Democratic Republic, 19 January 1961. Warsaw District Military Court. TELETECHNIK files BU_0_1911_97_1. Institute of National Remembrance, Warsaw.

18 Personal Statement of Michał Goleniewski. TELETECHNIK files BU_0_1911_97_1. Institute of National Remembrance, Warsaw.

19 Ibid.

20 Report by Erich Mielke, Minister for State Security, German Democratic. Republic, TELETECHNIK files BU_0_1911_97_1, op. cit.

21 Personal Statement of Michał Goleniewski. TELETECHNIK files BU_0_1911_97_1, op. cit.

22 Ibid.

23 Intercepted correspondence [undated] between Irmgard Kampf and Michał Goleniewski. TELETECHNIK files BU_0_1911_97_1. Institute of National Remembrance, Warsaw.

24 Ibid.

25 Personal Statement of Michał Goleniewski. TELETECHNIK files BU_0_1911_97_1, op. cit.

26 Report by Erich Mielke, Minister for State Security, German Democratic Republic, TELETECHNIK files BU_0_1911_97_1, op. cit.

27 Personal Statement of Michał Goleniewski. TELETECHNIK files BU_0_1911_97_1, op. cit.

28 Testimony of Col. Henryk Sokolac, Deputy Chief, Department 1, MSW, 18 April 1961. Warsaw District Military Court. TELETECHNIK files BU_0_1911_97_1. Institute of National Remembrance, Warsaw.

29 Testimony of Col. Witold Sienkiewicz, Chief, Department 1, MSW, 18 April 1961. Warsaw District Military Court; TELETECHNIK files BU_0_1911_97_1. Institute of National Remembrance, Warsaw.

30 Testimony of Col. Henryk Sokolac, Deputy Chief, Department 1, MSW, Institute of National Remembrance, Warsaw.

31 Report by Erich Mielke, Minister for State Security, German Democratic Republic. TELETECHNIK files BU_0_1911_97_1. Institute of National Remembrance, Warsaw.

32 Testimony of Col. Henryk Sokolac, Deputy Chief, Department 1, MSW, op. cit.

33 *Polish People's Republic v. Michał Goleniewski*: Verdict of Warsaw District
   Military Court, 18 April 1961. TELETECHNIK files BU_0_1911_97_1.
   Institute of National Remembrance, Warsaw.

34 Col. Witold Sienkiewicz, Chief, Department 1, MSW., *Report to Public
   Prosecutor* [undated, but apparently late January or early February 1961].
   Warsaw District Military Court. TELETECHNIK files BU_0_1911_97_1.
   Institute of National Remembrance, Warsaw.

35 UB cable to foreign stations, 13 January 1961. TELETECHNIK files
   BU_0_1911_97_1. Institute of National Remembrance, Warsaw.

36 Evidence of Col. Witold Sienkiewicz, *Polish People's Republic v. Michał
   Goleniewski*, 18 April 1961. Warsaw District Military Court. TELETECHNIK
   files BU_0_1911_97_1. Institute of National Remembrance, Warsaw.

37 *Polish People's Republic v. Michał Goleniewski*: Verdict of Warsaw District
   Military Court, 18 April 1961. TELETECHNIK files BU_0_1911_97_1, op. cit.

38 Ibid.

39 *Polish People's Republic v. Michał Goleniewski*: Affirmation of verdict and
   sentence, 21 May 1961. Warsaw District Military Court. TELETECHNIK
   files BU_0_1911_97_1. Institute of National Remembrance, Warsaw.

40 Testimony of Petr S. Deriabin, *The Kremlin's Espionage and Terror
   Organizations*. House Un-American Activities Committee, pp. 8–12, 17 May
   1959. US Congressional Archives, Washington DC.

41 CIA Memorandum for the Record, *Assassination of Stepan Bandera*, p. 14, 22
   April 1976. CIA Library. Declassified in 2006.

42 Operation TELETECHNIK files, Institute of National Remembrance,
   Warsaw.

15. LAMBDA 1

1 Jeffery, *MI6: The History of the Secret Intelligence Service 1909–1949*, op. cit.
   There is no successor volume detailing MI6's activities during the Cold War
   and its aftermath.

2 PBS 'Red Files'. Full transcript of an interview with George Blake, 1999.
   http://www.pbs.org/redfiles/kgb/deep/interv/k_int_george_blake.htm

3 Ibid.

4 Ibid.

5 Ibid.

6 Andrew, *Defence of the Realm*, op. cit., pp. 488–9.

7 PBS 'Red Files'. Full transcript of an interview with George Blake, 1999,
   op. cit.

8 Gillian Allen, an MI6 secretary, was at that time Blake's girlfriend. They
   married in October 1954.

9 Pathé News, *Return to Freedom*, September 1953.

10 Andrew, *Defence of the Realm*, pp. 488–9, op. cit.

11 Murphy, Kondrashev and Bailey, *Battleground Berlin*, op. cit., p. 215.

12 'Security Service Archive', quoted in Andrew, *Defence of the Realm*, op. cit., pp. 488–9.

13 'George Blake', CIA Memorandum, 4 May 1961. CIA Library. Declassified in October 2015.

14 Murphy, Kondrashev and Bailey, *Battleground Berlin*, op. cit., pp. 108–10.

15 PBS 'Red Files'. Full transcript of an interview with George Blake, 1999, op. cit.

16 'The Berlin Tunnel Operation 1952–1956', Clandestine Services Historical paper no. 150, August 1967. CIA Library. Declassified in June 2007.

17 Murphy, Kondrashev and Bailey, *Battleground Berlin*, op. cit., p. 218.

18 This was not entirely successful: according to Tennent Bagley, 'the CIA produced about 1,750 intelligence reports based on almost 400,000 telephone conversations' intercepted via the tunnel. Tennent H. Bagley, *Spymaster: Startling Cold War Revelations of a Soviet KGB Chief*, Skyhorse Publishing, 2013.

19 In 1992, KGB archivist Vasili Mitrokhin defected to the United Kingdom, bringing with him handwritten notes he had made over a thirty-year career in Soviet intelligence. The edited notes are held at Churchill College, Cambridge; in 1999 he collaborated with MI5's official historian, Professor Christopher Andrew, on a book detailing their contents. Christopher Andrew and Vasili Mitrokhin, *The Mitrokhin Archive*, Allen Lane, 1999.

20 'George Blake', CIA Memorandum, 4 May 1961, op. cit.

21 PBS 'Red Files'. Full transcript of an interview with George Blake, 1999, op. cit.

22 Letter from Tennent Bagley to Pierre de Villemarest, Centre Européen d'Information, Paris, 5 April 2001, op. cit.

23 'George Blake', CIA Memorandum, 4 May 1961, op. cit.

24 Ibid.

25 Blake served only five years of his sentence. In October 1966 he escaped from Wormwood Scrubs prison and eventually made his way to Moscow. In 2007, Russian President Vladimir Putin awarded him the Order of Friendship medal. He died, aged ninety-eight, on 26 December 2020, in Moscow. He remained unrepentant to the last.

26 *Hansard*, 4 May 1961.

27 George Blake, *No Other Choice*, Jonathan Cape, 1990, pp. 207–8.

28 Andrew, *Defence of the Realm*, op. cit., pp. 490–91.

29 'George Blake', CIA Memorandum, 4 May 1961, op. cit.

16. Felfe

1 'KGB Exploitation of Heinz Felfe', CIA report, March 1969, op. cit.

2 As with most other documents on its involvement with former Third Reich personnel, the CIA did not willingly divulge its records on Heinz Felfe – much less in timely fashion. Only after the Nazi War Crimes Disclosure Act came into force in 2005 was Felfe's file of 1,900 pages, and thousands of other files like it, declassified for public scrutiny.

3 Nineteen-page SS record for Heinz Felfe. CIA file Heinz Felfe, vol. 1_0007. CIA Library. Declassified in 2005.

4 Report by Capt. R. T. Robinson, Army Interrogation Pool Detachment, South Holland, 14 July 1945. CIA file Heinz Felfe, vol. 1_0009., op. cit.

5 'KGB Exploitation of Heinz Felfe', CIA report, March 1969, op. cit.

6 Ibid.

7 'Fiffi in IIIf', *Der Spiegel*, 24 February 1969.

8 Memo to James Angleton, head of counterintelligence, from Deputy-Director of Security, 8 October 1956. CIA file Heinz Felfe, vol. 1_0031, op. cit.

9 'KGB Exploitation of Heinz Felfe', CIA report, March 1969, op. cit.

10 Ibid.

11 CIA assessment of Heinz Felfe, 14 July 1959. CIA file Heinz Felfe, vol. 1_0045, op. cit.

12 No BND officer was permitted to travel to Berlin without permission and it was standard operating procedure for them to be given round-the-clock US surveillance and close protection when they did so. CIA file Heinz Felfe, vol. 1_0037, op. cit.

13 Report by Chief of East European Division to Chief of Station, Germany, 10 February 1960. CIA file Heinz Felfe, vol. 1_0053, op. cit.

14 'KGB Exploitation of Heinz Felfe', CIA report, March 1969, op. cit.

15 The Sicherheitsdienst, or SD, was the intelligence agency within the SS.

16 At the same trial, Herbert Kappler, SS police chief in Rome, was convicted by an Italian military court of crimes including the deportation to death camps of 2,000 Jews and the murder of 335 civilians in a reprisal, known as the Ardeatine massacre. He was jailed for life.

17 'KGB Exploitation of Heinz Felfe', CIA report, March 1969, op. cit.

18 Ibid.

19 Ibid.

20 Ibid.

21 Ibid.

22 Ibid.

23 The three spies did not come to trial until 22 July 1963. All were convicted; Felfe was jailed for fourteen years, Clemens nine and Tiebel two.

24 'Fiffi in IIIf', *Der Spiegel*, 24 February 1969.
25 Heinz Felfe: Damage Assessment Report. The CIA completed this report in 1963. It then hid it from public scrutiny until 2005, when the Nazi War Crimes Disclosure Act forced it to open its files.
26 Heinz Felfe: Damage Assessment Report; CIA internal document, 1 April 1963. CIA Library. Declassified in 2005.
27 Ibid.
28 'KGB Exploitation of Heinz Felfe', CIA report, March 1969, op. cit.
29 Ibid.
30 CIA file Heinz Felfe, vol. 1_0017, op. cit.
31 Ibid.

17. Glory Days

1 Equivalent to approximately $8,000 today.
2 Farndon, 'The Interrogation of Defectors', op. cit.
3 At the end of November 1961, following the Bay of Pigs and other fiascos, President Kennedy presented Dulles with the National Security Medal, then ordered him to resign.
4 Richards, *Imperial Agent*, op. cit., pp. 184–5.
5 Affidavit of Irmgard Romanoff [Goleniewski], 11 July 1967, op. cit.
6 Beer appealed to the Supreme Court, which took the unusual decision to increase his sentence to fifteen years. He died in jail in May 1966; he never disclosed his true identity. https://www.shabak.gov.il/english/heritage/affairs/Pages/YisraelBar.aspx
7 Letter from Michał Goleniewski to the *Government Employees' Exchange* newspaper, February 1968. US Legislative Archives, Washington DC.
8 Affidavit of Irmgard Romanoff [Goleniewski], 11 July 1967, op. cit.
9 Affidavit of Aleksei Nicholaevich Romanoff [Michał Goleniewski], 21 October 1969, op. cit.
10 Affidavit of Irmgard Romanoff [Goleniewski], 11 July 1967, op. cit.
11 Internal UB report, 14 March 1967. TELETECHNIK file BU_0_1911_97_2. Institute of National Remembrance, Warsaw.
12 Richards, *Imperial Agent*, op. cit., pp. 189–90.
13 Gen. Grzegorz Jan Korczyński, head of Polish military intelligence, 1956–71.
14 'Goleniewski's Work with the Soviets', op. cit.
15 NSA cryptologists William Martin and Bernon Mitchell defected to the Soviet Union in June 1960. Eight weeks later they appeared at a Moscow press conference and announced they had requested political asylum. A subsequent NSA analysis reported that the damage they caused was unprecedented.

16 'Goleniewski's Work with the Soviets', op. cit.

17 Affidavit of Aleksei Nicholaevich Romanoff [Michał Goleniewski], Exhibit H, 21 October 1969, op. cit.

18 Aleksei Nicholaevich Romanoff [Michał Goleniewski], Letter to Christopher Grose-Hodge, MI5, 10 December 1973. Herbert Romerstein Papers, Hoover Institution, Stanford University, California.

19 Report of unnamed UB officer, 1 August 1963. TELETECHNIK file BU_0_1911_97_1. Institute of National Remembrance, Warsaw.

20 The airport was renamed JFK International following the assassination of President John F. Kennedy on 22 November 1963.

21 Affidavit of Aleksei Nicholaevich Romanoff [Michał Goleniewski], 21 October 1969, op. cit.

22 'Goleniewski's Work with the Soviets', op. cit.

23 Ibid.

24 Testimony of Otto Otepka to the Senate Internal Security Subcommittee, 24 August 1964. US Congressional Archives, Washington DC.

25 John Vassall, *Vassall: The Autobiography of a Spy*, Sidgwick & Jackson, 1975, p. 67.

26 He served ten years and was released on parole in 1972.

27 Anatoliy Golitsyn.

28 Allen Dulles, 'The Craft of Intelligence', *Harpers Magazine*, 2 April 1963.

29 Affidavit of Aleksei Nicholaevich Romanoff [Michał Goleniewski], Exhibit K, 21 October 1969, op. cit.

30 Michał Goleniewski, Letter to 'David' and 'Paul', CIA East European Division, 20 March 1963. Edward J. Epstein Collection, Boston University.

31 MI5 letter to CIA. Affidavit of Irmgard Romanoff [Goleniewski], Exhibit B, 11 July 1967, op. cit.

32 The photocopy of this letter, attached as an exhibit to Irmgard Goleniewski's 1967 affidavit, shows the Security Service's reference number: PF: 776,206/D. Although there is no trace of this exact file reference in the UK National Archives, 'PF' was then the standard MI5 prefix for 'Personal Files' – a fact Goleniewski could not have known.

33 Michał Goleniewski, Letter to 'David' and 'Paul', CIA East European Division, 20 March 1963, op. cit.

34 Letter to Franz Oldenburg from 'Paul', 2 April 1963. Affidavit of Aleksei Nicholaevich Romanoff [Michał Goleniewski], Exhibit I, 21 October 1969, op. cit.

35 Affidavit of Aleksei Nicholaevich Romanoff [Michał Goleniewski], 21 October 1969, op. cit.

36 *The Bang-Jensen Case*. Senate Internal Security Subcommittee report, September 1961. US Legislative Archives, Washington DC.

37 Affidavit of Aleksei Nicholaevich Romanoff [Michał Goleniewski], 21 October 1969, op. cit.
38 UB POLA File BU_0_1739_9. Institute of National Remembrance, Warsaw.
39 Wennerström was subsequently sentenced to life in prison; he was paroled in 1974 after serving ten years.

18. Monster

1 Frank Friberg interview in Tom Mangold, *Cold War Warrior: James Jesus Angleton*, Simon & Schuster, 1991, p. 52.
2 Ibid.
3 'James J. Angleton, Anatoliy Golitsyn, and the "Monster Plot"', *CIA Studies in Intelligence*, vol. 55, no. 4, December 2011, marked 'SECRET'. CIA Library. Declassified in April 2013.
4 Equivalent to at least $85 million today.
5 'James J. Angleton, Anatoliy Golitsyn, and the "Monster Plot"', op. cit.
6 John Hart, 'The Monster Plot' [internal CIA report], 1976. US National Archives. Declassified in November 2017.
7 Ibid.
8 'James J. Angleton, Anatoliy Golitsyn, and the "Monster Plot"', op. cit.
9 Ibid.
10 Ibid.
11 Weisband was reported to the FBI by the US-based spy he handled. He was suspended from duty with the Army's Signals Intelligence Service and summoned to appear before a federal grand jury hearing concerning the American Communist Party; when he failed to appear, he was convicted of contempt and sentenced to a year in prison. He was never prosecuted for espionage, for fear that a trial would reveal US intelligence methods to Moscow. He died in 1967.
12 Hart, 'The Monster Plot', op. cit.
13 Ibid.
14 Ibid.
15 George Kisevalter interview with Joseph J. Trento, *The Secret History of the CIA*, op. cit., p. 286.
16 'James J. Angleton, Anatoliy Golitsyn, and the "Monster Plot"', op. cit.
17 David Robarge, 'Moles, Defectors and Deceptions – James Angleton and CIA Counter-Intelligence', *Journal of Intelligence History*, vol. 3, no. 2, Winter 2003.
18 Ibid.
19 Hart, *The Monster Plot*, op. cit.
20 Ibid.

21 Equivalent to almost $130 million today.

22 David Robarge, *John McCone as Director of Central Intelligence 1961–1965, Pt. 2*, Center for the Study of Intelligence, 2005. CIA Library. Declassified in April 2015.

23 'James J. Angleton, Anatoliy Golitsyn, and the "Monster Plot"', op. cit.

24 Ibid.

25 Equivalent to $1.6 million today.

26 Mangold, *Cold War Warrior*, op. cit., pp. 81–4.

27 'James J. Angleton, Anatoliy Golitsyn, and the "Monster Plot"', op. cit.

28 Ibid.

29 Robarge, 'Moles, Defectors and Deceptions', op. cit.

30 CIA Interview with Donald Deneslya, Arlington, Virginia, 24 September 1978; Agency file No: 012509. Provided to the US House Select Committee on Assassinations. US National Archives.

31 Hart, 'The Monster Plot', op. cit.

19. HR 5507

1 Michael A. Feighan Archives, Princeton University.

2 The Immigration and Nationality Act 1952, Section 313. US Legislative Archives, Washington DC.

3 Robarge, *John McCone as Director of Central Intelligence 1961–1965, Pt. 2*, op. cit.

4 Richards, *Imperial Agent*, op. cit., p. 16.

5 'An Interview with John S. Warner', Oral History Program, CIA Center for the Study of Intelligence [undated]. CIA Library. Declassified in September 2014.

6 Affidavit of Aleksei Nicholaevich Romanoff [Michał Goleniewski], 21 October 1969, op. cit.

7 Letter from 'Martin N. Cherico' to President John F. Kennedy, 15 June 1963. Affidavit of Aleksei Nicholaevich Romanoff [Michał Goleniewski], Exhibit K, 21 October 1969, op. cit.

8 Affidavit of Aleksei Nicholaevich Romanoff [Michał Goleniewski], 21 October 1969, op. cit.

9 Ibid.

10 Richards, *Imperial Agent*, op. cit., p. 18.

11 'Harassment of Spy Hero, Congressional Investigator, is Revealed', *Chicago Tribune*, 4 April 1965.

12 Richards, *Imperial Agent*, op. cit., p. 19.

13 US Senate Internal Security Subcommittee agenda, Friday, 9 August 1963. US Legislative Archives, Washington DC.

14 Letter from John E. Nolan, Administrative Assistant to Attorney General Robert F. Kennedy, 14 August 1963. Affidavit of Aleksei Nicholaevich Romanoff [Michał Goleniewski], Exhibit L, 21 October 1969, op. cit.

15 This contract has never been disclosed by the CIA, but it is contained in one of Goleniewski's sworn affidavits. Affidavit of Aleksei Nicholaevich Romanoff [Michał Goleniewski], 21 October 1969, op. cit.

16 Equivalent to $120,368 today.

17 'General Schedule' (GS) is the pay scale used for the majority of US federal government employees. An employee's base pay depends on two factors – the GS Paygrade of their job, and the Paygrade Step they have achieved (depending on seniority or performance). Paygrades start at GS-1 and run up to the top grade of GS-15 (so Goleniewski was being appointed to the top paygrade); the Paygrade Steps run from 1 (the base level) to 10. https://www.federalpay.org/gs/2019

18 This Act provided for federal employees – typically in the military, but also covering the FBI and intelligence agencies – to receive pay if they were reported missing in the line of duty.

19 Equivalent to $10,000 per month today.

20 A gross total for the twenty-one-year period of $126,000 – more than $1 million today.

21 Goleniewski identified this official as Col. Marcus Lipton. If accurate, the visit was distinctly unorthodox since Lipton was a Labour MP and the British government was then still in the hands of the Conservative Party. Lipton certainly had an interest in intelligence matters – in the 1950s he had been a thorn in the government's side about Kim Philby's suspected treachery – but there is no publicly available evidence that he represented MI5 overseas.

20. Downfall

1 Affidavit of Aleksei Nicholaevich Romanoff [Michał Goleniewski], 21 October 1969, op. cit.

2 Hart, *The Monster Plot*, op. cit.

3 Ibid.

4 Richards, *Imperial Agent*, op. cit., pp. 194–6, and Affidavit of Aleksei Nicholaevich Romanoff [Michał Goleniewski], 21 October 1969, op. cit.

5 Affidavit of Aleksei Nicholaevich Romanoff [Michał Goleniewski], Exhibit P, 21 October 1969, op. cit.

6 'Pour intelligences avec des agents étrangers le journaliste Joseph Bitonski est condamné à quatre ans de prison', *Le Monde*, 15 January 1964.

7 'Directive on the Need for Maintaining the Confidential Status of Employee Loyalty Records', 13 March 1948.

8 'Testimony of Victor H. Dikeos, Special Assistant to the Director of Personnel, Department of State, January 27, 1964'. SISS Report: *State Department Security, 1963–1965 – The Otepka Case, vol. XII*. US Legislative Archives, Washington DC.

9 'Goleniewski's Work with the Soviets', op. cit.

10 Affidavit of Aleksei Nicholaevich Romanoff [Michał Goleniewski], 21 October 1969, op. cit.

11 Affidavit of Aleksei Nicholaevich Romanoff [Michał Goleniewski], Exhibit Q, 21 October 1969, op. cit.

12 TELETECHNIK files BU_0_1911_97_1. Institute of National Remembrance, Warsaw.

21. Exposed

1 The *Journal-American* ceased publishing in April 1966, the victim of a general decline in the revenue of afternoon newspapers. It merged with the rival *World-Telegram and Sun* in September, but the resulting paper, *The New York World Journal Tribune* collapsed eight months later.

2 Guy Richards, 'US Secret Agencies Penetrated by Reds', *New York Journal-American*, 2 March 1964.

3 'Guy Richards': CIA Security Research Staff internal memo, 15 December 1965. CIA Library. Declassified in 1998.

4 Richards, 'US Secret Agencies Penetrated by Reds', op. cit.

5 Ibid.

6 Guy Richards, '4 US Envoys Linked to Red Spy Sex Net', *New York Journal-American*, 3 March 1964.

7 'Who Was John Ashbrook?' Ashbrook Ashland University: https://ashbrook. org/about/john-ashbrook

8 Congressional Record, 3 March 1964. US Legislative Archives, Washington DC.

9 'CIA Hiding Red Defector, Probers Seek to Quiz Him', *New York Journal-American*, 4 March 1964.

10 'Task Force Scrutinizes Security Files of 175', *Chicago Tribune*, 4 March 1964.

11 'Where Reds Put Spies', *New York Journal-American*, 5 March 1964.

12 Other documents in the Agency's files indicate that an officer called Eugene Winters used this cover name during the Goleniewski case. 'Memorandum for Director of Security', 9 December 1964. CIA Library. Declassified in 1993.

13 Affidavit of Aleksei Nicholaevich Romanoff [Michał Goleniewski], 21 October 1969, op. cit.

14 'Shield Diplomat-Turncoat Who Spied for the Soviets', *New York Journal-American*, 11 March 1964.

15 Affidavit of Aleksei Nicholaevich Romanoff [Michał Goleniewski], 21 October 1969, op. cit.

16 Michał Goleniewski, *Double Eagle*, August 1976. Howard Gottlieb Archival Research Center, Boston University.

17 'Anti-Red Group "Lost" in State Dept. Shuffle', *New York Journal-American*, 18 March 1964.

18 'The Questionables', *New York Journal-American*, 20 March 1964.

19 'The Smoot Report', 23 March 1964. CIA Library.

20 'Goleniewski's Work with the Soviets', op. cit.

22. Dirty Tricks

1 In later years he staunchly defended Richard Nixon during the Watergate scandal and refused to vote for the President's impeachment.

2 CIA Office of Legal Counsel: Memo, 17 March 1964. CIA Library. Declassified in January 2005.

3 Congressional record, 26 March 1964. US Legislative Archives, Washington DC.

4 Ibid.

5 Senate Internal Security Subcommittee Report: 'State Department Security 1963–1965, Part IV'. Undated, but first printed 'for the use of the subcommittee on the Judiciary', 1967. US Legislative Archives, Washington DC.

6 Congressional Record, 5 February 1969. Rep. John Rarick read into the record accounts of the saga published in the *Government Employees' Exchange* newspaper. Symans was never charged with espionage.

7 Senate Internal Security Subcommittee Report: 'State Department Security 1963–1965, Part IV', op. cit.

8 Ibid.

9 Affidavit of Aleksei Nicholaevich Romanoff [Michał Goleniewski], 21 October 1969, op. cit.

10 Ibid.

11 Letter from Senator James O. Eastland, 27 May 1964. Affidavit of Aleksei Nicholaevich Romanoff [Michał Goleniewski], Exhibit S, 21 October 1969, op. cit.

12 Congressional Record, 20 June 1944.

13 John R. Norpel, State Department. Sworn testimony to Senate Internal Security Subcommittee, 24 July 1964. SISS report: 'State Department Security, 1963–1965: The Otepka Case – VIII', printed 1965. US Legislative Archives, Washington DC.

14 UB retrospective report, 9 November 1964. TELETECHNIK files BU_0_1911_97_1. Institute of National Remembrance, Warsaw.

15 UB report, 1 December 1961. TELETECHNIK files BU_0_1911_97_1. Institute of National Remembrance, Warsaw.

16 'Update on operational enterprises', 7 April 1964. TELETECHNIK files BU_0_1911_97_1. Institute of National Remembrance, Warsaw.

23. Romanoff

1 Letter to Sen. James Eastland, 20 July 1964. Affidavit of Aleksei Nicholaevich Romanoff [Michał Goleniewski], Exhibit S, 21 October 1969, op. cit.

2 'Verbatim Transcript of Barry Farber Radio Program', 10 August 1964; Senate Internal Security Subcommittee, US Legislative Archives, Washington DC.

3 American spelling uses 'Czar' and 'Tsar', 'Romanov' and 'Romanoff' interchangeably.

4 Nikolai Sokolov was hired by the anti-communist White Army in 1919. He spent five years interviewing members of the Romanoff diaspora and recovered large quantities of the Imperial Family's belongings from the Ekaterinburg area. His investigation was cut short when Bolshevik forces recaptured the town. Sokolov died in exile in Paris in 1924. His report was published posthumously.

5 'Russia's Czar Lives!', *Manchester Union-Leader*, 17 August 1964.

6 Schuyler died in an aeroplane crash near Da Nang, Vietnam, in May 1967, aged thirty-five. She was helping escort young Vietnamese orphans to safety when their US Army helicopter plunged into the sea. She and a young boy who had been sitting on her lap drowned.

7 'Russia's Czar Lives!', *Manchester Union-Leader*, 17 August 1964.

8 'John McCone as Director of Central Intelligence, Pt. 2', internal CIA history. CIA Library. Declassified in April 2015.

9 'The Case of a New Anastasia', *Life*, 18 October 1963.

10 Ibid.

11 Author's interview with Kathleen Shedaker Speller, widow of Jon P. Speller, former editor-in-chief of Robert Speller & Sons, Publishers, 24 July 2018.

12 James Blair Lovell, *Anastasia: The Lost Princess*, Robson Books, 1991, p. 176.

13 'Biographical Sketch of Cleve Backster', Congressional Publication no. 31647, April 1964. Legislative Archives, Washington DC.

14 Cleve Backster, 'Statement about the Russian Imperial Family', *Novoye Russkoye Slovo*, 16 July 1965.

15 Internal CIA memo [author redacted], 22 January 1965; files on Herman E. Kimsey. CIA Library. Declassified in 1993.

16 Approximately $150 million today.

17 *New York Times*, 30 July and 11 August 1929.

18 The existence of this fabled wealth has never been proved, and even if it existed, the present-day Russian Federation would be its most likely inheritor. Nonetheless, the lost Romanoff fortune remains, like stories of a Nazi train, loaded with gold and buried in a hidden tunnel in Poland, a persistent urban myth.

19 Affidavit of Aleksei Nicholaevich Romanoff [Michał Goleniewski], 21 October 1969, op. cit.

20 Robert Speller on the Barry Farber radio show. 'Verbatim Transcript of Barry Farber Radio Program', 10 August 1964, op. cit.

21 Richards, *Imperial Agent*, op. cit., p. 254.

22 Richards, *Imperial Agent*, op. cit., pp. 254–5.

23 Affidavit of Aleksei Nicholaevich Romanoff [Michał Goleniewski], 21 October 1969, op. cit.

24 Polish intelligence reports on an intercepted letter from Goleniewski to Janina dated 7 July 1964. UB TELETECHNIK files BU_0_1911_97_1 and BU_0_1911_97_2. Institute of National Remembrance, Warsaw.

25 'Verbatim Transcript of Barry Farber Radio Program', 10 August 1964, op. cit.

26 'Russia's Czar Lives!', *Manchester Union-Leader*, 17 August 1964.

27 Certificate attached as an exhibit to Affidavit of Aleksei Nicholaevich Romanoff [Michał Goleniewski], 7 November 1966, op. cit.

28 'A Declaration by Aleksei Nicholaevich Romanoff (Goleniewski)'. *New York Journal-American*, 2 January 1965.

29 Richards, *Imperial Agent*, op. cit., p. 249.

30 The certificate was reproduced in a six-page, A3-format news sheet, issued by Robert Speller's Transglobal News Service. A copy is held in the Sergei L. Voitsekhovskii Collection at the Hoover Institution, Stanford University, California.

24. Support

1 'Did Lenin Spirit Royal Family Out of Russia?', *New York Journal-American*, 12 September 1964.

2 Donald G. Hanning (1913–2006) was a World War II veteran who became the FBI's 'personal representative' to the Americanism Commission and sat in on 'all its deliberations'. The Bureau also used him to ensure its responses to press attacks published in the Legion's magazine, *The Firing Line*.

3 The Commission is the American Legion body charged with supervising and coordinating the activities of the national executive.

4 Internal Memorandum, 22 October 1964; FBI files on Michał Goleniewski. FBI Vault.

5 *Novoye Russkoye Slovo*, 8 December 1964.

6 'A Declaration by Aleksei Nicholaevich Romanoff (Goleniewski)', *New York Journal-American*, 2 January 1965.

7 Robert Speller Snr and Robert Speller Jnr: Letter to the Synod of Bishops of the Russian Orthodox Church Outside of Russia, 13 January 1965. Affidavit of Aleksei Nicholaevich Romanoff [Michał Goleniewski], Exhibit T-G, 21 October 1969, op. cit.

8 Grand Duke Vladimir Kirrilovich (1938–1992) inherited his claim to the throne from his father who stemmed from a different line in the Romanoff family and who, in 1924, pronounced himself 'Emperor and Autocrat of all the Russias'.

9 'Cossack Exile Shifts Loyalties', UPI in [inter alia] *Miami Herald*, 28 January 1965.

10 'Defector Says He's the Czar's Son', UPI in *Miami Herald*, 10 January 1965.

11 'CIA Challenged to Bare Data on Czarevich Case', *New York Journal-American*, 19 January 1965.

12 Affidavit of Herman E. Kimsey, 3 June 1965. John F. Russell Collection, Hoover Institution Archives, Stanford University, California.

13 'Pictured: Last Image of Russian Royal Family Visiting King Edward VII in 1909', *Daily Express*, 22 March 2017.

14 Dr Alexander Wiener, 1907–1976. His pioneering work included the development of 'blood fingerprinting', the forerunner of modern DNA testing. He also discovered the Rh factor in blood, which led to the development of exchange transfusion methods that saved the lives of many young children.

15 Letter from Alexander S. Wiener MD to Herman E. Kimsey, 4 January 1965. US Legislative Archives, Washington DC.

16 'Memorandum for Director of Security from Ralph E. Tobiassen. Subject: [02] VISION #240 003', 9 December 1964. CIA files on Herman E. Kimsey, US National Archives, JFK Documents series, Box # JFK43; also in the CIA Library. Declassified in 1993.

17 Ibid.

18 Goleniewski, Michael aka: Oldenburg, Franz Roman: Memorandum for the Record by Harlan A. Westrell, ADDS(IOS), 28 January 1965. CIA files on Herman E. Kimsey, op. cit.

19 Memorandum for the Record, 25 January 1965. CIA files on Herman E. Kimsey, op. cit.

20 Memorandum from Helene Finan, Chief of Office of Security Research Staff, 15 December 1965. CIA Library. Declassified in 1998.

21 Letter from Marlo T. Noto, Immigration and Naturalization Service, 21 September 1965, in Irmgard Romanoff, 'Open Letter to President Lyndon B. Johnson, February 10, 1966'. CIA files on Herman E. Kimsey, op. cit.

22 Romanoff, 'Open Letter to President Lyndon B. Johnson, February 10, 1966', op. cit.

23 Legal Notice, *New York Herald Tribune*, 17 November 1965.

24 Affidavit of Aleksei Nicholaevich Romanoff [Michał Goleniewski], 21 October 1969, op. cit.

25. Wilderness

1 'Matter of Brevetti': New York Bar case 4 A.D.2d 579, 25 November 1957. https://ww.leagle.com/decision/19575834ad2d5791460

2 Contract between Goleniewski and Vincent P. Brevetti, 2 December 1965. CIA files on Herman E. Kimsey, US National Archives, op. cit.

3 Letter from Vincent P. Brevetti, attorney, to William F. Raborn, Director of the Central Intelligence Agency, 3 December 1965. CIA files on Herman E. Kimsey, US National Archives, op. cit.

4 Vincent P. Brevetti, letter to Congressman Joseph P. Addabbo, 1 March 1966. Affidavit of Aleksei Nicholaevich Romanoff [Michał Goleniewski], Exhibit S, 21 October 1969, op. cit.

5 Letter to John S. Warner, CIA, from Vincent P. Brevetti, attorney, 22 December 1965. Affidavit of Aleksei Nicholaevich Romanoff [Michał Goleniewski], 21 October 1969, op. cit.

6 Letter from Congressman Joseph P. Addabbo to Vincent P. Brevetti, 22 March 1966. CIA files on Herman E. Kimsey, US National Archives, op. cit.

7 Letter from Aleksei Nicholaevich Romanoff [Michał Goleniewski] to George F. Moran, Assistant Director, CIA, 10 May 1966. CIA files on Herman E. Kimsey, US National Archives, op. cit.

8 Letter from Charles A. Thompson, British Consul-General, New York, to L. C. W. Figg, Permanent Under Secretary, Foreign Office, London, 23 March 1966. Foreign Office files on Michał Goleniewski, released to author following FOI request, January 2019.

9 File note in Foreign Office files on Michał Goleniewski, released to author following FOI request, January 2019. The FO file referred to – NS 1691/1 – does not appear to exist in the UK National Archives.

10 In January 2020, MI5 confirmed, in an email to the author, that it held a file on Goleniewski, but declined to release it 'due to the continuing sensitivity of the material contained within it'.

11 Entered into the Congressional Record by Senator John Stennis: Congressional Record, 17 January 1962.

12 'The Time Has Come', John Birch Society Advertisement, *New York Times*, 15 December 1963.

13 Frank Capel, *Herald of Freedom*, 29 December 1971.

14 On 29 May 1945, Capel was given a one-year suspended jail sentence, two years' probation and ordered to pay $2,000 in fines. In 1965 he added to his criminal record when he was convicted of conspiracy to libel a US Senator and was handed a new 180-day suspended jail sentence, three more years on probation and a $500 fine. FBI files on Frank A. Capel. FBI Vault.

15 'The Strange Case of "Col. Goleniewski", Parts 1 & 2', *Herald of Freedom*, 11 February and 25 March 1966, Box 3, Zapareth, New Jersey. CIA Library.

16 *Testimony of Edward Hunter*: House Un-American Activities Committee, 13 March 1958. US Legislative Archives, Washington DC.

17 *POW: The Fight Continues after the Battle*, Report of the Secretary of Defense's Advisory Committee on Prisoners of War, August 1955. Library of Congress, https://www.loc.gov/rr/frd/Military_Law/pdf/POW-report.pdf

18 Michał Goleniewski: Telegram to Edward Hunter, Editor, *Tactics* magazine, 21 March 1968. Herbert Romerstein Collection, Hoover Institute Archives, Stanford University, California.

19 Letter from Edward Hunter to Michał Goleniewski, 8 August 1968. Herbert Romerstein Collection, Hoover Institution Archives, Stanford University, California.

20 Alan Cranston, Controller, State of California, 'John Birch Society – A Soiled Slip Is Showing', *Madera Tribune*, 3 August 1966.

21 Richard Cotten, *Conservative Viewpoint*, Script no. 163–166, broadcast 11–14 July 1966. CIA Library.

22 'List of Self-Styled or False Orders of St. John', Australian Government Department of Defence https://www.defence.gov.au/medals/_Master/docs/DHAM/48B.pdf

23 'Certificate of Recognition' of Grand Duke Aleksei Romanoff Order of Saint John of Jerusalem, Knights of Malta (America), 307 East 44th Street, New York City [undated]. Herbert Romerstein Collection, Hoover Institution Archives, Stanford University, California.

24 In 1983 a New York court ruled that Bassaraba had supplied a false 'passport' and knighthood to a gullible mark for the princely sum of $20,000. *Alhadeff v. Georg*, US District Court, Southern District of New York, November 1983.

25 'Statement – To Whom It May Concern', paid advertisement in the *New York Times*, 9 December 1966.

26 Letter from Aleksei Nicholaevich Romanoff [Michał Goleniewski] to Vincent Brevetti, 9 May 1966. CIA files on Herman E. Kimsey, US National Archives, op. cit.

27 Copies of these 'Open Letters' are reproduced in Irmgard's affidavit of 11 July 1967 and Goleniewski's affidavit of 21 October 1969, both at New York City Register Office, Queens.

28 Aleksei Nicholaevich Romanoff [Michał Goleniewski], 'Open Letter to Ramsey Clark, US Attorney General', advertisement published in [inter alia] *Ramparts Magazine*, October 1967. US Legislative Archives, Washington DC.

29 Affidavit of Aleksei Nicholaevich Romanoff [Michał Goleniewski], 21 October 1969, op. cit.

30 Steven L. Kuhn, Chief, Personnel Security Division (CIA): Memorandum for the Record, 14 April 1966. CIA files on Herman E. Kimsey, US National Archives, op. cit.

31 Memo from Sarah K. Hall, Office of Security (CIA) to 'Chief LEOB/SRS', 6 February 1968. CIA files on Herman E. Kimsey, US National Archives, op. cit.

32 'Guy Richards', Memo from Helene Finan, Chief of Office of Security Research Staff, CIA, to Deputy Chief, Research Staff, 15 December 1965. CIA Library. Declassified in 1998.

33 'The Romanov-Goleniewski Affair by Guy Richards', internal FBI memo, 18 April 1966. FBI Vault.

34 Ibid.

35 Press advertisement for *Imperial Agent – The Goleniewski-Romanov Case*. Devin Garrity Collection, Hoover Institution Archives, Stanford University, California.

36 Ibid.

37 'Statement – To Whom It May Concern', Aleksei Nicholaevich Romanoff [Michał Goleniewski], *New York Times*, 9 December 1966.

38 Internal CIA memo from Walter Pforzheim, Curator, Historical Intelligence Collection, 10 December 1966. CIA files on Herman E. Kimsey, US National Archives, op. cit. According to the Agency's website, Pforzheim was a World War II veteran who became 'a founding father of CIA', serving as its first legislative counsel and helping passage of the 1947 National Security Act which established its existence.

26. TELETECHNIK

1 Captain Józef Mędrzycki, Senior Operation Officer, Division III, Department I, Ministry of Internal Affairs: Report on operation 'TELETECHNIK', 4 February 1966. TELETECHNIK file BU_0_1911_97_2. Institute of National Remembrance, Warsaw.

2 Ibid.

3 David Wise's book *Molehunt* (Random House, 1992) was one of the first to detail the damage inflicted on the CIA by Anatoliy Golitsyn.

4 Major Józef Mędrzycki (he was promoted in Spring 1966), Report on operation 'TELETECHNIK', 7 January 1967. TELETECHNIK file BU_0_1911_97_2.

5 The Foreign Affairs Committee met to discuss the CIA on 29 July, not 27 July. In common with most closed-door hearings, there is no published transcript of the *in camera* session.

6 Major Józef Mędrzycki, Report on operation 'TELETECHNIK', 28 November 1966. TELETECHNIK file BU_0_1911_97_2.

7 'Soviet Says US Invents Heir to Russian Throne', UPI, 27 August 1966.

8 'L. Dende: Życiorys [Curriculum Vitae], 23 May 1949'. File ref: 01739/96/CD, 38–39. Institute of National Remembrance, Warsaw.

9 Captain Józef Mędrzycki, Report on operation 'TELETECHNIK', 9 November 1964. TELETECHNIK file BU_0_1911_97_1, op. cit.

10 Major Józef Mędrzycki, Report on operation 'TELETECHNIK', 12 June 1967. TELETECHNIK file BU_0_1911_97_2, op. cit.

11 Major Józef Mędrzycki, Report on operation 'TELETECHNIK', 8 February 1967. TELETECHNIK file BU_0_1911_97_1, op. cit.

12 Major Józef Mędrzycki, Report on operation 'TELETECHNIK', 14 March 1967. TELETECHNIK file BU_0_1911_97_2, op. cit.

13 Ibid.

14 Major Z. Zieliński, Report on operation 'TELETECHNIK', 20 March 1967. TELETECHNIK file BU_0_1911_97_2, op. cit.

15 Major Z. Zieliński, Report concerning Agent POLA's meeting with Robert Speller, 28 May 1967. TELETECHNIK file BU_0_1911_97_2, op. cit.

16 Ibid.

17 Major Z. Zieliński, Report concerning Agent POLA, 23 August 1967. POLA file BU_0_1739_96. Institute of National Remembrance, Warsaw.

18 Major Józef Mędrzycki, Report on operation 'TELETECHNIK', 20 July 1967. TELETECHNIK file BU_0_1911_97_2, op. cit.

19 Excerpts from a letter sent by Goleniewski to Father Jakubik, 15 July 1967. TELETECHNIK file BU_0_1911_97_2, op. cit.

20 Major Józef Mędrzycki, Report on operation 'TELETECHNIK', 20 July 1967. TELETECHNIK file BU_0_1911_97_2, op. cit.

21 Major Z. Zieliński, Report on operation 'TELETECHNIK', 17 May 1968. TELETECHNIK file BU_0_1911_97_2, op. cit.

22 Ibid.

23 Aleksei Nicholaevich Romanoff [Michał Goleniewski]: Public Notice, *New York Times*, 28 May 1968.

24 Affidavit of Aleksei Nicholaevich Romanoff [Michał Goleniewski],
   21 October 1969, op. cit.
25 Report and map by Agent JERZYM. Undated, but apparently late June 1968.
   TELETECHNIK file BU_0_1911_97_2, op. cit.
26 Report and map by Agent LESNY, 8 July 1968. TELETECHNIK file
   BU_0_1911_97_2, op. cit.
27 Ibid.
28 Reports by unnamed Soviet intelligence officers (handwritten in Cyrillic
   script), 23 April 1970 and 19 March 1971. TELETECHNIK file
   BU_0_1911_97_2, op. cit.
29 Equivalent to approximately $36,000 today.
30 Capt. St Ojrzyński: Report on operation 'TELETECHNIK', 13 June 1969.
   TELETECHNIK file BU_0_1911_97_2, op. cit.
31 Report on meeting with Janina Goleniewska by unidentified UB officer.
   Undated, but probably January 1969. TELETECHNIK file BU_0_1911_97_2,
   op. cit.
32 Col. Fr. Krawczik: Final report on Operation TELETECHNIK, 28 February
   1983. TELETECHNIK file BU_0_1911_97_2, op. cit.

27. Mole Hunts

1 Former CIA officer Bill Wagner, in Mark Bowden, *The Dark Art of
   Interrogation*, Atlantic Monthly Press, 2004, p. 103.
2 Hart, *The Monster Plot*, op. cit.
3 The equivalent today would be $4,200.
4 Hart, *The Monster Plot*, op. cit., p. 13.
5 Tennent Bagley: testimony to House Select Committee on Assassinations,
   16 November 1978. US Legislative Archives, Washington DC.
6 The CIA's 1976 report makes explicit the connection between the Nosenko
   material given to Golitsyn and Goleniewski. 'This ruse seemed plausible
   enough, since a previous defector, Michal Goleniewski, had written CIA a
   number of anonymous letters before eventually defecting'. Hart, *The Monster
   Plot*, op. cit., p. 15.
7 Hart, *The Monster Plot*, op. cit., p. 16.
8 The CIA used two-letter country-specific prefixes for its cryptonyms:
   AE was the code for the USSR.
9 Heuer, 'Nosenko – Five Paths to Judgment', op. cit.
10 Memo by David E. Murphy, Chief of SR Division, 17 February 1964;
   approved by Richard Helms, Deputy Director of the CIA, 17 February 1964.
   Hart, *The Monster Plot*, op. cit., p. 25.
11 Robarge, 'Moles, Defectors and Deceptions', op. cit.

12 Ibid, p. 30.

13 In September 1978, Nosenko told the House Select Committee on Assassinations that he was certain he had been administered hallucinogenic drugs. The CIA denied this, though admitted giving him tranquillizers.

14 Testimony of John Hart, CIA officer, to House Select Committee on Assassinations, 15 September 1978. US Legislative Archives, Washington DC.

15 Memo from Tennent Bagley, 19 November 1964. Hart, *The Monster Plot*, op. cit., pp. 41–2.

16 The officer who provided this account was identified only as 'Miles', and the story of his testimony offers an insight into the CIA's continuing determination – almost half a century on – to conceal the full extent of the damage that Golitsyn and Angleton caused. 'Miles' gave his evidence to Cleveland Cram, a senior Agency officer who was tasked in the early 1970s with writing a history of the Counter-Intelligence Staff. Cram's eventual study ran to twelve volumes – each more than 300 pages long; it has never been released, and when, after his death, his papers were given to George Washington University for public access, the CIA rushed to reclaim them; they remain closed, 'under review' by Langley. However, in the brief period between deposit and closure, a handful of pages, including the 'Miles' statement, were photographed by a British researcher. For a full account of this curious coda to the Agency's mole hunts, see Jefferson Morley, 'The Wilderness of Mirrors', *The Intercept*, 1 January 2018.

17 Heuer, 'Nosenko – Five Paths to Judgment', op. cit.

18 Ibid.

19 Clare Edward Petty, CIA officer, quoted in Wise, *Molehunt*, op. cit., pp. 234–7.

20 Wright, *Spycatcher*, p. 315.

21 Robarge, 'Moles, Defectors and Deceptions', op. cit.

22 'James J. Angleton, Anatoliy Golitsyn, and the "Monster Plot"', op. cit.

23 Andrew, *Defence of the Realm*, op. cit., p. 503.

24 One of the chief mole hunters, Arthur Martin, former head of MI5's Soviet counter-espionage section, subsequently gave detailed information to the intelligence writer, Nigel West. His account of events formed a central plank of West's book, *MI5 1945–72: A Matter of Trust*, Weidenfeld & Nicolson, 1982.

25 Wright, *Spycatcher*, op. cit., pp. 142–4.

26 Ibid.

27 Ibid., pp. 293–5.

28 Andrew, *Defence of the Realm*, op. cit., pp. 503–4.

29 Ibid., p. 510.

30 Ibid.

31 Wright, *Spycatcher*, op. cit., pp. 322–3.

32 Andrew, *Defence of the Realm*, op. cit., p. 512.

33 Wright, *Spycatcher*, op. cit., p. 324.

34 Ibid., pp. 170 and 315.

35 Andrew, *Defence of the Realm*, op. cit., p. 526.

36 Ibid., p. 517.

37 Cleveland Cram, 'Of Moles and Molehunters: A Review of Counter-Intelligence Literature, 1977–92', p. 8. CIA Center for the Study of Intelligence, October 1993. CIA Library.

38 Ibid., p. 519.

39 Hart, *The Monster Plot*, op. cit., pp. 76–9.

28. Double Eagle

1 'CIA Defector Watch List for the Secret Service': Memo for the Record, 14 June 1973. CIA Library.

2 Guy Richards, *The Rescue of the Romanovs*, Devin-Adair, 1975, p. 6.

3 Peter Bessell affidavit: 'In the Matter of My Investigations into the Theory of the Escape of the Former Czar Nicholas of Russia and His Family from Ekaterinburg and Related Matters', Los Angeles County, 28 May 1976. Courtesy of Paul Bessell.

4 *Hansard*, 14 May 1970.

5 Early Day Motion 291, May 1970, in Orbally Corbally Dunn column 'It's My Opinion', 2 June 1970, Columbia Features (Syndication) Inc., Herbert Romerstein Collection, Hoover Institution, Stanford University, California.

6 Peter Bessell affidavit, op. cit.

7 Letter from Peter Bessell to HIH Aleksei Nicholaevich Romanoff [Michał Goleniewski], 28 July 1970. Herbert Romerstein Collection, Hoover Institution, Stanford University, California.

8 Ibid., 11 January 1971.

9 Letter from Marshall H. Ward to HIH Aleksei Nicholaevich Romanoff [Michał Goleniewski], 25 January 1972. Herbert Romerstein Collection, Hoover Institution, Stanford University, California.

10 Letter from Marshall H. Ward to Superintendent, New York City Register Office, Queens, 31 January 1972. Herbert Romerstein Collection, Hoover Institution, Stanford University, California.

11 Memo from Victor M. Rivera, City Register, to John J. Lagutta, Acting Assistant Deputy Register, 31 January 1972. Herbert Romerstein Collection, Hoover Institution, Stanford University, California.

12 Equivalent to $3 million today.

13 Aleksei Nicholaevich Romanoff [Michał Goleniewski]: Memo of threat reported to FBI, 12 May 1971. Herbert Romerstein Collection, Hoover Institution, Stanford University, California.

14 Senate Internal Security Subcommittee staff memo, 21 May 1973. US Legislative Archives, Washington DC.

15 Equivalent to $900 today.

16 Reports from Michał Goleniewski to Christopher Grose-Hodge, MI5, and Cecil Shipp, Embassy, Washington DC, December 1973–January 1974. Herbert Romerstein Collection, Hoover Institution, Stanford University, California.

17 Letter from James Angleton, CIA, to Cecil Shipp, MI5, re: LAVINIA [Michał Goleniewski], 25 January 1974. CIA files on Heinz Felfe, vol. 4_0132. CIA Library. Declassified in 2005.

18 Angleton was on borrowed time within the CIA after the *New York Times* exposed his role in an illegal domestic surveillance scandal in December 1974. Soon afterwards, Director William Colby dismissed him from the Agency.

19 Report from Michał Goleniewski to Christopher Grose-Hodge, MI5, 10 December 1973. Herbert Romerstein Collection, Hoover Institution, Stanford University, California.

20 Ibid.

21 Appeal on behalf of 'Aleksei Nicholaevich Romanoff' [Michał Goleniewski] by Allen Mann Jnr *Manchester Union-Leader*, 1 August 1974.

22 Edward Hunter, file note of phone call with Goleniewski, 23 June 1969. Herbert Romerstein Collection, Hoover Institution, Stanford University, California.

23 Equivalent to $145 today.

24 *Double Eagle*, vol. II, no. 8, August 1976. Howard Gottlieb Archival Research Center, Boston University.

25 Ibid.

26 *Double Eagle*, November 1977.

27 Guy Richards, 'Memorandum to Criminal Court of the City of New York', 10 May 1976. Devin Garrity Collection, Hoover Institution, Stanford University, California.

28 *Double Eagle*, October 1977.

29 Alan Stang, 'The Tsar's Best Agent', *American Opinion* [John Birch Society journal], March 1976.

30 'Khomeini was Russ Agent, ex-Espionage Chief Claims', UPI, 24 November 1979.

31 Final report on Operation TELETECHNIK, 28 February 1983. TELETECHNIK file BU_0_1911_97_2, Institute of National Remembrance, Warsaw.

32 Notice of annulment of sentence, 23 June 1986. Warsaw District Military Court.

33 TELETECHNIK file BU_0_1911_97_2.

34 Robert K. Massie, *The Romanovs: The Final Chapter*, Random House, 1995.

35 William Clarke, *The Lost Fortune of the Tsars*, Weidenfeld and Nicolson, 1994.

36 Professor Leszek Pawlikowicz, Institute of Political Sciences, University of Rzeszów: 'Secret Front of the Cold War, Refugees from the Polish Special Services, 1956–1964'. http://niniwa22.cba.pl/podpulkownik_michal_goleniewski.htm

29. Who *Really* Was Michał Goleniewski?

1 Michael D. Coble, Odile M. Loreille, Mark J. Wadhams, Suni M. Edson, Kerry Maynard, Carner E. Meyer, Harald Niederstätter, Cordula Berger, Burkhard Berger, Anthony B. Falseti, Peter Gill, Walther Parsons, Louis N. Finelli, 'Mystery Solved: The Identification of the Two Missing Romanov Children Using DNA Analysis', PLOS ONE, 11 March 2009.

2 Anonymous CIA 'counterintelligence officer', quoted in Martin, *Wilderness of Mirrors*, p. 105.

3 Tennent H. Bagley, email to Col. Dick Blair, 8 March 1996, op. cit.

4 Second anonymous CIA officer, quoted in Martin, *Wilderness of Mirrors*, p. 104.

5 Tennent Bagley, *Spy Wars*, Yale University Press, 2007, pp. 48–9.

6 'Goleniewski's Work with the Soviets', op. cit.

Selected Bibliography

Books

Andrew, Christopher, *The Defence of the Realm: The Authorized History of MI5* (Allen Lane, 2009)

Bagley, Tennent H., *Spy Wars: Moles, Mysteries and Deadly Games* (Yale University Press, 2007)

Clarke, William, *The Lost Fortune of the Tsars* (Weidenfeld & Nicolson, 1994)

Epstein, Edward J., *Deception: The Invisible War between the KGB and the CIA* (Simon & Schuster, 1989)

—*Legend: The Secret World of Lee Harvey Oswald* (McGraw-Hill, 1978)

Hermiston, Roger, *The Greatest Traitor: The Secret Lives of Agent George Blake* (Arum Press, 2013)

Heuer, Richards J., *Psychology of Intelligence Analysis* (Globalytica/Pherson Publications, 2018)

Jeffery, Keith, *MI6: The History of the Secret Intelligence Service, 1909–1949* (Bloomsbury, 2010)

Kempe, Frederick, *Berlin 1961* (Putnam's, 2011)

Klier, John, *The Quest for Anastasia* (Smith Gryphon, 1995)

Lovell, James Blair, *Anastasia: The Lost Princess* (Regnery Publishing, 1989)

Mangold, Tom, *Cold War Warrior – James Jesus Angleton: The CIA's Master Spy Hunter* (Simon & Schuster, 1991)

Martin, David C., *Wilderness of Mirrors* (HarperCollins, 1980)

Massie, Robert K., *Nicholas and Alexandra* (Atheneum, 1967)

—*The Romanovs: The Final Chapter* (Random House, 1995)

Melman, Yossi, *Every Spy a Prince* (Houghton Mifflin, 1990)

Morley, Jefferson, *The Ghost: The Secret Life of CIA Spymaster James Jesus Angleton* (St. Martin's Press, 2017)

Murphy, David E., Sergei A. Kondrashev and George Bailey, *Battleground Berlin* (Yale University Press, 1997)

Richards, Guy, *Imperial Agent: The Goleniewski-Romanov Case* (Devin-Adair, 1966)

—*The Hunt for the Czar* (Doubleday, 1970)

—*The Rescue of the Romanovs* (Devin-Adair, 1975)

Shackley, Ted, *Spymaster: My Life in the CIA* (Potomac Books, 2005)

Sullivan, John F., *Gatekeeper: Memoirs of a CIA Polygraph Examiner* (Potomac Books, 2007)

Trento, Joseph J., *The Secret History of the CIA* (MJF Books, 2001)

Walters, Guy, *Hunting Evil* (Bantam Press, 2009)

Weiner, Tim, *Legacy of Ashes: The History of the CIA* (Allen Lane, 2005)

West, Nigel, *MI5 1945–72: A Matter of Trust* (Weidenfeld & Nicolson, 1982)

—*Molehunt: The Full Story of the Soviet Spy in MI5* (Weidenfeld & Nicolson, 1987)

Wise, David, *Molehunt: The Secret Search for Traitors that Shattered the CIA* (Random House, 1992)

Wright, Peter, *Spycatcher* (Heinemann Australia, 1987)

Journals and Academic Papers

Bagley, Tennent H., 'Ghosts of the Spy Wars: A Personal Reminder to Interested Parties', *International Journal of Intelligence and Counter-Intelligence*, vol. 28, no. 1 (2015), pp. 1–37

Robarge, David, 'Moles, Defectors and Deceptions: James Angleton and CIA Counter-Intelligence', *Journal of Intelligence History*, vol. 3, no. 2 (Winter 2003)

Acknowledgements

This book has been a long time in the making.

I first came across the name Michał Goleniewski fifty years ago, and over the decades thereafter slowly assembled what little reliable information was available. It took until 2017 for portions of the official files in Britain and the United States to emerge; while far from complete, they pointed to the location of many other documents – not least Goleniewski's own exhaustive writings.

Finding and acquiring these papers – many thousands of individual pages – required extensive travel to, and immersion in, archives across England, Europe and America. I am profoundly grateful to the Society of Authors for giving me the Eric Ambler Award, which provided funds to support this research. SoA works extremely hard on behalf of authors and I urge every writer to join.

The research teams in those archives also gave unstinting help. I must particularly thank the staff of New York City Register Office in Queens for burrowing deep into their vaults to locate the long-lost affidavits and exhibits filed by Goleniewski and his wife, Irmgard Kampf.

At the Hoover Institute, Stanford University, California, Sarah Patton enabled access to a treasure-trove of material collected by, amongst others, the late Herb Romerstein, a former card-carrying Communist Party member turned anti-communist activist, who ended up as chief investigator for the US House Committees on Internal Security and its more notorious precursor, the House Un-American Activities Committee.

At the US National Archives in Washington DC, the staff of the Legislative Archive section gave freely of their time and assistance to find dusty volumes of largely forgotten Congressional Committee hearings or reports. My particular thanks to Sarah Waitz and Kristen Wilhelm.

At Boston University, the research staff at the Howard Gottlieb Archival Research Center offered up the numerous boxes of both the Tennent H. Bagley and Edward J. Epstein Collections. Special thanks to Jane Parr and Laura Russo.

At Princeton University, Amanda Ferrara and her colleagues lugged the enormous Michael Feighan Collection into the Seeley G. Mudd Manuscript Library, not once but twice. I thank them for their patience.

In Poland, Dr Leszek Pawlikowicz at the University of Rzeszów kindly shared some of his research and pointed me towards the Polish Intelligence Services papers at the Institute for National Remembrance (IPN) in Warsaw. I am particularly grateful to IPN for providing copies of more than 1,100 pages from these files: the openness and availability of these historic records puts the security and intelligence agencies in the UK and the United States to shame. It is surely a sorry state of affairs when the Cold War records of the communist Polish Intelligence Services are more available than those of our own – especially since Goleniewski was ostensibly a traitor to his homeland but, initially at least, a hero to Britain and America.

Away from the archives, I was assisted with translations of the Russian and Polish documents by Yelena McCafferty and Eva Forbes respectively. And I have been very fortunate indeed with my editors: both Michael Flamini at St Martin's Press in New York and Simon Taylor at Transworld in London have given generous enthusiasm, warmth and support. My thanks are also due to the too-often-unsung professionals who worked on this book: copy editor Richard Mason, desk editor Kate Samano and designers Richard Shailer at Transworld and Nikolaas Eickelbeck at St Martin's. I also count myself truly lucky to be represented by Andrew Lownie: as a literary agent he simply has no equal, and his advice and encouragement – as well as his tireless work – were vital to getting this book off the ground.

Finally, and as always, I owe an immense debt of gratitude to my partner, Mia Pennal. Once again she cheerfully supported my lengthy disappearance into mounds of dusty files; her love and whole-souled goodness make everything possible.

Picture Credits

Page One

Michał Goleniewski in Polish Army uniform; Goleniewski with his mother and father; Goleniewski with his mother: Polish intelligence files, Institute of National Remembrance, Warsaw.

Page Two

Goleniewski during his employment as a Polish intelligence officer; Goleniewski with his mother, his first wife and two of their children: Polish intelligence files, Institute of National Remembrance, Warsaw. Bahnhoff Zoo, West Berlin: © Ullstein bild Dtl./Getty Images.

Page Three

The border between East and West Berlin in 1961: © Mary Evans Picture Library/Glasshouse Images. The Silver Towers apartment block in Kew Gardens, Queens, New York City: Tim Tate. Goleniewski in his Queens apartment, New York City; Irmgard Goleniewska (née Kampf) in the couple's Queens apartment, New York City: Polish intelligence files; Institute of National Remembrance, Warsaw.

Page Four

The Portland Spies Harry Houghton and Ethel Gee, photographed by an MI5 surveillance team in 1960: MI5 files on Harry Houghton/UK National Archives. Russian spy Konon Molody used the fictional identity of Gordon Lonsdale: © Keystone/Getty Images. Portland Spy Ring members Helen and Peter Kroger, in reality Lorna and Morris Cohen:

© Jeremy Fletcher/Getty Images. The Portland spies hid their one-time code pads in the hollowed-out bottoms of cigarette table lighters: © Mirrorpix/Getty Images.

Page Five

George Blake: © *Illustrated London News* Ltd/Mary Evans Picture Library. Heinz Felfe; Hans Tiebel; Stig Wennerström: © Topfoto.

Page Six

Anatoliy Golitsyn and his wife Svetlana, enjoying the high life at the Coconut Grove nightclub in the Ambassador Hotel, Los Angeles in 1961: source unknown. James Jesus Angleton: © Bettmann/Getty Images. Peter Wright: © Fairfax Media Archives/Getty Images.

Page Seven

Polish intelligence sketch maps of Goleniewski's location: Polish intelligence files; Institute of National Remembrance, Warsaw. New York City Marriage Registration Certificate for 'Aleksei N. Romanoff' (Goleniewski) and Irmgard M. Kampf, 30 September 1964: exhibit attached to an affidavit sworn 'Irmgard M. Romanoffa' (Irmgard Goleniewska), 11 July 1967, Queens County Register office, New York City. The Russian Orthodox Church New York City Parish Register recording the marriage of 'Aleksei Nicholaevich Romanoff' (Michał Goleniewski) and Irmgard M. Kampf, 30 September 1964: exhibit attached to an affidavit sworn 'Irmgard M. Romanoffa' (Irmgard Goleniewska), 11 July 1967, Queens County Register office, New York City.

Page Eight

Goleniewski's own monthly subscription 'bulletin', *Double Eagle*: Howard Gottllieb Archival Research Center, Boston University. Goleniewski in New York City, 1966: from publicity 'news sheets' issued by Goleniewski and publisher Robert Speller's Transglobal New Service, Sergei l. Voitsekhovskii Collection, Hoover Institute, Stanford University, California.

Index

Index